Contents

Apple Machine Language for Beginners

Richard Mansfield

COMPUTE!™ Publications, Inc. abc
One of the ABC Publishing Companies
Greensboro, North Carolina

Printed in the United States of America

10 9 8 7 6 5 4 3 2 1

ISBN 0-87455-002-5

COMPUTE! Publications, Inc., Post Office Box 5406, Greensboro, NC 27403, (919) 275-9809, is one of the ABC Publishing Companies and is not associated with any manufacturer of personal computers.

Preface

Something amazing lies beneath BASIC.

Several years ago I decided to learn to program in machine language, the computer's own language. I understood BASIC fairly well and I realized that it was simply not possible to accomplish all that I wanted to do with my computer using BASIC alone. BASIC is sometimes just too slow.

I faced the daunting (and exhilarating) prospect of learning to go below the surface of my computer, of finding out how to talk directly to a computer in *its* language, not the imitation-English of BASIC. I bought four books on 6502 machine language programming and spent several months practicing with them and puzzling out opcodes and hexadecimal arithmetic, and putting together small machine language programs.

Few events in learning to use a personal computer have had more impact on me than the moment that I could instantly fill the TV screen with any picture I wanted because of a machine language program I had written. I was amazed at its speed, but more than that, I realized that anytime large amounts of information were needed onscreen in the future—it could be done via machine language. I had, in effect, created a new BASIC "command" which could be added to any of my programs. This command—using a CALL instruction to send the computer to my custom-designed machine language routine—allowed me to have previously impossible control over the computer.

BASIC might be compared to a reliable, comfortable car. It will get you where you want to go. Machine language is like a sleek racing car—you get there with lots of time to spare. When programming involves large amounts of data, music, graphics, or games, speed can become the single most important factor.

After becoming accustomed to machine language, I decided to write an arcade game entirely without benefit of BASIC. It was to be in machine language from start to finish. I predicted that it would take about 20 to 30 hours. It was a space invaders game with mother ships, rows of aliens, sound . . . the works. It took closer to 80 hours, but I am probably more proud of that program than of any other I've written.

After I'd finished it, I realized that the next games would be easier and could be programmed more quickly. The modules handling scoring, sound, screen framing, delay, and player/enemy shapes were all written. I only had to write new sound effects, change details about the scoring, create new shapes. The essential routines were, for the most part, already written for a variety of new arcade-type games. When creating machine language programs, you build up a collection of reusable subroutines. For example, once you find out how to make sounds on your machine, you change the details, but not the underlying procedures, for any new songs.

The great majority of books about machine language assume a considerable familiarity with both the details of microprocessor chips and with programming technique. This book assumes only a working knowledge of BASIC. It was designed to speak directly to the amateur programmer, the part-time computerist. It should help you make the transition from BASIC to machine language with relative ease.

This book is dedicated to Florence, Jim, and Larry. I would also like to express my gratitude to Kevin Martin and Tim Victor for their work in translating the various versions of LADS.

Why Machine Language?

Sooner or later, many programmers find that they want to learn machine language. BASIC is a fine general-purpose tool, but it has its limitations. Machine language (often called *assembly language*) performs much faster. BASIC is fairly easy to learn, but most beginners do not realize that machine language can also be easy. And, just as learning Italian goes faster if you already know Spanish, if a programmer already knows BASIC, much of this knowledge will make learning machine language easier. There are many similarities.

This book is designed to teach machine language to those who have a working knowledge of BASIC. For example, Chapter 9 is a dictionary of BASIC commands. Following each BASIC command is a machine language routine which accomplishes the same task. In this way, if you know what you want to do in BASIC, you can find out how to do it in machine language.

To make it easier to write programs in machine language (called ML from here on), most programmers use a special program called an *assembler*. This is where the term *assembly language* comes from. ML and assembly language programs are both essentially the same thing. Using an assembler to create ML programs is far easier than being forced to look up and then POKE each byte into RAM memory. That's the way it used to be done, when there was too little memory in computers to hold *languages* (like BASIC or assemblers) at the same time as *programs* created by those languages. The old-style hand-programming was very laborious.

There is an assembler at the end of this book which will work on any Apple. It's called LADS, for Label Assembly Development System. It will let you type in ML instructions (like INC 2) and will translate them into the right numbers and POKE them for you wherever in memory you decide you want your ML program to be located. LADS will help you in a variety of other ways as well. It was designed to offer you a fast, convenient, and effective ML programming environment, a way of writing programs which is both natural and familiar.

ML *instructions* are like BASIC commands; you build an ML program by using the ML *instruction set*. A complete, descriptive table of all the 6502 ML instructions can be found in Appendix A. Whenever you see a three-letter abbreviation (like INC) in this book that you don't recognize, it's an ML instruction and you can look it up in Appendix A, where you'll find its purposes, modes, and syntax fully described.

It's a little premature, but if you're curious, INC 2 will increase the number in your computer's second memory cell (the second byte of RAM memory) by one. If 15 is the number currently in cell 2, it will become a 16 after INC 2. Think of it as "increment address two." Like BASIC, ML has a series of commands which you use to communicate with the computer when you write a program. ML commands are always three-letter abbreviations, like INC, and LADS will help you write your ML programs using these commands and numbers that you generally add to the commands as additional information, like INC 2.

Throughout the book you'll be learning how to handle a variety of ML instructions, and LADS will be of great help. You might want to familiarize yourself with it. Knowing what it does (and using it to enter the examples in this book), you will gradually build your understanding of ML, hexadecimal numbers, and the extraordinary range of new possibilities open to the computerist who knows ML. Knowing ML, being able to talk directly to your machine, changes things so much that it's like getting a whole new computer, a much more powerful computer.

Seeing It Work

Chapters 2–8 each examine a major aspect of ML where it differs from the way BASIC works. In each chapter, examples and exercises lead the programmer to a greater understanding of the methods of ML programming. By the end of the book, you should be able to write, in ML, most of the programs and subroutines you will want or need.

Let's examine some advantages of ML, starting with the main one—ML runs extremely fast.

Here are two programs which accomplish the same thing. The first is in ML, and the second is in BASIC. They get results at very different speeds indeed as you'll see:

Machine Language

```
169 193 160 0 153 0 4 200 208 250 153 0 5 200 208
250 153 0 6 200 208 250 153 0 7 200 208 250 96
```

BASIC
5 FOR I = 1 TO 1000: PRINT "A";: NEXT I

These two programs both print the letter *A* 1000 times on the screen. The ML version takes up 29 bytes of RAM (Random Access Memory). The BASIC version takes up 45 bytes and takes about 30 times as long to finish the job. If you want to see how quickly the ML works, you can POKE those numbers somewhere into RAM and run the ML program with a CALL command to the little program.

In both BASIC and ML, many instructions are followed by an *argument*. We mentioned the instruction INC 2. In that example, the number 2 is the argument. In BASIC, the CALL instruction must be given an argument which tells it where to CALL, where the ML program it's going to run is located in RAM. The CALL instruction will turn control of the computer over to the address given as its argument. There would be an ML program waiting there.

Just remember that an argument is the second item in a pair and that an argument modifies (makes more specific) a given instruction. In the pairs INC 2, CALL 151, and Send a Letter, the 2, *151*, and *Letter* are the arguments. The INC, CALL, and Send are the instructions.

To make it easy to see the speed of our 1000 *A*'s ML example program, we'll just load it into memory without yet knowing much about it. We'll use a BASIC loader program (on page *x*) that simply POKEs all the numbers of the ML program into memory; then you CALL from BASIC to activate the ML program.

A *disassembly* is like a BASIC program's LISTing. You can give the starting address of an ML program to a *disassembler*, and it will translate the numbers it finds in the computer's memory into a readable series of ML instructions. The built-in Apple monitor contains a disassembler that you can use to examine and study ML programs. Note that you have to give a start address whenever you write (with an assembler), list (with a disassembler), or run (with CALL) an ML program. That's because, unlike BASIC programs, ML programs can be located anywhere in RAM memory.

Here's what our little example ML program looks like when it has been translated by a disassembler:

```
0302-   A9 C1      LDA   #$C1
0304-   A0 00      LDY   #$00
0306-   99 00 04   STA   $0400,Y
0309-   C8         INY
030A-   D0 FA      BNE   $0306
030C-   99 00 05   STA   $0500,Y
030F-   C8         INY
0310-   D0 FA      BNE   $030C
0312-   99 00 06   STA   $0600,Y
0315-   C8         INY
0316-   D0 FA      BNE   $0312
0318-   99 00 07   STA   $0700,Y
031B-   C8         INY
031C-   D0 FA      BNE   $0318
031E-   60         RTS
```

The following BASIC program (called a *loader*) will POKE the ML instructions (and their arguments) into memory for you:

```
10 FOR I = 770 TO 798: READ A: POKE I,A: NEXT I
20 PRINT "CALL 770 TO ACTIVATE "
30 DATA 169,193,160,0,153,0,4,200,208,250,153,0,5,2
   00,208,250,153,0,6,200,208,250,153,0,7,200,208,2
   50,96
```

After running this program, type CALL 770 as instructed and the screen will instantly fill.

BASIC stands for Beginner's All-purpose Symbolic Instruction Code. Because it is all-purpose, it cannot be the perfect code for any specific job. The fact that ML speaks directly to the machine, in the machine's language, makes it far the more efficient language. This is because however cleverly a BASIC program is written, it will nevertheless always require extra running time to finish a job. This same problem slows down every other computer language as well: Logo, Forth, Pascal, C, whatever. None of them is the machine's language and, thus, none can run at maximum speed.

To see why this is, think of the common PRINT instruction in BASIC. A PRINT statement drags BASIC into a series of operations which ML avoids. BASIC must ask and answer a series of questions. Where is the text located that is to be PRINTed? Is it a variable? Where is the variable located? What's its length? Where on the screen is the text to be placed?

ML is far more efficient. As we will discover, ML does not need to hunt for a string variable. And screen addresses do not require a complicated series of searches in an ML program. Each of these tasks, and others, slows BASIC down because it must serve so many general purposes. The screen fills slowly because BASIC has to make so many more decisions about every action it attempts than does ML.

Inserting ML for Speed

A second benefit which you derive from learning ML is that your understanding of computing will be much greater. On the abstract level, you will be far more aware of just how computers work. On the practical level, you will be able to choose between BASIC or ML, whichever is best for the purpose at hand. This choice between two languages permits far more flexibility and allows a number of tasks to be programmed which are clumsy or even impossible in BASIC. Quite a few of your favorite BASIC programs would benefit from a small ML routine, "inserted" into BASIC with a CALL, to replace a heavily used, but slow, loop or subroutine. Large sorting tasks, smooth animation, and many arcade games and other kinds of programs *must* involve ML. And most programs can benefit from ML patches. It's no accident that nearly all commercial computer programs are written in machine language.

BASIC vs. Machine Language

Because of the great efficiency and speed of ML, it's not surprising that *BASIC itself is written in ML*. It's made up of many ML subprograms stored in your Apple's Read Only Memory (ROM). BASIC is a collection of special words such as *STOP* and *RUN*, each of which stands for a cluster of ML instructions. One such cluster might sit in ROM (unchanging memory) just waiting for you to type LIST. If you do type in that word, the computer turns control over to the ML routine which accomplishes a program listing. The BASIC programmer understands and uses these BASIC words to build a program. You hand instructions over to the computer and then rely on the convenience of referring to all those prepackaged ML routines by their BASIC names. The computer *always* works with ML instructions. That's why you cannot honestly say that you truly understand computing until you understand the computer's language: machine language.

Another reason to learn ML is that custom programming is then possible. Computers come with a disk operating system (DOS) and BASIC (or other higher-level languages). After awhile, you will likely find that you are limited by the rules or the commands available in these languages. You will want to add to them, to customize them. An understanding of ML is necessary if you want to add new words to BASIC, to modify a word processor (which was written in ML), to personalize your computer—to make it behave precisely as you want it to. This book will give you the knowledge and the tools to fully understand and to speak directly to your Apple.

BASIC's Strong Points

Of course, BASIC has its advantages and in some cases is to be preferred over ML. BASIC is usually simpler to *debug* (to get all the problems ironed out so that it works as it should). In Chapter 3 we'll examine some ML debugging techniques which work quite well, but BASIC is the easier of the two languages to correct. For one thing, BASIC often just comes out and tells you your programming mistakes by printing error messages on the screen. Nevertheless, if you use the LADS assembler from this book, it too will print error messages and identify the offending line number.

Contrary to popular opinion, ML is not necessarily a memory-saving process. ML can use up about as much memory as BASIC does when accomplishing the same task. Short programs can be somewhat more compact in ML, but longer programs generally use up bytes fast in both languages. However, worrying about using up computer memory is quickly becoming less and less important.

Soon programmers will probably have more memory space available than they will ever need. In any event, a talent for conserving bytes, like skill at trapping wild game, will likely become a victim of technology. It will always be a skill, but it seems as if it will not be an everyday necessity.

So, which language is best? They are both best—but for different purposes. Many programmers, after learning ML, find that they continue to construct some of their programs in BASIC or some other language, but add ML modules where speed is important. An all-ML program will, however, generally be more efficient, more flexible, and far faster than any alternative. Remember, it's no accident that the great majority of professional and commercial programs are written in pure ML.

But perhaps the best reason of all for learning ML is that it is fascinating and fun.

Chapter 1

How to Use This Book

How to Use This Book

Throughout this book there are short example programs in machine language for you to type in and experiment with. They vary in length, but most are quite brief and are intended to illustrate an ML concept or technique. The best way to learn something new is often to just jump in and do it. Machine language programming is no different. Machine language programs are written using a program called an *assembler*, just as BASIC programs are written using a program inside the computer called Applesoft BASIC.

In an earlier, not Apple-specific, version of this book, there was an assembler program written in BASIC. This book, however, offers a far more powerful assembler, LADS, in Appendix B. In addition to being versatile, LADS offers the beginner a number of conveniences such as error detection and a familiar environment. And the more sophisticated features of the assembler are there for you when you're ready to use them.

The First Step: Assembling

It is probably a good idea to first type LADS into your computer (ProDos and 3.3 versions and typing instructions are in Appendix B). Once you've got a working version, you're ready to use the assembler with the practice examples throughout the book. (If you prefer, you can order a 3.3/ProDos disk which contains LADS and other programs from this book. See the coupon in the back of this book for details.)

Frequently, the examples in the book are designed to do something to the screen. The reason for this is that you can then tell at once if things are working as planned. If you are trying to send the message TEST STRING and it comes out TEST STRI or TEST STRING@, you can go back and reassemble with LADS until you get it right. More important, you'll discover what you did wrong.

Normally, programs manipulate data within a database or make calculations with some numbers somewhere in RAM, but the action takes place offscreen. When learning ML, however, it's often helpful to put your data manipulations right up in front of your eyes on the screen so that you can see precisely how things are going. When everything is working correctly, you can redirect the data to some less visible place elsewhere in RAM.

A Sample Program

The following little ML program will show you how to go about entering and testing the practice examples in this book. At this point, of course, you won't yet recognize the ML instructions involved. This sample program is intended only to serve as a guide to working with the examples you will come upon later in the text.

After you've typed in and made a few backup copies of LADS, you can use it to create runnable ML programs. Detailed instructions on using all of LADS features are found in Appendix B, but for now, we just want to know how to enter a short, easy program.

Once you've booted up either DOS 3.3 or ProDOS, insert a disk with LADS on it in your disk drive. If you're using the ProDOS version of LADS, you must load and run the ProDOS LADS Loader (Program B-1); if you are using DOS 3.3, simply BRUN LADS.

You will now be in the LADS environment which is very like BASIC. You start out by writing a program using line numbers and colons separating statements. The first line, however, must tell LADS where you want your ML program located in memory (since ML can be placed anywhere in RAM). A safe place to have your programs put is address 768, so:

```
10 *= 768
20 .S
30 .O
40 LDA #193
50 STA 1024
60 RTS
70 .END TEST
```

After you've typed this in, save it to disk by typing

```
SAVE TEST
```

Now you're ready to call LADS into action, to have LADS assemble the program for you. It will print out the results on the screen while it works (the .S in line 20 tells LADS to show you what's happening), and it will store the resulting finished machine language program starting at address 768 in your RAM memory (the .O in line 30 tells LADS to store the bytes it assembles).

To make LADS assemble this program (we're calling it "TEST"), type

ASM TEST

and you'll see the assembler work through your program, creating an actual machine language program. This program is supposed to print the letter *A* in the upper left of your screen. You activate it by typing

CALL 768

It will do its job and return the control back to your normal environment. If you want to try making an adjustment, change the number 193 in line 40 to some other number to print a different character, then SAVE TEST, ASM TEST, and CALL 768 again to try it out. Raising the number in line 50 will print the character further down the screen (unless you fall into some of the reserved screen RAM bytes, but we'll get into that later).

By the way, the word *.END* (with the period before it) in line 70 isn't an ML instruction; it's a special command to LADS which tells the assembler that it has reached the end of your program. Such special commands are called *pseudo-ops* and we'll get to them later, too. They make ML programming much easier.

The main thing to learn here is how to type in, save, and assemble using LADS. Primarily, you should remember four things:

1. LADS always has to know where you want to store your ML program, so the first line of any program you give LADS must have *= 768 and nothing else on that line. We're generally going to start all our example programs at 768, so if an example doesn't have *= 768 as the first line, put it in.
2. LADS always has to know when your ML program is finished. Thus, the last line in each program must have .END *NAME* (and nothing else on the line), where you substitute whatever name you want to use.
3. Also always use a .O to send the finished ML program into RAM so that you can test it. Using the .S is optional, but it would probably be a good idea to see the actual assembly process onscreen while you're learning.

4. You must be in the LADS environment when typing in and saving programs that you plan to assemble with LADS. Although the LADS environment behaves just like BASIC for you, the user, it *is* different as far as your Apple is concerned.

And don't forget to SAVE *NAME* before trying to ASM. LADS looks to the disk for your program and so you must have saved it before assembling it. (There is another version of LADS, called RAMLADS, described in Appendix C, which doesn't use the disk, but for learning purposes, let's stick with the basic LADS model. Later on, you can graduate to RAMLADS after you're more comfortable with ML in general. RAMLADS assembles more quickly than regular LADS, but for beginners regular LADS is the best tool.)

Chapter 2

The Fundamentals

The Fundamentals

The difficulty of learning ML has sometimes been exaggerated. There are some new rules to learn and some new habits to acquire. But most ML programmers would probably agree that ML is not inherently more difficult to understand than BASIC. More of a challenge to debug in some cases, but it's not worlds beyond BASIC in complexity. In fact, in the 1970s, many of the first home computerists learned ML before they learned BASIC. This is because an average version of the BASIC language used in microcomputers takes up around 12,000 bytes of memory, and the early personal computers (KIM, AIM, etc.) were severely restricted—they had only a small amount of available memory. These early machines were unable to offer BASIC; it took up more space than they had, so everyone programmed in ML.

Interestingly, some of these pioneers reportedly found BASIC to be just as difficult to grasp as ML. In both cases, the problem seems to be that the rules of a new language simply are "obscure" until you know them. In general, though, learning either language probably requires roughly the same amount of effort.

The first thing to learn about ML is that it reflects the construction of computers. ML programmers often use a number system (hexadecimal) which is not based on ten. You will find a table in Appendix F which makes it easy to look up hex, decimal, or binary numbers.

We count by tens because it is a familiar (though arbitrary) grouping for us. Humans have ten fingers. If we had eleven fingers, the odds are that we would be counting by elevens.

What's a Natural Number?

Computers count in groups of twos. It is a fact of electronics that the easiest way to store and manipulate information is by on/off states. A light bulb is either on or off. This is a two-group; it's *binary*, and so the powers of two become the natural groupings for electronic counters: 2, 4, 8, 16, 32, 64, 128, 256. Finger counters (us) have been using tens so long that we have come to think of ten as *natural*, like thunder in April. Tens isn't natural at all. What's more, twos is a more efficient way to count.

To see how the powers of two relate to computers, we can run a short BASIC program which will give us some of these powers. *Powers* of a number is the number multiplied by itself.

Two to the power of two (2^2) means 2 times 2 (in other words, 4). Two to the power of three (2^3) means 2 times 2 times 2 (8).

```
10 FOR I = 0 TO 16
20 PRINT 2 ^ I
30 NEXT I
```

ML programming *can* be done entirely in the familiar decimal number system. For beginners, that's probably a wise thing to do. The LADS assembler in this book allows you to use either decimal or hex, as you wish. However, you'll probably see hex used in magazine articles and books, and hex does format on the screen or paper more neatly than decimal numbers. Another advantage of hex is that it relates visually to the binary numbers that the computer is using. The arguments for some advanced ML commands like ROL and EOR are more easily visualized with hex than with decimal.

Why not just always program in the familiar decimal numbers (as we do in BASIC)? Because hex is based on groups of 16 digits, not decimal's groups of 10. And 16 is one of the powers of two. Thus, 16 is a convenient grouping (or *base*) for ML because it organizes numbers the way the computer looks at numbers. For example, at the most elementary level all computers work with *bits*. A bit is the smallest piece of information possible: Something is either on or off, yes or no, plus or minus, true or false. This two-state condition (binary) can be remembered by a computer's smallest single memory cell. This single cell is called a bit. The computer can turn each bit *on* or *off* as if it were a light bulb, or a flag raised or lowered.

It's interesting that the word *bit* is frequently explained as a shortening of the phrase BInary digiT. In fact, the word *bit* goes back several centuries. There was a coin which was soft enough to be cut with a knife into eight pieces. Hence, *pieces of eight.* A single piece of this coin was called a bit and, as with computer memories, it meant that you couldn't slice it any further. We still use the word *bit* today as in the phrase *two bits,* meaning 25 cents.

Whatever it's called, the bit is a small, essential aspect of computing. Imagine that we wanted to remember the result of a subtraction. When two numbers are subtracted, they are actually being compared with each other. The result of the subtraction tells us which number is the larger or if they are equal. ML has an instruction, like a command in BASIC, which compares two numbers by subtraction. It is called CMP (for *compare*). This instruction sets *flags* in the CPU (Central Processing Unit) of the computer, and one of the flags always shows whether or not the result of the most recent action taken by the computer was a zero. We'll go into this again later. What we need to realize now is simply that each flag—like the flag on a mailbox—has two possible conditions: up or down. In other words, this information (that there's a zero result or a nonzero result) is *binary* and can be stored within a single bit. Each of the six flags within the 6502 chip is a bit. Together, the flags are all held within a single byte. That byte is called the status register.

Byte Assignments

Our computers group bits into units of eight, called *bytes*. This relationship between bits and bytes is easy to remember if you think of a bit as one of the "pieces of eight." Eight is a power of two also (two to the third power). Eight is a convenient number of bits to work with as a group since we can count from 0 to 255 using only eight bits. We'll see how this is done in a minute.

A byte—able to "hold" 256 different numbers—gives us enough room to assign all 26 letters of the alphabet (and the uppercase letters, punctuation marks, and so on) so that each character we might want to print will have its own particular number. The letter *A* (uppercase) has been assigned the number 65 (in the standard ASCII code that computers use to communicate). The letter *B* is 66, and so on. Most microcomputers, however, do not adhere strictly to the ASCII code, except when they are communicating with other computers, for example, through telephone links. The Apple code uses 193 for the ordinary letter *A*, whereas 65 is used for the flashing *A*. The Apple uses the following code for its internal operations:

Table 2-1. The Apple Version of the ASCII Code

	Normal		Inverse		Flash	
Character	Decimal	Hex	Decimal	Hex	Decimal	Hex
Space	160	A0	32	20	96	60
!	161	A1	33	21	97	61
"	162	A2	34	22	98	62
#	163	A3	35	23	99	63
$	164	A4	36	24	100	64
%	165	A5	37	25	101	65
&	166	A6	38	26	102	66
'	167	A7	39	27	103	67
(	168	A8	40	28	104	68
)	169	A9	41	29	105	69
*	170	AA	42	2A	106	6A
+	171	AB	43	2B	107	6B
,	172	AC	44	2C	108	6C
-	173	AD	45	2D	109	6D
.	174	AE	46	2E	110	6E
/	175	AF	47	2F	111	6F
0	176	B0	48	30	112	70
1	177	B1	49	31	113	71
2	178	B2	50	32	114	72
3	179	B3	51	33	115	73
4	180	B4	52	34	116	74
5	181	B5	53	35	117	75
6	182	B6	54	36	118	76
7	183	B7	55	37	119	77
8	184	B8	56	38	120	78
9	185	B9	57	39	121	79
:	186	BA	58	3A	122	7A
;	187	BB	59	3B	123	7B
<	188	BC	60	3C	124	7C
=	189	BD	61	3D	125	7D
>	190	BE	62	3E	126	7E
?	191	BF	63	3F	127	7F
@	192	C0	0	00	64	40
A	193	C1	1	01	65	41
B	194	C2	2	02	66	42
C	195	C3	3	03	67	43
D	196	C4	4	04	68	44
E	197	C5	5	05	69	45
F	198	C6	6	06	70	46
G	199	C7	7	07	71	47
H	200	C8	8	08	72	48

	Normal		Inverse		Flash	
Character	Decimal	Hex	Decimal	Hex	Decimal	Hex
I	201	C9	9	09	73	49
J	202	CA	10	0A	74	4A
K	203	CB	11	0B	75	4B
L	204	CC	12	0C	76	4C
M	205	CD	13	0D	77	4D
N	206	CE	14	0E	78	4E
O	207	CF	15	0F	79	4F
P	208	D0	16	10	80	50
Q	209	D1	17	11	81	51
R	210	D2	18	12	82	52
S	211	D3	19	13	83	53
T	212	D4	20	14	84	54
U	213	D5	21	15	85	55
V	214	D6	22	16	86	56
W	215	D7	23	17	87	57
X	216	D8	24	18	88	58
Y	217	D9	25	19	89	59
Z	218	DA	26	1A	90	5A
[	219	DB	27	1B	91	5B
\	220	DC	28	1C	92	5C
]	221	DD	29	1D	93	5D
^	222	DE	30	1E	94	5E
_	223	DF	31	1F	95	5F

Table 2-2. True ASCII

ASCII Code	Character	ASCII Code	Character	ASCII Code	Character
0	NUL	44	,	86	V
1	SOH	45	-	87	W
2	STX	46	.	88	X
3	ETX	47	/	89	Y
4	EOT	48	0	90	Z
5	ENQ	49	1	91	[
6	ACK	50	2	92	\
7	BEL	51	3	93	]
8	BS	52	4	94	^
9	HT	53	5	95	—
10	LF	54	6	96	`
11	VT	55	7	97	a
12	FF	56	8	98	b
13	CR	57	9	99	c
14	SO	58	:	100	d
15	SI	59	;	101	e
16	DLE	60	<	102	f
17	DC1	61	=	103	g
18	DC2	62	>	104	h
19	DC3	63	?	105	i
20	DC4	64	@	106	j
21	NAK	65	A	107	k
22	SYN	66	B	108	l
23	ETB	67	C	109	m
24	CAN	68	D	110	n
25	EM	69	E	111	o
26	SUB	70	F	112	p
27	ESC	71	G	113	q
28	FS	72	H	114	r
29	GS	73	I	115	s
30	RS	74	J	116	t
31	US	75	K	117	u
32	(space)	76	L	118	v
33	!	77	M	119	w
34	"	78	N	120	x
35	#	79	O	121	y
36	$	80	P	122	z
37	%	81	Q	123	{
38	&	82	R	124	|
39	'	83	S	125	}
40	(	84	T	126	~
41	)	85	U	127	DEL (appears onscreen as a blank)
42	*				
43	+				

The ASCII code, an assignment of numbers to letters and symbols, forms a convention by which computers worldwide can communicate with each other. Text can be sent via modems and telephone lines, and it will arrive meaning the same thing to an alien computer. It's important to visualize each byte, then, as being eight bits ganged together and that a byte is able to represent 256 different things. As you might have suspected, 256 is another power of two (two to the power of eight).

So these groupings of eight, these bytes, are a major aspect of computing; but we also want to simplify our counting from 0 to 255. We want the numbers to line up in a column on screen or on paper. Obviously, *decimal* numbers are erratic: The number 5 takes up one space, the number 230 takes up three spaces. Hex numbers between 0 and 255 will always, predictably, take up two spaces (here's 0–255 expressed in the hexadecimal format: $00–$FF).

In addition to being easier to format in printouts, hex is also somewhat easier to visualize in terms of the *binary* number system—the on/off, single-bit way that the computer manipulates numbers:

Decimal		**Hex**	**Binary**
1		01	00000001
2		02	00000010
3		03	00000011 (1+2)
4		04	00000100
5		05	00000101 (4+1)
6		06	00000110 (4+2)
7		07	00000111 (4+2+1)
8		08	00001000
9		09	00001001 (8+1)
10	(note new digits)——→	0A	00001010 (8+2)
11		0B	00001011 (8+2+1)
12		0C	00001100 (8+4)
13		0D	00001101 (8+4+1)
14		0E	00001110 (8+4+2)
15		0F	00001111 (8+4+2+1)
16	(note new column——→	10	00010000
17	in the hex)	11	00010001 (16+1)

See how hex $10 (hex numbers are usually preceded by a dollar sign to show that they are not decimal) *looks like* binary? If you split a hex number into two parts, 1 and 0, and the equivalent binary number into two parts, 0001 and 0000, you can see the relationship.

The Rationale for Hex Numbers

Many ML programmers like to use hexadecimal numbers because they are a superior visual analogue of the internal manipulations inside the computer; hex is simply more like binary because hex is a power of two and decimal (base ten) is not a power of two. It's really up to you whether or when you add hex to your bag of tricks. (In the early days of programming, another base, base eight, called *octal* was very popular. It's still used today when programming some large computers.) You will see that you can choose to use hex or decimal when writing ML with the LADS assembler in this book. And you can use them interchangeably, even on the same line of program code. You can write LDA $0A or LDA 10, whichever you prefer.

Here's what it looks like when you count up from zero in both systems:

Decimal
0 1 2 3 4 5 6 7 8 9

And now you start over by moving to a new column with the number 10.

Hex
00 01 02 03 04 05 06 07 08 09 0A 0B 0C 0D 0E 0F

And then you start over with $10, $11, and so on.

See how we ran out of digits when trying to count up to 16 in hex? Hex substitutes the first few letters of the alphabet to count past 09.

Program 2-1. Hex-Decimal Converter

```
10 HE$ = "0123456789ABCDEF": HOME
15 PRINT "PLEASE CHOOSE:"
20 PRINT "INPUT HEX & GET DECIMAL BACK (1)"
25 PRINT "INPUT DECIMAL TO GET HEX BACK (2)"
30 GET K
35 ON K GOTO 200,400
100 H$ = "": FOR M = 3 TO 0 STEP - 1:N% = DE / (16
    ^ M):DE = DE - N% * 16 ^ M:H$ = H$ + MID$ (HE$,
    N% + 1,1): NEXT M
```

```
101 RETURN
102 D = 0:Q = 3: FOR M = 1 TO 4: FOR W = 0 TO 15: I
    F MID$ (H$,M,1) = MID$ (HE$,W + 1,1) THEN 104
103 NEXT W
104 D1 = W * (16 ^ (Q)):D = D + D1:Q = Q - 1: NEXT
    M
105 DE = INT (D): RETURN
200 INPUT "HEX  ";H$: IF LEN (H$) < > 4 THEN PRINT
    "NEED FOUR DIGITS": GOTO 200
205 GOSUB 102: PRINT DE
210 GOTO 200
400 INPUT "DECIMAL  ";DE: GOSUB 100: PRINT H$
410 GOTO 400
```

The first thing to notice is that instead of the familiar decimal symbol 10, hex uses the letter *A* because this is where we run out of symbols and must start over again with a 1 and a 0. Zero always reappears at the start of each new grouping in any number system: 0, 10, 20, and so on. The same thing happens with the groupings in hex: 0, 10, 20, 30, and so on. The difference is that, in hex, the 1 in the "10's" column is actually what we would call a 16 (in our normal decimal way of counting).

The second column is now a 16's column; 11 (hex) means 17 (decimal), and 21 means 33 (2 times 16 plus 1). Learning hex is probably the single biggest hurdle to overcome when getting to know ML.

Don't be discouraged if it's not immediately clear what's going on. (It probably never will be totally clear—hex is, after all, unnatural.) And remember that hex is an *option,* not a requirement, when programming in ML.

It's just that much ML printed in magazines and books uses hex. That's why you at least need to be able to make the conversion (you can use Appendix F to convert between decimal and hex if you don't want to get deeply into hex). Nobody really knows it that well. Most ML programmers use one of the calculators sold by Sharp, TI, or Hewlett-Packard that perform hex/decimal conversions. Hex is one of those things, like telephone books and dictionaries, that you have to know how to use, but you don't have to memorize.

It's possible that someday hex will go the way of octal, and we'll stick to the easy, obvious decimal mode entirely (except for excursions into binary numbers from time to time). If you want more understanding, you might want to practice the exercises at the end of this chapter. As you work with hex, it will gradually seem less and less alien.

To figure out a hex number, multiply the second column by 16 and add the other number to it. So, $2A would be 2 times 16 plus 10 (recall that A stands for 10).

Hex does seem impossibly confusing when you come upon it for the first time. It will never become second nature, but it should be at least generally understood. You need not memorize hex beyond learning to count from 1 to 16; this teaches you the symbols. Be able to count from 00 up to 0F. (By convention, even the smallest hex number is listed as two digits as in 03 or 0B. The other distinguishing characteristic is the dollar sign that is usually placed in front of the digits: $05 or $0E.)

It's enough to know what they look like and be able to find them when you need them.

The First 255

Another thing that makes all this easier is that if you *do* need to work with hex, most ML programming involves working with hex numbers only between 0 and 255. This is because a single byte (eight bits) can hold no number larger than 255. Manipulating numbers larger than 255 is of no real importance in ML programming until you are ready to work with more advanced ML programs. This comes later in the book. For example, all 6502 ML instructions are coded into one byte, all the flags are held in one byte, and many addressing modes use one byte.

To learn all we need to know about hex for now, we can try some problems and look at some ML code to see how hex is used in the majority of ML work. But first, let's take an imaginary flight over computer memory. Let's get a visual sense of what bits and bytes and the inner workings of the computer's RAM look like.

The City of Bytes

Imagine a city with a single long row of houses. It's night. Each house has a peculiar Christmas display: On the roof is a row of eight lights. The houses represent bytes; each light is a single bit. (See Figure 2-1.)

Figure 2-1. Night in the City of Bytes

If we fly over the City of Bytes, at first we see only darkness. Each byte contains nothing (zero), so all eight of its bulbs are off. (On the horizon we can see a glow, however, because the computer has memory up there, called ROM memory, which is very active and contains built-in programs.) But we are down in RAM, our free user-memory, and there are no programs in RAM yet, so every house is dark. Let's observe what happens to an individual byte when different numbers are stored there; we can randomly choose byte 1504. We hover over that house to see what information is "contained" in the light display. (See Figure 2-2.)

Figure 2-2

Like everywhere else in the City of Bytes, this byte is dark. Each bulb is off. Observing this, we know that the byte here is "holding," or representing, a zero. If someone at the computer types in POKE 1504,1, suddenly the rightmost light bulb goes on and the byte holds a one instead of a zero:

Figure 2-3

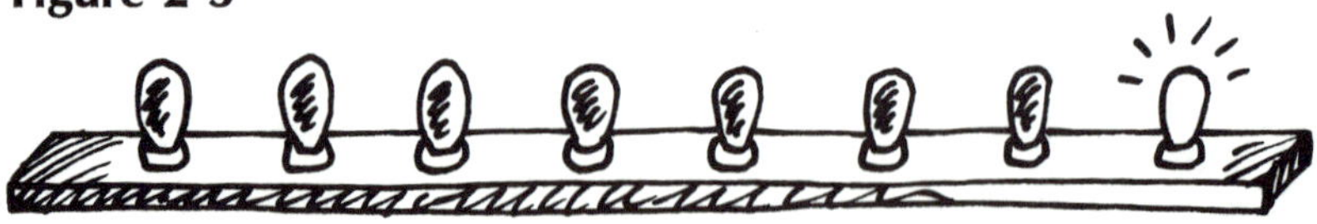

This rightmost bulb is the one's column (so far, this is exactly the way things would work in our usual way of counting by tens, our familiar *decimal* system). But the next bulb is in the two's column, so POKE 1504, 2 would be:

Figure 2-4

And three would be one and two:

Figure 2-5

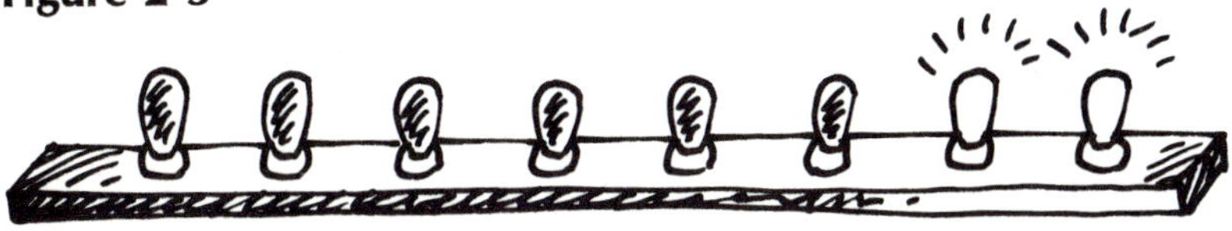

In this way—by checking which bits are turned on and then adding them together—the computer can look at a byte and know what number is there. Each light bulb, each *bit,* is in its own special position in the row of eight and has a value twice the value of the one just before it:

Figure 2-6

Eight bits together make a byte. A byte can hold a number from 0 through 255 decimal. We can think of bytes, though, in any number system we wish—in hex, decimal, or binary. Because the computer uses binary, it's useful to be able to visualize it. Hex has its uses in ML programming. And decimal is familiar. But a number is still a number, no matter what we call it. After all, five pennies are always five pennies, whether we symbolize them by 5 (decimal) or $05 (hex) or 00000101 (binary) or just call them a nickel.

A Binary Quiz

BASIC doesn't understand numbers expressed in hex or binary. Binary, for humans, is very *visual.* It forms patterns out of zeros and ones and lets you see an x-ray of the interior of a byte. The following program will let you quiz yourself on these patterns.

Here is a game which will show you a byte as it looks in binary. You then try to give the number in decimal:

Program 2-2. Binary Quiz

```
1ØØ REM B1NARY QUIZ
11Ø C1 = 177:CØ = 79
14Ø X = INT (256 * RND (1)):D = X:P = 128
17Ø HOME
18Ø FOR I = 1 TO 8
19Ø IF INT (D / P) = 1 THEN PRINT CHR$ (C1);:D = D
    - P: GOTO 21Ø
2ØØ PRINT CHR$ (CØ);
21Ø P = P / 2: NEXT I: PRINT
22Ø PRINT "WHAT IS THIS IN DECIMAL": PRINT
23Ø INPUT Q: IF Q = X THEN PRINT "CORRECT": GOTO 25
    Ø
24Ø PRINT "SORRY, IT WAS ";X
25Ø FOR T = 1 TO 1ØØØ: NEXT T
26Ø GOTO 14Ø
```

This next program will print out an entire table of binary numbers from 0 to 255:

Program 2-3. Binary Table

```
1ØØ REM COMPLETE BINARY TABLE
12Ø FOR X = Ø TO 255: PRINT X;
13Ø Z = X:L = 7
14Ø FOR Q = Ø TO 7:T = INT (X / 2)
15Ø K$(L) = CHR$ (48 + (X - T * 2))
16Ø L = L - 1:X = T: NEXT Q
18Ø X = Z
19Ø PRINT TAB( 1Ø);
2ØØ FOR I = Ø TO 7: PRINT K$(I);: NEXT I
2Ø5 PRINT
21Ø NEXT X
```

Examples and Practice

Here are several ordinary decimal numbers. Try to work out the hex equivalent:

1. 10 ______________
2. 15 ______________
3. 5 ______________
4. 16 ______________
5. 17 ______________
6. 32 ______________

7. 128 ____________
8. 129 ____________
9. 255 ____________
10. 254 ____________

We are not making an issue of learning hex or binary. If you needed to look up the answers in the table in Appendix F, fine. As you work with ML, you will familiarize yourself with some of the common hex numbers. And remember, you can program in ML without needing to worry about hex numbers. For now, we only want to be able to recognize what hex is. The LADS assembler will do the translations for you anytime you need them.

One other reason that we're not stressing hex too much is that ML is generally not programmed without the help of an assembler. The LADS assembler provided in this book will handle your input automatically. It allows you to choose whether you prefer to program in hex or decimal. With LADS, just use the $ symbol when you intend a number to be interpreted as hex.

This short BASIC program is good for practicing hex and also shows you how a two-byte hex number relates to a one-byte hex number. It will take decimal in and give back the correct hex.

Program 2-4. Hex Practice

```
10 H$ = "0123456789ABCDEF"
20 HOME
30 PRINT "ENTER DECIMAL NUMBER";: INPUT X
40 IF X > 255 THEN GOTO 30: REM NO NUMBERS BIGGER T
   HAN 255 ALLOWED
50 FOR I = 1 TO 0 STEP - 1
60 N = INT (X / (16 ^ I)):X = X - N * 16 ^ I
70 HE$ = HE$ + MID$ (H$,N + 1,1)
80 NEXT I
90 PRINT HE$
100 HE$ = "": GOTO 30
```

For larger hex numbers (up to two bytes, $FFFF equals 65535), we can just make a simple change to the above program. Change line 40 to IF x>65535 THEN 30, and change line 50 to FOR I = 3 TO 0 STEP − 1. This will give us four-place hex numbers. These larger hex numbers are used in ML mainly for addresses, since the 6502 can directly address 65536 bytes (bytes with addresses from 0 to 65535). This is the reason that many microcomputers max out at 64K. There are special ways to get around this, but an eight-bit microprocessor like the 6502 is generally limited in the total amount of RAM memory it can access directly.

The number 65535 is interesting because it represents the limit of our computers' memories. In special cases, with additional hardware, memory *can* be expanded beyond this. But this is the normal upper limit because the 6502 chip is designed to be able to *address* (put bytes in or take them out of memory cells) up to $FFFF.

Ganging Two Bytes Together to Form an Address

The 6502 often addresses by attaching two bytes together and looking at them as if they formed a unit. It's like the way that putting eight bits together forms the unit we call a *byte*. The largest number that two bytes can represent is $FFFF (65535), and the most that *one* byte can represent is $FF (255). Three-byte addressing is not possible for the 6502 chip. *Machine language* means programming instructions which are understood directly by the 6502 chip itself. There are other CPU (Central Processing Unit) chips, but the 6502 is the Apple's CPU. It's the one covered in this book.

Reading a Machine Language Program

Before getting into an in-depth look at the *monitor,* that bridge between you and your machine's language—we should first learn how to read ML program listings. You've probably seen them often enough in magazines.

These commented, labeled, but very strange-looking programs are called *source code* (see Program 2-8 for an example). Source code is what you write when you want to create an ML program. It can be translated by an *assembler program* (like LADS) into an ML program. When you have an assembler program attack your source code, it looks at the keywords (the instructions and their arguments, and their addresses) and then POKEs a series of numbers into the computer. This series of numbers is called the *object code* and is the runnable ML program. You can CALL object code and it will do whatever you've designed it to do.

Source code usually contains a great deal of information

in the form of comments which are of interest to the programmer, but which the computer ignores. It's rather like the way a BASIC program has REMarks to which the computer pays no attention.

The computer needs only a list of numbers which it can execute in order. That's what an ML program is. But for most people, lists of numbers are only slightly more understandable than Morse code. The solution is to let us use words which are then translated into numbers for the computer. The primary job of an assembler is to recognize an ML instruction. These instructions are called *mnemonics,* which means "memory aids." They are like BASIC words, except that they are always three letters long and are somewhat less like standard English.

If you type the mnemonic instruction JMP, the assembler POKEs a 76 into RAM memory. It's easier for us to remember something like JMP than the number 76. Seeing a 76, however, the computer immediately knows that it's supposed to perform a JMP. The number 76 is an *operation code,* or *opcode,* to the computer.

We write the mnemonic instruction JMP, an assembler translates this into the number 76, and the computer recognizes 76 as the command JUMP. These three-letter words we use in ML programming were designed to sound like what they do. JMP does a JUMP (like a GOTO in BASIC). Deluxe assemblers like LADS also let you use labels instead of numbers. These labels can refer to individual memory locations, special values like the score in a game, or entire subroutines. (See the instructions for using LADS for more information about using labels.)

Four Ways to List a Program

Labeled, commented source code listings are the most elaborate kind of ML program representation. There are also three other kinds of ML listings. Let's see how these four styles of representing an ML program would look by using a simple example program that just adds 2 + 5 and stores the result in RAM memory location 848. The first two styles are simply ways for you to type a program into the computer. The last two styles show you what to type in, but also illustrate what is going on in the ML program. First, let's look at the most elementary kind of ML found in books and magazines: the BASIC loader.

Program 2-5. BASIC Loader

```
10 FOR ADDRESS = 768 TO 776
20 READ BYTE
30 POKE ADDRESS, BYTE
40 NEXT ADDRESS
50 DATA 24,169,2,105,5,141,80,3,96
```

This is a series of decimal numbers in DATA statements which are POKEd into memory beginning at decimal address 768. This is a BASIC program. When these numbers are stashed into RAM, they form a little routine which clears the carry (so there won't be any holdover from previous addition—you always clear the carry before any addition in ML), then puts the number 2 into the *accumulator*—a special location in the computer that we'll get to later—and then adds 5. The result of the addition is then moved from the accumulator to decimal address 848. If you try this program out, you can CALL 768 to execute the ML program and then PRINT PEEK (848) and you'll see the answer: 7. BASIC loaders are convenient for magazines to publish because the user doesn't need to know anything at all about ML to enter and use these programs. The BASIC loader POKEs the ML program into memory, and then the only thing the user has to do is CALL the right address and the ML transfers control back to BASIC when its job is done. Many ML programs end with an RTS (ReTurn from Subroutine) instruction which reverts to BASIC mode.

Getting even closer to the machine level is the second way you might see ML printed in books or magazines: the hex dump. The Apple has a special monitor program in ROM which lets you list memory addresses and their contents as hex numbers.

More than that, you can type in new numbers and change the program. That's what a hex dump listing is for. You copy its numbers into your computer's RAM by using your computer's monitor.

A hex dump, like a BASIC loader, tells you nothing about the functions or strategies employed within an ML program.

Here's the hex dump version of the same 2 + 5 addition program:

Program 2-6. Hex Dump

```
0300- 18 A9 02 69 05 8D 50 03
0308- 60 00 00 00 00 00 00 00
```

The third type of listing is called a *disassembly.* It's the opposite of an assembly: A program called a *disassembler* takes machine language (the series of numbers, the opcodes in the computer's memory) and translates it into the words, the mnemonics, which humans can read and understand. The instruction (the mnemonic) you use when you want to put something into the accumulator is called LDA, and you store what's in the accumulator by using an STA. We'll get to them later. In this version of our example addition routine, it's a bit clearer what's going on and how the program works. Notice that on the far left we have the memory addresses (in hex), then hex numbers representing the actual bytes of the program and, on the right, the translation into ML instructions. ADC means ADd with Carry and RTS means ReTurn from Subroutine. A disassembly is to ML what LIST is to BASIC. Your monitor has a disassembler built-in which will produce these listings:

Program 2-7. Disassembly

```
., Ø3ØØ 18          CLC
., Ø3Ø1 A9 Ø2       LDA #$Ø2
., Ø3Ø3 69 Ø5       ADC #$Ø5
., Ø3Ø5 8D 5Ø Ø3 STA $Ø35Ø
., Ø3Ø8 6Ø          RTS
.
```

The Deluxe Version

Finally, we come to that full, luxurious, commented, labeled, deluxe source code we spoke of earlier. It includes the hex dump and the disassembly, but it also has labels and comments and line numbers added to further clarify the purposes of things and to make it easier for programmers to enter and edit their programs. This kind of listing can be produced with the LADS assembler by invoking the .S or .P features to create a full listing on screen or printer during the assembly process.

Note that in Program 2-8 all the numbers (except the line numbers on the far left) are in hex. LADS makes this optional. To make them decimal, use the .NH option and your listing will be entirely in decimal.

On the far left are the line numbers for the convenience of the programmer when writing the source code (the program you write to feed into the assembler). The line numbers can be used the way BASIC line numbers are used: deleted, inserted, and so on. Next are the memory addresses where each individual instruction in this routine is located in RAM. Then come the hex numbers of the instructions. (So far, it resembles the traditional hex dump.) Next are the disassembled translations of the hex, but note that you can replace numbers with labels as we'll see in Program 2-9. Last are the comments. They are the same as REM statements in BASIC.

Program 2-9 is functionally the same as 2-8, but we've defined some labels and used them instead of numbers. That can be a good way to remember the purpose of various things, just the way variable names in BASIC assist the programmer.

Where Programs 2-9 and 2-8 show you what LADS prints out during an assembly if you request a listing, Program 2-10 illustrates just the *source code* part, what you would type into your Apple and save to disk. Source code is the program you write; it's what's fed to the assembler to produce object code (the runnable ML program.) The object code has not yet been generated from this source code. The code has not been *assembled* yet. Once LADS is activated, you can save or load source code in the same way that you can save or load programs via BASIC. Once 2-10 is saved on disk, you could use the LADS ASM command, and the assembler would translate the instructions and print them on the screen and/or POKE them into memory if so instructed.

Those few differences between Programs 2-9 and 2-10 are conveniences for the programmer. The *= symbol tells the assembler where you want the ML program located in memory. The .P turns on the printer, and .S turns on listing to screen during assembly. The semicolons announce that a remark follows and the assembler should ignore the rest of the line, just like REM in BASIC. Finally, the .END symbol tells the assembler that there are no other files on the disk which contain additional parts of this program. This is the total program.

A simple assembler, like the one found in Apple's monitor, operates differently. It translates, prints, and POKEs as soon as you hit RETURN on each line of code. You can save and load the object, but not source code, with a simple assembler.

Before we get into the heart of ML programming, a study of the opcodes and ways of moving information around

Program 2-8. A Full Assembly Listing

```
                              ┌────────Source Code────────┐
Line   Memory  Object        Disassembly                Comments
Number Address Code
100    0300    18            CLC                CLEAR THE CARRY FLAG
110    0301    A9 02         LDA #$02           LOAD A WITH 2
120    0303    69 05         ADC #$05           ADD 5
130    0305    8D 50 03      STA $0350          STORE AT DECIMAL LOCATION 848
140    0308    60            RTS                RETURN
```

Program 2-9. Labeled Assembly

```
10  0300                TWO = 2             DEFINE LABEL "TWO" AS 2
20  0300                ADDER = 5           DEFINE "ADDER" AS A 5
30  0300                STORAGE = 848       DEFINE STORAGE ADDRESS
40
100 0300 18             CLC                 CLEAR THE CARRY FLAG
110 0301 A9 02          LDA #TWO            LOAD A WITH 2
120 0303 69 05          ADC #ADDER          ADD 5
130 0305 8D 50 03       STA STORAGE         STORE AT DECIMAL LOCATION 848
140 0308 60             RTS                 RETURN
```

(called *addressing*), we should look at a major ML programming aid: the monitor. It deserves its own chapter.

Program 2-10. The Source Code by Itself

```
5 *= 768
6 .P
7 .S
10 TWO = 2;              DEFINE LABEL "TWO" AS 2
20 ADDER = 5;            DEFINE "ADDER" AS A 5
30 STORAGE = 848;        DEFINE STORAGE ADDRESS
40 ;
100 CLC;                 CLEAR THE CARRY FLAG
110 LDA #TWO;            LOAD A WITH 2
120 ADC #ADDER;          ADD 5
130 STA STORAGE;         STORE AT DECIMAL LOCATION 848
140 RTS;                 RETURN
150 .END ADDITION
```

Answers to quiz:

1. 0A	6. 20
2. 0F	7. 80
3. 05	8. 81
4. 10	9. FF
5. 11	10. FE

Chapter 3

The Monitor

The Monitor

A monitor is a program which allows you to work directly with your computer's memory cells. When you "fall below" BASIC into the monitor mode, BASIC is no longer active. If you type RUN, it will not execute anything. BASIC commands are not recognized. The computer waits, as usual, for you to type in some instructions. There are only a few instructions to give to a monitor. When you're working with it, you're pretty close to talking directly to the machine in machine language.

The Apple has a monitor in ROM. This means that you do not need to load the monitor program into the computer; it's always available to you.

Debugging is the main purpose of a monitor. You use it to check your ML code, to find errors.

You enter the Apple monitor by typing **CALL −151.** You will see the * monitor prompt and the cursor immediately after it. Here are the monitor instructions:

1. Typing an address (in hex) will show you the number contained in that memory cell; ***2000** (hit RETURN) will show 2000–FF, if, in fact, 255 decimal ($FF hex) is in that location.
2. You can examine a larger amount of memory in hex (this is called a *memory dump* or a *hex dump*). The Apple monitor remembers the address of the last number displayed. This can be used as a starting address for the dump. If you type the instruction in number 1, above, and then type ***.2010,** you will see a dump of memory between 2001 and 2010. The only difference between this and instruction 1 is the period (.) before the requested address.
3. You can directly cause a dump by putting the period between two addresses: ***2000.2010** combines the actions of instructions 1 and 2 above.
4. Hitting RETURN will continue a dump, one line at a time.
5. The last displayed memory location can be *changed* by using the colon (:). This is the equivalent of BASIC's POKE.

   If *2000 results in FF on the screen (or whatever), you can change this FF to 0 by typing *:00. To see the change, type ***2000** again. Or you could type ***2000:00** and make the change directly.

The Apple II reference manual contains excellent descriptions of the monitor instructions. We will list the rest of them only briefly here:

6. Change a series of locations at once: ***2000: 00 69 15 65 12.**
7. Move (transfer) a section of memory: ***4000<2000.2010M** will copy what's between 2000 and 2010 up to address 4000. (All these addresses are hex.)
8. Compare two sections of memory: ***4000<2000.2010V.** This looks like Move, but its job is to see if there are any differences between the numbers in the memory cells from 2000 to 2010 and those from 4000 to 4010. If differences are found, the address where the difference occurs appears onscreen. If the two memory ranges are identical, nothing is printed onscreen.
9. Saving (writing) a section of ML to tape: ***2000.2010W.** This is how you would save an ML program. You specify the addresses of the start and end of your program. Note that all your normal DOS functions are available as well, while in the monitor mode.
10. Loading (reading) a section of memory (or an ML program) back into the computer from tape: ***2000.2010R** will put the bytes saved, in instruction 9, above, back where they were when you saved them. Disk users save and load ML programs using the BSAVE and BLOAD commands, just as in BASIC mode.

An interesting additional feature is that you could send the bytes to *any* address in the computer. To put them at 4000, you would just type ***4000.4010R.** This gives you another way to relocate subroutines or entire ML programs (in addition to the Move instruction, number 7, above). If you move an ML program to reside at a different address from the one it was originally intended during assembly, any JMP or JSR (Jump to SubRoutine, like BASIC's GOSUB) instruction which points to within your program must be adjusted to point to the new addresses. If your subroutine contained an instruction such as 2000 JSR 2005, and you loaded at 4000, it would still say 4000 JSR 2005. You would have to change it to read 4000 JSR 4005. All the BNE, BPL, BEQ *branching* instructions, though, will make the move without damage. They are *relative* addresses (as opposed to the *absolute* addressing of JSR

2005). They will not need any adjusting. We'll go into this in detail later.

11. Run (go): ***2000G** will start executing the ML program which begins at address 2000. There had better be a program there or the machine is likely to lock up, performing some nonsense, an endless loop, until you turn off the power or press a RESET key. The program or subroutine will finish and return control of the computer to the monitor when it encounters an RTS.

    This is like BASIC's SYS command, except the computer returns to the monitor mode.

12. Disassemble (list): ***2000L** will list 20 lines of ML on the screen. It will contain three *fields* (a field is a "zone" of information). The first field will contain the address of an instruction (in hex). The address field is somewhat comparable to BASIC's line numbers. It defines the order in which instructions will normally be carried out.

    Here's a brief review of *disassembly* listings. The second field shows the hex numbers for the instruction, and the third field is where a disassembly differs from a "memory" or "hex" dump (see numbers 1 and 2, above). This third field translates the hex numbers of the second field back into a mnemonic and its argument. Here's an example of a disassembly:

```
2000    A9 41       LDA #$41
2002    8D 23 32    STA $3223
2005    A4 99       LDY $99
```

    Recall that a dollar sign ($) shows that a number is in hexadecimal. The pound sign (#) means *immediate* addressing (put the *number itself* into the A register at 2000 above).

    Confusing these two symbols is a major source of errors for beginning ML programmers. You should pay careful attention to the distinction between LDA #$41 and LDA $41. The second instruction (without the pound sign) means to load A with whatever number is found in *address* $41 hex. LDA #$41 means put the *actual number 41 itself* into the accumulator. If you are debugging a routine, check to see that you've got these two types of numbers straight, that you've loaded from addresses where you meant to (and, vice versa, that you've loaded *immediately* where you intended).

13. Mini-assembler. This assembler program is part of the Integer BASIC ROM, and must be placed in memory by booting the DOS 3.3 *System Master* disk and loading Integer BASIC into the Language card. Type INT from BASIC and press RETURN. Your prompt symbol should change to the > symbol for Integer BASIC. Then enter the monitor program by typing CALL −151, and press RETURN.

    From the monitor, type F666G to enter the assembler. The prompt symbol should change to the exclamation point (!) to insure that you are in fact in the assembler.

    Enter your starting address, followed by a colon (:), the mnemonic, and the argument for your first instruction. Press RETURN, and the assembler will erase your line and display the assembled code, placing the ! prompt on the next line. Type

    !2000:LDA #15

    The assembler program replaces your line with

    2000-   A9 15   LDA #$15

    To enter the next instruction, type a space following the ! prompt, and then the mnemonic and the argument. The assembler will place the code in memory correctly.

    ! LDY #01

    .

    If you mistyped LDA as LDDA, your Apple mini-assembler would sound a beep and put a caret (^) near the error. In any case, you are not going to get elaborate SYNTAX ERROR messages. Unless you are using a very sophisticated assembler like LADS, the only error that a simple assembler can usually detect is an impossible opcode.

    To reenter the monitor program from the assembler, type $FF69G and press RETURN. The dollar sign ($) must be typed before this hexadecimal address. Your prompt will change to an asterisk indicating that you are in the monitor program.

14. Changing registers. ***(CONTROL) E,** in the monitor, will display the contents of the accumulator, the X and Y registers, the status register (P), and the stack pointer (S). You can then change the contents of these registers by typing them in onscreen, following a colon. Note that to change

the Y register, you must type in the A and X registers as well:

***(CONTROL) E** (and hit RETURN)

You'll see A=01 X=05 Y=FF P=30 S=FE (whatever's in the registers at the time).

To change the Y register to 00, type in the A, X, and then the new version of Y:

***:01 05 00** (and hit RETURN)

15. Going back to BASIC. You can use ***(CONTROL) B** to go to BASIC (but it will wipe out any BASIC program that might have been there). Or you can use ***(CONTROL) C** to go back to BASIC, nondestructively.

Using the Monitor

You will make mistakes. Monitors are for checking and fixing ML programs. ML is an exacting programming process, and causing bugs is as unavoidable as mistyping when writing a letter. It will happen, be sure, and the only thing for it is to go back and try to locate and fix the slip-up. It is said that every Persian rug is made with a deliberate mistake somewhere in its pattern. The purpose of this is to show that only Allah is perfect. This isn't our motivation when causing bugs in an ML program, but we'll cause them nonetheless. The best you can do is try to get rid of them when they appear.

Probably the most effective tactic, especially when you are just starting out with ML, is to write very short subroutines. Because they are short, you can more easily check and examine them to make sure that they are functioning the way they should. Let's assume that you want to write an ML subroutine to ask a question on the screen. (This is often called a *prompt* since it prompts the user to do something.)

The message can be PRESS ANY KEY. First, we'll have to store the message in RAM somewhere. Let's put it at hex $1500. That's as good a place as anywhere else.

```
      ASCII
1500  208 P
1501  210 R
1502  197 E
1503  211 S
1504  211 S
1505  160
```

1506 193 A
1507 206 N
1508 217 Y
1509 160
150A 203 K
150B 197 E
150C 217 Y
150D 0 (This is a special signal to the computer called the *delimiter* which shows that the message is concluded.)

We'll put our "print-it-out" subroutine at address $1000. So, we've got the data at address $1500 and the subroutine that uses the data located at $1000. All this is entirely arbitrary. The ML programmer can put things wherever in RAM he or she wishes.

We haven't got into actual programming yet, but this example is a good place to see if you can spot an error in ML programming. This subroutine will not work as printed. There are two errors in this program. See if you can spot them:

```
1000 LDY #$00;        (Set up the Y register to count events.)
1002 LDA $1500,Y;     (Get the first character from the data.)
1005 CMP $00;         (Is it the delimiter?)
1007 BNE $100A;       (If not, continue on.)
1009 RTS;             (It was zero, so quit and return to whatever
                      JSRed, or called, this subroutine.)
100A STA $0400,Y;     (Apple text display area)
100D INY;             (Raise the counter by one.)
100E JMP $1000;       (Always JMP back to address $1000.)
```

Since we haven't yet gone into addressing or opcodes much, this is like learning to swim by the throw-them-in-the-water method. Nevertheless, see if you can make out how these instructions interact. Here's some help, a BASIC version (containing the same errors) of the same routine:

```
10 DATA 208,210,197,211,211,160,193,206,217,160,203,197,217,0
20 Y = 0
30 READ X: IF X < PEEK(0) THEN 50
40 RETURN
50 POKE 1024 + Y,X
60 Y = Y + 1
70 GOTO 20
```

This subroutine won't work. In the ML version, you'll find two of the most common bugs in ML programming. Unfortunately, they are not obvious bugs. An obvious bug would be typing LDS when you meant LDA. Any assembler would alert you to this error by printing an error message to let you know that no such instruction as LDS exists in 6502 ML.

No, the bugs in this program are errors in logic, in the flow or sense of the thing. If you disassemble it, it will also look just fine to the disassembler program, and no error messages will be printed out in this situation either.

But, the routine will not work the way you want it to. Before reading on, see if you can spot the two errors. Also, see if you can follow the events as the ML routine runs through its loop, picking up the characters in the message and supposedly depositing them onscreen. Where does the computer go after the first pass through the code? When and how does it know that it's finished with its job?

Two Common Errors

A very common bug, perhaps the most common ML bug, is caused by accidentally using *zero page addressing* when you mean to use *immediate addressing*. We mentioned this distinction before, but it is the cause of so much puzzlement to the beginning ML programmer that we're going to pound away at it several times in this book. Zero page addressing looks very similar to immediate addressing. Zero page means that you are dealing with one of the cells, or bytes, in the first 256 addresses in RAM memory in the computer, the lowest locations possible.

A *page* of memory is 256 bytes. Page 1 is from addresses 256 to 511 ($0100 to $01FF) and is special. It's called the *stack*, and the computer has a special use for it. We'll get to it later, but don't try storing anything in page 1 unless you're fond of havoc. Addresses 512–767 ($0200–$02FF) comprise page 2. The Apple text screen memory starts at address $0400 (1024 in decimal), and this is the start of page 4. And so on, in 256-byte blocks, up memory to the very top, page 255.

By contrast to zero page addressing is immediate addressing. Immediate addressing means that the number you're dealing with is right within the ML code (not somewhere else in memory). It means that you knew what number you were dealing with and put it right into your program when you wrote the program. Immediate addressing means that the number directly follows an instruction; it's the argument, the operand, of an instruction. LDY #$00 is immediate addressing.

It puts the number 0 into the Y register (see line 1000 in the example routine).

LDY $0 is *not* immediate addressing, and you very well might not get a 0 into the Y register. LDY $0 is zero page addressing. LDY $34 is also zero page addressing. Using any address lower than 256 would mean zero page addressing. LDY $34 might put anything, any number, into the Y register because *whatever number is in address $34* will be placed into the Y register. The key is that # symbol, the number symbol. If you mean to load the number $34 into the Y register, use LDY #$34. If you mean to fetch whatever is currently in address $34, use LDY $34. It's easy and very common to mix up these two modes. So, look for this error first when debugging a faulty program. Check to see that all your zero page addressing is supposed to fetch from the zero page of RAM and that all your immediate mode numbers are supposed to come from within the ML code itself, *immediately* following the instruction.

In our example ML program, LDY #$0 is correct—we do want to set the Y register to 0 so that it can help us put the characters in the proper places on the screen (STA $0400,Y stores each character at address $0400, the screen, *plus* the current value of Y). For this purpose, we want the immediate, the *actual,* number 0.

Take a close look, however, at the instruction at location $1005. Here, we are trying to see if we've picked out that zero in the message that tells us the message is finished. We want to CoMPare to the *number* 0. But, we left off the # symbol that tells the computer to use the number 0. Instead, we're going to cause a comparison against whatever might be in location 0, address 0. To fix this bug, the instruction should be changed to read CMP #$0 so that it will be immediate mode, not zero page mode. (If this confuses you, take a look at line 30 in the BASIC version to see the flaw. If it still confuses you, don't worry, we'll be going over all this in much greater detail in Chapters 4 and 6.)

The second bug in this example routine is also a very common one. The subroutine, as written, can never leave itself, will endlessly loop. Loop structures are usually preceded by a short setup of some kind. You have to initialize counters before the loop can begin because you have to tell it where to start and how many times to loop. In BASIC, FOR I = 1 TO 10 tells the computer to cycle ten times. In ML, we set the Y register to zero and let it act as our counter. In this particular routine, we don't use Y to tell us when to stop (that's the job of the embedded zero at the end of the message itself). Instead, Y serves two other purposes. It kills two birds with one stone. It is the offset (the pointer to the current position in a list or series) to load the message in the data and is also the offset to position the letters of the message on the screen. Without Y going up one (INY) each time through this loop, we would always print the first letter of the message and always print it in the first position on the screen.

What's the problem? It's that JMP instruction at $100E. We should be jumping back to address $1002, but the JMP tells us to jump back to $1000. As things stand, the Y register will always be reset to zero, there will never be a chance to read through the message and pick up that zero that ends things, and we cannot therefore ever exit this loop. We will endlessly cycle, printing *P* over and over again. Y will never go up past zero because each loop puts a zero back into Y. Look at the relationship between lines 70 and 20 in the BASIC example.

Tracking Them Down

The monitor will let you locate these and other errors. You can replace an instruction with a zero (the BReaK command) which will stop a program run and let you see the condition of your variables and what's going on in the registers at the *breakpoint*. If this doesn't help, you can get more specific by single-stepping through your program in order to discover, for example, that you are using CMP $0 when you meant CMP #$0.

It would also be easy, by stepping, to notice that your Y register is being reset to zero every time through the loop. For single-stepping, it's good to first make a printout of the suspect area of your program so that you can follow along during the single-stepping. If the Y register keeps turning back into zero, that clues you that this register isn't cooperating, it's not counting up each time through the loop the way you intended it to. These and other errors, if not always immediately obvious, are at least discoverable from within the monitor.

Also, the disassembler function of the monitor will permit you to study the program and look, deliberately, for the correct use of #$00 and $00. Since that mixup between immediate and zero page addressing is so common an error, always check for it first.

Programming Tools

The single most significant quality of monitors which contributes to easing the ML programmer's job is that monitors, like BASIC, are *interactive*. This means that you can make changes and test them right away, right then. In BASIC, you can find an error in line 120, make the correction, and run a test immediately.

It's not always that easy to locate and fix bugs in ML: There are few error messages, so finding the location of a bug can be difficult. But a monitor does allow interactivity: You make changes and test them on the spot. This is one of the drawbacks of complex assemblers, especially those which have several steps between the writing of the source code and the final assembly of executable object code (ML which can be executed). LADS, however, was designed to maximize interactivity, and you should find that its speed of assembly, its open architecture (you can easily modify it, add your own error messages and bug traps), and its BASIC-like environment will all contribute to quick program adjustments and quick testing.

Unfortunately, other sophisticated assemblers often require several steps between writing an ML program and being able to test it. These assemblers can require linkers, relocatable loaders, mapping, global/local variable definition, macros, separate and clumsy source code editors, and other "features" which contribute little to the actual assembly of a program or to the comfort of the programmer. If you don't already know the function of these "enhancements," count it as a blessing. They greatly retard program development except in professional, programming-by-committee situations. These functions make it easier to rearrange ML subroutines, put them anywhere in memory without modification, and so forth. They make ML more modular (composed of small, self-sufficient modules or subroutines), but they also make it far less interactive. You cannot easily make a change and see the effects at once.

However, using the monitor's mini-assembler, or the LADS assembler from this book, you are right near the monitor level, and fixes can easily and quickly be tested. In other words, the assemblers which are best for individual programmers trade efficiency for group-programming communication flexibility. Personal assemblers, like personal computers, should reflect the needs of the programmer, not the needs of industrial, programming teams. Personal assemblers should involve little, if any, preplanning, less forethought, less abstract analysis, and no rules for communicating between one programmer and another. If something goes awry, you can just try something else until it all works. Not only does this help you learn, it's also significantly the fastest way to program.

Plan Ahead or Plunge In?

Some people find such trial and error programming uncomfortable, disgraceful even. Industrial assemblers (and many assemblers currently sold for personal use) discourage interactivity, requiring flowcharts, even expecting the programmer to write out a program ahead of time on paper and debug it before even sitting down at the computer.

In one sense, these large assemblers are a holdover from the early years of computing, when computer time was extremely expensive. There was a clear advantage to coming to the terminal as prepared as possible. Interactivity was costly. But, like the increasingly outdated advice urging programmers to worry about saving computer memory space, it seems that strategies designed to conserve computer time are also anachronistic. You can spend all the time you want on your personal computer.

Complex assemblers tend to downgrade the importance of a monitor, to reduce its function in the assembly process. Some programmers who've worked on large IBM mainframe computers for 20 years do not know what the word *monitor* means in the sense we are using it. To them, monitors are CRT screens. The machine language tools used for years by mainframe programmers often have what we call a monitor, but it will be seriously restrictive. It will often, for example, have no single-step function and no provision for saving an ML program to disk or tape from within the monitor.

Whether or not you prefer the interactive style of personal programming, its greater reliance on the monitor, and on trial and error programming is your decision. If you're used to group programming, you might find it difficult to abandon the preplanning, the flowcharts, and all the rest. The choice is ultimately a matter of personal style.

Some programmers are uncomfortable unless they have a fairly complete plan before they even get to the computer keyboard. Others are quickly bored by elaborate flowcharting, "dry computing" on paper, and can't wait to get on the computer and see-what-happens-if.

Perhaps a good analogy can be found in the various ways that people make telephone calls. When long-distance calls were extremely expensive, most people made lists of what they wanted to say and carefully planned the call before dialing. They would also watch the clock during the call. (Some still do this today.) As the costs of phoning came down, many people found that spontaneous conversation was more satisfying. It's up to you.

Computer time, though, is now extremely cheap. If your computer uses 100 watts and your electric company charges 5 cents per kilowatt-hour, never turning your machine off would cost only about 12 cents a day.

Chapter 4

Addressing

Addressing

The 6502 processor is an electronic brain. It performs a variety of manipulations with numbers to allow us to write words, draw pictures, control outside machines such as tape recorders, calculate, and do many other things. It was designed to be logical and fast, to work accurately and efficiently.

If you could peer down into the CPU (Central Processing Unit), the heart of the processor, you would see numbers being delivered and received from memory locations all over the computer. Sometimes the numbers arrive and are sent out, unchanged, to some other address. Other times they are compared, added, or otherwise modified, before being sent back to RAM or to a peripheral. Writing an ML program can be compared with planning the activities of this message center. This can be illustrated by thinking of computer memory as a City of Bytes with the CPU acting as the main post office (see Figure 4-1). The CPU uses four tools to do its job: three *registers,* a program counter, a stack pointer, and seven little one-bit flags.

The monitor, if you type CONTROL-E, will display the present status of these tools. It looks something like this:

A=01 X=05 Y=FF P=30 S=FE

A, X, and Y are the registers, P is the processor status flags (each bit in this byte is a flag), and S is the stack pointer. You can more or less let the computer handle the stack pointer. It keeps track of numbers, usually return-from-subroutine addresses, which are kept together in a list called the stack.

The computer will automatically handle the stack pointer for us. It will also handle the program counter (PC) which keeps track of where you are located at any given time within the computer. For example, each ML instruction can be either one, two, or three bytes long. TYA has no argument and is the instruction to transfer a number from the Y register to the accumulator. Since it has no argument, the PC can locate the next instruction to be carried out by adding one to itself. If the PC held $4000, it would hold $4001 after execution of a TYA.

LDA #$01 is a two-byte instruction. It takes up two bytes in memory, so the next instruction to be executed after LDA #$01 will be two bytes beyond it. In this case, the PC will raise itself from $4000 to $4002. But we can just let it work merrily away without worrying about it.

Figure 4-1. Postal Executives at Work on an Instruction: 21254 STA $3300,Y

The Accumulator: The Busiest Register

S, A, X, and Y, however, are our business. They are all eight-bits, or one byte, in size. They are not located in memory proper. You can't PEEK them since they have no address like the rest of memory. They are zones of the CPU. The A register, most often called the *accumulator,* is the busiest place in the computer. The great bulk of the mail comes to rest here, if only briefly, before being sent to another destination.

Any logical transformations (EOR, AND, ORA) or arithmetic operations leave their results in the accumulator. Most of the bytes streaming through the computer come through the accumulator. You can compare one byte against another using the accumulator. And nearly everything that happens which involves the accumulator will have an effect on the *status register* (S, the flags). We won't need to actually work directly with the status register, but the information it holds will be important because several important instructions, like Branch if EQual (BEQ) test to see if a flag is up or down when deciding where to send the program for the next task.

The X and Y registers are similar to each other in that one of their main purposes is to assist the accumulator. They are used as addressing indexes. There are some methods of addressing that we'll get to in a minute which add an index value to another number. For example, if the X register is currently holding a five, LDA $4000,X will load the byte in address $4005 into A. In other words, the real address when you're using indexed addressing is the number *plus* the index value. If X has a six, then we load from $4006. Why not just LDA $4006? The reason is that it's far easier to raise or lower an index inside a loop structure than it would be to write in each specific address literally.

A second major use of X and Y is in counting and looping. We'll go into this more in the chapter on the instruction set.

We'll also have some things to learn later about S, the status register, which holds some flags showing current conditions. Among other things, the S can tell a program or the CPU if there has been a zero, a carry, or a negative number as the result of some operation. Although it's not important to be able to work directly with the status register, knowing about carry and zero flags is especially significant in ML. The branching instructions will check these flags for you, but you should be aware of what some of the flags signify.

But we can leave learning about the instructions until we get to Chapter 6. For now, the task at hand is to explore the various "classes" of mail delivery, the 6502 addressing modes.

The computer must have a logical way to pick up and send information. Rather like a postal service in a dream—everything should be picked up and delivered rapidly, and nothing should be lost, damaged, or delivered to the wrong address.

The 6502 accomplishes its important function of getting and sending bytes (GET and PRINT would be examples of the same activity in BASIC) by using several *addressing modes.* There are 13 different ways that a byte might be "mailed" either to or from the central processor.

When programming, in addition to picking an instruction (of the 56 available to you) to accomplish the job you are working on, you must also make one other decision. You must decide how you want to *address* the instruction—how, in other words, you want the mail sent or delivered. There is some room for maneuvering, however. It will rarely matter if you should choose a slower delivery method than you could have. Nevertheless, it is worth knowing about the various addressing modes; most of them are designed to be helpful during some particular programming activity.

Absolute and Zero

Let's picture a postman's dream city, a city so well planned from a postal-delivery point of view that no byte is ever lost, damaged, or sent to the wrong address. It's the City of Bytes we first toured in Chapter 2. It has 65536 houses all lined up on one side of a street (a long street). Each house is clearly labeled with its number, starting with house 0 and ending with house 65535. When you want to get a byte from, or send a byte to, a house (each house holds one byte), you must "address" the package. (See Figure 4-2.)

Let's look at the most elementary mode of addressing. It's quite popular and could be thought of as "first class." Called *absolute* addressing it can send a number to, or receive one from, any house in the city. It's what we normally think of first when the idea of *addressing* something comes up. You just put the number on the package and send it off. No indexing or special instructions. If it says 2500, then it means house 2500.

Figure 4-2. The First Few Addresses on a Street with 65536 Houses

1000 STA $2500

or

1000 LDA $2500

These two, STore A and LoaD A, STA and LDA, are the instructions which get a byte from, or send it to, the accumulator. The *address*, though, is those numbers following the instruction. The item following an instruction is sometimes called the instruction's *argument*. You could have written the above addresses several ways. Writing $2500, however, tells the computer to carry out the instruction with respect to address $2500, to store or load the byte from that location. This kind of addressing uses just a simple $ (to show that this is a hex, not decimal, number) and a four-digit number. You can send the byte in the accumulator to anywhere in memory by this method (or retrieve it from anywhere). Remember, too, that if you send a byte from the accumulator, it also remains in the accumulator. It's more a copying than a literal sending.

Heavy Traffic in Zero Page

A second addressing mode, called *zero page*, we've touched on before. If you are sending a byte down to anywhere between addresses 0 and 255 ($0000 and $00FF), the *zero page*, you can just leave off the first two numbers: 1000 STA $07. (Remember that the 1000 is the address, the location, of the *instruction*, not the argument, or target, of the instruction.)

Zero page addressing, using only two hex digits or decimal numbers lower than 256, is pretty fast mail service: The mail carrier has to worry about choosing between only 256 instead of 65536 possible houses. And, also, the computer is specially wired to service these special addresses. Think of them being close to the post office. Things get picked up and delivered rapidly in zero page. That's precisely why your BASIC and operating systems tend to use it so often.

Although zero page addressing works only with the first 256 locations in your computer, it gets more than its share of the mail. Apple's BASIC language, its operating system, and disk operating systems use up most of zero page to hold flags and other temporary information they need. Why? Because zero page addressing is the fastest of all the addressing modes. It's nearly instantaneous. Since the Apple has appropriated these first 256 houses for its own use, there's not much room left over down there for you to store your own ML pointers or flags, not to mention entire subroutines. You will, however, want to squeeze in some address *pointers* which we'll get to in a minute. After all, your programs, too, will sometimes want the fastest possible service.

These two addressing modes, absolute and zero page, are very common ones. In your programming, however, you probably won't get to use zero page as much as you might want to. You will notice on a map of the Apple that zero page is heavily trafficked. You could cause a problem by storing things in zero page where the Apple expects to use it for its own purposes. You can find excellent maps of your machine in its *Reference Manual* from Apple. Earlier Apples included these reference manuals with the computer; the IIc manual costs extra, but it's well worth it for ML programming. (Maps not only tell you what space must be avoided, but also where to access the many built-in BASIC routines in your computer. More about this later.)

There are, however, safe areas for you to use down there in those exclusive locations in lower RAM memory. Buffers for the cassette player or for BASIC activities like floating-point arithmetic are safe when you're not using a tape drive or BASIC. So, if you put your pointers and flags into these addresses, things will be fine. In any case, zero page is a popular, busy neighborhood. Don't put any of your actual ML programs there. Your main use of zero page will be to hold pointers for an especially useful addressing mode called *zero Y* that we're going to look at in detail. But you've always got to make sure that you aren't interfering with the Apple's own requirements for space in zero page.

Here is a list of the places you can safely store things in zero page without worrying that there will be a conflict with your Apple's needs:

6–9 (You can use addresses 6, 7, 8, or 9.)
25–31
206–207
214–215
235–239
249–255

While we're on the subject of places to avoid, keep out of page 1, too (decimal addresses 256–511). That's for the *stack,* about which more later. We'll get to the safe places in RAM that you can use for your ML programs and their flags, variables, tables, and so on. It's always okay to use ordinary higher RAM as long as you keep BASIC programs from putting their variables on top of the ML and keep the ML from writing over BASIC (if you want them to coexist during a program run).

The safest place of all for short ML routines is between addresses 768 ($300) and 1023 ($3FF) since the Apple leaves these RAM locations essentially undisturbed. So, when you want to practice with the examples in this book, it's always okay to give the LADS assembler a start address instruction of *= $300 or its decimal equivalent *= 768.

Immediate

Another very common addressing mode is called *immediate* addressing—it deals directly with a number. Instead of sending away for the number, we can just shove it directly into the accumulator by putting the number right in the same place where the other addressing modes have an address. Let's illustrate this:

1000 LDA $2500	(Absolute mode, loading from address 2500)
1000 LDA #$9	(Immediate mode, put number 9 into the accumulator)

The first example will load the accumulator with whatever number is found in address $2500. In the second example, we simply wanted to put a $9 into the accumulator. We know that we want the number $9. So, instead of sending off for the $9, we just type in a $9 where we normally would put a memory address. And we tack on the # symbol to show that the $9 is the number we're after. Without that #, the computer would load the accumulator with whatever it finds at *address* $9 (as in LDA $9). Without the #, it would be zero page addressing, not immediate addressing.

In any case, immediate addressing is very commonly used, since you often know already what number you are after and do not need to send away for it at all. One example would be printing out a carriage return on the screen. You already know what the code is for a carriage return, so you just load it into the accumulator with #. This is similar to BASIC where you define a variable (10 VARIABLE = 9). In this case, we have a variable being given a known value. LDA #9 is the same idea. To repeat, immediate addressing is used when you know what number you're dealing with; you're not sending off for it. It's put right into the ML program code *as a number, not as an address*. To illustrate immediate and absolute addressing working together, imagine that you wanted to copy the number 15 ($0F) into address $4000. (See Program 4-1.)

Implied

Here's an easy one. You don't use *any* address or argument with this one. You just type the instruction; it sits alone, needs no argument.

This is among the more obvious modes. It's called *implied*, since the mnemonic, the instruction itself, implies what is being sent where: TXA means Transfer the X register's contents to the Accumulator. Implied addressing means that you do not type anything following the instruction.

TYA and others are similar short-haul moves from one register to another. Included in this implied group are the SEC, CLC, SED, CLD instructions as well. They merely clear or set the flags in the status register, thereby letting you and the computer keep track of whether or not the most recent arithmetic resulted in a zero, whether or not a carry occurred, and so forth.

Also "implied" are such instructions as RTS (ReTurn from Subroutine), BRK (BReaK which is the ML equivalent of BASIC's STOP command), PLP, PHP, PLA, PHA (which "push" or "pull" the processor status register or accumulator onto or off the stack).

Increasing by one (incrementing) the X or Y register's number (INX, INY) or decreasing it (DEX, DEY) are also "implied." What all of these implied addressing modes have in common is the fact that you do not need to actually give any address. By comparison, an LDA $2500 (the absolute mode) must have that $2500 address to know where to pick up the package. TXA already says, in the instruction itself, that the address, the destination, is the accumulator. Likewise, you do not put an address after RTS since the computer always memorizes its jump-off address when it does a JSR. NOP (NO oPeration) is, of course, implied mode, too.

Program 4-1. Putting an Immediate 15 into Absolute Address $4000

```
20     ML PROGRAM STARTS AT $2000 (*= MEANS START ADDRESS)
30
40 2000 A9 0F                   LDA #15       LOAD A WITH THE NUMBER (NOT THE ADDRESS)
50 2002 8D 00 40                STA $4000     STORE IT IN ADDRESS $4000
60
70  NOTE THAT IN SOME ASSEMBLERS YOU CAN SWITCH BETWEEN
80  HEX AND DECIMAL AT WILL.  LADS ALLOWS THIS.  THE 15
90  IS DECIMAL.  IN HEX IT WOULD BE WRITTEN #$0F
```

Relative

One particular addressing mode, the *relative* mode, used to be a real headache for programmers. Not so long ago, in the days when ML programming was done "by hand," this was a frequent source of errors. Hand computing—entering each byte by flipping eight switches up or down and then pressing an ENTER key—meant that the programmer had to write a program out on paper, translate the mnemonics into their number equivalents, and then "key" the whole thing into the machine with that set of switches.

It was a big advance when hexadecimal numbers permitted entering $0F instead of eight switches: 00001111. This reduced errors and fatigue.

An even greater advance was having enough free memory so that an assembler program could be in the computer while the ML program was being written. An assembler not only takes care of translating LDA $2500 into its three (eight-switch) numbers—10101101 (the code for the instruction LDA) and 00000000 00100101 (the number $2500)—but an assembler also does relative addressing. So, for the same reason that you can program in ML without knowing how to deal with binary numbers, you can also forget about relative addressing. The assembler will do it for you. All you need to remember about it is that you can't go very far away from the current instruction when using relative addressing.

Relative addressing is used with eight instructions only: BCC, BCS, BEQ, BMI, BNE, BPL, BVC, BVS. They are all branching instructions. They force the control of the program to *branch* (jump) when the overflow flag is set (or cleared); when the carry flag is set (or cleared); or if the most recent arithmetic resulted in equal, less than, not equal, or more than.

Branch if EQual (BEQ) would look like this in BASIC: IF X = 0 THEN GOTO. It forces the computer to branch somewhere else in a program if something is equal to zero.

All these B instructions can branch only as far as 128 addresses forward or 127 backward from where the instruction is located. If you were delivering the mail in the City of Bytes, you would probably dislike relative addresses; it would mean extra work. You would be going peacefully from house to house up the road and then, suddenly, one of the letters has a giant *B* on it and a number like −5 or +47. You've then got to stop your orderly progress up the road and take this letter 5 houses back from the current house or 47 houses forward.

Remember that these branches, these jumps, can be a distance of only 128 bytes from their own address, but they can go in either direction. Thus, if a BNE instruction above is located in RAM at address $3500, you cannot specify $5600 as its target. That would be much too big a branch. You specify *where* the branch should go by giving an address within the boundaries of 128 bytes in either direction. Here's an example:

```
1000 LDX #$00
1002 INX
1003 BNE $1002
1005 BRK
```

(The X register in this example will count up by ones until it hits 255 decimal. At that point, it resets itself to zero. When it does become zero, that will fail to trigger the Branch if Not Equal to zero instruction, and we will "fall through" the branch to the BRK at $1005.)

This is how you create an ML FOR-NEXT loop. You are branching *relative* to address 1003, which means that the assembler will calculate what address to place into the computer that will get you to address $1002. You might wonder what's wrong with the computer just accepting the number $1002 as the address to which you want to branch. Absolute addressing *does* give the computer the actual address, but the branching instructions all need addresses which are offsets of the starting address. After assembling the example above, the assembler puts the following into the computer:

```
1000 A2 00
1002 E8
1003 D0 FD
1005 00
```

The odd thing about this piece of code is that FD at address $1004. How does $FD tell the computer to branch back to $1002? The $FD is 253 decimal. Now it begins to be clear why relative addressing is so messy. If you are curious, numbers larger than 127, when used as arguments for the B instructions, tell the computer to go *back down* to lower addresses. What's worse, the larger the number, the *less* far down it goes. In this case, the computer counts the address $1005 as zero and counts backward thus:

1005 = 0 = $00
1004 = 255 = $FF
1003 = 254 = $FE
1002 = 253 = $FD

Not a very pretty counting method! It's easy for the computer to deal with this, but to us it's awkward and strange. Fortunately, all that we assembler users need do is to assign a label to the address we're branching to and use the label as the address (as if it were an *absolute* address). The assembler will do the hard part.

This strange counting method is the way that the computer handles negative numbers. It thinks of the leftmost bit in a byte as the sign bit. Whether the bit is on or off signifies a positive or negative number. For the beginning ML programmer, however, it's just as well to forget all about negative numbers. You won't find that you'll need to use them since practically everything you'll want to do can be done with positive integers.

Before leaving our discussion of branching, let's look at one special problem that you *will* need to deal with if you use a simple assembler. When you are using one of the branch instructions, you sometimes branch forward. Let's say that you want to have a different kind of FOR-NEXT loop:

```
1000  LDX #$0
1002  INX
1003  BEQ $100A
1005  JMP $1002
1008  BRK
1009  BRK
100A BRK
```

When jumping forward, you often do not yet know the precise address you want to branch to. In the example above, we really wanted to go to $1008 when the loop was finished (when X was equal to zero), but we just entered an approximate address ($100A) and made a note of the place where this guess appeared ($1004). Then, using the direct memory changing function in the monitor, we can change location $1004 to the correct offset when we know what it should be.

Forward counting is easy. When we learned that we wanted to go to $1008, we would change the number $5 in address $1004 to $3.

Remember that you start counting from zero from the address immediately following the branch instruction. For example, a jump to $1008 would be three because you count $1005=0, $1006=1, $1007=2, $1008=3. All this confusion disappears after writing a few programs and practicing with estimated branch addresses. Luckily, the assembler does all the backward branches. That's lucky because they are much harder to calculate.

Unknown Forward Branches

If you are using LADS, all branches are given *names* rather than addresses. These names are called *labels,* and they are automatically calculated for you by the assembler. You would write the above example with LADS in this way:

```
LDX #0
COUNTUP INX
BEQ MORETHINGS;  (or any other label you want to give it)
JMP COUNTUP;     (jumps also have labels as their targets)
MORETHINGS BRK
```

With LADS and other advanced assemblers, you'll often use labels instead of actual addresses. This makes things pretty easy on the programmer. LADS does much of the busywork for you, particularly if you make good use of its pseudo-ops.

By the way, we'll get to pseudo-ops later. Essentially, they are instructions directly to the assembler such as "please insert the following as pure ASCII text," but which are not normal 6502 instructions that get translated into ML object code. Instead, a pseudo-op is a request to the assembler program to perform some extra service for the programmer.

Absolute,X and Absolute,Y

Another important mode provides you with an easy way to manipulate lists or tables. This method looks like absolute addressing, but it attaches an X or a Y to the address. The X and Y stand for the X and Y registers, which are being used in this technique as offsets. That is, if the X register contains the number 3, then whatever address you type in will have 3 added to it. If X holds a 3 and you type LDA $1000,X, you will LoaD Accumulator with the value (number) which is in memory cell $1003. *The register value is added to the absolute address.*

Another addressing method called *zero page,X* works the same way: LDA $05,X. (Load from cell 5 plus whatever's in the X register.) These indexed addressing modes let you easily transfer or search through messages, lists, or tables. Error messages can be sent to the screen using such a method. Assume that you set it up so that the words SYNTAX ERROR are held in some part of memory because you sometimes need to send them to the screen from your program. You might have a whole *table* of such messages. But we'll say that the words SYNTAX ERROR are stored at address $3000. Assuming that your screen memory address is 1024 ($0400 hex), here's how you would send the message:

1000 LDX #$00	(Set the counter register to zero.)
1002 LDA $3000,X	(Get a letter at 3000 + X.)
1005 BEQ $100E	(If the letter is a zero, we've reached the end of the message, so we branch to the end of this routine.)
1007 STA $0400,X	(Send the letter to 0400 + X.)
100A CMP #$00	(If the accumulator picked up a zero, the message is finished. Each message ends with a zero—called a *delimiter*—to alert the computer to stop sending.)
100A INX	(Increment the counter so that the next letter in the message, as well as the next screen position, are pointed to.)
100B JMP $1002	(Jump to the load instruction to fetch the next character.)
1010 BRK	(Task completed, message transferred.)

This sort of indexed looping is an extremely common ML programming device. It can be used to create delays (FOR T = 1 TO 5000: NEXT T), to transfer any kind of memory to another place, to check the status of memory (to see, for example, if a particular word appeared somewhere on the screen), and to perform many other tasks. It is a fundamental, all-purpose machine language technique.

Here's a fast way to fill your screen or any other area of memory. This is a full source code for the demonstration screen-fill example we tried in Chapter 1. See if you can follow how this indexed addressing works. What bytes are filled in, and when? At ML speeds, it isn't necessary to fill them in order—nobody would see an irregular filling pattern because, like magic, it all happens too fast for the eye to see. (See Program 4-2.)

Program 4-2. Filling the Screen with the letter *A*

```
20
30 9C40                    A = $C1   THE "A" CHARACTER
40
50 9C40 A0 00              LDY #0         SET COUNTER TO ZERO
60 9C42 A9 C1              LDA #A
70 9C44 99 00 04   LOOP    STA $0400,Y
80 9C47 99 00 05           STA $0500,Y
90 9C4A 99 00 06           STA $0600,Y
100 9C4D 99 00 07          STA $0700,Y
110 9C50 C8                INY            RAISE COUNTER BY 1
120 9C51 D0 F1             BNE LOOP       IF Y IS NOT YET ZERO, KEEP GOING
130 9C53 60                RTS
```

Compare this with the program on page *x* to see the effects of using a different screen starting address and how source code is a more elaborate version of what you get when you run a disassembler to get an ML program listing.

Indirect Y

This addressing mode is a real workhorse; you'll use it often. Several of the examples in this book refer to it and explain it in context. The argument you use with this mode isn't so much an *address in itself* as a method of *creating* an address. It looks like this:

```
4000 STA ($80),Y
```

Seems innocent enough. That Y works like the other kinds of index modes we've discussed before. Whatever is in the Y register is added to the final address.

But watch out for those parentheses. They mean that $80 is *not* the real address here. We're not going to put the byte in the accumulator into address $80. Instead, addresses $80 and $81 are themselves *holding* the address we are sending our byte to. We are not sending to $0080; hence, the name for this mode is *indirect* Y.

Where does the byte in the accumulator end up? If $80 and $81 have these numbers in them:

```
$0080 01
$0081 20
```

and Y is holding a five, then the byte in A will end up in address $2006! How did we get $2006?

First, you've got to mentally swap the numbers in $80 and $81. The 6502 requires that *address pointers* be listed in backward order: The pointer is holding $2001, not $0120. Then, you've got to add the value in the Y register, 5, and you get $2006.

This is a valuable tool, even if it's perplexing at first. You should familiarize yourself with it. It lets you get easy access to many memory locations very quickly by just changing the Y register (using INY or DEY) or by directly changing the address pointer itself (using INC or DEC, instructions that raise or lower a byte in RAM memory by one). You can make radical shifts with this pointer changing technique. You can shift up a whole page (256 bytes) by simply INC $81: That will change your target address from $2001 to $2101. To go down four pages, subtract four from address $81. Combine this with the indexing that the Y register is doing for you, and you've got greater efficiency, greater reach to all the RAM you want to manipulate.

Right now you're paying the only price you'll ever pay for this valuable tool: It's not one of the more obvious things in learning ML. You've got to try it a few times, scratch your head, and get the concept.

Let's clear away some of the fog. How were those bytes at $80 and $81 selected to be the ones holding our indirect address? The programmer decides where *address pointers* are stashed (they must be in zero page). You figure out where the safe places are in zero page and you use them for your pointers. That's the main use that you'll have for zero page.

How did the numbers $20 and $01 get into the pointer? The programmer put them there. As part of the initial activities of an ML program, you stick byte-pairs (these address pointers) into zero page. If you're using a simple assembler, you'll need to keep a record of the pointers on paper. If you're using LADS, you give the pointers labels like this:

```
TOSCREEN = $80
```

And you can also have a label for the actual screen address:

```
SCREEN = $0400
```

Then, to set up a pointer, you use some pseudo-ops in LADS which break a two-byte address like $0400 into halves for storage in pointers:

```
LDA #<SCREEN; loads the low byte
STA TOSCREEN
LDA #>SCREEN; loads the high byte
STA TOSCREEN+1; stores into address TOSCREEN plus 1 ($81)
```

When an address is set up in a pointer, it's split in half. The address $0400 was split in the example above. When programming in ML, it's useful to distinguish between the two halves by saying that one of the bytes is the LSB (least significant byte) and the other is the MSB (most significant). In our example, the $00 is the LSB and the $04 is the MSB. That's not because one number is smaller than the other; rather, it's because they are in different positions in the two-byte address. The position on the left is of far more significance than the position on the right in $0400. It's the same for decimal numbers: 5015 when chopped in half means that the left half stands for fifty 100's and the right half only stands for fifteen 1's.

Note that every time you add one to the MSB of a double-byte hex number in ML, you are adding one page, 256. This is how you can INC or DEC the MSB of your pointer and move quickly through the "pages" of memory. And remember, you store pointers in reverse order when you are setting up a pointer, LSB, MSB:

0080 00
0081 04; a pointer to the screen memory of the Apple

Indirect X

This addressing mode is rarely used. It makes it possible to set up a *group* of pointers, a cluster of them, in zero page. It's like indirect Y except the X register value is not added to the address pointer to form the ultimate address target. Rather, X points to the *pointer* you desire to use. Nothing is added to the address held in the pointer. It looks like this:

5000 STA ($90,X)

To see it in action, let's assume that you've already set up a cluster of pointers in zero page. It's a table of pointers, not just one:

0090 $00;	**Pointer 1**
0091 $04;	points to $0400
0092 $05;	**Pointer 2**
0093 $70;	points to $7005
0094 $EA;	**Pointer 3**
0095 $81;	points to $81EA

If X holds a two when we STA ($90,X), then the byte in the accumulator will be sent to address $7005. If X holds a four, the byte will go to $81EA.

All things considered, this addressing mode has little to recommend it. If you set up the same table, you could access these pointers just as easily and have the flexibility of that Y index into the bargain. Who knows why the designers of the 6502 chip included this mode?

Accumulator Mode

ASL, LSR, ROL, and ROR shift the *bits* in the byte held in the accumulator. We'll touch on this shifting in Chapter 6 when we discuss the instruction set. This mode doesn't really have much to do with addressing as such, but it's always listed as a separate mode.

Zero Page,Y

This mode can be used with only two instructions: LDX and STX. Otherwise, it operates just like zero page,X discussed above.

What to Remember

There you have them, 13 addressing modes to choose from. However, there are only 6 that you should focus on and practice with until you understand their uses: immediate, absolute (plus absolute,X and ,Y), zero page, and indirect Y. The rest are either unimportant when you're programming because they are automatic (like the *implied* mode) or not really worth bothering with. Now that we've surveyed the ways you can move numbers around, it's time to see how to do arithmetic in ML.

Chapter 5

Arithmetic

Arithmetic

There'll be many things that you'll want to do in ML, but complicated math is not one of them. Mathematics beyond simple addition, subtraction, multiplication, and division will not be covered in this book. For games and most other ML for personal computing, you won't need to use complex math. In this chapter we'll cover what you are likely to use. BASIC is well-suited to sophisticated mathematical programming and is far easier to work with for such tasks. If you're planning a program that's going to involve trigonometry or quadratic equations, use BASIC.

But before we look at ML arithmetic, let's briefly review an important concept: how the computer tells the difference between addresses, numbers as such, and instructions. It is valuable to be able to visualize what the computer is going to do as it comes upon each byte in your ML routine.

Even when a computer appears to be working with words, letters of the alphabet, graphics symbols, and the like, *it is still working with numbers*. A computer works *only* with numbers. The ASCII code is a convention by which a computer understands that when the context is alphabetic, the number 193 means the letter *A*. At first this is confusing. How does it know when 193 is *A* and when it is just 193? And there's a third possibility: The 193 could represent the cell 193 in the computer's memory, the one hundred ninety-third address. (In the Apple character code, the letter *A* is 193, but true ASCII would use the number 65 for *A*. We'll use the Apple code in this discussion since it's important to become familiar with it.)

It is worth remembering that, like us, the computer means different things at different times when it uses a symbol (like 193). We can mean a street address by it, a temperature, or a code. We could agree that whenever we used the symbol 193, we were ready to leave the party. We would look meaningfully at our companion and say, "We always cook our pork to a temperature of *one hundred ninety-three.*" Then hope they got the hint.

The point is that symbols aren't anything in themselves. They *stand* for other things, and what they stand for must be agreed upon in advance. There must be rules. A code is an agreement in advance that one thing symbolizes another.

The Computer's Rules

Inside your machine, at the most basic level, there is a stream of input. The stream flows continually past a "gate" like a river through a canal. For 99 percent of the time, this input is 0's. (BASICs differ; some see continuous 255's, but the idea is the same.)

When you first turn it on, the computer just sits there.

What's it doing? It might be updating a clock, if you have one, and it's holding things coherent on the TV screen—but it mainly waits in an endless loop for you to press a key on your keyboard to let it know what it's supposed to do.

There is a memory cell inside your Apple which the computer constantly checks. This byte in the Apple is located at 49152 ($C000 in hexadecimal). While no key is pressed, the leftmost bit (the "high bit") in this byte is off, is zero. When a key is hit on the keyboard, however, the leftmost bit flips on, and that's the signal that someone is trying to type something in. If you press the RETURN key, a 141 will appear in location 49152. Finally, after centuries (the computer's sense of time differs from ours) here is something to work with! Something has come up to the gate at last.

By the way, it's interesting that 49152 is not a RAM memory byte. You can't POKE something in there; you can only look at it, PEEK it. Thus, when you need to test this byte, you must set its seventh bit off (a seventh bit *on* in 49152 signals that someone has pressed a key on the keyboard). But you can't set the seventh bit off by LDA #0:STA $C000 because you can't store something in this location. Instead, you can only turn the seventh bit off by *any* reference to location $C010 (LDA, STA, whatever). Anytime you mention $C010, that location appears on the computer's *address bus,* and this act has the effect of clearing out the seventh bit in $C000. This is one of those things you memorize but don't question. It works; use it.

But assume that someone hits the RETURN key and, thus, a 141 appears in location 49152. You notice the effect at once—everything on the screen moves up one line, because 141 (in the Apple code) stands for a carriage return. How did the Apple know that you were not intending to type the *number* 141 when it saw 141 in the keyboard sampling cell? Simple. The number 141, and any other keyboard input, is *always* read as an ASCII number. Besides, there's a difference between the *number* 141 and the *three characters required* to indicate the characters 1, 4, 1.

In ASCII, the digits from 0 through 9 are the only number symbols. There is no single symbol for the three characters in 1 4 1. So, when you type in a 1 followed immediately by a 4 and then another 1, the computer's input-from-keyboard routine notices that you have *not* pressed one of the "instant action" keys (such as the ESC, TAB, cursor-control keys). Rather, you typed 1 and 4 and another 1—the keyboard sampling cell, the "which key pressed" location in zero page, received the ASCII value for 1, and then for 4, and finally another 1.

The point is that hitting the key labeled 1 followed by the key labeled 4 followed by another 1 is not storing those numbers into that sampling cell at 49152. Instead, these things are stored as *characters*. On the ML level, numbers are distinct from characters. Characters like 3 have an ASCII code value which differs from their numeric value. In other words, typing 1-4-1 will not result in the computer seeing a 1-3-1. If you looked, you would find that the computer saw a $B1, $B4, and $B1 (177, 180, 177 decimal).

Incidentally, Apple ASCII code representations of the digits are easy to remember in hex: 0 is $B0, 1 is $B1, up to $B9 for 9. In decimal, the digits would be 176 to 185.

The computer decides the "meaning" of the numbers which flow into and through it by each number's *context*. If it is in "alphabetic" mode, the computer will see the number 193 as *A;* or if it has just received an *A,* it might see a subsequent number 193 as an address to store the *A*. It all depends on the events that surround a given number. We can illustrate this with a simple example:

```
2000   LDA #$C1   $A9 (169)   $C1 (193)
2002   STA $C1    $85 (133)   $C1 (193)
```

This short ML program (the numbers in parentheses are the decimal values) shows how the computer can "expect" different meanings from the number 193 ($C1 hex). When it receives an *instruction* to perform an action, it is then prepared to act *upon* a number. The instruction comes first and, since it is the first thing the computer sees when it starts a job, it *knows that the number $A9 (169) is not a number.*

It has to be one of the ML instructions from its set of instructions (see Appendix A).

Instructions and Their Arguments

The computer would no more think of this first 169 as the *number* 169 than you would seal an envelope before the letter was inside. If you are sending out a pile of Christmas cards, you perform instruction-argument just the way the computer does: You (1) fill the envelope (instruction) (2) with a card (argument or operand). You don't get the envelopes confused with the cards and try to stuff an envelope into a card.

All actions do something *to* something. A computer's action is called an instruction (or, in its numeric form as part of an ML program inside the computer's memory, it's called an *opcode* for *operation code*). The target of the action is called its argument (operand). In our program above, the computer must LoaD Accumulator with 193. The # symbol means *immediate;* the target is right there in the next memory cell following the LDA instruction, so it isn't supposed to be fetched from a distant memory cell. That 193, however, is not another instruction; it's the number 193.

Then, after this action has been completed, after the accumulator contains the number 193, the next number (the 133 which means STore Accumulator in zero page, the first 256 cells) *must be* an instruction, the start of another complete action. And, once again, the computer knows that the instruction 133 must be followed by an address of a cell in memory to store to. So, in the example, we've got a total of four numbers: 169, 193, 133, and 193. If you PEEKed at this little ML routine, you'd find these numbers in this order. But when this ML program is run, is executed by the 6502, it will see 169 as an instruction, 193 as a number, 133 as another instruction, and the 193 following that instruction as an address in memory. Instructions, numbers, addresses—they are all mixed in together, but the chip can figure out which is which based upon their context. It knows that LDA # will be followed by a single byte *number* because that's what LDA in the immediate addressing mode demands. The computer would no more expect an address to come after LDA # than you would expect someone to say "1700 Taylor Street" when you asked what time it was.

Think of the computer as completing each action and then looking for another instruction. It moves through your list of instructions logically. Recall from the last chapter that the target can be "implied" in the sense that INX simply increases the X register by one. The one is "implied" by the instruction itself, so there is no target argument in these cases. The next cell in this case *must* also contain an instruction for a new instruction-argument cycle.

Some instructions call for a single-byte argument. LDA #193 is of this type. You cannot LoaD Accumulator with anything greater than 255. The accumulator is only one byte large, so anything that can be loaded into it can also be only a single byte large. (Recall that 255, $FF, is the largest number that can be represented by a single byte.)

STA $C1 also has a one-byte argument because the target address for the STore Accumulator is, in this case, in zero page.

Storing to zero page, or loading from it, will need only a one-byte argument—the address. Zero page addressing is a special case, but an assembler program will take care of it for you. It will pick the correct opcode for this addressing mode when you type LDA $C1. Typing in LDA $00C1 would create ML code that performs the same operation, though it would use three bytes instead of two to do it.

But how does the chip know that a given instruction is self-contained like the INY, implied addressing mode? Or another instruction uses up two bytes like zero page addressing (STA $15 uses one byte for the STA command and one byte for the $15)? Or the biggest addressing modes, like STA $1500, absolute addressing, take three bytes before they can look for the next instruction in a program?

Inside the chip is a *program counter*. It has a list of all the ML instructions. And it knows how many bytes—one, two, or three—that each instruction takes up. During an ML program's execution, the program counter acts like a finger that keeps track of where the computer is located at any given time in its trip up the series of ML instructions that comprise your program. Each instruction takes up one, two, or three bytes, depending on what type of addressing is going on. The program counter looks at its list and moves up the appropriate number of bytes to show where the next instruction will be.

Context Defines Meaning

TXA uses only one byte, so the program counter (PC) moves ahead one byte and stops and waits until the value in the X register is moved over into the accumulator. TXA is supposed to transfer into the accumulator whatever number is in the X register. Then the computer asks the PC, "Where are we?" and the PC is pointing to the address of the next instruction. The PC never points to an argument. It skips over them because it knows how many bytes each addressing mode uses up in a program.

Say that the next instruction after TXA is LDA $15. This is a two-byte-long, zero page addressing mode. The PC looks on its list and moves up two bytes. The longest possible instruction would use three bytes, such as LDA $5000 (absolute addressing). The PC counts up three and points. Your assembler would translate LDA $15 into $A5 and POKE it. It would translate LDA $1500 into $AD and POKE that. Since the opcodes that get POKEd are different, even though the LDA mnemonics are identical, the computer can know how many bytes a given instruction will use up. That's how it knows where the next instruction must be in your program.

Having reviewed the way that your computer makes *contextual* sense out of the mass of seemingly similar numbers of which an ML program is composed, we can now move on to see how elementary arithmetic is performed in ML.

Addition

Arithmetic is performed in the accumulator. The accumulator holds the first number, the target address holds the second number (but is not affected by the activities), and the result is left in the accumulator. So

```
LDA #$40   (Remember, the # means immediate, the $ means hex.)
ADC #$01
```

will result in the number $41 being left in the accumulator. We could then STA that number wherever we wanted. Simple enough.

The ADC means ADd with Carry. If an addition results in a number higher than 256 (if we added, say, 250 + 7), then there would have to be a way to show that the number left behind in the accumulator isn't the correct result—that what's in the accumulator isn't the total, it's the *carry*.

After adding 250 + 7, you would find a 1 in the accumulator and the *carry flag* would be up. That means that you must add 256 to whatever is in the accumulator to find the real answer: 257.

To make sure that things never get confused, always CLC

(CLear the Carry flag) before you do any addition. CLC will push the carry flag down (in case it was up from some previous event in your program). Then, if you find that it is up after the addition (ADC), you'll know that you need to add 256 to whatever is in the accumulator. You'll know that the accumulator is holding the carry, not the total result.

One other point about the status register: There is another flag, the *decimal* flag. If you ever set this flag up (with the SED, SEt Decimal instruction), all addition and subtraction is performed in a *decimal mode* in which the carry flag is set whenever an addition exceeds 99. In this book, we are not going into the decimal mode at all, so it's a good precaution to put a CLear Decimal mode (CLD) instruction as the first instruction of any ML program you write. After you type CLD, the flag will be put down and the assembler will move on to ask for your next instruction, but the arithmetic from then on will all be handled as we are describing it. Decimal mode has little value in ML programming. It's another one of those things that sounds good, but doesn't do much in practice.

Adding Numbers Larger Than 255

We have already discussed the idea of setting aside some memory cells as a table for data. To do this, we simply make a note to ourselves that, say, addresses $D6 and $D7 are declared a zone for our personal use as a storage area. Using a typical example, let's think of this two-byte zone as the place that holds the address of a "moving finger" going through a list of names we've stored in RAM. As long as the zone is not in ROM or used by our program elsewhere or used by the computer (see your computer's memory map in the *Reference Manual* from Apple or use the safe areas we discussed earlier), it's fine to declare an area a data zone. It is a good idea (especially with longer programs) to make notes on a piece of paper to show where you intend to have your subroutines, your main loop, your initialization, and your miscellaneous data—names, messages for the screen, input from the keyboard, and so on. This is one of those things that BASIC does for you automatically, but which you must do for yourself in ML. However, you can set up data zones with the LADS assembler by using the .BYTE, =, or *= pseudo-ops.

When BASIC creates a string variable, it sets aside an area to store variables. This is what DIM does. In ML, you set aside your own areas by simply finding a clear memory space and not writing a part of your program into it (or by staking out some memory with .BYTE or *= in LADS). Part of your data zone can be special registers you declare to hold the results of addition or subtraction.

But back to our example: You might make a note to yourself that $D6 and $D7 will hold the current position within a list of names in your database. This is a *pointer,* and we can look at all the bytes within our database by adjusting this pointer in $D6 and $D7. In this way we can efficiently search through the database.

Since the "moving finger" searching through the database is constantly in motion, this pointer will be changing all the time as it looks for your target information. Notice that you need *two* bytes for this pointer. That is because one byte could hold only a number from 0 to 255. Two bytes together, though, can hold a number up to 65535 (all the possible addresses in the Apple).

To define the pointer location, you could do this in LADS:

```
FINGER = $D7
```

If you needed another two-byte pointer to hold another address, you could write this:

```
OTHER = $EB
```

and so on, using safe areas, for as many pointers as you needed.

Since your Apple can address only a total of 65536 memory cells at any moment, two-byte registers like these can address *any* addressable cell in your computer. So if your "moving finger" is supposed to look up the name "Mitchell, Nancy" in the database, you'll want to start off by looking for the letter *M*. In setting up your list of names, you decided that each entry, each "record," would be given 40 bytes of space. Thus, you are going to be adding 40 to the FINGER if the first character in the first record isn't an *M*. Let's say that the list of records starts in memory at address $8000.

Before accessing the list, we punch in the target address:

```
LDA #0:STA $D6:LDA #80:STA $D7
```

Or you could accomplish the same thing with the LADS assembler by using labels and the #> and #< pseudo-ops which extract the MSB and LSB of a label's address:

```
LDA #<DATA:STA FINGER:LDA #>DATA:STA FINGER+1
```

The FINGER address register now looks like this in the monitor: $00D6 00 80 (remember that the higher, most significant byte, comes *after* the LSB, the least significant byte). To move to the next name in the list, we want FINGER to be $00D6 28 80. (The 28 is hex for 40.) In other words, we're going to move the finger up one record in the database list. To do this, we need to add $28 (40 decimal) to the pointer, the FINGER.

Remember the indirect Y addressing mode which lets us use an address in zero page as a *pointer* to another address in memory? The number in the Y register is added to whatever address sits in D6, D7, so we don't STA to $D6 or $D7, but rather to the address that they *contain:* STA ($D6),Y.

How to add $28 to the FINGER pointer? First of all, CLC, CLear the Carry, to be sure that flag is down. This example uses the mini-assembler in the monitor:

1000 CLC	(1000 is the location of our "add 40 to FINGER" subroutine)
1001 LDA $D6	(We fetch the LSB of FINGER)
1003 ADC #$28	(Add 40)
1006 STA $D6	(Put the new result into FINGER)
1008 LDA $D7	(Get the MSB of FINGER)
100A ADC #$0	(Add *with carry* to the MSB of FINGER)
1010 STA $D7	(Update FINGER'S MSB)

That's it. Any carry will automatically set the carry flag up during the ADC action on the LSB and will be added into the result when we ADC to the MSB. It's all quite similar to the way that we add numbers, putting a carry onto the next column when we get more than a ten in the first column. And this carrying is why we always CLC (clear the carry flag; put it down) just before additions. If the carry is set, we could get the wrong answer if our problem did not result in a carry. Did the addition above cause a carry? (Remember, we started with a value of $8000 in FINGER.)

Note that we need not check for any carries during the MSB+MSB addition. Any carries resulting in a database address greater than $FFFF (65535) would be impossible on our machines.

The 6502 is permitted to address $FFFF tops, under normal conditions. However, it is possible to add numbers larger than 65535 by simply using more than two bytes and continuing to add *with carry* across a multibyte chain.

The example above would be somewhat easier with LADS because you would substitute label names (FINGER and DATA in this case) for the numbers. Also, you could define another label to hold the size of a record (RECORD = 40), and then line 1003 would read ADC #RECORD.

Subtraction

As you might expect, subtracting single-byte numbers is a snap:

```
LDA #$41
SBC #$01
```

results in a $40 being left in the accumulator. As before, though, it is good to make it a habit to deal with the carry flag before each calculation. When subtracting, however, you *set* the carry flag: SEC. Why is unimportant. Just always SEC before any subtractions, and your answers will be correct. Here's double subtracting that will move the FINGER back down one record in the data list:

```
$1020 SEC       ($1020 is where we arbitrarily decided to locate
                our "take 40 from FINGER" subroutine)
 1021 LDA $D6   (Get the LSB of FINGER)
 1023 SBC #$28  (LSB of the size of a single record)
 1026 STA $D6   (Put the new result into FINGER)
 1028 LDA $D7   (Get FINGER's MSB)
 102A SBC #$00  (Subtract the MSB of the size of a single record)
 102D STA $D7   (Update FINGER's MSB)
```

Multiplication and Division

Multiplying could be done by repeated adding. To multiply 5 × 4, you could just add 4 + 4 + 4 + 4 + 4. One way would be to set up two registers like the ones we've used before. Both registers (or storage zones) could contain a 4, and then you could loop through an add-these-two-registers subroutine five times. For practical purposes, however, multiplying and dividing are more easily accomplished in BASIC. They are simply not worth the trouble of setting up in ML, especially if you need to involve decimal-point fractions (floating-point arithmetic). Perhaps surprisingly, for games and most personal computing tasks where ML routines and programs are created, there is little use either for negative numbers or arithmetic beyond simple addition and subtraction. When we get into division and multiplication, we've gone beyond the simple arithmetic that you'll need—unless you're writing an accounting program or a spreadsheet program.

If you find that you do need complicated mathematical structures, create the program in BASIC, adding ML where super speeds are desirable. Such hybrid programs are efficient and, in their way, elegant.

One final note: An easy way to divide the number in the accumulator by two is to LSR. Try it. Similarly, you can multiply by two with ASL. We'll define LSR and ASL in the next chapter. If you're interested in using these techniques, take a look at the "Library of Subroutines" (Appendix E).

Double Comparison

One rather tricky technique is used fairly often in ML and should be learned. It is tricky because there are two branch instructions which *seem* to be worth using in this context, but which are best avoided for this kind of comparing. If you're trying to keep track of the location of a record within a database, this will be a two-byte address. If you need to compare those two bytes against another two-byte address, you'll need a "double-compare" subroutine. You might, for example, want to check whether or not one record is located higher in the database than another.

Double-compare is also useful in any other ML where you need to manipulate numbers larger than can be held in one byte (where the single CMP instruction would be able to compare them for you).

The problem is the BPL instruction (Branch on PLus) and its companion, BMI (Branch on MInus). *Don't use them* for comparisons. In any comparisons, whether single- or double-byte, use BEQ to test if two numbers are equal; BNE for not equal; BCS for equal or higher; and BCC for lower. You can remember BCS because its *S* is *higher* and BCC because its *C* is *lower* in the alphabet. To see how to perform a double-compare, Program 5-1 shows one easy way to do it.

This is LADS at work. Recall that with assemblers like LADS, you can use line numbers and labels, add numbers to labels (see the TESTED + 1 in line 110), add comments, and all the rest.

To try out this double comparison from the monitor, type in the hex bytes on the left (starting at $0310 with the AD) and put zeros (BRK instructions to stop the program) in

Program 5-1. Double-Compare

```
20 Ø31Ø                         TESTED = $Ø38Ø     LOCATION OF OUR FIRST NUMBER
30 Ø31Ø                         SECOND = $Ø382     LOCATION OF OUR SECOND NUMBER
40
90 Ø31Ø AD 8Ø Ø3   START        LDA TESTED         COMPARE THE LOW BYTES
100 Ø313 CD 82 Ø3               CMP SECOND
110 Ø316 AD 81 Ø3               LDA TESTED+1             COMPARE THE HIGH BYTES
120 Ø319 ED 83 Ø3               SBC SECOND+1
130 Ø31C FØ Ø5                  BEQ EQUAL                TESTED = SECOND
140 Ø31E BØ Ø4                  BCS HIGHER               TESTED > SECOND
150 Ø32Ø 9Ø ØØ                  BCC LOWER                TESTED < SECOND
160
240 Ø322 LOWER .BYTE Ø
250 Ø323 EQUAL .BYTE Ø        LANDING PLACES
260 Ø324 HIGHER .BYTE Ø
```

$0322–$0324. Then try putting different numbers into $0380 and $0381 (this is the "tested" number) and $0382, $0383 (the number it is being tested against, the second number in our label scheme here). As you can see, you've got to keep it straight in your mind which number is being tested, or the results won't make much sense.

Then, when you've set up two double-byte numbers in the registers ($0380 to $0383), you can run this routine by 1010G, where it starts. All that will happen is that you will land on a BRK instruction and halt further activity. *Where* you land tells you the results of the comparison. If the numbers are equal, you land at $323. If the tested number is less than the second number, you'll end up in location $322, and so forth. You could test using only a BNE if all you needed to know is whether or not the two numbers are equal. You could leave out some of these branch tests if you're not interested in them. Play around with this until you've understood the ideas involved.

In a real program, you would be branching to addresses in your ML program which *do something* if the numbers under comparison are equal or one is greater or whatever. This example sends the computer to $322, $323, or $324, where it comes to an abrupt halt just to let you see the effects of a double-compare subroutine. Above all, remember that you should use BCC and BCS (*not* BPL or BMI) when comparing in ML.

Some might wonder why we use CMP to test the low bytes and then switch to SBC to test the high bytes. It's just a convenience. CoMPare is a subtraction of one number from another. The only difference between CMP and SBC, really, is that subtraction replaces the number in the accumulator with the result. LDA #5:SBC #2 will leave 3 in the accumulator. Using LDA #5:CMP #2 leaves the 5 in the accumulator, and all that happens is that flags are affected. Both SBC and CMP have an effect on the zero, negative, and carry flags. In our double-compare we don't care if there is a result left in the accumulator or not. So, we can use either SBC or CMP. The reason for starting off with CMP, however, is that we don't have to SEC (set the carry flag) as we always need to do before an SBC.

Chapter 6

The Instruction Set

The Instruction Set

There are 56 instructions (commands) available in 6502 machine language. Most versions of BASIC have about 50 commands. Some BASIC instructions are rarely used by the majority of programmers, for example, END, SGN, TAN, USR. Some, such as LET, contribute nothing to a program and seem to have remained in the language for nostalgic reasons. Others, like TAN, have uses that are highly specialized. There are surplus commands in computer languages just as there are surplus words in English. People don't often say *culpability*. They usually just say *guilt*. The message gets across without using the entire dictionary. The simple, common words can do the job.

Machine language is the same as any other language in this respect. There are around 20 heavily used instructions. The 36 remaining ones are used far less often. You can switch into the Apple monitor with CALL −151 and look at part of your computer's ROM. To look at BASIC ROM, once in the monitor, enter at the * prompt D36AL, and press RETURN. To see more, just enter L, and press RETURN a few times. You can now read the machine language routines which comprise BASIC. You will quickly discover that the accumulator is heavily trafficked (LDA and STA appear frequently in the disassembly), but you will have to hunt to find BVC, CLV, ROR, RTI, or SED.

ML, like BASIC, offers you many ways to accomplish the same job. Some programming solutions, of course, are better than others, but the main thing is to get the job done. An influence still lingers from the early days of computing when memory space was rare and expensive. This influence—that you should try to write programs using up as little memory as possible—can be safely ignored. Efficient memory use will often be at the bottom of your list of objectives when programming ML. It could hardly matter whether you use 25 instead of 15 bytes to print a message to the screen when your computer has space for programming which exceeds 30,000 bytes.

Rather than memorize each ML instruction individually, we will concentrate on the workhorses. Bizarre or arcane instructions will get only passing mention. Unless you are planning to use ML programs to interface to strange peripherals or need to do complex mathematical calculations and such, you will be able to write excellent machine language programs for nearly any application with the instructions we'll focus on in this book.

For each instruction group, we will describe three things before getting down to the details about programming with them: (1) what the instructions accomplish, (2) the addressing modes you can use with them, and (3) what they do, if anything, to the flags in the status register. All of this information is also found in Appendix A.

The Six Instruction Groups

The best way to approach the instruction set might be to break it down into the following six categories which group the instructions according to their functions:

1. Transporters
2. Arithmetic Group
3. Decision-Makers
4. Loop Group
5. Subroutine and Jump Group
6. Debuggers

We will deal with each group in order, pointing out similarities to BASIC and describing the major uses for each.

As always, the best way to learn is by doing. Move bytes around. Use each instruction, typing a BRK as the final instruction to see the effects. If you LDA #65, look in the A register to see what happened. Then, STA $12 and check to see what was copied into address $12. If you send the byte in the accumulator (STA), what is left behind in the accumulator? Is it better to think of bytes being *copied* rather than being *sent*?

Play with each instruction to get a feel for it. Discover the effects, qualities, and limitations of these ML commands.

1. The Transporters: LDA, LDX, LDY STA, STX, STY TAX, TAY TXA, TYA

These instructions move a byte from one place in memory to another. To be more precise, they *copy* whatever value is in a source location into a target location. The source location still contains the byte, but after a "transporter" instruction, a copy of the byte is also in the target location. This *does* replace whatever was in the target.

All of them affect the N and Z flags, except STA, STX, and STY which do nothing to any flag.

There are a variety of addressing modes available to different instructions in this group. Check the chart in Appendix A for specifics.

Remember that the computer does things *one at a time*. Unlike the human brain which can carry out a thousand different instructions simultaneously (walk, talk, and smile, all at once), the computer goes from one tiny job to the next. It works through a series of instructions, raising the *program counter* (PC) each time it handles an instruction.

If you do a TYA, the PC goes up by one to the next address, and the computer looks at that next instruction. STA $80 is a two-byte-long instruction; it's zero page addressing, so the PC=PC+2. STA $8600 is a three-byte-long absolute addressing mode and PC=PC+3.

Recall that there's nothing larger than a three-byte increment of the PC. However, in each case, the PC is cranked up the right amount to make it point to the address for the next instruction. Things would get quickly out of control if the PC pointed to some argument (some address) thinking it was an instruction. It would be incorrect (and soon disastrous) if the PC pointed to the $15 in LDA $15.

If you type CALL 15000, the program counter is loaded with 15000 and the computer transfers control to the ML instructions which are (we hope!) sitting at address 15000 (decimal) on up. It will then look at byte 15000 (decimal), expecting it to be an instruction. Since the computer does all this very fast, it can seem to be keeping score, bouncing the ball, moving the paddle, and everything else—simultaneously. It's not, though. It's flashing from one task to another and doing it so fast that it creates the illusion of simultaneity much the way that 24 still pictures per second look like motion in movies.

The Programmer's Time Warp

Movies are, of course, lots of still pictures flipping by in rapid succession. Computer programs are composed of lots of individual instructions performed in rapid succession.

Grasping this sequential, step-by-step activity makes our programming job easier: We can think of large programs as single steps, coordinated into meaningful, harmonious actions. Now the computer will put a blank over the ball at the ball's current address, then adjust the ball address to move it slightly downward on the screen, then print the ball character to the new address. The main single-step action is moving information, as single-byte numbers, from here to there, in memory. We are always creating, updating, modifying, moving, and destroying single-byte variables. The moving is generally done from one double-byte address to another. But it all looks smooth to the player during a game.

Programming in ML can pull you into an eerie time warp. You might spend several hours constructing a program which executes in seconds. You are putting together instructions which will later be read and acted upon by coordinated electrons, moving at electron speeds. It's as if you spent an afternoon slowly and carefully drawing up pathways and patterns which would later be a single bolt of lightning.

Registers

In ML there are three primary places where variables rest briefly on their way to memory cells: the X, the Y, and the A registers. And the A register (the *accumulator*) is the most frequently used. X and Y are used for looping and indexing. Each of these registers can grab a byte from anywhere in memory or can grab the byte from the address right after its own opcode (immediate mode addressing):

LDY $8000 (Puts the number at hex address 8000 into Y, without destroying it at $8000)
LDY #65 (Puts the *decimal number* 65 into Y)
LDA and **LDX** work the same

Be sure you understand what is happening here. LDY $1500 does not copy the byte in the Y register into address $1500. It's just the opposite. The number (or *value*, as it's sometimes called) in $1500 is copied into the Y register.

To copy a byte from X, Y, or A, use STX, STY, or STA. For these "store-bytes" instructions, however, there is no immediate addressing mode. No STA #$15. It would make no sense to have STA #$15. That would be disruptive, for it *would modify the ML program itself. It would put the number 15 into the next cell beyond the STA instruction within the ML program itself.*

Another type of transporter moves bytes *between* registers—TAY, TAX, TYA, TXA. See the effect of writing the following. Look at the registers after executing this:

```
1000 LDA #$65
1002 TAY
1003 TAX
```

The number $65 is placed into the accumulator, then transferred to the Y register, then sent from the accumulator to X. All the while, however, the A register (the accumulator) is *not* being emptied. Sending bytes is not a transfer in the usual sense of the term *sending*. It is more as if a photocopy were made of the number, and then the *copy* was sent. The original stays behind after the copy is sent.

LDA #$15 followed by TAY would leave the $15 in the accumulator, sending a copy of $15 into the Y register.

Notice that you cannot directly move a byte from the X to the Y register, or vice versa. There is no TXY or TYX.

Flags Up and Down

Another effect of moving bytes around is that it sometimes throws a flag up or down in the status register. LDA (or LDX or LDY) will affect the N and Z, negative and zero, flags.

We will ignore the N flag. It changes when you used "signed numbers," a special technique to allow for negative numbers. For our purposes, the N flag will fly up and down all the time, and we won't care. We won't pay any attention to it; we won't test to see where it is. If you're curious, signed numbers are manipulated by allowing the seven bits on the right to hold the number, the leftmost bit to stand for positive or negative. We normally use a byte to hold values from 0 through 255. If we were working with "signed" numbers, anything higher than 127 would be considered a negative number, since the leftmost bit would be "on"—and an LDA #255 would be thought of as −1.

This is another example of how the same thing (the number 255 in this case) can signify several different conditions, depending on the context in which it is being interpreted.

The Z flag, on the other hand, is quite important; we can't ignore this flag. It shows whether or not some action during a program run resulted in a zero. The branching instructions and looping depend on this flag, and we'll deal with the important zero-result effects below with the BNE and INX instructions, and so on.

No flags are affected by the STA, STX, or STY instruction.

The Stack Can Take Care of Itself

There are some instructions which move bytes to and from the stack. These are for advanced ML programmers. PHA and PLA copy a byte from A to the stack, and vice versa. PHP and PLP move the status register to and from the stack. TSX and TXS move the stack pointer to or from the X register. Forget them. Unless you know precisely what you are doing, you can cause havoc with your program by fooling with the stack. The main job for the stack is to hold the return addresses pushed into it when you JSR (Jump to SubRoutine). Then, when you come back from a subroutine (RTS), the computer pulls the addresses off the stack to find out where to go back to.

For most ML programming, avoid stack manipulation until you are an advanced programmer. If you manipulate the stack without great care, you'll cause an RTS to the wrong return address, and the computer will travel far, far beyond your control. If you are lucky, it sometimes lands on a BRK instruction and you fall into the monitor mode. The odds are that you would get lucky roughly once every 256 times. Don't count on it. Since BRK is rare in your BASIC ROM, the chances are pretty low.

You could fill large amounts of RAM with "snow" by putting zeros everywhere. This greatly improves the odds that a crash *will* hit a BRK. But why bother? Play it safe when you're writing a program.

As an aside, there is another use for snow, a blanket of

"zero page snow." Recall that you can safely use some locations in zero page (addresses 0–255), but that your computer and many commercial programs compete for space in zero page because it's such a fast place to access. If you are planning to modify, say, a commercial word processor and need to make sure that it's not using a particular area of zero page for its own purposes, fill zero page with 00 (snow), put the word processor through its paces, and then take a look at the tracks, the nonzeros, in the snow.

2. The Arithmetic Group: ADC, SBC, SEC, CLC

Here are the commands which add, subtract, and set or clear the carry flag. ADC and SBC trigger the N, Z, C, and V (overflow) flags. CLC and SEC, needless to say, affect the C flag, and their only addressing mode is implied.

ADC and SBC can be used in eight addressing modes: immediate, absolute, zero page, (indirect,X), (indirect),Y, zero page,X, and absolute,X and ,Y.

Arithmetic was covered in the previous chapter. To review, before any addition, the carry flag must be cleared with CLC. Before any subtraction, it must be set with SEC. The decimal mode should be cleared at the start of any program (the initialization) with CLD. You can multiply by two with ASL and divide by two with LSR. You can divide by four with LSR LSR or by eight with LSR LSR LSR. You could multiply a number by eight with ASL ASL ASL. What would this do to a number: ASL ASL ASL ASL? To multiply by numbers which aren't powers of two, use addition plus multiplication. To multiply by ten, for example, copy the original number temporarily to a vacant byte somewhere in memory. Then ASL ASL ASL to multiply it by eight. Multiply the original number by two with a single ASL. Then add them together.

If you're wondering about the V flag, it is rarely used for anything. You can forget about the branch which depends on it, BVC, too. Only five instructions affect it, and it relates to twos complement arithmetic which we've not touched on in this book. Like decimal mode or negative numbers, you will be able to construct your ML programs very effectively if you remain in complete ignorance of this mode. We have largely avoided discussion of most of the flags in the status register: B,

D, I, N, and V. This avoidance has also removed several branch instructions from our consideration: BMI, BPL, BVC, and BVS. These flags and instructions are not usually found in ML programs, and their use is confined to specialized mathematical or interfacing applications. They will not be of use or interest to the majority of ML programmers.

The two flags of interest to most ML programmers are the carry flag and the zero flag. That is why, in the following section, we will examine only the four branch instructions which test the C and Z flags. They are likely to be the only branching instructions that you'll ever find occasion to use.

3. The Decision-Makers: BCC, BCS, BEQ, BNE, CMP

The four "branchers" here—they all begin with a *B*—have only one addressing mode. In fact, it's an interesting mode unique to the B instructions and created especially for them: *relative* addressing. They do not address a memory location as an *absolute* thing; rather, they address a location which is just a certain distance from their position in the ML code. Put another way, the argument of a B instruction is an offset which is *relative* to the position of the instruction itself. You never have to worry about relative instructions if you relocate an ML program, if you locate the ML program in some other place in RAM memory. The B instructions will work just as well no matter where your ML program is moved.

That's because their argument just says "add 5 to the present address" or "subtract 27" or whatever argument you give them. You *do* give the branchers actual addresses as you would in absolute addressing: BEQ $3560. However, your assembler will translate that $3560 into a different, somewhat strange, number that is used in relative addressing. (If you are using an advanced assembler like LADS, you will give label names as the argument of the branchers instead of actual numeric addresses.)

The branchers cannot branch further back than 127 or further forward than 128 bytes.

None of the brancher instructions have any effect whatsoever on any flags; instead, they are the instructions which *look at* the flags. They are the only instructions which base their activity on the condition of the status register and its flags. They're why the flags exist at all.

CMP is an exception. Many times it is the instruction that comes just before the branchers and sets flags for them to look at and make decisions about. Lots of instructions—LDA is one—will set or clear (put down) flags—but sometimes you need to use CMP to find out what's going on with the flags. CMP affects the N, Z, and C flags. CMP has many addressing modes available to it: immediate, absolute, zero page, (indirect,X), (indirect),Y, zero page,X, and absolute,X and ,Y.

The Foundations of Computer Power

This decision-maker group and the following group (loops) are the basis of our computers' enormous strength. The decision-makers allow the computer to decide between two or more possible courses of action. This decision is based on comparisons. *If* the ball hits a wall, *then* reverse its direction. In BASIC, we use IF-THEN and ON-GOTO structures to make decisions and to make appropriate responses to conditions as they arise during a program run.

Recall that the Apple uses *memory-mapped video*, which means that you can treat the screen like an area of RAM memory. You can PEEK and POKE into it to create animation, text, or other visual events. In ML, you PEEK by LDA SCREEN and examine what you've PEEKed with CMP. You POKE via STA SCREEN.

CMP does comparisons. It tests the value at an address against what is in the accumulator. Less common are CPX and CPY.

Assume that we have just added 40 to a register we set aside to hold the current address-location of FINGER which points to records in our database. We want to POKE in a new record, but we need to locate a vacant record. We don't want to cover over a record that's in use.

In practical terms, you might have deleted several records within your database and, each time one is deleted, you just stick a zero into the first byte of the record's 40-byte space to show that it's empty. Thus, we can bounce along the records, looking at the first byte of each, to find an available empty record.

Recall that the very useful indirect Y addressing mode allows us to use an address in zero page as a *pointer* to another address in memory. The number in the Y register is added to whatever address sits in \$D6,\$D7; so we don't LDA from \$D6 or $D7, but rather from the address that they *contain*, plus Y's value.

To see what's in the first byte of a record, we can do the following:

LDY #$0 (We want to fetch from the first byte, so we don't want to add anything to it. Y is set to zero.)

LDA ($D6),Y (Fetch whatever is sitting there. To review indirect,Y addressing once more, say that the address we are fetching from here is $1077. Address $D6 would hold the least significant byte, LSB [$77], and address $D7 would hold the MSB [$10]. Notice that the argument of an indirect,Y instruction only mentions the lower address of the two-byte pointer, the $D6. The computer knows that it has to combine $D6 and $D7 to get the full address—and it does this automatically.)

At this point, there might be a $CD (Apple ASCII for the letter *M)* or some other number which we would know indicated that this record was not deleted. Now that this questionable number sits in the accumulator, we will CMP it against a $0 which signals a deleted record. We could compare it with other numbers, too, numbers which we—in setting up the database—had decided would mean "old record" or "duplicated record" or some other housekeeping information which would help us in managing the data. It doesn't matter. The main thing is to compare it and find out the condition of this particular record:

2000 CMP #$0 (Is it a zero?)

2002 BNE $200A (Branch if Not Equal [if not zero] to address $200A, which contains the first of a series of comparisons to see if it's an "old" or "duplicated" record, or the like. On the other hand, if the comparison *worked,* if it was a zero, so we didn't Branch Not Equal, then the next thing that happens is the instruction in address $2004. We "fall through" the BNE to an instruction which jumps to the subroutine, JSR, which moves the new record into the vacant record space, thus jumping past the series of comparisons for old, duplicated, and so forth.)

2004 JSR $3000 (Insert new record subroutine.)

2007 JMP $2020 (Jump over the rest of the comparisons.)

200A CMP #$1 (Is it an old record?)

200C BNE $2014 (If not, continue to next comparison.)

200E JSR $3050	(Perform the "old records" subroutine and...
2011 JMP $2020	jump over the rest, as before in $2007.)
2014 CMP #$2	(Is it a duplicated record?...and so forth with as many comparisons as needed.)

This structure is to ML what ON-GOTO or ON-GOSUB is to BASIC. It allows you to take multiple actions based on a single LDA. Doing the CMP only once would be like IF-THEN.

Other Branching Instructions

In addition to the BNE we just looked at, there are BCC, BCS, BEQ, BMI, BPL, BVC, and BVS. Learn BCC, BCS, BEQ, and BNE and you can safely ignore the others.

All of them are branching, if-then, instructions. They work in the same way that BNE does. You would write BEQ followed by the address you want to go to. If the result of the comparison is "yes, equal-to-zero is true," then the ML program will jump (branch) to the address which is the argument of the BEQ instruction. "True" here means that something EQuals zero. One example that would send up the Z flag (thereby triggering a branch with BEQ) is LDA #$00. The action of loading a zero into the accumulator sets the Z flag up.

You are allowed to branch either forward or backward from the address that holds the B instruction. However, you cannot branch any further than 128 bytes in either direction. If you want to go further, you must JMP (JuMP) or JSR (Jump to SubRoutine). For all practical purposes, you will usually be branching to instructions located within 30 bytes of your B instruction in either direction. You will be taking care of most things right near where the CoMPare, or other flag-flipping event, takes place.

If you need to use an elaborate, big subroutine which cannot reside within 128 bytes of a branch, simply JSR to it at the target address of your branch:

2000 LDA $65	
2002 CMP $85	(Is what was in address 65 equal to what was in address 85?)
2004 BNE $2009	(If Not Equal, branch over the next three bytes which perform some elaborate job.)
2006 JSR $4000	(At $4000 sits the elaborate subroutine to take care of cases where addresses $65 and $85 turn out to be equal.)
2009	(Continue with the program here.)

If you are branching backward, you've already written that part of your program, so you know the address to type in after a BNE or one of the other branches. But, if you are branching forward, to an address in part of the program not yet written—how do you know what to give as the address to branch to? In sophisticated, two-pass assemblers like LADS, you can just use a word like BRANCHTARGET, and the assembler will pass twice through your program when it assembles it. The first pass simply notes that your BNE is supposed to branch to BRANCHTARGET, but it doesn't yet know where that is.

When it finally finds the actual address of BRANCHTARGET, it makes a note of the correct address in a special *label table*. Then, it makes a second pass through the program and fills in (as the next byte after your BNE or whatever) the correct address of BRANCHTARGET.

All of this is automatic, and the labels make the program you write (called the *source code*) look almost like English. In fact, LADS includes so many special features that it gets close to *higher-level* languages, like BASIC:

```
  2000 TESTBYTE = $80       (These initial definitions of labels
  2002 NEWBYTE = $99        are sometimes called equates.)
  2004 LDA TESTBYTE
  2006 CMP NEWBYTE
  2008 BNE BRANCHTARGET
  200A JSR SUBROUTINE
BRANCHTARGET        200D     ...etc.
```

Instead of using lots of numbers (as you do when using the built-in mini-assembler in the monitor) for the target/argument of each instruction, LADS allows you to *define* (equate) the meanings of words like *testbyte* and then use the word instead of the number. And LADS does simplify the problem of forward branching since you just give (as above) address $200D a name, BRANCHTARGET, and the word at address $2009 is later replaced with $200D when the assembler does its passes.

Program 6-1 shows how the example above looks as source code to be fed into a deluxe, two-pass assembler like LADS.

Actually, we should point out in passing that a $200D will not be the number which finally appears at address $2009 to replace BRANCHTARGET. (Take a look at Program 6-1.)

Program 6-1

```
20 2004                          TESTBYTE = $80
30 2004                          NEWBYTE = $99
40
50 2004 A5 80       START        LDA TESTBYTE         IMMEDIATE ADDRESSING
60 2006 C5 99                    CMP NEWBYTE                   ZERO PAGE ADDRESSING
70 2008 D0 03                    BNE BRANCHTARGET              RELATIVE ADDRESSING
80 200A 20 10 20                 JSR SUBROUTINE                ABSOLUTE ADDRESSING
90 200D AD 00 04    BRANCHTARGET LDA $400       YOU CAN FREELY MIX LABELS
100  AND SUBROUTINES.  ALSO, COMMENTS WILL BE IGNORED
110  BY LADS AND CAN BE STUCK ANYWHERE WITH A SEMICOLON,
120  AS YOU SEE.
130
140 2010 A5 21      SUBROUTINE LDA 33
150  ETC.    ETC.
```

As we mentioned, all branches are relative, an offset from the address of the branch. The number which will finally replace BRANCHTARGET at $2009 is, as you can see, a three. This is similar to the way that the value of the Y register is *added* to an address in zero page during indirect Y addressing: The number given as an argument of a branch instruction is *added* to the address of the next instruction. So, $2008 + $3 = $200B. If this seems confusing, forget about it. LADS, or even the mini-assembler in the monitor, will take care of all this for you. All you need to do is give $200D as the argument to the mini-assembler, or a label name to LADS, and they will compute the three for you.

Forward Branch Solutions

There is one responsibility that you do have, though, if you are using the mini-assembler. When you are writing 2008 BNE $200D, how do you know to write in $200D? You can't yet know to exactly which address up ahead you want to branch. There are two ways to deal with this. Perhaps easiest is just to put in BNE $2008 (have it branch to itself). This will result in an $FE being temporarily left as the target of your BNE. Then, you can make a note on paper to later change the byte at $2009 to point to the correct address, $200B. You've got to remember to "resolve" that $FE, to POKE in the correct offset to the target address, or you will leave a little bomb in your program—an endless loop.

The other, even simpler, way to deal with forward branch addresses will come after you are familiar with which instructions use one, two, or three bytes. The BNE–JSR–TARGET construction is common and will always be three above the current address, an *offset* of three. If your branch instruction is at $2008, you just count off three: $200A,B,C and write BNE 200D.

Other, more complex branches such as ON-GOTO constructions will also become easy to count off when you're familiar with the instruction byte-lengths. In any case, it's simple enough to make a note of any unsolved branches and correct them before running the program.

Of course, LADS is the easiest assembler to use for forward branching: It allows you to branch to any address by just giving the label name of that address.

Recall our previous warning about not using the infamous BPL and BMI instructions? BPL (Branch on PLus) and BMI (Branch on MInus) sound good, but should be avoided. To test for less-than or more-than situations, use BCC and BCS respectively. (Recall that BCC is alphabetically *less-than* BCS—an easy way to remember which to use.) The reasons for this are exotic. We don't need to go into them. Just be warned that BPL and BMI which sound so logical and useful are not. They can fail you and neither one lives up to its name. Stick with the always trustworthy BCC, BCS.

Also remember that BNE and the other three main B group branching instructions often don't need to have a CMP come in front of them to affect a flag that can be tested by a following B instruction. Many actions of many opcodes will automatically affect flags. For example, LDA $80 will affect the Z flag so you can tell (using BNE or BEQ) if the number in address $80 was or wasn't zero. LDA $80 followed by BNE would branch away if there were anything besides a zero in address $80. If in doubt about which flags are affected by which instructions, check in Appendix A. You'll soon get to know the common ones. If you are really in doubt, go ahead and stick in a CMP. It can't do any harm.

4. The Loop Group: DEY, DEX, INY, INX, INC, DEC

INY and INX raise the Y and X register values *by one* each time they are used. If Y is a 17 and you INY, Y becomes an 18. Likewise, DEY and DEX decrease the values in these registers by one. There is no such increment or decrement instruction for the accumulator.

Similarly, INC and DEC will raise or lower a memory address by one. You can give arguments to these instructions in four addressing modes: absolute, zero page, zero page,X, and absolute,X. These instructions affect the N and Z flags.

The Loop Group are usually used to set up FOR-NEXT structures. The X register is used most often as a counter to allow a certain number of events to take place. In the structure FOR I = 1 TO 10:NEXT I, the value of the variable I goes up by one each time the loop cycles around. The same effect is created by:

```
2000 LDX #$0A   (Decimal 10)
2002 DEX        ("DEcrement" or "DEcrease X" by one)
2003 BNE $2002  (Branch if Not Equal [to zero] back up to address
                $2002)
```

Notice that DEX is tested by BNE (which sees if the Z flag, the zero flag, is up). DEX sets the Z flag up when X finally gets down to zero after ten cycles of this loop. The only other flag affected by this loop group is the N (negative) flag for signed arithmetic.

Why didn't we use INX, INcrease X by one? This would parallel exactly the FOR I = 1 TO 10, but it would be clumsy since our starting count which is #10 above would have to be #245. This is because X will not become a zero *going up* until it hits 255. So, for clarity and simplicity, it is customary to set the count of X and then DEX it downward to zero. The following program will accomplish the same thing as the one above, and allow us to INX, but it too is somewhat clumsy:

```
2000 LDX #$0
2002 INX
2003 CPX #$0A
2005 BNE $2002
```

Here, we had to use zero to start the loop because, right off the bat, the number in X is INXed to one by the instruction at $2002. In any case, it is a good idea simply to memorize the simple loop structure in the first example. It is easy and obvious and works very well.

Big Loops

How would you create a loop which has to be larger than 256 cycles? When we wanted to add large numbers, numbers too big to be held in a single byte, we simply used two-byte units instead of single-byte units to hold our information. Likewise, to do large loops, you can count down using two bytes, rather than one. In fact, this is quite similar to the idea of nested loops (loops within loops) in BASIC.

```
2000 LDX #$0A   (Start of first loop)
2002 LDY #$0    (Start of second loop)
2004 DEY
2005 BNE $2004  (If Y isn't yet zero, loop back to DEcrease Y
                again—this is the inner loop.)
2007 DEX        (Reduce the outer loop by one.)
```

```
2008 BNE $2002 (If X isn't yet zero, go through the entire DEY loop
               again.)
200A           (Continue with the rest of the program....)
```

One thing to watch out for: Be sure that a loop BNE's back up to *one address after* the start of its loop. The start of the loop sets a number into a register and, if you keep looping up to it, you'll always be putting the same number into it. The DEcrement (decrease by one) instruction would then never bring it down to zero to end the looping. You'll have created an endless loop.

The example above could be used for a timing loop in a similar way to the method that BASIC creates delays with FOR T = 1 TO 2000: NEXT T. Also, sometimes you *do* want to create a pseudo endless loop (the BEGIN–UNTIL in structured programming). A useful pseudo endless loop in BASIC waits until the user hits any key: 10 GET K$: IF K$ = "" THEN 10.

The simplest way to accomplish this in ML is to look on the map of your computer to find which byte holds the *last keypressed* number. On the Apple II, it's 49152. In any event, when a key is pressed, it deposits its special numeric value into this cell. If no key is pressed, the leftmost bit in this cell remains off:

```
2000 LDA $C010; THIS SETS THE LEFTMOST BIT IN $C000
          (49152) TO 0
2003 LOOP LDA $C000
2006 BPL LOOP; IF THE LEFTMOST BIT IS OFF, KEEP
          LOOPING
```

If the BPL is triggered, this means that the LDA found the leftmost bit off in address $C000 (49152) and, thus, no key has been pressed. So, we keep looping until the value in address $C000 has the leftmost bit on. This setup is the same as GET in BASIC, because not only does it wait until a key is pressed, but it also leaves the value of the key in the accumulator when it's finished.

The BPL instruction is triggered when the LDA loads in the byte from address $C000, *if the value loaded in has a zero in the leftmost bit*. Thus, 01111111 would cause a branch back to the loop to keep looking for a legitimate keypress; 10000000 would "fall through" the BPL test because BPL is not triggered when the leftmost bit is on—regardless of the condition of the rest of the bits in the byte. The leftmost bit is on, in effect, if the number in address $C000 is higher than 127. Although it's best to avoid BMI and BPL when dealing with quantities like less-than or greater-than, here is one of the legitimate uses of these instructions.

Dealing with Strings

You've probably been wondering how ML handles strings.

It's pretty straightforward. There are essentially two ways: known-length and zero-delimit. If you know how many characters there are in a message, you can store this number at the very start of the text: 5ERROR. (The number 5 will fit into one byte.) If this little message is stored in your "message zone"—some arbitrary area of free memory set aside by you at the beginning to hold all of your messages—you would make a note of the particular address of the "ERROR" message. Say it's stored at address $0FE6 (4070).

To print out the message, you pluck off the length and then repeatedly JSR to $FDED, the Apple character output routine in ROM.

Alternatively, you could simply set up your own zero page pointers to the screen and use the STA (NN),Y addressing mode.

For Apple II, the screen memory starts at $0400 (1024). You can set up a "cursor management" system for yourself. To simplify, we'll send our message to the beginning of Apple's screen and just use the simple absolute,Y addressing mode:

2000 LDX $0FE6	(Remember, we put the length of the message as the first byte of the message, so we load our counter with the length.)
2003 LDY #$0	(Y will be our message offset.)
2005 LDA $0FE7,Y	(Gets the character at the address plus Y. Y is zero the first time through the loop, so the "e" from here lands in the accumulator. It also stays in $0FE7 [4071]. It's just being copied into the accumulator.)
2008 STA $0400,Y	(We can make Y do double duty as the message and the screen-printout offset. Y is still zero, so the "e" goes to $0400 the first time through the loop.)
200B INY	(Prepare to add one to the message-storage location and to the screen-print location.)
200C DEX	(Lower the counter.)

200D BNE $2005	(If X isn't used up yet, go back and get-and-print the next character, the "r.")

If the Length Is Not Known

Yet another way to print to the screen—probably the most common and the easiest, and doesn't require that you know the length of the string. You just put a special character (usually zero) at the end of each message to show its limit. This is called a *delimiter*. A zero works well because, in ASCII, the value 0 has no character or function (such as a carriage return) coded to it. Consequently, any time the computer loads a zero into the accumulator (which will flip up the Z flag), it will then know that it is at the end of your message. At $0FE6, we might have a couple of error messages: "Ball out of range0Time nearly up!0". (These zeros are not ASCII zeros, remember. ASCII zero, the zero *character* that can be printed, has a value of 176.)

To print the time warning message to the top of the Apple screen:

2000 LDY #$0	
2002 LDA $0FF8,Y	(Get the "T.")
2005 BEQ $2005	(The LDA just above will flip the zero flag up if it loads a zero, so we *forward branch* out of our message-printing loop.)
2007 STA $0400,Y	(We're using the Y as a double-duty offset again.)
200A INY	
200B JMP $2002	(In this loop, we always jump back. Our exit from the loop is not here, at the end. Rather, it is the Branch if EQual which is within the loop. This is similar to the BEGIN–UNTIL structure in structured programming.)
200E	(Continue with another part of the program.)

Now that we know the address which follows the loop ($2014), we can store that address into the "false forward branch" we left in address $2006. What number do we store into $2006? Just subtract $2007 from $200E which is 7.

Of these two ways of handling strings, the zero-delimit method is the most popular and probably the easiest to use. It's even easier if you use LADS. With LADS, you don't need to remember the address of the stored string, you just give each string a label. Also, you don't need to translate the message into ASCII, just use the .BYTE pseudo-op in LADS.

Here's how you would write the source code for LADS using the zero-delimit technique example above:

100 SCREEN = 1024 (This variable is defined at the start of the program, not in with the body of the ML. The numbers on the left are *not* addresses. They are line numbers that you use when writing the source code. The assembler handles memory addresses for you.)

.
.
.

500 LDY #0
510 MESSAGE LDA TIMEOUT,Y (Get the "T.")
520 BEQ MORE
530 STA SCREEN,Y
540 INY
550 JMP MESSAGE
560 MORE (Continue with another part of the program.)

.
.
.

1000 TIMEOUT .BYTE "TIME NEARLY UP!": .BYTE 0
(Message stored with a true zero at the end. This is stored at the very end of the ML program, not in with the instructions themselves.)

The .BYTE pseudo-op in LADS is designed to work with true ASCII. This means that your messages would be understood by other computers, over modems, by printers, and so forth. However, the Apple's internal version of the ASCII code (which prints messages to the screen) differs from true ASCII. True ASCII characters appear in reverse field on the Apple screen. For more information, see the discussion of the .BYTE and #" pseudo-ops in Appendix B.

All the ways of handling messages discussed above are effective, but you must keep a list on paper of the starting addresses of each message if you are using the monitor assembler so that you can remember from where to pick off the letters of the message. In ML, you have the responsibility for some of the tasks that BASIC (at an expense of speed) does for you. If you're using a more advanced assembler like LADS, however, you can simply define the location of the message with a label.

Also, when using these techniques, no message can be larger than 255 characters because the offset and counter registers (X and Y) can count only that high before starting over at zero again. To print two strings back-to-back gives a longer, but still less than 255-byte-long, message:

2000	**LDY #$0**	
2002	**LDX #$2**	(In this example, we use X as a counter which represents the *number* of messages we are printing.)
2004	**LDA $4000,Y**	(Get the "B" from "Ball out of....")
2007	**BEQ $2011**	(Go to increment Y, reduce [and check] the value of X.)
2009	**STA $1024,Y**	(We're using the Y as a double-duty offset again.)
200D	**INY**	
200E	**JMP $2004**	
2011	**INY**	(We need to raise Y since we skipped that step when we branched out of the loop.)
2012	**DEX**	(At the end of the first message, X will be a one; at the end of the second message, it will be zero.)
2013	**BNE $2004**	(If X isn't down to zero yet, reenter the loop to print out the second message.)

This example, too, could not deliver a message longer than 255 characters. To fill your screen with instructions instantly (say, at the start of a game), you can use the following mass-move. We'll assume that the instructions go from $5000 to $6024 in memory and you want to transfer them to the screen (at $0400):

2000	**LDY #$0**	
2002	**LDA $5000,Y**	
2005	**STA $0400,Y**	
2008	**LDA $5100,Y**	
200B	**STA $0500,Y**	
200E	**LDA $5200,Y**	
2011	**STA $0600,Y**	
2014	**LDA $5300,Y**	
2017	**STA $0700,Y**	
201A	**INY**	
201B	**BNE $2002**	(If Y hasn't counted *up to* 0—which comes just above 255—go back and load-store the next character in each quarter of the large message.)

This technique is fast and easy anytime you want to mass-move one area of memory to another. It makes a copy and does not disturb the original memory. To mass-clear a memory zone (to clear the screen, for example), you can use a similar loop, but instead of loading the accumulator each time with a different character, you load it at the start with $A0 (160 decimal), the Apple ASCII code for the character that the Apple uses to print a space:

```
2000  LDA #$A0
2002  LDY #$0
2004  STA $0400,Y
2007  STA $0500,Y
200A STA $0600,Y
200D STA $0700,Y
2011  INY
2012  BNE $2004
```

Of course, you could simply JSR to the routine which already exists in BASIC to clear the screen (JSR $FC58 or JSR 64600). In Chapter 7 we will explore the techniques of using BASIC as examples to learn from and also as a collection of ready-made ML subroutines. Now, though, we can look at how subroutines are handled in ML.

5. The Subroutine and Jump Group: JMP, JSR, RTS

JMP has only one useful addressing mode: absolute. You give it a firm, two-byte argument and it goes there. The computer puts the argument into the program counter, and control is transferred to this new address where an instruction located there is acted upon. (There is a second addressing mode, JMP indirect which has a bug and is best left unused.)

JSR can use only absolute addressing.

RTS's addressing mode is implied. The address is on the stack, put there during the JSR.

JSR (Jump to SubRoutine) is the same as GOSUB in BASIC, but instead of giving a line number, you give an address in memory where the subroutine sits (or, with LADS, you give a label name). BASIC's CALL is a kind of JSR, too. It acts like GOSUB except the destination is an ML routine rather than a BASIC subroutine.

RTS (ReTurn from Subroutine) is the same as RETURN in

BASIC, but instead of returning to the next BASIC command, you return to the address following the JSR instruction (it's a three-byte-long instruction containing JSR and the two-byte target address). JMP (JuMP) is GOTO. Again, you JMP to an address or label name, not a line number. As in BASIC, there is no RETURN from a JMP.

Some Further Cautions About the Stack

The stack is like a pile of coins. The last one you put on top of the pile is the first one you'll pull off later. The main reason that the 6502 chip sets aside an entire page of memory for the stack is that it has to know where to go back to after GOSUBs and JSRs.

A JSR instruction "pushes" the address held in the program counter plus two onto the stack and, later, the next RTS "pulls" the top two numbers off the stack, increments the result, and uses this number as its argument (target address) for the return. Some programmers, as we noted before, like to play with the stack and use it as a temporary register to PHA (PusH Accumulator onto stack). This sort of thing is best avoided until you are an advanced ML programmer. Stack manipulations often result in a very confusing program. Handling the stack is one of the few things that the computer does *for you* in ML. Let it.

The main function of the stack (as far as we're concerned) is to hold return addresses. It's done automatically for us by "pushes" with the JSR and, later, "pulls" (sometimes called *pops*) with the RTS instruction. If we don't bother the stack, it will serve us well. There are thousands upon thousands of cells where you could temporarily leave the accumulator—or any other value—without fouling up the orderly arrangement of your return addresses.

Subroutines are extremely important to ML programming.

ML programs are designed around them, as we'll see. There are times when you'll be several subroutines deep (one will call another which calls another); this is not as confusing as it sounds. Your main Player-input routine might call a Print-message subroutine which itself calls a Wait-until-key-is-pressed subroutine. If any of these routines PHA (PusH the Accumulator onto the stack), they then disturb the addresses on the stack. If the extra number on top of the stack isn't PLAed off (PulL Accumulator), the next RTS will pull off the number that was PHAed along with half the correct address. It will then merrily return to what it thinks is the correct address: It might land somewhere in the RAM, it might go to an address somewhere in the outer reaches of your operating system—but it certainly won't go where it should.

Some programmers like to change a GOSUB into a GOTO (in the middle of the action of a program) by PLA PLA. Pulling the two top stack values off with PLA PLA has the effect of eliminating the most recently stored RTS address. It does leave a clean stack, but why bother to JSR in the first place if you later want to change it to a GOTO? Why not use JMP in the first place. (There is some use for this technique, but it's for advanced ML programming where you want to speed up a program by returning directly to some routine elsewhere in the calling subprogram. LADS uses this method in places.)

There are cases, too, when the stack has been used to hold the current condition of the flags (the status register byte).

This is pushed/pulled from the stack with PHP and PLP. You probably never will, but if you should need to "remember" the condition of the status flags, why not just PHP PLA STA $*NN (NN* means the address is your choice)? Set aside a byte somewhere that can hold the flags (they are always changing inside the status register during a program run) for later and keep the stack clean. Leave stack acrobatics to Forth programmers. The stack, except for advanced ML, should be inviolate.

Forth, an interesting language, requires frequent stack manipulations. But in the Forth environment, the reasons for this and its protocol make excellent sense. In ML, though, stack manipulations are a sticky business.

Saving the Current Environment

There are two exceptions to our leave-the-stack-alone rule. Sometimes (especially when you are "borrowing" a routine from BASIC by JSRing into the ROM) you will want to take up with your own program from where it left off. That is, you might not want to write a "clear the screen" subroutine because you find the address of such a routine on your map (in your computer's *Reference Guide*) of BASIC. (The HOME subroutine is located at address $FC58, 64600 decimal.)

However, when you JSR into one of these ready-made

subroutines, you don't know what sorts of things the subroutine will do to your accumulator or X and Y registers. In other words, you just want to clear the screen, but you might well need to retain the status of the registers because your program is going to need them. You sometimes cannot afford to have unpredictable things happen to your X, Y, A, and status registers. If you know you don't need to preserve the state of the accumulator or the X or Y registers, then JSR blithely away. The JSR into ROM will probably change the registers, but you don't care.

However, sometimes you are using, let's say, Y to hold the offset of a line of information or a screen line. You can't allow it to suffer from some unknown event in the ROM subroutine. In such cases, you can use the following "save the state of things" routine:

2000	**PHP**	(Push the status register onto the stack.)
2001	**PHA**	
2002	**TXA**	
2003	**PHA**	
2004	**TYA**	
2005	**PHA**	
2006	**JSR $FC58**	(To the clear-the-screen routine in BASIC. When the BASIC routine is finished, it will end with an RTS. This RTS will remove the return address ($2009), and you'll have a mirror image of the things you had pushed onto the stack. They are pulled out in reverse order, as you can see below. This is because the first pull from the stack will get the *most recently pushed* number. If you make a little stack of coins, the *first* one you pull off will be the *last* one you put onto the stack.)
2009	**PLA**	(Now we reverse the order to get them back.)
200A	**TAY**	
200B	**PLA**	
200C	**TAX**	
200D	**PLA**	(This one stays in A.)
200E	**PLP**	(The status register)

This little routine will enter your JSR while preserving everything as it was before you JSRed. Use it when you're unsure. Nearly *every* ROM routine mentioned in this book will mess with one or more of the registers. The only truly safe one is JSR $FDED, the output-a-character routine. You can use this one with impunity.

Saving the current state of things before visiting an uncharted, unpredictable subroutine is probably the only valid excuse for playing with the stack as a beginner in ML. The routine above is constructed to leave the stack intact. Everything that was pushed on has been pulled back off.

If you dare, you can also use the stack as a temporary storage place when you need to save something briefly. You could save the accumulator (while JSRing to the HOME routine in BASIC) by PHA:JSR $FC58:PLA. That would temporarily push the accumulator onto the stack, hold it there beneath the two-byte return address pushed onto the stack by the JSR, and then pull it off again after the RTS had fetched the return address (leaving your accumulator on top of the stack). This pushing is sometimes considered a dangerous practice because, if you forget to match every push with a subsequent pull, the stack will overflow and you might not realize why. Use this trick at your own risk. For simple register saves, it's pretty easy to define register "holding bytes" using LADS and then stuff things there whenever you need temporary storage:

```
10 HOME = $FC58
100 STY Y:STA A:JSR HOME:LDA A:LDY Y
```

While, somewhere after the end of your program proper, down with the messages and other things that are data, not program, you have:

```
5000 A .BYTE 0
5010 Y .BYTE 0
5020 X .BYTE 0
```

A third alternative is to use the built-in "save registers" and "restore registers" routines in ROM:

```
10 SAVER = $FF4A
20 RESTORE = $FF3F
```

which would be used thus:

```
 30 HOME = $FC58
100 JSR SAVER:JSR HOME:JSR RESTORE
```

The Significance of Subroutines

Possibly the best way to approach ML program writing—especially a large program—is to think of it as a collection of subroutines. Each of these subroutines should be small. It should be listed on a piece of paper followed by a note on what it needs as input and what it gives back as *parameters*. "Parameter passing" simply means that a subroutine needs to know things from the main program (parameters) which are handed to it (passed) in some way. Alternatively, if you are using LADS, you can insert parameter information into the body of the source code of the program using the ";" remark pseudo-op.

The current position of the record in a database is a parameter which has its own "register" (we would have set aside a register for it at the start when we were assigning memory space either on paper for simple assemblers or by using the *equate* pseudo-op for LADS). So, the "look at the next record in the database" subroutine is a double-adder which adds 40 or whatever to the "current position register." This value always sits in the register to be used anytime any subroutine needs this information. In other words, the register (we called it FINGER in a previous example) is always pointing to our current position within the database. This is why such registers are called *pointers*.

The "look at the next register" subroutine *sends* the current-position parameter by *passing* it to the current-position register.

This is one example of a way that parameters are passed. Another example might be when you are telling a delay loop how long to delay. Ideally, your delay subroutine will be multipurpose. That is, it can delay for anywhere from 1/2 second to 60 seconds or something. This means that the subroutine itself isn't locked into a particular length of delay.

The main program will "pass" the amount of delay to the subroutine.

```
3000 LDY #$0
3002 INY
3003 BNE $3002
3005 DEX
3006 BNE $3000
3008 RTS
```

Notice that X never is initialized (set up) here with any particular value. This is because the value of X is passed to this subroutine from the main program. If you want a short delay, you would:

```
2000 LDX #$5
2002 JSR $3000
```

And for a delay which is twice as long as that:

2000 LDX #$0A (10 decimal)
2002 JSR $3000

In some ways, the less a subroutine does, the better. If it's not entirely self-sufficient, and the shorter and simpler it is, the more versatile it will be. For example, our delay above could function to time responses, to hold sounds for specific durations, and so on. When you make remarks about a general-purpose routine, write something like this: 3000 ; DELAY LOOP (expects duration in X; returns zero in X).

The longest duration delay would be set up with LDX #0. This is because the first thing that happens to X in the delay subroutine is DEX. If you DEX a zero, you get 255. If you need longer delays than the maximum value of X, simply:

2000 LDX #$0
2002 JSR $3000
2005 JSR $3000 (Notice that we don't need to set X to zero this second time. It returns from the subroutine with a zeroed X.)

You could even make a loop out of the JSRs above for extremely long delays. The point to notice here is that it helps to document each subroutine in your library: what parameters it expects; what registers, flags, and so on, it changes; and what it leaves behind as a result. This documentation—on a single sheet of paper or within LADS source—helps you remember each routine's address and lets you know what effects and preconditions are involved.

JMP

Like BASIC's GOTO, JMP is easy to understand. It goes to an address: JMP $5000 leaps from wherever it is to start carrying out the instructions which start at $5000. It doesn't affect any flags. It doesn't do anything to the stack. It's clean and simple. Yet some advocates of structured programming suggest avoiding JMP (and GOTO). Their reasoning is that JMP is a shortcut and a poor programming habit.

For one thing, they argue, using GOTO makes programs confusing. If you drew lines to show a program's "flow" (the order in which instructions are carried out), a program with lots of GOTOs would look like boiled spaghetti. Many programmers feel, however, that JMP has its uses. Clearly, you should not overdo it and lean heavily on JMP. In fact, you might see if there isn't a better way to accomplish something if you find yourself using it all the time and your programs are becoming impossibly awkward. But JMP is convenient, often necessary, in ML.

A 6502 Chip Bug

On the other hand, there is another, rather peculiar JMP addressing mode which is hardly, if ever, used in ML: JMP ($5000). This is an *indirect* jump which works like the indirect addressing we've seen before. Remember that with the indirect,Y addressing mode, LDA ($81),Y, the number in Y is added to the *address* found in $81 and $82. This address is the *real* place we are LDAing from, sometimes called the *effective address*. If $81 holds a 00, $82 holds a $40, and Y holds a 2, the address we LDA from is going to be $4002. Similarly (but without adding Y), the effective address found at the two bytes within the parentheses becomes the place we JMP to in JMP ($5000).

There are no necessary uses for this instruction. Best avoid it the same way you avoid playing around with the stack until you're an ML expert. If you find it in your computer's BASIC code, it will probably be involved in an "indirect jump table," a series of registers which are dynamic. That is, they can be changed as the program progresses. Such a technique is very close to a self-altering program and would have few applications in ML. But worse than than, there is a bug in the 6502 chip itself which causes the indirect JMP instruction to malfunction under certain circumstances. Just put JMP ($*NNNN)* into the same category as BPL and BMI. Avoid them.

If you decide that for some reason you must use indirect JMP, be sure to avoid the edge of pages, such as JMP ($*NN*FF). (The *NN* means "any number.") Whenever the low byte is right on the edge of a page ($FF is on the edge, it's ready to reset to $00), an indirect JMP will correctly use the low byte (LSB) from the pointer at $*NN*FF, but it will not pick up the high byte (MSB) from $*NN*FF+1 as it should. Instead, it gets the high byte from $*NN*00!

Here's how this error would work if you had set up a pointer to address $5043 with the pointer located at $40FF:

$40FF 43
$4100 50

Your intention would be to JMP to $5043 by bouncing off this pointer. You would write JMP ($40FF) and expect that the next instruction the computer would follow would be the instruction located at $5043. Unfortunately, your pointer would malfunction in this example. You would land at $0043 (if address $4000 held a zero). The indirect JMP would get its MSB from $4000.

This bug does not apply to any other addressing modes, just JMP (indirect). So, unless you want to take a chance with an addressing mode that's strictly for advanced programmers, contains a bug, and has no compelling uses, avoid JMP (indirect).

6. Debuggers: BRK and NOP

BRK and NOP have no arguments and are therefore members of that class of instructions which use only the implied addressing mode. They also affect no flags in any way with which we would be concerned. BRK does affect the I and B flags, but since it is a rare situation which would require testing those flags, we can ignore this flag activity altogether.

After you've assembled your program and it doesn't work as expected (few do), you start *debugging*. Some studies have shown that debugging takes up more than 50 percent of programming time. Such surveys can be misleading, however, because "making improvements and adding options" frequently take place after the program is allegedly finished, and would be thereby categorized as part of the debugging process.

Another factor is that these surveys reflect the sometimes inefficient programming styles adopted by professional or academic programming teams. Some assemblers and compilers used by professionals are extraordinarily cumbersome, requiring heroic efforts with linkers, maps, variable definition, and so forth, before a piece of program can be tested. LADS, by contrast, is virtually instantaneous. It will make the process of debugging very efficient.

In ML, debugging is facilitated by setting *breakpoints* with BRK and then seeing what's happening in the registers or memory. If you insert a BRK, it has the effect of halting the program and throwing you into the monitor where you can examine, say, the Y register to see if it contains what you would expect it to at this point in the program. It's similar to BASIC's STOP instruction:

```
2000 LDA #$15
2002 TAY
2003 BRK
```

At this point, you could use the monitor to examine any areas of memory just as you would examine variables after having your BASIC program STOP.

Debugging Methods

In practice, you debug whenever your program runs merrily along and then does something unexpected. It might crash and lock you out. You look for a likely place where you think it is failing and just insert a BRK right over some other instruction.

Remember that when you're in the monitor mode, you can directly change bytes, you can insert $00 (BRK) where you want.

In the example above, imagine that we put the BRK over a STY $8000. Make a note of the instruction you covered over with the BRK so that you can restore it later. After checking the registers and memory, you might find something wrong, some variable or register isn't behaving as it should or you somehow never even arrive at the break (some branch or JMP is being incorrectly activated). Now you have narrowed things down. Now you can locate and fix the error.

Sometimes it helps to have a printed listing of the suspect area in a program. You can turn your printer on and off with the .P and .NP options in LADS, printing out only the suspect zone of the program and use that to help you locate errors while working with the monitor. Alternatively, you can check the program with the built-in disassembler.

If nothing seems wrong at this point, restore the original STY over the BRK, and put BRK in somewhere further on. By this process, you can isolate the cause of the oddity in your program. Setting breakpoints (like putting STOP into BASIC programs) is an effective way to run part of a program and then examine the variables.

If your monitor or assembler allows *single-stepping*, this can be an excellent, though more time-consuming, way to debug. Your computer performs each instruction in your program one step at a time. This is like having BRK between each instruction in the program. You can control the speed of the stepping from the keyboard. Single-stepping automates breakpoint checking. It is like the TRACE command sometimes used to debug BASIC programs.

Like BRK ($00), the hex number of NOP ($EA) is worth memorizing. If you're working within your monitor, you will need to use hex numbers, and these two are particularly worth knowing.

NOP means NO oPeration. The computer slides over NOPs without taking any action other than increasing the program counter. There are two ways in which NOP can be effectively used.

First, it can be an eraser. If you suspect that JSR $8000 is causing all the trouble, try running your program with everything else the same, but with JSR $8000 erased. Simply put three $EAs over the instruction and argument. (Make a note, though, of what was under the $EAs so that you can restore it.) Then, the program will run without this instruction, without going to that subroutine at $8000, and you can watch the effects.

Second, it is sometimes useful to use $EA to temporarily hold open some space. If you don't know something (an address, a graphics value) during assembly, $EA can mark that this space needs to be filled in later before the program is run. As an instruction, it will let the program slide by. $EA could become your "fill this in" alert within programs in the way that we use self-branching (leaving a zero) to show that we need to put in a forward branch's address when using a mini-assembler.

Less Common Instructions

The following instructions are not often necessary for beginning applications, but we can briefly touch on their main uses. There are several logical instructions which can manipulate or test individual bits within each byte. This is most often necessary when interfacing. If you need to test what's coming in from a disk drive, or translate on a bit-by-bit level for I/O (input/output), you might work with the logical group.

In general, I/O is handled for you by your machine's operating system and is well beyond beginning ML programming. I/O is perhaps the most difficult, or at least the most complicated, aspect of ML programming. When putting things on the screen, programming is fairly straightforward, but handling the data stream into and out of a disk is pretty involved. Timing must be precise, and the preconditions which need to be established are complex.

For example, if you need to *mask* a byte by changing some of its bits to zero, you can use the AND instruction. After an AND, *both* numbers must have contained a one in any particular bit position for it to result in a one in the answer. This lets you set up a mask: 00001111 will zero any bits within the left four positions. So, 00001111 and 11001100 result in 00001100.

The unmasked bits remained unchanged, but the four high bits were all masked and, thus, zeroed.

There is a minor use for AND when you want to change a character to a reverse (black on white) or flashing character. The letter *A*, for example, has a value of $C1 which looks like this in binary (all the bits within the byte showing): 11000001. Notice that the left two bits are "on." To change this to a flashing *A* character, we need to turn the leftmost bit off so that we end up with 01000001, which is $41. You can turn off the leftmost bit by 11000001 AND 01111111, which will leave 01000001. Expressed in hex numbers you take the ordinary *A* ($C1) and AND it with 01111111 ($7F) to get the flasher, $41. Likewise, B ($C2) AND $7F results in a flashing B ($42). To change *A* into a reverse character, $C1 AND $3F.

Going the other way, you can change a flashing *A* back into a stable ordinary *A* by $41 ORA $80 (10000000). The ORA instruction is the same as AND, except it lets you mask to *set* bits (make them a one). Thus, 11110000 ORA 11001100 results in 11111100. The accumulator will hold the results when these instructions are used.

EOR (Exclusive OR) permits you to toggle bits. If a bit is 1, it will go to 0. If it's 0, it will flip to 1. EOR is sometimes useful in games. If you are heading in one direction and you want to go back when bouncing a ball off a wall, you could toggle. Let's say that you use a register to show direction: When the ball's going up, the byte contains the number 1 (00000001), but down is 0 (00000000). To toggle this least significant bit, you would EOR with 00000001. This would flip 1 to 0, and 0 to 1. This action results in the *complement* of a number. Thus, 11111111 EOR 11001100 results in 00110011.

To know the effects of these logical operators, we can look them up in *truth tables* which give the results of all possible combinations of zeros and ones:

AND	OR	EOR
0 AND 0 = 0	0 OR 0 = 0	0 EOR 0 = 0
0 AND 1 = 0	0 OR 1 = 1	0 EOR 1 = 1
1 AND 0 = 0	1 OR 0 = 1	1 EOR 0 = 1
1 AND 1 = 1	1 OR 1 = 1	1 EOR 1 = 0

Another instruction, BIT, also tests (it does an AND), but, like the BNE and so forth, branch instructions, it does not affect the number in the accumulator—its sole purpose is to set flags in the status register. The N flag is set (has a one) if bit 7 has a one (and vice versa). The V flag responds similarly to whatever value is in the sixth bit of the tested byte. The Z flag shows whether or not the result of the AND resulted in a zero. Instructions, like BIT, which do not affect the numbers being tested are called *nondestructive.*

We discussed LSR and ASL in the chapter on arithmetic: They can conveniently divide and multiply by two. ROL and ROR *rotate* the bits left or right in a byte, but, unlike with the Logical Shift Right or Arithmetic Shift Left, no bits are lost off one end during the shift. ROL will leave the seventh (most significant) bit in the carry flag, leave the carry flag in the zeroth bit (least significant bit), and move every other bit one space to the left:

ROL 11001100 (with the carry flag set results in:)
10011001 (carry is still set, it got the leftmost one)

If you disassemble your computer's BASIC, you may well look in vain for an example of ROL, but it and ROR are available in the 6502 instruction set if you should ever find a use for them.

Should you go into advanced ML arithmetic, they can be used for multiplication and division routines. Please see Appendix A for more details on some of these obscure instructions if you're interested.

Three other instructions remain to be discussed: SEI (SEt Interrupt), RTI (ReTurn from Interrupt), and CLI (CLear Interrupt). These operations are also beyond the scope of a book on beginning ML programming, but we'll briefly note their effects. Your computer gets busy as soon as the power goes on. Things are always happening: Timing registers are being updated; the keyboard, the video, and the peripheral connectors are being refreshed or examined for signals. To *interrupt* all this activity, you can SEI, perform some task, and then CLI to let things pick up where they left off. This description applies to a degree to the IIc, but the Apple II does not use the interrupt option. The following is simply for your information should you later decide to try some sophisticated ML interrupt programming on the IIc or another computer.

SEI sets the interrupt flag. Following this, all *maskable* interruptions (things which can be blocked from interrupting when the interrupt status flag is up) are no longer possible.

There are also *nonmaskable* interrupts which, as you might guess, will jump in anytime, ignoring the status register.

The RTI instruction (ReTurn from Interrupt) restores the program counter and status register (takes them from the stack), but the X and Y registers, and so on, might have been changed during the interrupt. Recall that our discussion of the BRK instruction involved the above actions. The key difference is that BRK stores the program counter plus two on the stack and sets the B flag on the status register. CLI puts the interrupt flag down and lets all interrupts take place.

If these last instructions are confusing to you, it doesn't matter. They are essentially hardware and interface related.

You can do nearly everything you will want to do in ML without them. How often have you used WAIT in BASIC?

A Newer Chip

The venerable 6502 chip, which has been the brains of most of the popular home computers for years, is being replaced in newer Apples with a slightly different younger sibling, the 65C02 chip. The C version is identical to the 6502, but has a few additional instructions. These new instructions offer nothing which cannot be done by the 6502, but in a couple of cases, they simplify things. For example, the STZ (STore Zero) instruction would simplify putting a zero into a memory location. Now, we have to LDA #$0:STA $5000. With the new instruction, we could STZ $5000. Not much of an advantage, but useful.

There is a new branching instruction, BRA, which means BRanch Always and is like the rest of the branchers, but doesn't check the flags. It always branches.

DEA and INA decrement or increment the accumulator.

That, too, is something you want to do once in awhile and would be easier with these new instructions. Normally, though, you use the X and Y registers as counters and they can be INY/DEY in the 6502.

There are PHX, PHY, PLX, and PLY which directly push or pull the X or Y registers to or from the stack. Now, if you want to put the X register on the stack, you have to TXA:PHA, because X and Y can't directly address the stack in the 6502 instruction set.

Finally, TRB and TSB will test and turn on (or off) bits within a given byte, somewhat simplifying the job.

There is also a new addressing mode, called zero page indirect addressing, which can operate much like the useful indirect,Y mode, but without adding the Y offset.

In general, it would be best to ignore these additional instructions. While they do offer, in some cases, minor conveniences, any program you write with them will not work on the majority of Apples. The 65C02 is inside all IIc's and any IIe's sold after March 1984. Using the extra instructions in the 65C02 will limit your programs to these recent models. Using the 6502 instruction set, however, will permit your programs to run on any Apple, including the new models.

LADS does not support the 65C02's new instructions, but LADS can be customized. (You could even make up commands for LADS which added clusters of frequently used instructions which were inserted into your ML program automatically.) Customizing LADS is for programmers who are relatively conversant in ML, but approaches and examples are described in Appendix C.

Chapter 7

Borrowing from BASIC

Borrowing from BASIC

BASIC is a collection of ML subroutines. It is a large web of hundreds of short ML programs. Why not use some of them by JSRing to them? At times, this is in fact the best solution to a problem.

How would this differ from BASIC itself? Doesn't BASIC just create a series of JSRs when it runs? Wouldn't using BASIC's ML routines in this way be just as slow as BASIC is?

In practice, you will not be borrowing from BASIC all that much. One reason is that such JSRing makes your program far less *portable*, less easily run on other computers or other models of your computer. When you JSR to an address within your ROM set to save yourself the trouble of reinventing the wheel, you are, unfortunately, making your program applicable only to machines which are the same model as yours.

While Apple has been better than many computer companies at keeping important ROM addresses like $FDED in the same place in new Apple models, there are no guarantees that this will always be the case.

However, if you want your program to work on many different computer brands, you'll need to limit the degree to which you make it ROM-specific. Stick to the few essential ones (input/output, clear screen, and so on, listed in this book and in your *Reference Guide*). If you try to get too tricky—using your BASIC's or operating system's ROM to the maximum—your programs will be pretty hard to translate to other Apple models, not to mention other computer brands. For example, the subroutine to allocate space for a string in memory is found at $D3D2 in the earliest Commodore PET model. A later version of PET BASIC (Upgrade) used $D3CE, and the current models use $C61D. Although Microsoft BASIC is nearly universally used in personal computers (Atari is the exception), each computer's version differs in both the order and the addresses of key subroutines.

Jump Tables and Other Menus

To help overcome this lack of portability, some computer manufacturers set aside a group of frequently used subroutines and create a "Jump Table," or "Kernal," for them. The idea is that future, upgraded BASIC versions will still retain this table. It would look something like this:

```
FFCF  4C  15  F2  (INPUT one byte)
FFD2  4C  66  F2  (OUTPUT one byte)
FFD5  4C  01  F4  (LOAD something)
FFD8  4C  DD  F6  (SAVE something)
```

This example is part of the Commodore Kernal and is intended to apply to all future versions of BASIC on Commodore machines.

The interesting thing about this table of jumps for Apple users is that there is a trick to the way this sort of table works, and you might want to use it yourself sometime. Notice that each member of the table begins with 4C. That's the JMP instruction and, if you land on it, the computer bounces right off to the address which follows.

Now, at that address following the 4C, there is going to be a subroutine (so it will end in RTS). So when we JSR to one of the JMPs inside this table, to, say, FFD2, we're going to land on a JMP and rebound, just bounce right off the JMP table to the correct subroutine. When that subroutine finally finishes its work and ends in RTS, we will be returned to our starting place. That's how a JMP table works and it can be a useful technique.

By the way, the PRINT subroutine is a fundamental one in any computer because it offers you so much value. For one thing, it keeps track of the cursor position which is incremented each time you access PRINT. It works semi-automatically, and you don't have to keep track of where you are on the screen. The PRINT-the-character routine in the Apple is $FDED (65005 decimal). This is a very important address; you should memorize it.

For convenience, you might want to make a standard "header" for all your ML source programs that you use with LADS. It would consist of a series of "equates" which define frequently used internal subroutines by giving them labels:

```
30 PRINTIT = $FDED; PRINTS CHARACTER IN
   ACCUMULATOR
40 HOME = $FC58; CLEAR SCREEN
50 SCREEN = $0400; LOCATION OF TEXT SCREEN
60 TEXT = $FB2F; SET TEXT MODE
70 GRAPHICS = $FB40; SET GRAPHICS MODE (LIKE GR)
```

Then, when you're writing an ML source program using LADS and want to print some character, you just JSR PRINTIT. Whenever you want to clear the text screen, you JSR HOME.

You would write JSR TEXT to set the text mode; JSR GRAPHICS to set graphics mode. ML can thus be very similar to BASIC in that, when you are going to use a known subroutine, a subroutine that you've given a label at the beginning of your program in the manner illustrated above, you just type a word like TEXT that means something to your program and also means something memorable to you.

The same PRINT routine will work for a printer or a disk or a tape—anything that the computer sees as an output device. However, unless you open a file to one of the other devices (it's simplest to do this from BASIC in the normal way and then SYS to an ML subroutine), the computer defaults to (assumes) the screen as the output device, and $FDED prints there. To see how to set up different output targets, see the Open1 source code of LADS in Appendix D.

So, if you look into any ML program and discover a series of JMPs (4C xx xx 4C xx xx), you've found a jump table. Using a jump table should help make your programs compatible with later versions of BASIC which might be released. Though this is the purpose of such tables, there are never any guarantees that the manufacturer will consistently observe them. And, of course, the program which depends on them will certainly not work on any other brand.

What's Fastest?

Since, when a BASIC program runs, it is JSRing around inside itself, how, then, is a JSR into BASIC code faster than a BASIC program? The answer is that a program written entirely in ML, aside from the fact that it borrows only sparingly from BASIC prewritten routines, differs from BASIC in an important way.

A finished ML program is like *compiled* code; that is, it is ready to execute without any overhead. BASIC, for each command or instruction, must be interpreted *as it runs.* This is why BASIC is called an *interpreter.* Each instruction must be looked up in a table to find its address in ROM. And many other aspects of a BASIC instruction need to be interpreted. All this takes time. Your ML code will contain the direct addresses for its JSRs. When that ML program runs, the instructions don't need elaborate interpretation, time-consuming cross-checking, table lookups, or any other delay. The JSR just leaps into the right area of BASIC ROM without further ado.

There are special programs called *compilers* which can take a BASIC program and transform (compile) it into ML-like code which can then be executed like ML, without having to interpret each command during the program's run. The JSRs are within the compiled program, just as in ML. Compiled programs will run perhaps 20 to 40 times faster than the BASIC program they grew out of. (Generally, there is a small price to pay in that the compiled version is almost always larger than its BASIC equivalent.)

Compilers are interesting; they act almost like automatic ML writers. You write it in BASIC, and they translate it into an ML-like program. Even greater improvements in speed can be achieved if a program uses no floating point (decimal points) in the arithmetic. Also, there are "optimized" compilers which take longer during the translation phase to compile the finished program, but which try to create the fastest, most efficient compiled program design possible. No compiler is excessively slow, however. A good optimizing compiler can translate an 8K BASIC program in two or three minutes. Well, why not just compile BASIC programs and forget about ML altogether? The main reason is that ML is always far faster than even optimized compilations. You just can't beat the efficiency of hand-crafted communications which speak directly to the chip in its own language.

GET and PRINT

Two of the most common activities of a computer program are getting characters from the keyboard and printing them to the screen. To illustrate how to use BASIC from within an ML program, we'll show how both of these tasks can be accomplished from within ML.

Try this program and hit a key on the keyboard. Notice that the code number for whatever character you typed on the keyboard appears in the accumulator.

Apple Microsoft BASIC's GET waits for user input:

2000 JSR $FD1B (GET a byte from the keyboard)

This address, $FD1B, will wait until the user types in a character, but will not show a cursor on the screen. It will position a flashing cursor at the correct position. However, it will not print an "echo," an image of the character on the screen.

To print to the screen:

```
2000 LDA #$C1   (Put "A" into the accumulator)
2002 JSR $FDED  (Print it)
```

If you combine these routines into a "GET and PRINT," you can leave out the LDA #$C1, because JSR $FD0C will have left the value of whatever key you typed in the accumulator, and JSR $FDED will print it to the next available location on screen:

```
2000 JSR $FD0C;  (Get a keypress)
2003 JSR $FDED;  (Print it)
```

However, if you intend to use or analyze what's being typed into the computer, you must also store each character somewhere in RAM:

```
2000 LDY #$0;           (Use Y as an offset into your buffer)
2002 LOOP JSR $FD0C
2005 STA BUFFER,Y
2008 INY;               (Raise the offset)
2009 JSR $FDED;         (Echo the character to the screen)
2012 JMP LOOP;          (Return to fetch the next character)
```

Notice that this example is an endless loop: It has no way to exit its loop. You would need to add a CMP #141 if you wanted to exit when the typist hit the RETURN key. You would CMP #141:BEQ END to branch to a label called END which you put somewhere beyond this loop, beyond that JMP LOOP instruction in line 2012.

In any event, an ML routine within BASIC which keeps track of the current cursor position and will help you print things to the screen is often needed in ML programming. Apple uses $FDED. You can safely use the Y register to print out a series of letters, by having Y hold the index, the counter, that keeps moving through the message and, simultaneously, through the screen RAM. You could print out an entire word or paragraph of text or graphics using the method illustrated in Program 7-1.

If you look at a map of the ROM chips in your computer's *Reference Manual* from Apple, you will discover that there are many freeze-dried ML modules sitting in BASIC. These routines were written by the professionals who built BASIC itself, and their methods can seem intimidating at first. However, disassembling some of these routines and picking them apart is a good way to discover new techniques, new efficiencies, and to see how the best ML programs are constructed.

Studying your computer's BASIC is worth the effort, and it's something you can do for yourself. You won't understand everything (some shortcuts are taken which are obscure in the extreme). Nevertheless, if you've got some time, take a look at a particular routine and see if you can see the logic in it, its purpose and structure.

Program 7-1

```
20 8000                          COUNTER = $55
30 8000                          LENGTH = 11     ONE LARGER THAN THE TRUE LENGTH
40 8000                          PRINTIT = $FDED
50
60 8000 A0 00         START      LDY #0
70 8002 B9 0E 80      LOOP       LDA STRING,Y
80 8005 20 ED FD                 JSR PRINTIT
90 8008 C8                       INY
100 8009 C0 0B                   CPY #LENGTH
120 800B D0 F5                   BNE LOOP
130 800D 60                      RTS
140
150 800E STRING .BYTE "SUPERDUPER
```

Chapter 8

Building a Program

Building a Program

Using what we've learned so far, and adding a couple of new techniques, let's build a useful program. This example will demonstrate many of the techniques we've discussed and will also show some of the thought processes involved in writing ML.

Among the computer's more impressive talents is searching. It can run through a mass of information and find something very quickly. We can write an ML routine which looks through any area of memory to find matches with anything else. Based on an idea by Michael Erperstorfer published in *COMPUTE!* magazine, this ML program will report the line number of all the matches it finds.

Safe Havens

Before we go through some typical ML program-building methods, let's clear up the "where do I put it?" question. ML can't be just dropped anywhere in RAM. When you give the starting address to LADS at the beginning of your source code with the *= symbol, you can't just put in any address that pops into mind.

There are other things going on in the computer in addition to your hard-won ML program. RAM is used in many ways. There is always the possibility that you want to have a BASIC program coresident with your ML program. If so, you'll need to figure out where to put the ML so that it won't cover up, or be covered up by, the BASIC. Too, BASIC needs to use part of RAM to store some of its variables. During execution, these variables might be written (POKEd) into your vulnerable ML if you located it in a vulnerable zone. That would fatally corrupt your ML.

Also, the operating system, the disk operating system, cassette or disk loads, printers—they all use parts of RAM for their housekeeping activities. There are other things going on besides your ML. And you obviously can't put your ML program into ROM addresses. That's impossible. Nothing can be POKEd into those frozen ROM addresses; they're *read only memory*, no writing allowed.

Where to put ML? There are some fairly safe areas. Addresses 768–1023 ($300–$3FF), also called page 3, is safe.

The "safe storage problem" is solved most easily by knowing about this free zone, or by creating artificial space by changing the computer's knowledge about the start or end of your BASIC RAM storage space. When BASIC is running, it will set up arrays and strings in RAM memory. The RAM of a BASIC program's text (the line numbers, commands, and so on, up to the top line number) isn't the only RAM that a BASIC program uses. Sometimes it stores strings just after the program itself. Sometimes it builds them down from the "top of memory," the highest RAM address. Where are you going to hide your ML routine if you want to use it along with a BASIC program? How are you going to keep BASIC from overwriting the ML code?

Misleading the Computer

If the ML is a short piece of program, you can stash it into the safe $0300–3FF zone mentioned above. Because this safe area is only a couple hundred bytes long, and because so many ML routines want to use that area, it can become crowded. Worse yet, we've been putting the word "safe" in quotes because it isn't 100 percent safe. Apple uses this page 3 for high-res work, for example. The alternative is to deceive the computer into thinking that its RAM is smaller than it really is. This is usually the best solution, unless you are writing short routines or practicing with the examples in this book where you can just go ahead and use $0300–03FF.

Your ML will be truly safe if your computer doesn't even suspect the existence of some set-aside RAM. It will leave the now-safe RAM alone because you've told it that it has less RAM than it really does. Nothing can overwrite your ML program after you've misled your computer's operating system about the size of its RAM memory. There are two bytes in zero page which tell the computer what its highest RAM address is. You just change those bytes to point to a lower address. You can have your ML program do this as its first job.

These crucial bytes are 115,116 ($73,$74 hex).

To repeat, pointers such as these are stored in LSB,MSB order. That is, the more significant byte (the one that's multiplied by 256) comes second (this is the reverse of normality). For example, $8000, divided between two bytes in this top-of-RAM pointer, would look like this:

```
0073 00
0074 80
```

As we mentioned earlier, this odd inversion of normal numeric representation is a peculiarity of the 6502 that you just have to get used to. You can take comfort in the fact that the 6502 and its family of chips have far fewer peculiarities and illogical rules than their main rivals, the Z80 family. You can be driven to distraction with chips where the language is frequently at odds with the way humans think. Destinations precede sources, and so on. It's maddening. Fortunately, the 68000 chip, the chip in the Mac, is a sensible, programmer-friendly chip, too. If you go on to learn how to work with this new generation of chips, the 6502 family will seem both familiar and reasonable. But do beware of the pointer inversion: The LSB is stored in the *lower* byte in memory. It's a small price to pay for an otherwise well-designed microprocessor.

Anyway, you can lower the computer's opinion of the top-of-RAM-memory, thereby making a safe place for your ML, by changing only the MSB. If you need one page (256 bytes), POKE 116, PEEK (116)−1. For four pages, POKE 116, PEEK (116)−4, and so on. You don't need to fiddle around with the LSB of the pointer. Give yourself plenty of room.

If you want to reserve safe RAM as the first act of your ML program (so that it protects itself), just take a look at the LADS source code in the Eval subprogram. It protects itself by stuffing its START into the top-of-RAM pointer. Take a look at lines 80–150 in Eval; here, LADS is setting some of its own pointers, but is also protecting itself by inserting its START into the BMEMTOP (BASIC memory top) variable. BMEMTOP was defined in the Defs subprogram.

For details on how to protect ML programs in high RAM with ProDOS, see CALL in Chapter 9.

Building the Code

Now we return to the subject at hand—building an ML program. Most people find it easiest to mentally divide a task into several tasks, solve the individual small tasks, and then weave them all together into a complete program. That's how we'll attack the job of building a search program.

We will build our ML program in pieces and then tie them all together at the end. The first phase, as always, is the initialization. We set up the variables and fill in the pointers. Lines 20 and 30 define two, two-byte zero page pointers. L1L is going to point at the address of the BASIC line we are currently searching through; L2L points to the starting address of the line following it.

BASIC stores four important bytes just prior to the start of the code in each BASIC line. Take a look at Figure 8-1. The first two bytes contain the address of the next line in the BASIC program. Thus, when BASIC has finished evaluating and acting upon the current line, it will already know where to go to find the next line. This is called *linking*.

The second two bytes hold the line number. The end of a BASIC line is signaled by a zero. Zero does not stand for anything in the ASCII code or for any BASIC command. This is quite similar to the way we signal in ML programs that a text message is finished—by storing a zero at the end of the text. We discussed this earlier when we talked of *delimiting* an ASCII message.

If there are three zeros in a row, it tells BASIC that it has reached the end of the program in memory. Three zeros is a super delimiter.

But back to our examination of the ML program. In line 40 is a definition of the zero page location which holds a two-byte number that BASIC looks at when it is going to print a line number on the screen. We'll want to store line numbers in this location as we come upon them during the execution of our ML search. Each line number will temporarily sit waiting in case a match is found. If a match is found, the program will JSR to the BASIC ROM routine we're calling PLINE, as defined in line 70. This routine prints a line number on the screen, and it will need to have the "current line number" where it expects to find it.

Line 50 establishes that BASIC RAM starts at $0800, and line 60 gives the address of the "print the character in the accumulator" ROM routine. Use *=768 to put the object code into the traditional "safe" RAM area to store short ML programs.

Refer to Program 8-1 to follow the logic of constructing our search program. The search is initiated by typing in line 0 followed by a colon and the item we want to locate. It might be that we are interested in removing all REM statements from a program to shorten it. We would type 0:REM and hit RETURN to enter this line into the BASIC program. Then we would start the search by a CALL to the starting address of the ML program: CALL 768.

Figure 8-1. A BASIC Program's Structure

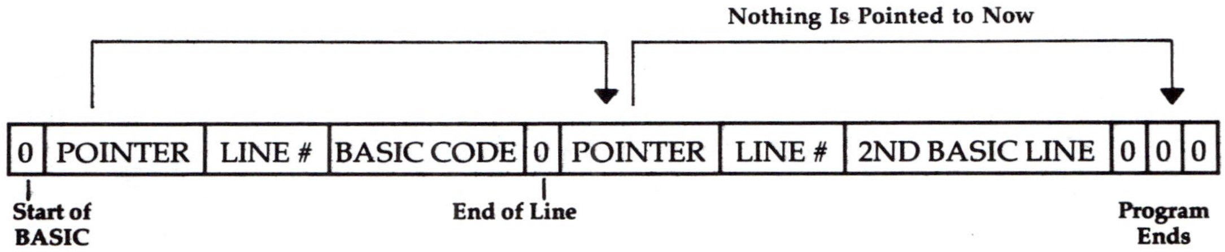


```
10 PRINT"HI"
20 END

0800                                 080B                0811
00 0B 08 0A  00 99 22 48 49 22 00 11 08 14  00  80 00 00 00
         LINE    ?  "   H  I  "          LINE END
          10                              20
```

By entering the "sample" string or command into the BASIC program, we simplify our task in two ways. First, if the thing we're searching for is a string, it will be automatically stored as the ASCII code for that string, just as BASIC stores strings.

If it is a keyword like REM, it will be translated into the "tokenized," one-byte representation of the keyword, just as BASIC stores keywords.

The second problem this method solves is that our sample is located in a known area of RAM. By looking at Figure 8-1, you can tell that the sample's starting address will always be the start of BASIC plus six. In Program 8-1 that means $0806 (see line 550).

Set Up the Pointers

We will have to get the address of the next line in the BASIC program we are searching. And then we need to store it while we look through the current line. The way that BASIC lines are arranged, we come upon the link to the next line's address and the line number before we see any BASIC code itself. Therefore, the first order of business is to put the address of the next line into our L1L location for safekeeping. Lines 150–180 take the link found in start-of-BASIC RAM (plus one) and move it to the storage pointer L1L.

Next, lines 190–250 check to see if we have reached the end of the BASIC program. It would be the end if we had found two zeros in a row as the pointer to the next line's address. If it is the end, the RTS sends us back to BASIC mode.

The subroutine in lines 260–440 saves the pointer to the following line's address and also the current line number.

Note the double-byte addition in lines 390–440. We *always* CLC before any addition. If adding four to the LSB (line 400) results in a carry, we want to be sure that the MSB goes up by one during the add-with-carry in line 430. At first glance, it seems to make no sense to add a zero in that line. What's the point? We're doing an addition *with carry;* in other words, if the carry flag has been set up by the addition of four to the LSB in line 400, then the MSB will have one added to it. That's the carry. The carry flag makes this happen.

First Characters

When you're searching for something, say, your car in a parking lot, you look for something distinctive. You might search for the color blue, or perhaps a plastic flower that you've attached to the antenna. You certainly don't look at each entire car, at the hood, the wheels, the windows, the size, the color, etcetera, etcetera. You look for a single attribute; then, if the car is blue, you compare other attributes to see if it is indeed entirely the same as yours.

Likewise, it's better just to compare the first character in a word against each byte in the searched memory than to try to compare the entire sample word. If you are looking for the word MEM, you don't want to stop at each byte in memory and see if M-E-M starts there. Just look for *M*'s. When you come upon an *M*, *then* go through the full string comparison. If line 490 finds a first-character match, it transfers the program to the subroutine labeled SAME (line 520) which will perform a thorough comparison.

On the other hand, if the routine starting at line 460 comes upon a zero (line 470), it knows that the BASIC line has ended (all BASIC lines end with zero, and zero is not used in any other way within a BASIC program). Our search program then goes down to STOPLINE (line 610) which puts the "next line" address pointer into the "current line" pointer and the whole process of reading a new BASIC line begins anew.

If, however, a perfect match *was* found (line 560 found a zero at the end of the 0:REM line, showing that we had come to the end of the sample string), we go to PERFECT and it makes a JSR to print out the line number (line 660). The PERFECT subroutine bounces back (RTS) to STOPLINE which replaces the "current line" (L1L) pointer with the "next line" pointer (L2L).

Then we JMP back to READLINE which, once again, pays very close attention to zeros to see if the whole BASIC program has ended with a pair of zeros. We have now returned to the start of the main loop of this ML program.

This all sounds more complicated than it is. If you've followed it so far, you can see that there is enormous flexibility in constructing ML programs. If you want to put the STOPLINE segment before the SAME subroutine—go ahead.

It is quite common to see a structure like this:

```
Definitions
SCREEN = $0400
Initialization
LDA #15
STA $83
Main Loop
START JSR 1
      JSR 2
      JSR 3
BEQ START  (Until some index runs out)
RTS        (To BASIC)
Subroutines
1
2          (Each ends with RTS back to the Main Loop)
3
DATA
Table 1
Table 2
Table 3
```

These are the main subdivisions of machine language programs. If you use this structure, you will find that it simplifies locating the different parts of a program and it also prevents nonprogram data (such as tables, messages, definitions) from getting mixed in with the program code proper. LADS is designed using this nearly universal format. Since all but the shortest programs will have defined variables, initialization, a main loop, a cluster of subroutines, and, finally, a collection of data tables, why not organize all your programs in this simple, straightforward, and sensible way?

There is a BASIC loader program which will POKE in the ML for you if you don't want to assemble the source code. Remember from Chapter 2 that a loader is a BASIC program that creates an ML program. It POKEs numbers that are held in DATA statements. These numbers form the ML. Once you have entered and run the loader, you could examine the resulting ML program by using the Apple built-in monitor.

Use CALL 768 to activate the program; that's where it sits in RAM when it's POKEd from the BASIC loader or created via an assembler.

As your skills improve, you will likely begin to appreciate, and finally embrace, the extraordinary freedom that ML confers on the programmer.

At first, learning ML can seem fraught with apparently

endless obscure tricks and rules. It can even seem menacing, beyond your understanding. It's this way with every new language because the words are still new, still odd.

Everyone, this author included, passes through this (surprisingly brief) sense of dread. Once you know how to tell your computer, directly in its language, how to print something on the screen, you don't need to relearn this trick. Things fall into place. It won't take as long as it might now seem for you to begin to grasp the relatively few novelties involved when programming in ML. ML isn't the theory of relativity; it's no more difficult than BASIC. It's just a new vocabulary for the same programming techniques you've been using with BASIC.

And this brief sensation, this brief confusion, is a very small price to pay for the flights you will soon be taking through your computer. Work at it. Try things. Learn how to find your errors. It's not circular—there will be steady advances in your understanding. One day soon, you'll be able to easily turbocharge your BASIC programs with ML; to write convenient, custom utilities like our search routine; and to do pretty much anything you could want to do with your machine.

Program 8-1. Search Source Code

```
14 ------------------------
15    DEFINE VARIABLES BY GIVING THEM LABELS.
16
20 0300                        L1L = $F9
30 0300                        L2L = $FB
40 0300                        FOUND = $75
50 0300                        BASIC = $0800
60 0300                        PRINT = $FDED
70 0300                        PLINE = $ED20  PRINT LINE #
80
90 -------------------------
100    INITIALIZE POINTERS
110
150 0300 AD 01 08              LDA BASIC+1
160 0303 85 F9                 STA L1L
170 0305 AD 02 08              LDA BASIC+2
180 0308 85 FA                 STA L1L+1
185 -------------------------
186   SUBROUTINE TO CHECK FOR 2 ZEROS.
187  IF WE DON'T FIND THEM, WE ARE NOT
188  YET AT THE END OF THE PROGRAM.
189
190 030A A0 00       READLINE  LDY #0
200 030C B1 F9                 LDA (L1L),Y
210 030E D0 06                 BNE GOON
220 0310 C8                    INY
230 0311 B1 F9                 LDA (L1L),Y
240 0313 D0 01                 BNE GOON
250 0315 60          END       RTS      RETURN TO BASIC
```

```
251 -----------------------------
252     SUBROUTINE TO UPDATE POINTERS TO THE NEXT LINE
253  AND STORE THE CURRENT LINE NUMBER IN CASE WE
254  FIND A MATCH AND NEED TO PRINT THE LINE #.
255  ALSO, WE ADD 4 TO THE CURRENT LINE POINTER SO THAT
256  WE ARE PAST THE LINE # AND "POINTER-TO-NEXT-LINE"
257  INFORMATION. WE ARE THEN POINTING AT THE 1ST CHAR.
258  IN THE CURRENT LINE AND CAN COMPARE IT TO THE SAMPLE.
259
260 0316 A0 00      GOON      LDY #0
270 0318 B1 F9                LDA (L1L),Y   GET NEXT LINE
280 031A 85 FB                STA L2L       ADDRESS AND
290 031C C8                   INY           STORE IT IN L2L
300 031D B1 F9                LDA (L1L),Y
310 031F 85 FC                STA L2L+1
320 0321 C8                   INY
330 0322 B1 F9                LDA (L1L),Y   PUT LINE #
340 0324 85 75                STA FOUND     IN STORAGE TOO
350 0326 C8                   INY           IN CASE IT
360 0327 B1 F9                LDA (L1L),Y   NEEDS TO BE
370 0329 85 76                STA FOUND+1   PRINTED OUT LATER
380 032B A5 F9                LDA L1L
390 032D 18                   CLC   MOVE FORWARD TO FIRST
400 032E 69 04                ADC #$04   PART OF BASIC TEXT
410 0330 85 F9                STA L1L    (PAST LINE # AND
420 0332 A5 FA                LDA L1L+1   POINTER TO NEXT LINE)
430 0334 69 00                ADC #0
440 0336 85 FA                STA L1L+1
441 -----------------------------
442  SUBROUTINE TO CHECK FOR ZERO (LINE IS FINISHED?)
443  AND THEN CHECK 1ST CHARACTER IN BASIC LINE AGAINST
```

```
444  1ST CHARACTER IN SAMPLE STRING AT LINE Ø.  IF THE
445  1ST CHARACTERS MATCH, WE MOVE TO A FULL STRING
446  COMPARISON IN THE SUBROUTINE CALLED "SAME".  IF 1ST
447  CHARS. DON'T MATCH, WE RAISE THE "Y" COUNTER AND
448  CHECK FOR A MATCH IN THE 2ND CHAR. OF THE CURRENT
449  BASIC LINE'S TEXT.
450
451 Ø338 AØ ØØ                LDY #Ø
460 Ø33A B1 F9       LOOP     LDA (L1L),Y
470 Ø33C FØ 1C                BEQ STOPLINE   Ø MEANS LINE FINISHED
480 Ø33E CD Ø6 Ø8             CMP BASIC+6    SAME AS 1ST SAMPLE CHAR?
490 Ø341 FØ Ø4                BEQ SAME       YES?  CHECK WHOLE STRING
500 Ø343 C8                   INY            NO?  CONTINUE SEARCH
510 Ø344 4C 3A Ø3             JMP LOOP
511 -------------------------------
512  SUBROUTINE TO LOOK AT EACH CHARACTER IN BOTH
513  THE SAMPLE (LINE Ø) AND THE TARGET (CURRENT LINE) TO
514  SEE IF THERE IS A PERFECT MATCH.  Y KEEPS TRACK OF
515  TARGET. X INDEXES SAMPLE. IF WE FIND A MISMATCH
516  BEFORE A LINE-END ZERO, WE FALL THROUGH TO LINE
517  59Ø AND JUMP BACK UP TO 46Ø WHERE WE CONTINUE ON
518  LOOKING FOR 1ST CHAR. MATCHES IN CURRENT LINE.
519
52Ø Ø347 A2 ØØ       SAME     LDX #Ø    COMPARE SAMPLE TO
53Ø Ø349 E8          COMPARE  INX     TARGET
54Ø Ø34A C8                   INY
55Ø Ø34B BD Ø6 Ø8             LDA BASIC+6,X
56Ø Ø34E FØ Ø7                BEQ PERFECT    LINE ENDS SO PRINT
57Ø Ø35Ø D1 F9                CMP (L1L),Y
58Ø Ø352 FØ F5                BEQ COMPARE    CONTINUE COMPARE
59Ø Ø354 4C 3A Ø3             JMP LOOP       NO MATCH
```

```
600 0357 20 65 03   PERFECT   JSR PRINTOUT
601 ----------------------------
602  SUBROUTINE TO REPLACE "CURRENT LINE" POINTER
603  WITH THE "NEXT LINE" POINTER WE SAVED IN THE
604  SUBROUTINE STARTING AT LINE 260.
605  THEN JUMP BACK TO THE START WITH THE CHECK FOR THE
606  END-OF-PROGRAM DOUBLE ZERO.  THIS IS THE LAST
607  SUBROUTINE IN THE MAIN LOOP OF THE PROGRAM.
608
610 035A A5 FB      STOPLINE  LDA L2L
620 035C 85 F9                STA L1L
630 035E A5 FC                LDA L2L+1
640 0360 85 FA                STA L1L+1
650 0362 4C 0A 03             JMP READLINE
651 -----------------------------
652  SUBROUTINE TO PRINT OUT A BASIC LINE NUMBER.
653  THIS ROM ROUTINE PRINTS THE NUMBER AT THE
654  NEXT CURSOR POSITION ON THE SCREEN.
655  THEN WE PRINT A BLANK SPACE
656  AND RETURN TO LINE 610 TO CONTINUE ON WITH
657  THE MAIN LOOP AND FIND ANY MORE MATCHES.
658
660 0365 20 20 ED   PRINTOUT  JSR PLINE
670 0368 A9 A0                LDA #$A0   THIS IS A BLANK
680 036A 20 ED FD             JSR PRINT  TO PRINT BETWEEN LINE #'S
690 036D 60                   RTS
691 -----------------------------
692
COM8
= 768
```

Program 8-2. Search BASIC Loader

```
10 FOR X = 768 TO 880: READ A:CK = CK + A: POKE X,A
   : NEXT X
20 IF CK < > 15786 THEN PRINT "ERROR IN DATA STATEM
   ENTS": END
100 DATA 173,1,8,133,249,173
110 DATA 2,8,133,250,160,0
120 DATA 177,249,208,6,200,177
130 DATA 249,208,1,96,160,0
140 DATA 177,249,133,251,200,177
150 DATA 249,133,252,200,177,249
160 DATA 133,117,200,177,249,133
170 DATA 118,165,249,24,105,4
180 DATA 133,249,165,250,105,0
190 DATA 133,250,160,0,177,249
200 DATA 240,28,205,6,8,240
210 DATA 4,200,76,58,3,162
220 DATA 0,232,200,189,6,8
230 DATA 240,7,209,249,240,245
240 DATA 76,58,3,32,101,3
250 DATA 165,251,133,249,165,252
260 DATA 133,250,76,10,3,32
270 DATA 32,237,169,160,32,237
280 DATA 253,96,254,254,2
```

Chapter 9

ML Equivalents of BASIC Commands

ML Equivalents of BASIC Commands

What follows is a small dictionary, arranged alphabetically, of the major BASIC commands. If you need to accomplish something in ML—TAB, for example—look it up in this chapter to see one way of doing it in ML. Often, because ML is so much freer than BASIC, there will be several ways to go about a given task.

Of these choices, one might work faster, one might take up less memory, and one might be easier to program and understand. When faced with this choice, I have selected example routines for this chapter which are easier to program and understand.

At ML's extraordinary speeds, and with the large amounts of RAM memory available to today's computerists, it will be rare that you will need to opt for velocity or memory efficiency.

CALL

This is BASIC's way of using a piece of ML code, an ML routine, as a subroutine. The only difference between CALL and GOSUB is that the computer is alerted to the fact that it needs to switch mental gears: The next series of instructions will be ML. In other words, the computer shouldn't try to interpret what it finds at the CALL address as more BASIC instructions. When it comes upon an RTS instruction in the ML program which was not matched by a previous JSR instruction, it will then revert to the BASIC program and pick up where it left off, following the CALL instruction.

There are times when you want to write in ML and use it as a subroutine for a BASIC program. This can greatly speed up the execution of the BASIC program. To put an ML program in RAM where it will be safe from BASIC's dynamic variable storage (where it won't be overwritten by BASIC), you boot DOS and then lower the HIMEM pointer ($73,74) to create some space in high RAM of which the computer is "unaware." HIMEM contains the address (in the usual LSB,MSB format discussed earlier) beyond which BASIC is forbidden to intrude.

After resetting this pointer, you are free to load in your ML program into the now-safe RAM between HIMEM and the true highest RAM byte in your computer.

The new ProDOS system, however, requires a slightly more complicated way of setting aside safe RAM. In effect, you access a routine which will lower the location of ProDOS's buffers and then you can put your ML program between these buffers and the ROM operating system starting location.

You put the number of *pages* (256-byte increments) of RAM memory you will require for your ML into the accumulator and then JSR $BEF5. When finished, this subroutine returns the MSB of the start address of your safe, reserved block of RAM. As an example, if you LDA #1:JSR $BEF5, you will have secured 256 bytes of RAM for your ML program between $9900 and $99FF. One page.

Short ML routines can always be stored in the page between $0300 and $03FF without any special preliminaries.

CLR

In BASIC, this clears all variables. Its primary effect is to reset pointers. It is a somewhat abbreviated form of NEW since it does not "blank out" your program, as NEW does.

CLR, in fact, is rarely used.

We might think of CLR, in ML, as the *initialization* phase of a program which erases (fills with zeros) the memory locations you've set aside to hold your ML flags, pointers, counters, and so on. You can see an example of this in the LADS source code in Eval between lines 30 and 70.

Before an ML program runs, you will usually want to be sure that some of these variables are set to zero. If they are in different places in memory, you will need to zero them individually:

2000 LDA #$0	
2002 STA $1990	(Put zero into one of the "variables.")
2005 STA $1994	(Continue putting zero into each byte which needs to be initialized.)

On the other hand, if you've put all your variables together at the end, the job is easy: Just loop through the list, putting zero in each variable. BASIC sets up a group of its variables (pointers) in zero page, so you can use a loop to zero them out:

2000 LDA #$0
2002 LDY #$0F (Y will be the counter. There are 15 bytes to zero out in this example.)
2004 STA $199,Y (The highest of the 15 bytes)
2007 DEY
2008 BNE $2004 (Let Y count down to zero, BNEing until Y is zero, then the Branch if Not Equal will let the program fall through to the next instruction at $200A.)

CONT

This BASIC command allows your program to pick up where it left off after a STOP command (or after hitting the system break key combination). You might want to look at STOP, below. In ML, you can't usually get a running program to stop with the break (or STOP) key. If you like, you could write a subroutine which checks to see if a particular key is being held down on the keyboard and, if it is, BRK:

3000 LDA $C000; (The "key currently pressed" location)
3002 CMP #$8D (This is the RETURN key on your machine, but you'll want CMP here to the value that appears in the "currently pressed" byte for the key you select as your STOP key. It could be any key. If you want to use A for your "stop" key, try CMP #$C1.)
3004 BNE $3007 (If it's not your target key, jump to RTS.)
3006 BRK (If it *is* the target, BRK.)
3007 RTS (Back to the routine which called this subroutine)

The 6502 places the program counter (plus two) on the stack after a BRK.

A close analogy to BASIC is the placement of BRK within ML code to cause a halt to program execution. Then, after examining registers or variables or *buffers* (places that hold input or output before it's received or sent), you can restart your program by using the monitor G (go) command. G is the equivalent of CONT.

DATA

In BASIC, DATA announces that the items following the word DATA are to be considered pieces of information (as opposed to being thought of as parts of the program). That is, the program will probably *use* this data, but the data are not BASIC commands. In ML, such a zone of "nonprogram" is called a *table*. It is unique only in that the program counter never starts trying to run through a table to carry out instructions. This never happens because you never transfer program control to anything within a table. (This is similar to the way that BASIC slides right over DATA lines.) There are no meaningful instructions inside a table. To see what a table looks like and what it does, see the Tables subprogram in the LADS source code in this book.

To keep things simple, tables of data are usually stored together either above or below the program. Usually, tables are stored above, at the very end of the ML program. (See Figure 9-1.)

Tables can hold messages that are to be printed to the screen, hold variables, hold flags (temporary indicators), and so on. If you disassemble your BASIC in ROM, you'll find the words STOP, RUN, LIST, and so forth, gathered together in a table. You can suspect a data table when your disassembler starts giving lots of error messages. It cannot find groups of meaningful opcodes within tables.

Figure 9-1. Typical ML Program Organization

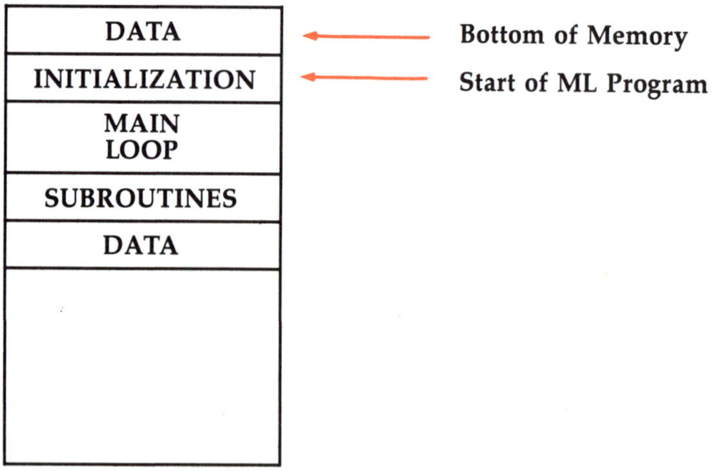

DIM

With its automatic string handling, array management, and error messages, BASIC makes life easy for the programmer.

The price you pay for this hand-holding is that it slows down the program when it's run. In ML, the DIMensioning of space in memory for variables is not explicitly handled by the computer. You must make a note that you are setting aside memory from $6000 to $6500, or whatever, to hold variables. It helps to make a simple map of this "dimensioned" memory so that you know where permanent strings, constants, variable strings, and variables, flags, and so on, are *within* the dimensioned zone. Because this set-aside memory will not contain meaningful ML instructions, it is generally placed at the end of the actual ML program. With LADS, you can make Tables the final file in your chain of files. That will automatically put the tables at the end of your program proper. To define data (string or numeric), you use the .BYTE instruction; .BYTE automatically makes space, like DIM.

A particular chunk of memory (where, and how much, is up to you) is set aside; that's all. You don't write any instructions in 6502 ML to set aside the memory; you just start using the .BYTE pseudo-op and it fills in your tables.

END

There are several ways to make a graceful exit from ML programs. You can use the "warm start" address in the map of its BASIC locations and JMP to that address. Or you can go to the "cold start" address.

If you went into the ML *from* BASIC with a CALL, you can return to BASIC with an RTS. Recall that every JSR matches up with its own RTS. Every time you use a JSR, it shoves its "return here" address onto the top of the stack. If the computer finds another JSR (before any RTS), it will shove another return address on top of the first one. So, after two JSRs, the stack contains two return addresses. When the first RTS is encountered, the top return address is lifted from the stack and put into the program counter so that the program returns control to the current instruction following the most recent JSR.

When the next RTS is encountered, it pulls *its* appropriate return (waiting for it on the stack), and so on. The effect of a

CALL from BASIC is like a JSR from within ML. The return address to the correct spot *within BASIC* is put on the stack. In this way, if you are within ML and there is an RTS (without any preceding JSR), what's on the stack had better be a return-to-BASIC address left there by CALL when you first went into ML.

Another way to END is to put a BRK in your ML code. This drops you into the machine's monitor. Normally, you use BRKs during program debugging. When the program is finished, though, you would not want this ungraceful exit any more than you would want to end a BASIC program with STOP.

In fact, many ML programs, if they stand alone and are not part of a larger BASIC program, never END at all. They are an endless loop. The main loop just keeps cycling over and over. A game will not end until you turn off the power. After each game, you see the score and are asked to press a key when you are ready for the next game. Arcade games which cost a quarter will ask for another quarter, but they don't end. They go into "attract mode." The game graphics are left running onscreen to interest new customers.

An ML word processor will cycle through its main loop, waiting for keys to be pressed, words to be written, format or disk instructions to be given. Here, too, it is common to find that the word processor takes over the machine, and you cannot stop it without turning the computer off. Among other things, such an endless loop protects software from being pirated. Since it takes control of the machine, how is someone going to save it or examine it once it's in RAM? Some such programs are "auto-booting" in that they start themselves running as soon as they are loaded into the computer.

BASIC, itself an ML program, also loops endlessly until you power down. When a program is running, all sorts of things are happening. BASIC is an *interpreter*, which means that it must look up each word (like INT) it comes across during a RUN (interpreting, or *translating*, its meaning into machine-understandable JSRs). Then, BASIC executes the correct sequence of ML actions from its collection of routines.

In contrast to BASIC RUNs, BASIC spends 99 percent of its time waiting for you to *program* with it. This waiting for you to press keys is its endless loop, a tight, small loop indeed.

It would look like our "which key is pressed?" routine:

```
2000 LDA 49168; THIS SETS THE LEFTMOST BIT IN 49152 TO 0
2003 LOOP LDA 49152; THE APPLE'S "WHICH KEY IS BEING
     PRESSED" LOCATION
2006 BMI LOOP; IF THE LEFTMOST BIT IS OFF, KEEP
     LOOPING
```

If the BMI is triggered, this means that the LDA found the leftmost bit off in address 49152 and, thus, no key has been pressed. So, we keep looping until the value in address 49152 has the leftmost bit on. This setup is the same as GET in BASIC because not only does it wait until a key is pressed, but it also leaves the value of the key in the accumulator when it's finished.

FOR-NEXT

Everyone has had to use delay loops in BASIC (FOR T = 1 TO 1000: NEXT T) which are also tight loops, sometimes called do-nothing loops because nothing happens between the FOR and the NEXT except the passage of time. For example, when you need to let the user read something on the screen, it's sometimes easier just to use a delay loop than to say, "When finished reading, press any key."

In any case, you'll need to use delay loops in ML just to *slow ML itself down*. In a game, the ball can fly across the screen. It can get so fast, in fact, that you can't see it. It just "appears" when it bounces off a wall. And, of course, you'll need to use loops in many other situations. Loops of all kinds are fundamental programming techniques.

In ML, you don't have that convenient little counter (T in the BASIC FOR-NEXT example above) which decides when to stop the loop. When T becomes 1000, go to the instructions beyond the word NEXT. Again, you must set up and check your *counter variable* by yourself.

If the loop is going to be smaller than 255 cycles, you can use the X register as the counter (Y is saved for the very useful *indirect indexed* addressing discussed in Chapter 4: LDA (96),Y). Anyway, by using X, you can count to 200 by:

```
2000 LDX #200 (or $C8 hex)
2002 DEX
2003 BNE $2002
```

For loops involving counters larger than 255, you'll need to use two bytes to count down, one going from 255 to 0 and then clicking (like a gear) the other (more significant) byte.

To count to 512:

```
2000 LDA #$2
2002 STA $0      (Put the 2 into address 0, our MSB, most signifi-
                 cant byte, counter.)
2004 LDX #$0     (Set X to 0 so that its first DEX will make it 255.
                 Further DEXs will count down again to 0, when it
                 will click the MSB down from 2 to 1 and then fi-
                 nally 0.)
2006 DEX
2007 BNE $2006
2009 DEC $0      (Click the number in address 0 down 1.)
200B BNE $2006
```

Here we used the X register as the LSB (least significant byte) and address 0 as the MSB. Why use address 0? Why not? Use any RAM byte you want that won't interfere with other things going on in the computer.

We could use addresses 0 *and 1* to hold the MSB/LSB if we wanted. This is commonly useful because then address 0 (or some available, two-byte space in zero page) can be used for LDA ($0),Y. You would print a message to the screen using the combination of a zero page counter and LDA (zero page address),Y.

FOR-NEXT-STEP

Here you would just increase your counter (usually X or Y) more than once. To create FOR I = 100 TO 1 STEP −2 you could use:

```
2000 LDX # 100
2002 DEX
2003 DEX
2004 BNE $2002
```

For larger numbers you create a counter which uses two bytes, working together, to keep count of the events. Following our example above for FOR-NEXT, we could translate FOR I = 512 TO 0 STEP −2:

```
2000 LDA #$2
2002 STA $0      (This is going to hold our MSB.)
2004 LDX #$0     (X is holding our LSB.)
```

```
2006 DEX
2007 DEX          (Here we click X down a second time, for −2.)
2008 BNE $2006
200A DEC $0
200c BNE $2006
```

To count up, use the CoMPare instruction. FOR I = 1 TO 50 STEP 3:

```
2000 LDX #$0
2002 INX
2003 INX
2004 INX
2005 CPX #$50
2007 BNE $2002
```

For larger STEP sizes, you can use a *nested loop* within the larger one. This would avoid a whole slew of INXs. To write the ML equivalent of FOR I = 1 TO 50 STEP 10:

```
2000 LDX #$0
2002 LDY #$0
2004 INY
2005 CPY #$0A
2007 BNE $2004
2009 CPX #$32
200B BNE $2002
```

GET

Every computer must have that important "which key is being pressed?" address, where it holds the value of a character typed in from the keyboard. To GET, you create a very small loop which just keeps testing this address. In the Apple:

```
2000 LDA $C000 ("Which key pressed?" Note: this is in hex.)
2003 BPL $2000  (If the seventh bit of $C000 is clear—meaning no
                key was pressed—the BPL branch instruction is trig-
                gered and we jump back to keep waiting until the
                seventh bit in $C000 is set which, on the Apple,
                means a key was struck on the keyboard.)
2005 STA $C010 (Clears the keyboard)
2008 AND #$7F  (To give the correct character value)
```

This routine will wait until a key is pressed. For most programming purposes, you want the computer to wait until a key has actually been pressed. However, if your program is supposed to fly around doing things *until* a key is pressed, you might use the above routine without the loop structure. Just use a CMP to test for the particular key that would stop the routine and branch the program somewhere else when a particular key is pressed. This flexibility would never be permitted in BASIC, but that's one of the signal advantages of ML. How you utilize and construct a GET-type command in ML is up to you, tailored to each application.

GOSUB

This is nearly identical to BASIC in ML. Use JSR $*NNNN* and you will go to a subroutine at address *NNNN* instead of a line number as in BASIC. (*NNNN* just means that you can substitute any hex number for the *NNNN* that you want to. This is a form of math shorthand.) LADS allows you to give *labels,* names to JSR to, instead of addresses. A simple assembler like the one in the monitor does not allow labels. You are responsible (as with DATA tables, variables, and so on) for keeping a list of your subroutine addresses *and the parameters involved* if you're not using LADS.

Parameters are the number or numbers handed to a subroutine to give it information it needs. Quite often, BASIC subroutines work with the variables already established within the BASIC program. In ML, though, managing variables is up to you. Subroutines are useful because they can perform tasks repeatedly without needing to be written into the body of the program each time the task is to be carried out. Beyond this, they can be *generalized* so that a single subroutine can act in a variety of ways, depending upon the variable (the parameter) which is passed to it.

A delay loop to slow up a program could be general in the sense that the amount of delay is handed to the subroutine each time. The delay can, in this way, be of differing durations, depending on what it gets as a parameter from the main routine.

Let's say that we've decided to use address 0 to pass parameters to subroutines. We could pass a delay of five cycles of the loop by:

```
                    2000 LDA #$5
The Main Program    2002 STA $0
                    2004 JSR $5000
                    .
                    .
                    .
                    .
                    5000 DEC $0
                    5002 BEQ $500C  (If address 0 has counted all
                                    the way down from five to
                                    zero, RTS back to the Main
                                    Program.)
                    5004 LDY #$0
                    5006 DEY
The Subroutine      5007 BNE $5006
                    5009 JMP $5000
                    500C RTS
```

A delay which lasted twice as long as the above would merely require a single change to the calling routine: 2000 LDA #$0A.

GOTO

In ML, it's JMP. JMP is like JSR, except the address you leap away from is not saved anywhere. You jump, but cannot use an RTS to find your way back. A *conditional* branch would be CMP #0:BEQ 5000. The condition of equality is tested by BEQ, Branch if EQual. BNE tests a condition of inequality, Branch if Not Equal. Likewise, BCC (Branch if Carry is Clear) and the rest of these branches are testing conditions within the program.

GOTO and JMP do not depend on any conditions within the program, so they are *unconditional* branches. The question arises, when you use a GOTO: Why did you write a part of your program that you must *always* (unconditionally) jump over? GOTO and JMP are sometimes used to patch up a program, but used without restraint, they can make your program hard to understand later. On the other hand, JMP can many times be the best solution to a programming problem. In fact, it is hard to imagine ML programming without it.

One additional note about JMP: It makes a program nonrelocatable. If you later need to move your whole ML program to a different part of memory, all the JMPs (and JSRs) need to be checked to see if they are pointing to addresses which are no longer correct. (JMP or JSR into your BASIC ROMs will still be the same, but not those which are targeted to addresses *within* the ML program.)

2000 JMP $2005
2003 LDY #$3
2005 LDA #$5

If you moved this little program up to $5000, everything would survive intact and work correctly except the JMP $2005. It would still say to jump to $2005, but it should say to jump to $5005, after the move. You have to go through with a disassembly and check for all these incorrect JMPs. To make your programs more "relocatable," you can use a special trick with unconditional branching which *will* move without needing to be fixed:

2000 LDY #$0
2002 BEQ $2005 (Since we just loaded Y with a zero, this Branch if EQual to zero instruction will always be true and cause a pseudo-JMP.)
2004 NOP
2005 LDA #$5

Various monitors and assemblers include a "moveit" routine, which will take an ML program and relocate it somewhere else in memory for you. On the Apple, you can go into the monitor and type *5000<2000.2006M (you give the monitor these numbers in hex). The first number is the target address. The second and third are the start and end of the program you want to move.

The best solution to relocatability, however, is LADS. With it, you never JMP to actual addresses; rather, you JMP or JSR or branch to labels. This way, relocating your program couldn't be simpler. You just change the start address with *= and reassemble. Everything is taken care of and the program reassembles to the new location flawlessly. With LADS, the example above is written like this:

100 JMP NEXTROUTINE
110 LDY #3
120 NEXTROUTINE LDA #5

(The numbers at the left are not addresses; they are line numbers for your convenience when writing the program, and they have no effect on the resulting ML code after assembly.)

GR(APHICS)

JSR $FB40 switches to the graphics screen.

HOME

JSR $FC58 clears the screen and puts the cursor in the upper-left-hand corner, just like BASIC.

IF-THEN

This familiar and fundamental computing structure is accomplished in ML with the combination CMP-BNE or any other conditional branch: BEQ, BCC, and so forth. Sometimes, the IF half isn't even necessary. Here's how it would look:

```
2000 LDA $57     (What's in address $57?)
2002 CMP #$0F    (Is it $0F, 15 decimal?)
2004 BEQ $200D   (IF it is, branch up to $200D)
2006 LDA #$0A    (or ELSE, put a $0A, 10 decimal, into address
                 $57)
2008 STA $57
200A JMP $2011   (and jump over the THEN part.)
200D LDA #$14    (THEN, put a $14, 20 decimal, into address $57.)
200F STA $57
2011             (Continue with the program....)
```

Often, though, your flags are already set by an action, making the CMP unnecessary. For example, if you want to branch to $200D if the number in address $57 is zero, just LDA $57:BEQ $200D. This works because the act of loading the accumulator will affect the status register flags. You don't need to CMP #0 because the zero flag will be set if a zero was just loaded into the accumulator. It won't hurt anything to use a CMP, but you'll find many cases in ML programming where you can shorten and simplify your coding if you wish to. As you gain experience, you will see these patterns and learn how and what affects the status register flags.

INPUT

This is a series of GETs, echoed to the screen as they are typed in, which end when the typist hits the RETURN key. The reason for the *echo* (the symbol for each key typed is reproduced on the screen) is that few people enjoy typing without seeing what they've typed. This also allows for error correction using cursor control keys or DELETE and INSERT keys.

To handle all of these actions, an INPUT routine must be fairly complicated. We don't want, for example, the DELETE to become a character within the string. We want it to immediately act on the string being entered during the INPUT, to erase a mistake.

Our INPUT routine must also be smart enough to know what to add to the string and what keys are intended only to modify it. Here is the basis for constructing your own ML INPUT. It simply receives a character from the keyboard, stores it in the screen RAM cells, and ends when the RETURN key is pressed. We'll write this INPUT as a subroutine. That simply means that when the 141 (Apple ASCII for carriage return) is encountered, we'll perform an RTS back to a point just following the main program address which JSRed to our INPUT routine:

```
5000 LDY #$0       (Y will act here as an offset for storing the
                   characters to the screen as they come in.)
5002 LDA $9E       (This is the "number of keys in the keyboard
                   buffer" location. If it's zero, nothing has been
                   typed yet.)
5004 BNE $5002     (So we go back to $5002.)
5006 LDA $26F      (Get the character from the keyboard buffer.)
5009 CMP #$8D      (Is it a carriage return?)
500B BNE $500F     (If not, continue.)
500D RTS           (Otherwise, return to the main program.)
500E STA $8000,Y   (Echo it to the screen.)
500F INY
5010 LDA #$0
5012 STA $96       (Reset the "number of keys" counter to zero.)
5014 JMP $5002     (Continue looking for the next key.)
```

This INPUT could be much more complex. As it stands, it will hold the string on the screen only. To save the string, you would need to read it from screen RAM and store it elsewhere where it will not be erased. Or, you could have it echo to the screen, but (also using Y as the offset) store it into some safe location where you are keeping string variables. The routine above does not make provisions for DELETE or INSERT, either. The great freedom you have with ML is that you can redefine anything you want. You can *softkey*: define a key's meaning via software; have any key perform any task you want. You might even decide to use the $ key to DELETE.

Along with this freedom goes the responsibility for organizing, writing, and debugging these routines.

LET

Although this word is still available on most BASICs, it is a holdover from the early days of computing. It is supposed to remind you that statements like LET NAME = NAME + 4 is an *assignment* of a value to a variable, not an algebraic equation. The two numbers on either side of the equal sign, in BASIC, are not intended to be equal in the algebraic sense. Most people write NAME = NAME + 4 without using LET. The function of LET applies though to ML as well as to BASIC: We must assign values to variables.

In the Apple, for example, where the address of the screen RAM can change depending on how much memory is in the computer, and so on, there has to be a place where we find out the starting address of screen RAM. Likewise, a program will sometimes require that you *assign* meanings to string variables, counters, and the like. This can be part of the initialization process, the tasks performed before the real program, your main routine, gets started. Or it can happen during the execution of the main loop. In either case, there has to be an ML way to establish, to *assign*, variables. This also means that you must have zones of memory set aside to hold these variables. Normally, you will store your variables as a group at the end of an ML program.

For strings, you can think of LET as the establishment of a location in memory. In our INPUT example above, we might have included an instruction which would have sent the characters from the keyboard to a table of strings as well as echoing them to the screen. If so, there would have to be a way of managing these strings. For a discussion on the two most common ways of dealing with strings in ML, see Chapter 6 under the subhead "Dealing with Strings."

In general, you will probably find that you program in ML using somewhat fewer variables than in BASIC. There are three reasons for this:

1. You will probably not write many programs in ML like databases where you manipulate hundreds of names, addresses, and so forth. It might be somewhat inefficient to create an *entire database management program*, an inventory

program for example, in ML. Keeping track of the variables would require careful programming. (For an example database manager, see LADS's Equate and Array subprograms.)

The value of ML is its speed of execution, but its drawback is that it requires more precise programming and, at least for beginners, can take more time to write. So, for an inventory program, you could write the bulk of the program in BASIC and simply attach ML routines for *sorting* and *searching* tasks within the program.

2. The variables in ML are often handled within a series of instructions (not held elsewhere as BASIC variables are). FOR I = 1 TO 10 : NEXT I becomes LDY #1:INY:CPY #10:BNE.

   Here, the BASIC variable is counted for you and stored outside the body of the program. The ML "variable," though, is counted by the program itself. ML has no *interpreter* which handles such things. If you want a loop, you must construct all of its components yourself.

3. In BASIC, it is tempting to assign values to variables at the start of the program and then to refer to them later by their variable names, as in 10 BALL = 79. Then, anytime you want to PRINT the BALL to the screen, you could say, PRINT CHR$(BALL). Alternatively, you might define it this way in BASIC: 10 BALL$ = "O". In either case, your program will later refer to the word BALL. In this example we are assuming that the number 207 will place a ball character on your screen (the letter *O).*

In ML we can use variable names precisely the same way if we are programming with an advanced assembler like LADS. However, with an elementary assembler like the one in the monitor, you will just LDA #207, STA (screen position) each time. Some people like to put the 207 into their zone of variables (that arbitrary area of memory set up at the end of a program to hold tables, counters, and important addresses). They can pull it out of that zone whenever it's needed. That is somewhat cumbersome, though, and slower. You would LDA 1015, STA (screen position), assuming you had put a 207 into this "ball" address, 1015, earlier.

Obviously a value like BALL will always remain the same throughout a program. The ball will look like a ball in your game, whatever else happens. So, it's not a true variable; it does not *vary*. It is constant. A true variable *must* be located in your "zone of variables," your variable *table*.

It cannot be part of the body of your program itself (as in LDA #207) because it will change. You don't know when writing your program what the variable will be. So you can't use *immediate mode* addressing because it might not be a #207. You have to LDA 1015 from within your table of variables.

Elsewhere in the program you have one or more STA 1015 or INC 1015 or some other manipulation of this address which keeps updating this variable. In effect, ML makes you responsible for setting aside areas which are safe to hold variables if you are using the monitor assembler. What's more, you have to remember the addresses and update the variables in those addresses whenever necessary. This is why it is so useful to keep a piece of paper next to you when you are writing ML. The paper lists the start and end addresses of the zone of variables, the table. You write down the specific address of each variable as you write your program. LADS, of course, makes variable zones and names automatic with the .BYTE pseudo-op. See LADS's Tables subprogram to see how variables (and constants) can be handled efficiently.

LIST

This is done via a *disassembler*. It will not have line numbers (though, again, advanced assembler-disassembler packages like LADS do have line numbers). You will see the address of each instruction in memory. You can look over your work and plan debugging strategies, where to set BRKs into problem areas, and so on.

The most common way to list and check your work, however, is to read over the source code. This does not require a disassembler. You write LADS source code as if it were a BASIC program and, thus, can LIST it and modify it as if it were a BASIC program.

LOAD

The method of saving and loading an ML program varies from computer to computer. Normally, you have several options which can include loading from within the monitor, from BASIC, or even from an assembler. When you finish working on a program, or a piece of a program, on the mini-assembler you will know the starting and ending addresses of your work. Using these, you can save to tape using the W monitor command (described in Chapter 3) or to disk using BSAVE in the manner you would from BASIC. To LOAD, the simplest way is just to BLOAD. (From tape, you use the monitor R command.)

To see how to save and load from *within* your ML programs, to write ML which itself saves and loads files, please refer to the Open1 subprogram of LADS in Appendix D.

NEW

In Microsoft BASIC, this has the effect of resetting some pointers which make the machine think that you are going to start over again. The next program line you type in will be put at the "start-of-a-BASIC-program" area of memory. Some computers, the Atari for example, even *wash* memory by filling it with zeros. There is no special command in ML for NEWing an area of memory, though the monitor has a "fill memory" option which will fill an area of memory as large as you want with whatever value you choose.

The reason that NEW is not found in ML is that you do not always write your programs in the same area of memory as you do in BASIC, building up from some predictable address. You might have a subroutine floating up in high memory, another way down low, your table of variables at the end, and your main program in the middle. Or you might not. We've been using $2000 as our starting address for many of the examples in this book and $5000 for subroutines, but this is entirely arbitrary.

To "NEW" in ML, just start assembling over the old program.

Alternatively, you could just turn the power off and then back on again. This would, however, have the disadvantage of wiping out LADS along with your program.

ON-GOSUB

In BASIC, you are expecting to test values from among a group of numbers: 1, 2, 3, 4, 5.... The value of X must fall within this narrow range: ON X GOSUB 100, 200, 300 ... (X must be 1 or 2 or 3 here). In other words, you could not conveniently test for widely separated values of X (18, 55,

220). Some languages feature an improved form of ON-GOSUB where you can test for any values. If your computer were testing the temperature of your bath water:

```
CASE
     80 OF GOSUB HOT ENDOF
    100 OF GOSUB VERYHOT ENDOF
    120 OF GOSUB INTOLERABLE ENDOF
ENDCASE
```

ML permits you the greater freedom of the CASE structure. Using CMP, you can perform a *multiple branch* test:

```
2000 LDA $96   (Get a value, perhaps input from the keyboard)
2002 CMP #$50  (Decimal 80)
2004 BNE $2009
2006 JSR $5000 (Where you would print "hot," following our ex-
                ample of CASE)
2009 CMP #$64  (Decimal 100)
200B BNE $2011
200D JSR $5020 (Print "very hot")
2010 CMP #$78  (Decimal 120)
2012 BNE $2017
2014 JSR $5030 (Print "intolerable")
```

This illustrates one way that bugs get into ML—by not cleanly entering and leaving subroutines. The potential problem here is triggering the CMPs more than once. Since you are JSRing and then will be RTSing back to *within* the multiple branch test above, you will have to be sure that the subroutines up at $5000 do not change the value of the accumulator. If the accumulator started out with a value of $50 and, somehow, the subroutine at $5000 left a $64 in the accumulator, you would print "hot" and then also print "very hot." One way around this would be to put a zero into the accumulator before returning from each of the subroutines (LDA #$0). This assumes that none of your tests, none of your cases, responds to a zero.

ON-GOTO

This is more common in ML than the ON-GOSUB structure above. It eliminates the need to worry about what is in the accumulator when you return from the subroutines. Instead of RTSing back, you jump back, *following all the branch tests.*

```
2000 LDA $96
2002 CMP #$50
2004 BNE $2009
2006 JMP $5000  (Print "hot")
2009 CMP #$64
200B BNE $2010
200D JMP $5020  (Print "very hot")
2010 CMP #$78
2012 BNE $2017
2014 JMP $5030  (Print "intolerable")
2017 (All the subroutines JMP $2017 when they finish.)
```

Instead of RTS, each of the subroutines will JMP back to $2017, which lets the program continue without accidentally "triggering" one of the other tests with something left in the accumulator during the execution of one of the subroutines.

PLOT

You can use the BASIC PLOT command by putting the row into the accumulator, the column into the Y register, and then JSR to $F800. However, Program 9-1, written by my associate Tim Victor, illustrates how you can construct an arcade-style game from within ML by using a flexible routine in BASIC ROM which calculates the start address of any screen line. By then using the Y register as an offset from the line (in other words, Y holds the number of the column you're after), you can print and erase a character as it flies around the screen.

A great variety of player/enemy action games can be constructed by using the techniques illustrated in Program 9-1, so let's look at the structure of this program.

Between lines 50 and 120, we define the labels of this program. We're going to move a ball-like character around the screen. The current position of the ball must be known at all times, so we'll keep its row (on which line on the screen it currently resides) in $FF, labeled ROW, and the column number in the location called COL.

But we also need to erase the ball every time it moves to a new location, so we create places that will hold the previous position of the ball and we call these places OLDROW and OLDCOL. Now we're ready to move the ball around.

In lines 150–160 we set the row to zero which means we'll start on the first screen line, and we set the column to zero so that we'll be in the leftmost space on that line.

Program 9-1

```
10 *= 768
15 .D BALL.OBJ
20 ; SUBROUTINE TO MOVE A BALL AROUND THE SCREEN.
30 ;
40 ;
50 BASCALC = $FBC1; CALCULATES THE START ADDRESS OF A LINE
60 ;  (WHEN GIVEN THE LINE'S #)
70 ;
80 BASE = $28; (PLACE WHERE BASCALC LEAVES ITS POINTER)
90 COL = $FE
100 ROW = $FF; (WE SAVE THE CURRENT LINE NUMBER HERE)
110 OLDCOL = $EE; (WE NEED TO ERASE IN THIS COLUMN)
120 OLDROW = $EF; ( AND IN THIS ROW)
130 ;
140 ;------------------------
150 LDA #0
160 STA ROW:STA COL; START AT UPPER LEFT OF SCREEN
165 ;
166 ;--MAIN LOOP, HORIZONTAL MOVE
167 ;
170 LOOP LDA COL:STA OLDCOL;  SAVE POSITION
180 INC COL
190 CMP #39:BNE NOTRIGHT; AT RIGHT EDGE?
200 LDA #0:STA COL
210 ;
213 ;
214 ;-- VERTICAL MOVE
215 ;
220 NOTRIGHT LDA ROW:STA OLDROW; SAVE POSITION
```

```
230 INC ROW
240 CMP #23:BNE NOTBOTT; AT BOTTOM OF SCREEN?
250 LDA #Ø:STA ROW
263 ;
264 ;-- ERASE OLD BALL
265 ;
270 NOTBOTT LDA OLDROW:JSR BASCALC; FIND START OF LINE FOR ERASE
280 LDY OLDCOL:LDA #16Ø:STA (BASE),Y
283 ;
284 ;-- DRAW NEW BALL
285 ;
290 LDA ROW:JSR BASCALC; FIND START OF LINE FOR DRAWING
300 LDY COL:LDA #2Ø7:STA (BASE),Y; STORE THE BALL
302 ;
303 ;-- DELAY
304 ;
310 LDX #2ØØ
315 DLUP1 LDY #Ø
320 DLUP2 INY:BNE DLUP2
330 INX:BNE DLUP1
340 JMP LOOP
350 .END PROGRAM9.1
```

To illustrate horizontal, vertical, and diagonal movement, we'll cause the ball to move down the screen from the upper left to the lower right. We'll have it move diagonally because that's simply a combination of horizontal and vertical movement: one down, one to the right, one down, and so on.

The first thing we're going to do is save the current column and row locations for future reference. We'll need their locations when we go to erase the ball character after printing a new ball lower down on the screen. Since we're going to calculate the new row and column (and place them into our holding areas called ROW and COL), we need to have holding places which remember the location we need to erase. Without erasing the old balls, the illusion that a ball is moving would be destroyed and the graphics on the screen would look like a string of pearls. (Some games, however, make use of this. To create a firing ray gun, you can print a line of characters and then erase the line all the way from the end, all at once. This looks like a whip shoots out and then recoils.)

In any case, after saving the column position, we then raise it by one (INC) to move the ball one space to the right (if we were simply moving the ball horizontally, we'd now be ready to print the ball).

Next, we check to see if we've gone off the screen to the right (a column number of 39 would cause us to reset our column number in line 200). Then, between lines 220 and 250, we perform the same steps for the vertical move downward by one line.

Now we are ready to call upon the built-in ROM routine which, if we give it the screen line we're interested in (by putting the line number in the accumulator), will give us back the address in RAM of that line. BASE was defined in line 80 as the location where this ROM routine leaves the address of the BASIC line.

We get our offset out of COL and put it into the Y register, load the blank character into the accumulator, and store the blank character at the proper line and offset the proper number of columns from the start of that line (lines 270–280).

Then we repeat these steps to print the ball character in the new location. Because ML is so fast, we have to delay things before printing the next ball, so lines 310–330 simply waste some time counting up the X and Y registers. It's here that you would raise or lower the LDX and LDY values to adjust the speed of the game or to provide various "skill levels" of play.

If your game involved several things bouncing around on the screen, you would control each of them with their own OLDCOL/COL, OLDROW/ROW pairs. If you needed to detect whether or not a player had hit a missile or had run into a wall or some other object, you could insert the following starting at line 300:

```
300 LDY COL:LDA (BASE),Y:CMP #MISSILE:BEQ
    HITSOMETHING
302 LDA #207:STA (BASE),Y:JMP DELAY
303 HITSOMETHING  (Raise or lower the score or take other
                  action)
310 DELAY LDX #200
```

You would have defined the missile character as MISSILE at the top of the program. The HITSOMETHING routine could cause an explosion, could damage or transform the player, or could simply affect the score—it depends on the rules of the game.

PRINT

You *could* print out a message in the following way:

```
2000  LDY #$0
2002  LDA #$C8     (the letter H)
2004  STA $0400,Y  (an address on the screen)
2007  INY
2008  LDA #$C5     (the letter E)
200A  STA $0400,Y
200D  INY
200E  LDA #$CC     (the letter L)
2010  STA $0400,Y
2013  INY
2014  LDA #$CC     (the letter L)
2016  STA $0400,Y
2019  INY
201A  LDA #$CF     (the letter O)
201C  STA $0400,Y
```

But this is clearly a cumbersome, memory-eating way to go about it. In fact, it would be absurd to print out a long message this way. The most common ML method involves putting message strings into a data table and ending each message with a zero. Zero is never a printing character in computers; to print the *number* zero, you use 176: LDA #176, STA $0400. So, zero itself can be used as a delimiter to let the printing routine know that you've finished the message. In a data table, we first put in the message "hello":

```
1000 $C8  H
1001 $C5  E
1002 $CC  L
1003 $CC  L
1004 $CF  O
1005 $0        (the delimiter)
1006 $C8  H
1007 $C9  I    (another message)
1008 $0        (another delimiter)
```

Such a message table can be as long as you need; it holds all your messages and they can be used again and again:

```
2000 LDY #$0
2002 LDA $1000,Y
2005 BEQ $200F     (If the zero flag is set, it must mean that we've
                   reached the delimiter, so we branch out of this
                   printing routine.)
2007 STA $0400,Y   (Put it on the screen.)
200A INY
200B JMP $2002     (Go back and get the next letter in the message.)
200F               (Continue with the program.)
```

Had we wanted to print HI, the only change necessary would have been to put $1006 into the LDA at address $2003. To change the location on the screen that the message starts printing, we could just put some other address into $2008. The message table, then, is just a mass of words, separated by zeros, in RAM memory.

The process of printing messages is even simpler using the LADS label-based assembler and its .BYTE trick for storing numbers or words:

```
 10 SCREEN = $0400
100 LDY #0:MORE LDA MESSAGE,Y:BEQ FINISH
110 STA SCREEN,Y:INY:JMP MORE
```

with, at the end of your source code, the following line included somewhere in your table of variables, your data:

```
400 MESSAGE .BYTE "HELLO":.BYTE 0
410 MESSAGE1 .BYTE "HI":.BYTE 0
```

The fastest way to print to the screen, especially if your program will be doing a lot of printing, is to create a subroutine which will print any of your messages. It can use some bytes in zero page (addresses 0–255) to hold the location of the message within your table of data.

To put an address into zero page, you will need to put it into two bytes. Addresses are too big to fit into one byte. With LADS, you can use the #< and #> pseudo-ops to extract the LSB and MSB of a label and thus store the address of your message into a zero page pointer:

```
 10 MSGADDRESS = 56
 20 SCREEN = $0400
100 LDA #<MESSAGE:STA MSGADDRESS; set up pointer
110 LDA #>MESSAGE:STA MSGADDRESS+1
120 JSR PRINTMSG; go to universal print subroutine
500 PRINTMSG LDY #0:LOOP LDA (MSGADDRESS),Y:BEQ
    END:STA SCREEN,Y
510 STA SCREEN,Y:INY:JMP LOOP
520 END RTS
```

This same trick can be done with the simple assembler in the monitor, but it is more cumbersome.

First, you split the hex number in two. The left two digits, $10, are the MSB (most significant byte) and the right digits, $00, make up the LSB (least significant byte). If you are going to put this target address into zero page at 56 (decimal):

```
2000  LDA #$00     (LSB)
2002  STA $56
2004  LDA #$10     (MSB)
2006  STA $57
2008  JSR $5000    (Printout subroutine)

5000  LDY #$0
5002  LDA ($56)Y
5004  BEQ $5013    (If zero, return from subroutine)
5006  STA $0400,Y  (to screen)
5009  INY
500A JMP $5002
500D RTS
```

One drawback to this PRINT subroutine we've constructed is that it will always print any messages to the same place on the screen. That $0400 is frozen into your subroutine. Solution? Use another zero page pair of bytes to hold the screen address. Then, your calling routine sets up the message address as above, but also goes on to specify a screen address as well.

We are using the Apple II's low-resolution graphics screen for the examples in this book, so you will want to put 0 and 4 into the LSB and MSB respectively for your screen pointer.

```
2000 LDA #$00    (LSB)
2002 STA $56     (Set up message address)
2004 LDA #$10    (MSB)
2006 STA $57
2008 LDA #$0     (LSB)

200A STA $58     (We'll just use the next two bytes in zero page
                 above our message address for the screen
                 address.)
200C LDA #$4     (MSB)
200E STA $59
2010 JSR $5000
5000 LDY #$0
5002 LDA ($56)Y
5004 BEQ $500D   (If zero, return from subroutine)
5006 STA ($58),Y (to screen)
5009 INY
500A JMP $5002
500D RTS
```

The easiest way to print messages to particular places on the screen, however, is to use the Apple's built-in BASIC PRINT routine to send the characters, one by one, each to the next cursor position onscreen. The built-in routine updates and keeps track of the current cursor position for you. So, you can get around having to keep a screen pointer in zero page this way. In the example immediately above, just replace line 5006 with JSR $FDED (the Apple PRINT routine) and remove lines 2008–200E.

RANDOM

To pick off a random number, look in address $4E or $4F which is erratically updated whenever input is requested from the user. The reason this works so well is that these locations are furiously cycled whenever the computer waits for user input. Since the amount of time it takes you to type something in after an INPUT prompt is thoroughly unpredictable in milliseconds, very high quality randomness is achieved. In other words, nothing within the machine can achieve the high degree of temporal randomness of the human nervous system organizing itself to put a finger to a particular key on a keyboard. If you are looking for a random number between certain limits, mask the bytes (described at the end of Chapter 6 under the subhead "Less Common Instructions").

READ

There is no reason for a *read*ing of data in ML. Variables are not placed into "DATA statements." They are entered into a table when you are programming. The purpose of READ, in BASIC, is to assign variable names to raw data, or to take a group of data and move it somewhere, or to manipulate it into an array of variables. These things are handled by you, not by the computer, in ML programming.

If you need to access a piece of information, *you* set up the addresses of the datum and the target address to which you are moving it. (See the "PRINT" routines above.) As always, in ML you are expected to keep track of the locations of your variables. If you are using the simple assembler in the monitor, you must keep a map of data locations, vectors, tables, and subroutine locations. This pad of paper is always next to you as you program in ML. It would seem that you would need many notes, but in practice an average program of, say, 1000 bytes could be mapped out and commented on, using only one sheet.

Alternatively, with more sophisticated assemblers like LADS, the labels themselves within the program will keep track of things for you, and embedded comments serve to remind you of the use and function of all data.

REM

You do this on a pad of paper, too, when working with a simple assembler. If you want to comment or make notes about your program (and it can be a necessary, valuable explanation of what's going on), you can disassemble some ML code like a BASIC LISTing. If you have a printer, you can make notes on the printed disassembly. If you don't use a printer, make notes on your pad to explain the purpose of each subroutine, the parameters it expects to get, and the results or changes it effects.

The more sophisticated assemblers like LADS will permit comments within the source code. As you program, you can include REMarks by typing a semicolon, which is a signal to the assembler to ignore the REMarks when it is assembling your program. In these assemblers, you are working much closer to the way you work in BASIC. Your REMarks remain part of the source program and can be listed out and studied.

RETURN

RTS works the same way that RETURN does in BASIC: It takes you back to *just after* the JSR (GOSUB) that sent control of the program away from the main program and into a subroutine. JSR pushes, onto the stack, the address which immediately follows the JSR itself. That address, then, sits on the stack, waiting until the next RTS is encountered. When an RTS occurs, the address is pulled from the stack and placed into the *program counter*. This has the effect of transferring program control back to the instruction just after the JSR.

RUN

There are several ways to start an ML program. If you are taking off into ML from BASIC, you just CALL it. This acts just like JSR and will return control to BASIC, just like RETURN would, when there is an unmatched RTS in the ML program. By *unmatched* we mean the first RTS which is not part of a JSR/RTS pair. CALL can take you into ML either in *immediate mode* (directly from the keyboard) or from within a BASIC program as one of the BASIC commands.

If you need to "pass" information from BASIC to ML, it is easiest to use integer numbers and just POKE them into some predetermined ML variable zone that you've set aside and noted on your notepad. Then just CALL your ML routine, which will look into the set-aside, POKEd area when it needs the values from BASIC.

If you are not going between BASIC and ML, you can start (RUN) your ML program from within the built-in monitor. To enter the monitor on Apple II, type CALL −151 and you will see an asterisk as your prompt. To run an ML program from within the monitor, you type 2000G (that's address 8192 in decimal).

The Apple expects to encounter an unmatched RTS or a BRK instruction to end the run and return control to the monitor.

SAVE

When you save a BASIC program, the computer automatically handles it. The starting address and the ending address of your program are calculated for you. In ML, you must know the start address and the length (size in bytes) of the program if you are BSAVEing. For tape users, use the W function of the monitor (described in Chapter 3). From the Apple II monitor, you type the starting and ending address of what you want saved, and then W for *write*:

2000.2010W (Note that these commands are in hex. These addresses are 8192 and 8208, in decimal.)

For more information about BSAVE and BLOAD, please see your *User's Guide*.

Saving object code is automatic with LADS; you use the .O pseudo-op. To see how to save and load from *within* your ML programs—to write ML which itself saves and loads files—please refer to the Open1 subprogram of LADS in Appendix D.

STOP

BRK (or an RTS with no preceding JSR) throws you back into the monitor mode after running an ML program. BRK is most often used for debugging programs because you can set "breakpoints" in the same way that you would use STOP to examine variables when debugging a BASIC program.

TEXT

JSR $FB39. Sets text mode, just like BASIC.

String Handling

ASC

In BASIC, this will give you the number of the ASCII code which stands for the character you are testing. ?ASC("A") will result in a 193 being displayed. There is never any need for this in ML. If you are manipulating the character *A* in ML, you *are using ASCII already*. In other words, the letter *A is* 193 in ML programming. The Apple ASCII isn't standard ASCII; it stores character symbols in nonstandard ways, so you will need to write a special program to be able to translate to standard ASCII if you are using a modem or some other peripheral which uses true ASCII.

CHR$

This is most useful in BASIC to let you use characters which cannot be represented within normal strings, will not show up on your screen, or cannot be typed from the keyboard.

For example, if you have a printer attached to your computer, you could send CHR$(13) to it, and it would perform a carriage return. (The correct numbers which accomplish various things sometimes differ, though decimal 13—an ASCII code standard—is nearly universally recognized as carriage return, except that the Apple internal code for a carriage return on the screen is 141.)

Or, you could send the combination CHR$(27) CHR$(8), and the printer would backspace.

There is no real use for CHR$ within ML. If you want to specify a carriage return, just LDA #141. In ML, you are not limited to the character values which can appear onscreen or within strings. Any value can be dealt with directly.

LEFT$

As usual in ML, *you* are in charge of manipulating data. Here's one way to extract a certain "substring" from the left side of a string as in the BASIC statement LEFT$(X$,5):

```
2000 LDY #$5
2002 LDX #$0        (Use X as the offset for buffer storage)
2004 LDA $1000,Y    (The location of X$)
2007 STA $4000,X    (The "buffer," or temporary storage area, for the
                    substring)
200A INX
200B DEY
200C BNE $2004
```

LEN

In some cases, you will already know the length of a string in ML. One of the ways to store and manipulate strings is to know beforehand the length and address of a string. Then you could use the subroutine given for LEFT$, above. More commonly, though, you will store your strings with delimiters (zeros) at the end of each string. To find out the length of a certain string:

```
2000 LDY #$0
2002 LDA $1000,Y (The address of the string you are testing)
2003 BEQ $2009   (Remember, if you LDA a zero, the zero flag is
                 set. So you don't really need to use a CMP #0
                 here to test whether you've loaded the zero
                 delimiter.)
2005 INY
2006 BNE $2002   (We are not using a JMP here because we assume
                 that all your strings are less than 256 characters
                 long.)
2008 BRK         (If we still haven't found a zero after 256 INYs,
                 we avoid an endless loop by just BRKing out of
                 the subroutine.)
2009 DEY         (The LENgth of the string is now in the Y
                 register.)
```

We had to DEY at the end because the final INY picked up the zero delimiter. So, the true count of the LENgth of the string is one less than Y shows, and we must DEY one time to make this adjustment.

MID$

To extract a substring which starts at the fourth character from within the string and is five characters long (MID$(X$,4,5)):

```
2000 LDY #$5      (The size of the substring we're after)
2002 LDX #$0      (X is the offset for storing the substring.)
2004 LDA $1003,Y  (To start at the fourth character from within the
                  X$ located at $1000, simply add three to that ad-
                  dress. Instead of starting our LDA,Y at $1000,
                  skip to $1003. This is because the first character
                  is not in position 1. Rather, it is at the zeroth po-
                  sition, at $1000.)
2007 STA $4000,X  (The temporary buffer to hold the substring)
200A INX
200B DEY
200C BNE $2004
```

RIGHT$

This, too, is complicated because normally we do not know the LENgth of a given string. To find RIGHT$(X$,5) if X$ starts at $1000, we should find the LEN first and then move the substring to our holding zone (buffer) at $4000:

```
2000  LDY #$0
2002  LDX #$0
2004  LDA $1000,Y
2007  BEQ $200D    (The delimiting zero is found.)
2009  INY
200A  JMP $2004
200D  TYA          (Put LEN into A so that we can subtract the
                   substring size from it.)
200E  SEC          (Always set carry before any subtraction.)
200F  SBC #$5      (Subtract the size of the substring you want to
                   extract.)
2011  TAY          (Put the offset back into Y, now adjusted to
                   point to five characters from the end of X$.)
2012  LDA $1000,Y
2015  BEQ $201E    (We found the delimiter, so end.)
2017  STA $4000,X
201A  INX
201B  DEY
201C  BNE $2012
201E  RTS
```

TAB

This formatting instruction moves you to a specified column on a given line. TAB 10 moves you ten spaces from the left side of the screen.

In ML, you have more direct control over what happens: You would just add or subtract the amount you want to TAB over to. If you were printing to the screen and wanted ten spaces between A and B so it looked like this:

A   B

you could write:

```
2000 LDA #$C1  (A)
2002 STA $0400 (Screen RAM address)
2005 LDA #$C2  (B)
2007 STA $040A (You've added ten to the target address.)
```

Alternatively, you could add ten to the Y offset (this is LADS format):

```
 10 SCREEN = $0400
100 LDY #0:LDA #"A:STA SCREEN,Y:LDY #10:LDA #"B:STA
SCREEN,Y
```

An even simpler LADS method uses the + pseudo-op to add whatever amount you wish to a label:

```
 10 SCREEN = $0400
100 LDA #"A:STA SCREEN:STA SCREEN+10
```

As an example, we are writing to the screen here, but messages that were longer than 40 characters would behave strangely on the Apple screen because the RAM bytes which map it are not contiguous across lines. In practice, you would print to the screen using $FDED as described below. The examples above, using Y as an offset, are more applicable to storing, say, items in a database or printing hardcopy.

Nonetheless, if you are printing out many columns of numbers and need a subroutine to correctly space your printout, you might want to use a subroutine which will add ten to the Y offset each time you call the subroutine:

```
5000 TYA
5001 CLC
5002 ADC #10
5004 TAY
5005 RTS
```

This subroutine directly adds ten to the Y register whenever you JSR $5000. To accomplish TAB onscreen correctly, however, and to take into account the entire screen, you should use blanks (character 160) and feed them to the screen via the built-in ROM routine which prints the number of blanks you've requested in the X register: $F94A. So, LDX #45:JSR $F94A will print 45 blanks. Then, send your actual message via the PRINT subroutine in ROM: $FDED. The Apple screen is not orderly, and, thus, $F94A in combination with $FDED will do all the hard work for you. Just stuff blanks onto the screen whenever you need to SPC forward to format text. To tab backward, use JSR $FC10 to print a backspace character.

Related formatting routines in ROM are

JSR $FC1A; (Moves the cursor up one line)
JSR $FC66; (Moves the cursor down one line—not a carriage return since the cursor remains in the same column)

Appendix A

6502 Instruction Set

6502 Instruction Set

Here are the 56 mnemonics, the 56 instructions you can give the 6502 (or 6510) chip. Each of them is described in several ways: what it does, what major uses it has in ML programming, what addressing modes it can use, what flags it affects, its opcode (hex/decimal), and the number of bytes it uses up.

ADC

What it does: Adds byte in memory to the byte in the accumulator, plus the carry flag if set. Sets the carry flag if result exceeds 255. The result is left in the accumulator.

Major uses: Adds two numbers together. If the carry flag is set prior to an ADC, the resulting number will be *one* greater than the total of the two numbers being added (the carry is added to the result). Thus, one always clears the carry (CLC) before beginning any addition operation. Following an ADC, a set (up) carry flag indicates that the result exceeded one byte's capacity (was greater than 255), so you can chain-add bytes by subsequent ADCs without any further CLCs (see "Multibyte Addition" in Appendix E).

Other flags affected by addition include the V (overflow) flag. This flag is rarely of any interest to the programmer. It merely indicates that a result became larger than could be held within bits 0–6. In other words, the result "overflowed" into bit 7, the highest bit in a byte. Of greater importance is the fact that the Z is set if the result of an addition is zero. Also the N flag is set if bit 7 is set. This N flag is called the "negative" flag because you can manipulate bytes thinking of the seventh bit as a sign (+ or −) to accomplish "signed arithmetic" if you want to. In this mode, each byte can hold a maximum value of 127 (since the seventh bit is used to reveal the number's sign). The B branching instruction's relative addressing mode uses this kind of arithmetic.

ADC can be used following an SED which puts the 6502 into "decimal mode." Here's an example. Note that the number 75 is *decimal* after you SED:

```
SED
CLC
LDA #75
ADC #$05  (this will result in 80)
CLD       (always get rid of decimal mode as soon as you've
          finished)
```

Attractive as it sounds, the decimal mode isn't of much real value to the programmer. LADS will let you work in decimal if you want to without requiring that you enter the 6502's mode. Just leave off the $ and LADS will handle the decimal numbers for you.

Addressing Modes:

Name	Format	Opcode	Number of Bytes Used
Immediate	ADC #15	$69/105	2
Zero Page	ADC 15	$65/101	2
Zero Page,X	ADC 15,X	$75/117	2
Absolute	ADC 1500	$6D/109	3
Absolute,X	ADC 1500,X	$7D/125	3
Absolute,Y	ADC 1500,Y	$79/121	3
Indirect,X	ADC (15,X)	$61/97	2
Indirect,Y	ADC (15),Y	$71/113	2

Affected flags: N Z C V

AND

What it does: Logical ANDs the byte in memory with the byte in the accumulator. The result is left in the accumulator. All bits in both bytes are compared, and if both bits are 1, the result is 1. If either or both bits are 0, the result is 0.

Major uses: Most of the time, AND is used to turn bits off. Let's say that you are pulling in numbers higher than 128 (10000000 and higher) and you want to "unshift" them and print them as lowercase letters. You can then put a zero into the seventh bit of your "mask" and then AND the mask with the number being unshifted:

```
LDA ?      (test number)
AND #$7F   (01111111)
```

(If *either* bit is 0, the result will be 0. So the seventh bit of the test number is turned off here and all the other bits in the test number are unaffected.)

Addressing Modes:

Name	Format	Opcode	Number of Bytes Used
Immediate	AND #15	$29/41	2
Zero Page	AND 15	$25/37	2
Zero Page,X	AND 15,X	$35/53	2
Absolute	AND 1500	$2D/45	3
Absolute,X	AND 1500,X	$3D/61	3
Absolute,Y	AND 1500,Y	$39/57	3
Indirect,X	AND (15,X)	$21/33	2
Indirect,Y	AND (15),Y	$31/49	2

Affected flags: N Z

ASL

What it does: Shifts the bits in a byte to the left by 1. This byte can be in the accumulator or in memory, depending on the addressing mode. The shift moves the seventh bit into the carry flag and shoves a 0 into the zeroth bit.

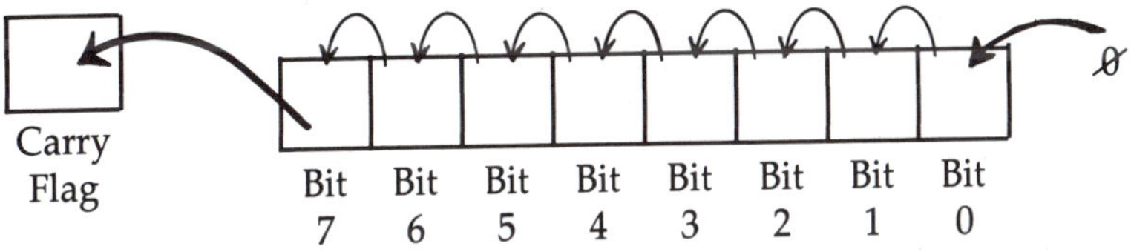

Major uses: Allows you to multiply a number by 2. Numbers bigger than 255 can be manipulated using ASL with ROL (see "Multiplication" in Appendix E).

A secondary use is to move the lower four bits in a byte (a four-bit unit is often called a *nybble*) into the higher four bits. The lower bits are replaced by zeros, since ASL stuffs zeros into the zeroth bit of a byte. You move the lower to the higher nybble of a byte by ASL ASL ASL ASL.

Addressing Modes:

Name	Format	Opcode	Number of Bytes Used
Accumulator	ASL	$0A/10	1
Zero Page	ASL 15	$06/6	2
Zero Page,X	ASL 15,X	$16/22	2
Absolute	ASL 1500	$0E/14	3
Absolute,X	ASL 1500,X	$1E/30	3

Affected flags: N Z C

BCC

What it does: Branches up to 127 bytes forward or 128 bytes backward from its own address if the carry flag is clear. In effect, it branches if the first item is lower than the second, as in LDA #150: CMP #149 or LDA #22: SBC #15. These actions would clear the carry and, triggering BCC, a branch would take place.

Major uses: For testing the results of CMP or ADC or other operations which affect the carry flag. IF-THEN or ON-GOTO type structures in ML can involve the BCC test. It is similar to BASIC's > instruction.

Addressing Modes:

Name	Format	Opcode	Number of Bytes Used
Relative	BCC addr.	$90/144	2

Affected flags: none

BCS

What it does: Branches up to 127 bytes forward or 128 bytes backward from its own address if the carry flag is set. In effect, it branches if the first item is higher than the second, as in LDA #150: CMP #249 or LDA #22: SBC #85. These actions would set the carry and, triggering BCS, a branch would take place.

Major uses: For testing the results of LDA or ADC or other operations which affect the carry flag. IF-THEN or ON-GOTO type structures in ML can involve the BCC test. It is similar to BASIC's < instruction.

Addressing Modes:

Name	Format	Opcode	Number of Bytes Used
Relative	BCS addr.	$B0/176	2

Affected flags: none

BEQ

What it does: Branches up to 127 bytes forward or 128 bytes backward from its own address if the zero flag (Z) is set. In other words, it branches if an action on two bytes results in a 0, as in LDA #150: CMP #150 or LDA #22: SBC #22. These actions would set the zero flag, so the branch would take place.

Major uses: For testing the results of LDA or ADC or other operations which affect the carry flag. IF-THEN or ON-GOTO type structures in ML can involve the BEQ test. It is similar to BASIC's = instruction.

Addressing Modes:

Name	Format	Opcode	Number of Bytes Used
Relative	BEQ addr.	$F0/240	2

Affected flags: none

BIT

What it does: Tests the bits in the byte in memory against the bits in the byte held in the accumulator. The bytes (memory and accumulator) are unaffected. BIT merely sets flags. The Z flag is set as if an accumulator AND memory had been performed. The V flag and the N flag receive *copies* of the sixth and seventh bits of the tested number.

Major uses: Although BIT has the advantage of not having any effect on the tested numbers, it is infrequently used because you cannot employ the immediate addressing mode with it. Other tests (CMP and AND, for example) can be used instead.

Addressing Modes:

Name	Format	Opcode	Number of Bytes Used
Zero Page	BIT 15	$24/36	2
Absolute	BIT 1500	$2C/44	3

Affected flags: N Z V

BMI

What it does: Branches up to 127 bytes forward or 128 bytes backward from its own address if the negative (N) flag is set. In effect, it branches if the seventh bit has been set by the most recent event: LDA #150 or LDA #128 would set the seventh bit. These actions would set the N flag, signifying that a *minus number* is present if you are using signed arithmetic or that there is a *shifted character* (or a BASIC keyword) if you are thinking of a byte in terms of the ASCII code.

Major uses: Testing for BASIC keywords, shifted ASCII, or graphics symbols. Testing for + or − in signed arithmetic.

Addressing Modes:

Name	Format	Opcode	Number of Bytes Used
Relative	BMI addr.	$30/48	2

Affected flags: none

BNE

What it does: Branches up to 127 bytes forward or 128 bytes backward from its own address if the zero flag is clear. In other words, it branches if the result of the most recent event is not zero, as in LDA #150: SBC #120 or LDA #128: CMP #125. These actions would clear the Z flag, signifying that a result was not 0.

Major uses: The reverse of BEQ. BNE means Branch if Not Equal. Since a CMP subtracts one number from another to perform its comparison, a 0 result means that they are equal. Any other result will trigger a BNE (not equal). Like the other B branch instructions, it has uses in IF-THEN, ON-

GOTO type structures and is used as a way to exit loops (for example, BNE will branch back to the start of a loop until a 0 delimiter is encountered at the end of a text message). BNE is like BASIC's <> instruction.

Addressing Modes:

Name	Format	Opcode	Number of Bytes Used
Relative	BNE addr.	$D0/208	2

Affected flags: none

BPL

What it does: Branches up to 127 bytes forward or 128 bytes backward from its own address if the N flag is clear. In effect, it branches if the seventh bit is clear in the most recent event, as in LDA #12 or LDA #127. These actions would clear the N flag, signifying that a *plus number* (or zero) is present in signed arithmetic mode.

Major uses: For testing the results of LDA or ADC or other operations which affect the negative (N) flag. IF-THEN or ON-GOTO type structures in ML can involve the BCC test. It is the opposite of the BMI instruction. BPL can be used for tests of "unshifted" ASCII characters and other bytes which have the seventh bit off and so are lower than 128 (0XXXXXXX).

Addressing Modes:

Name	Format	Opcode	Number of Bytes Used
Relative	BPL addr.	$10/16	2

Affected flags: none

BRK

What it does: Causes a forced interrupt. This interrupt cannot be masked (prevented) by setting the I (interrupt) flag within the status register. If there is a Break Interrupt Vector (a vector is like a pointer) in the computer, it may point to a resident monitor if the computer has one. The PC and the status register are saved on the stack. The PC points to the location of the BRK + 2.

Major uses: Debugging an ML program can often start with a sprinkling of BRKs into suspicious locations within the code. The ML is executed, a BRK stops execution and drops you into the monitor, you examine registers or tables or variables to see if they are as they should be at this point in the execution, and then you restart execution from the breakpoint. This instruction is essentially identical to the actions and uses of the STOP command in BASIC.

Addressing Modes:

Name	Format	Opcode	Number of Bytes Used
Implied	BRK	$00/0	1

Affected flags: Break (B) flag is set.

BVC

What it does: Branches up to 127 bytes forward or 128 bytes backward from its own address if the V (overflow) flag is clear.

Major uses: None. In practice, few programmers use "signed" arithmetic where the seventh bit is devoted to indicating a positive or negative number (a set seventh bit means a negative number). The V flag has the job of notifying you when you've added, say, 120 + 30, and have therefore set the seventh bit via an "overflow" (a result greater than 127). The result of your addition of two positive numbers should not be seen as a negative number, but the seventh bit *is* set. The V flag can be tested and will then reveal that your answer is still positive, but an overflow took place.

Addressing Modes:

Name	Format	Opcode	Number of Bytes Used
Relative	BVC addr.	$50/80	2

Affected flags: none

BVS

What it does: Branches up to 127 bytes forward or 128 bytes backward from its own address if the V (overflow) flag is set).

Major uses: None. See BVC above.

Addressing Modes:

Name	Format	Opcode	Number of Bytes Used
Relative	BVS addr.	$70/112	2

Affected flags: none

CLC

What it does: Clears the carry flag. (Puts a 0 into it.)

Major uses: Always used before any addition (ADC). If there are to be a series of additions (multiple-byte addition), only the first ADC is preceded by CLC since the carry feature is necessary. There might be a carry, and the result will be incorrect if it is not taken into account.

The 6502 does not offer an addition instruction without the carry feature. Thus, you must always clear it before the first ADC so a carry won't be accidentally added.

Addressing Modes:

Name	Format	Opcode	Number of Bytes Used
Implied	CLC	$18/24	1

Affected flags: Carry (C) flag is set to zero.

CLD

What it does: Clears the decimal mode flag. (Puts a 0 into it.)

Major uses: Commodore computers execute a CLD when first turned on as well as upon entry to monitor modes (PET/CBM models) and when the SYS command occurs. Apple and Atari, however, can arrive in an ML environment with the D flag in an indeterminant state. An attempt to execute ML with this flag set would cause disaster—all mathematics would be performed in "decimal mode." It is therefore suggested that owners of Apple and Atari computers CLD during the early phase, the initialization phase, of their programs. Though this is an unlikely bug, it would be a difficult one to recognize should it occur.

For further detail about the 6502's decimal mode, see SED below.

Addressing Modes:

Name	Format	Opcode	Number of Bytes Used
Implied	CLD	$D8/216	1

Affected flags: Decimal (D) flag is set to zero.

CLI

What it does: Clears the interrupt-disable flag. All interrupts will therefore be serviced (including maskable ones).

Major uses: To restore normal interrupt routine processing following a temporary suspension of interrupts for the purpose of redirecting the interrupt vector. For more detail, see SEI below.

Addressing Modes:

Name	Format	Opcode	Number of Bytes Used
Implied	CLI	$58/88	1

Affected flags: Interrupt (I) flag is set to zero.

CLV

What it does: Clears the overflow flag. (Puts a 0 into it.)

Major uses: None. (See BVC above.)

Addressing Modes:

Name	Format	Opcode	Number of Bytes Used
Implied	CLV	$B8/184	1

Affected flags: Overflow (V) flag is set to zero.

CMP

What it does: Compares the byte in memory to the byte in the accumulator. Three flags are affected, but the bytes in memory and in the accumulator are undisturbed. A CMP is actually a subtraction of the byte in memory from the byte in the accumulator. Therefore, if you LDA #15:CMP #15—the result (of the subtraction) will be zero, and BEQ would be triggered since the CMP would have set the Z flag.

Major uses: This is an important instruction in ML. It is central to IF-THEN and ON-GOTO type structures. In combination with the B branching instructions like BEQ, CMP allows the 6502 chip to make decisions, to take alternative pathways depending on comparisons. CMP throws the N, Z, or C flag up or down. Then a B instruction can branch, depending on the condition of a flag.

Often, an action will affect flags by itself, and a CMP will not be necessary. For example, LDA #15 will put a 0 into the N flag (seventh bit not set) and will put a 0 into the Z flag (the result was not 0). LDA does not affect the C flag. In any event, you could LDA #15: BPL TARGET, and the branch would take effect. However, if you LDA $20 and need to know if the byte loaded is *precisely* $0D, you must CMP #$0D:BEQ TARGET. So, while CMP is sometimes not absolutely necessary, it will never hurt to include it prior to branching.

Another important branch decision is based on > or < situations. In this case, you use BCC and BCS to test the C (carry) flag. And you've got to keep in mind the *order* of the numbers being compared. The memory byte is compared to the byte sitting in the accumulator. The structure is memory *is less than or equal to* the accumulator (BCC is triggered because the carry flag was cleared). Or memory *is more than* accumulator (BCS is triggered because the carry flag was set). Here's an example. If you want to find out if the number in the accumulator is less than $40, just CMP #$41:BCC LESSTHAN (be sure to remember that the carry flag is cleared if a number is less than *or equal*; that's why we test for less than $40 by comparing with a $41):

```
LDA #75
CMP #$41; IS IT LESS THAN $40?
BCC LESSTHAN
```

One final comment about the useful BCC/BCS tests following CMP: It's easy to remember that BCC means *less than or equal* and BCS means *more than* if you notice that C is less than S in the alphabet.

The other flag affected by CMPs is the N flag. Its uses are limited since it merely reports the status of the seventh bit; BPL triggers if that bit is clear, BMI triggers if it's set. However, that seventh bit does show whether the number is greater than (or equal to) or less than 128, and you can apply this information to the ASCII code or to look for BASIC keywords or to search databases (BPL and BMI are used by LADS's database search routines in the Array subprogram). Nevertheless, since LDA and many other instructions affect the N flag, you can often directly BPL or BMI without any need to CMP first.

Addressing Modes:

Name	Format	Opcode	Number of Bytes Used
Immediate	CMP #15	$C9/201	2
Zero Page	CMP 15	$C5/197	2
Zero Page,X	CMP 15,X	$D5/213	2
Absolute	CMP 1500	$CD/205	3
Absolute,X	CMP 1500,X	$DD/221	3
Absolute,Y	CMP 1500,Y	$D9/217	3
Indirect,X	CMP (15,X)	$C1/193	2
Indirect,Y	CMP (15),Y	$D1/209	2

Affected flags: N Z C

CPX

What it does: Compares the byte in memory to the byte in the X register. Three flags are affected, but the bytes in memory and in the X register are undisturbed. A CPX is actually a subtraction of the byte in memory from the byte in the X register. Therefore, if you LDA #15:CPX #15—the result (of the subtraction) will be zero and BEQ would be triggered since the CPX would have set the Z flag.

Major uses: X is generally used as an index, a counter within loops. Though the Y register is often preferred as an index since it can serve for the very useful indirect Y addressing mode (LDA (15),Y)—the X register is nevertheless pressed into service when more than one index is necessary or when Y is busy with other tasks.

In any case, the flags, conditions, and purposes of CPX are quite similar to CMP (the equivalent comparison instruction for the accumulator). For further information on the various possible comparisons (greater than, equal, less than, not equal), see CMP above.

Addressing Modes:

Name	Format	Opcode	Number of Bytes Used
Immediate	CPX #15	$E0/224	2
Zero Page	CPX 15	$E4/228	2
Absolute	CPX 1500	$EC/236	3

Affected flags: N Z C

CPY

What it does: Compares the byte in memory to the byte in the Y register. Three flags are affected, but the bytes in memory and in the Y register are undisturbed. A CPX is actually a subtraction of the byte in memory from the byte in the Y register. Therefore, if you LDA #15: CPY #15—the result (of the subtraction) will be zero, and BEQ would be triggered since the CPY would have set the Z flag.

Major uses: Y is the most popular index, the most heavily used counter within loops since it can serve two purposes: It permits the very useful indirect Y addressing mode (LDA (15),Y) and can simultaneously maintain a count of loop events.

See CMP above for a detailed discussion of the various branch comparisons which CPY can implement.

Addressing Modes:

Name	Format	Opcode	Number of Bytes Used
Immediate	CPY #15	$C0/192	2
Zero Page	CPY 15	$C4/196	2
Absolute	CPY 1500	$CC/204	3

Affected flags: N Z C

DEC

What it does: Reduces the value of a byte in memory by 1. The N and Z flags are affected.

Major uses: A useful alternative to SBC when you are reducing the value of a memory address. DEC is simpler and shorter than SBC, and although DEC doesn't affect the C flag, you can still decrement double-byte numbers (see "Decrement Double-Byte Numbers" in Appendix E).

The other main use for DEC is to control a memory index when the X and Y registers are too busy to provide this service. For example, you could define, say, address $505 as a counter for a loop structure. Then: LOOP STA $8000:DEC $505:BEQ END:JMP LOOP. This structure would continue storing A into $8000 until address $505 was decremented down to zero. This imitates DEX or DEY and allows you to set up as many nested loop structures (loops within loops) as you wish.

Addressing Modes:

Name	Format	Opcode	Number of Bytes Used
Zero Page	DEC 15	$C6/198	2
Zero Page,X	DEC 15,X	$D6/214	2
Absolute	DEC 1500	$CE/206	3
Absolute,X	DEC 1500,X	$DE/222	3

Affected flags: N Z

DEX

What it does: Reduces the X register by 1.

Major uses: Used as a counter (an index) within loops. Normally, you LDX with some number (the number of times you want the loop executed) and then DEX:BEQ END as a way of counting events and exiting the loop at the right time.

Addressing Modes:

Name	Format	Opcode	Number of Bytes Used
Implied	DEX	$CA/202	1

Affected flags: N Z

DEY

What it does: Reduces the Y register by 1.

Major uses: Like DEX, DEY is often used as a counter for loop structures. But DEY is the more common of the two since the Y register can simultaneously serve two purposes within a loop by permitting the very popular indirect Y addressing mode. A common way to print a screen message (the ASCII form of the message is at $5000 in this example, and the message ends with 0): LDY #0:LOOP LDA $5000,Y:BEQ END:STA SCREEN,Y:INY:JMP LOOP:END continue with the program.

Addressing Modes:

Name	Format	Opcode	Number of Bytes Used
Implied	DEY	$88/136	1

Affected flags: N Z

EOR

What it does: Exclusive ORs a byte in memory with the accumulator. Each bit in memory is compared with each bit in the accumulator, and the bits are then set (given a 1) if *one of the compared bits* is 1. However, bits are cleared if both are 0 or if both are 1. The bits in the byte held in the accumulator are the only ones affected by this comparison.

Major uses: EOR doesn't have too many uses. Its main value is to *toggle* a bit. If a bit is clear (is a 0), it will be set (to a 1); if a bit is set, it will be cleared. For example, if you want to reverse the current state of the sixth bit in a given byte: LDA BYTE:EOR #$40:STA BYTE. This will set bit 6 in BYTE if it was 0 (and clear it if it was 1). This selective bit toggling could be used to "shift" an unshifted ASCII character via EOR #$80 (1000000). Or if the character were shifted, EOR #$80 would make it lowercase. EOR toggles.

Addressing Modes:

Name	Format	Opcode	Number of Bytes Used
Immediate	EOR #15	$49/73	2
Zero Page	EOR 15	$45/69	2
Zero Page,X	EOR 15,X	$55/85	2
Absolute	EOR 1500	$4D/77	3
Absolute,X	EOR 1500,X	$5D/93	3
Absolute,Y	EOR 1500,Y	$59/89	3
Indirect,X	EOR (15,X)	$41/65	2
Indirect,Y	EOR (15),Y	$51/81	2

Affected flags: N Z

INC

What it does: Increases the value of a byte in memory by 1.

Major uses: Used exactly as DEC (see DEC above), except it counts up instead of down. For raising address pointers or supplementing the X and Y registers as loop indexes.

Addressing Modes:

Name	Format	Opcode	Number of Bytes Used
Zero Page	INC 15	$E6/230	2
Zero Page,X	INC 15,X	$F6/246	2
Absolute	INC 1500	$EE/238	3
Absolute,X	INC 1500,X	$FE/254	3

Affected flags: N Z

INX

What it does: Increases the X register by 1.

Major uses: Used exactly as DEX (see DEX above), except it counts up instead of down. For loop indexing.

Addressing Modes:

Name	Format	Opcode	Number of Bytes Used
Implied	INX	$E8/232	1

Affected flags: N Z

INY

What it does: Increases the Y register by 1.

Major uses: Used exactly as DEY (see DEY above), except it counts up instead of down. For loop indexing and working with the indirect Y addressing mode (LDA (15),Y).

Addressing Modes:

Name	Format	Opcode	Number of Bytes Used
Implied	INY	$C8/200	1

Affected flags: N Z

JMP

What it does: Jumps to any location in memory.

Major uses: Branching long range. It is the equivalent of BASIC's GOTO instruction. The bytes in the program counter are replaced with the address (the argument) following the JMP instruction and, therefore, program execution continues from this new address.

Indirect jumping—JMP (1500)—is not recommended, although some programmers find it useful. It allows you to set up a table of jump targets and bounce off them indirectly. For example, if you had placed the numbers $00 $04 in addresses $88 and $89, a JMP ($0088) instruction would send the program to whatever ML routine was located in address $0400. Unfortunately, if you should locate one of your pointers on the edge of a *page* (for example, $00FF or $17FF), this indirect JMP addressing mode reveals its great weakness. There is a bug which causes the jump to travel to the wrong place—JMP ($00FF) picks up the first byte of the pointer from $00FF, but the second byte of the pointer will be incorrectly taken from $0000. With JMP ($17FF), the second byte of the pointer would come from what's in address $1700.

Since there is this bug, and since there are no compelling reasons to set up JMP tables, you might want to forget you ever heard of indirect jumping.

Addressing Modes:

Name	Format	Opcode	Number of Bytes Used
Absolute	JMP 1500	$4C/76	3
Indirect	JMP (1500)	$6C/108	3

Affected flags: none

JSR

What it does: Jumps to a subroutine anywhere in memory. Saves the PC (Program Counter) address, plus three, of the JSR instruction by pushing it onto the stack. The next RTS in the program will then pull that address off the stack and return to the instruction following the JSR.

Major uses: As the direct equivalent of BASIC's GOSUB command, JSR is heavily used in ML programming to send control to a subroutine and then (via RTS) to return and pick up where you left off. The larger and more sophisticated a program becomes, the more often JSR will be invoked. In LADS, whenever something is printed to screen or printer, you'll often see a chain of JSRs performing necessary tasks: JSR PRNTCR: JSR PRNTSA:JSR PRNTSPACE:JSR PRNTNUM:JSR PRNTSPACE. This JSR chain prints a carriage return, the current assembly address, a space, a number, and another space.

Another thing you might notice in LADS and other ML programs is a PLA:PLA pair. Since JSR stuffs the correct return address onto the stack before leaving for a subroutine, you need to do something about that return address if you later decide *not to RTS* back to the position of the JSR in the program. This might be the case if you *usually* want to RTS, but in some particular cases, you don't. For those cases, you can take control of program flow by removing the return address from the stack (PLA:PLA will clean off the two-byte address) and then performing a direct JMP to wherever you want to go.

If you JMP out of a subroutine without PLA:PLA, you could easily overflow the stack and crash the program.

Addressing Modes:

Name	Format	Opcode	Number of Bytes Used
Absolute	JSR 1500	$20/32	3

Affected flags: none

LDA

What it does: Loads the accumulator with a byte from memory. *Copy* might be a better word than *load,* since the byte in memory is unaffected by the transfer.

Major uses: The busiest place in the computer. Bytes coming in from disk, tape, or keyboard all flow through the accumulator, as do bytes on their way to screen or peripherals. Also, because the accumulator differs in some important ways from the X and Y registers, the accumulator is used by ML programmers in a different way from the other registers.

Since INY/DEY and INX/DEX make those registers useful as counters for loops (the accumulator couldn't be conveniently employed as an index; there is no INA instruction), the accumulator is the main temporary storage register for bytes during their manipulation in an ML program. ML programming, in fact, can be defined as essentially the rapid, organized maneuvering of single bytes in memory. And it is the accumulator where these bytes often briefly rest before being sent elsewhere.

Addressing Modes:

Name	Format	Opcode	Number of Bytes Used
Immediate	LDA #15	$A9/169	2
Zero Page	LDA 15	$A5/165	2
Zero Page,X	LDA 15,X	$B5/181	2
Absolute	LDA 1500	$AD/173	3
Absolute,X	LDA 1500,X	$BD/189	3
Absolute,Y	LDA 1500,Y	$B9/185	3
Indirect,X	LDA (15,X)	$A1/161	2
Indirect,Y	LDA (15),Y	$B1/177	2

Affected flags: N Z

LDX

What it does: Loads the X register with a byte from memory.

Major uses: The X register can perform many of the tasks that the accumulator performs, but it is generally used as an index for loops. In preparation for its role as an index, LDX puts a value into the register.

Addressing Modes:

Name	Format	Opcode	Number of Bytes Used
Immediate	LDX #15	$A2/162	2
Zero Page	LDX 15	$A6/166	2
Zero Page,Y	LDX 15,Y	$B6/182	2
Absolute	LDX 1500	$AE/174	3
Absolute,Y	LDX 1500,Y	$BE/190	3

Affected flags: N Z

LDY

What it does: Loads the Y register with a byte from memory.

Major uses: The Y register can perform many of the tasks that the accumulator performs, but it is generally used as an index for loops. In preparation for its role as an index, LDY puts a value into the register.

Addressing Modes:

Name	Format	Opcode	Number of Bytes Used
Immediate	LDY #15	$A0/160	2
Zero Page	LDY 15	$A4/164	2
Zero Page,X	LDY 15,X	$B4/180	2
Absolute	LDY 1500	$AC/172	3
Absolute,X	LDY 1500,X	$BC/188	3

Affected flags: N Z

LSR

What it does: Shifts the bits in the accumulator or in a byte in memory to the right, by one bit. A zero is stuffed into bit 7, and bit 0 is put into the carry flag.

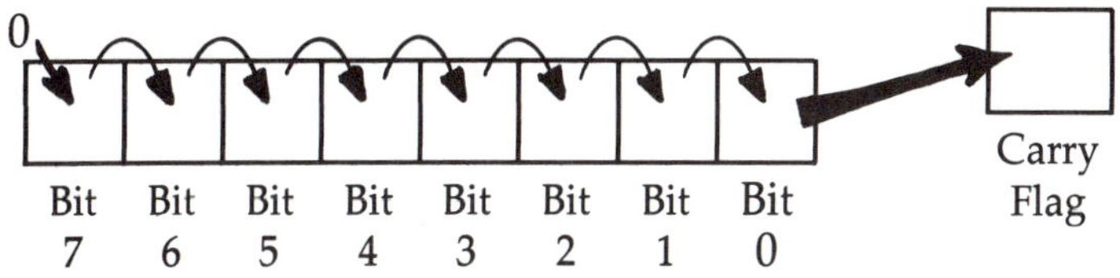

Major uses: To divide a byte by 2. In combination with the ROR instruction, LSR can divide a two-byte or larger number (see Appendix E).

LSR:LSR:LSR:LSR will put the high four bits (the high nybble) into the low nybble (with the high nybble replaced by the zeros being stuffed into the seventh bit and then shifted to the right).

Addressing Modes:

Name	Format	Opcode	Number of Bytes Used
Accumulator	LSR	$4A/74	2
Zero Page	LSR 15	$46/70	2
Zero Page,X	LSR 15,X	$56/86	2
Absolute	LSR 1500	$4E/78	3
Absolute,X	LSR 1500,X	$5E/94	3

Affected flags: N Z C

NOP

What it does: Nothing. No operation.

Major uses: Debugging. When setting breakpoints with BRK, you will often discover that a breakpoint, when examined, passes the test. That is, there is nothing wrong at that place in the program. So, to allow the program to execute to the next breakpoint, you cover the BRK with a NOP. Then, when you run the program, the computer will slide over the NOP with no effect on the program. Three NOPs could cover a JSR XXXX, and you could see the effect on the program when that particular JSR is eliminated.

Addressing Modes:

Name	Format	Opcode	Number of Bytes Used
Implied	NOP	$EA/234	1

Affected flags: none

ORA

What it does: Logically ORs a byte in memory with the byte in the accumulator. The result is in the accumulator. An OR results in a 1 if either the bit in memory or the bit in the accumulator is 1.

Major uses: Like an AND mask which turns bits off, ORA masks can be used to turn bits on. For example, if you wanted to "shift" an ASCII character by setting the seventh bit, you could LDA CHARACTER:ORA #$80. The number $80 in binary is 10000000, so all the bits in CHARACTER which are ORed with zeros here will be left unchanged. (If a bit in CHARACTER is a 1, it stays a 1. If it is a 0, it stays 0.) But the 1 in the seventh bit of $80 will cause a 0 in the CHARACTER to turn into a 1. (If CHARACTER already has a 1 in its seventh bit, it will remain a 1.)

Addressing Modes:

Name	Format	Opcode	Number of Bytes Used
Immediate	ORA #15	$09/9	2
Zero Page	ORA 15	$05/5	2
Zero Page,X	ORA 15,X	$15/21	2
Absolute	ORA 1500	$0D/13	3
Absolute,X	ORA 1500,X	$1D/29	3
Absolute,Y	ORA 1500,Y	$19/25	3
Indirect,X	ORA (15,X)	$01/1	2
Indirect,Y	ORA (15),Y	$11/17	2

Affected flags: N Z

PHA

What it does: Pushes the accumulator onto the stack.

Major uses: To temporarily *(very temporarily)* save the byte in the accumulator. If you are within a particular subroutine and you need to save a value for a brief time, you can PHA it. But beware that you must PLA it back into the accumulator *before any RTS* so that it won't misdirect the computer to the wrong RTS address. All RTS addresses are saved on the stack. Probably a safer way to temporarily save a value (a number) would be to STA TEMP or put it in some other temporary variable that you've set aside to hold things. Also, the values of A, X, and Y need to be temporarily saved, and the programmer will combine TYA and TXA with several PHAs to stuff all three registers onto the stack. But, again, matching PLAs must restore the stack as soon as possible and certainly prior to any RTS.

Addressing Modes:

Name	Format	Opcode	Number of Bytes Used
Implied	PHA	$48/72	1

Affected flags: none

PHP

What it does: Pushes the "processor status" onto the top of the stack. This byte is the status register, the byte which holds all the flags: N Z C I D V.

Major uses: To temporarily *(very temporarily)* save the state of the flags. If you need to preserve all the current conditions for a minute (see description of PHA above), you may also want to preserve the status register as well. You must, however, restore the status register byte and clean up the stack by using a PLP before the next RTS.

Addressing Modes:

Name	Format	Opcode	Number of Bytes Used
Implied	PHP	$08/8	1

Affected flags: none

PLA

What it does: Pulls the top byte off the stack and puts it into the accumulator.

Major uses: To restore a number which was temporarily stored on top of the stack (with the PHA instruction). It is the opposite action of PHA (see above). Note that PLA does affect the N and Z flags. Each PHA must be matched by a corresponding PLA if the stack is to correctly maintain RTS addresses, which is the main purpose of the stack.

Addressing Modes:

Name	Format	Opcode	Number of Bytes Used
Implied	PLA	$68/104	1

Affected flags: N Z

PLP

What it does: Pulls the top byte off the stack and puts it into the status register (where the flags are). PLP is a mnemonic for PuLl Processor status.

Major uses: To restore the condition of the flags after the status register has been temporarily stored on top of the stack (with the PHP instruction). It is the opposite action of PHP (see above). PLP, of course, affects *all* the flags. Any PHP must be matched by a corresponding PLP if the stack is to correctly maintain RTS addresses, which is the main purpose of the stack.

Addressing Modes:

Name	Format	Opcode	Number of Bytes Used
Implied	PLP	$28/40	1

Affected flags: all

ROL

What it does: Rotates the bits in the accumulator or in a byte in memory to the left, by one bit. A rotate left (as opposed to an ASL, Arithmetic Shift Left) moves bit 7 to the carry, *moves the carry into bit 0,* and every other bit moves one position to its left. (ASL operates quite similarly, except it always puts a 0 into bit 0.)

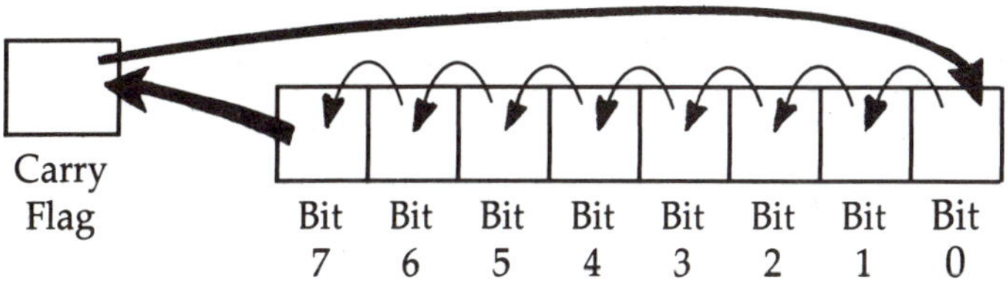

Major uses: To multiply a byte by 2. ROL can be used with ASL to multiply multiple-byte numbers since ROL pulls any carry into bit 0. If an ASL resulted in a carry, it would be thus taken into account in the next higher byte in a multiple-byte number. (See Appendix E.)

Notice how the act of moving columns of binary numbers to the left has the effect of multiplying by 2:

0010 (the number 2 in binary)
0100 (the number 4)

This same effect can be observed with decimal numbers, except the columns represent powers of 10:

0010 (the number 10 in decimal)
0100 (the number 100)

Addressing Modes:

Name	Format	Opcode	Number of Bytes Used
Accumulator	ROL	$2A/42	1
Zero Page	ROL 15	$26/38	2
Zero Page,X	ROL 15,X	$36/54	2
Absolute	ROL 1500	$2E/46	3
Absolute,X	ROL 1500,X	$3E/62	3

Affected flags: N Z C

ROR

What it does: Rotates the bits in the accumulator or in a byte in memory to the right, by one bit. A rotate right (as opposed to a LSR, Logical Shift Right) moves bit 0 into the carry, *moves the carry into bit 7,* and every other bit moves one position to its right. (LSR operates quite similarly, except it always puts a 0 into bit 7.)

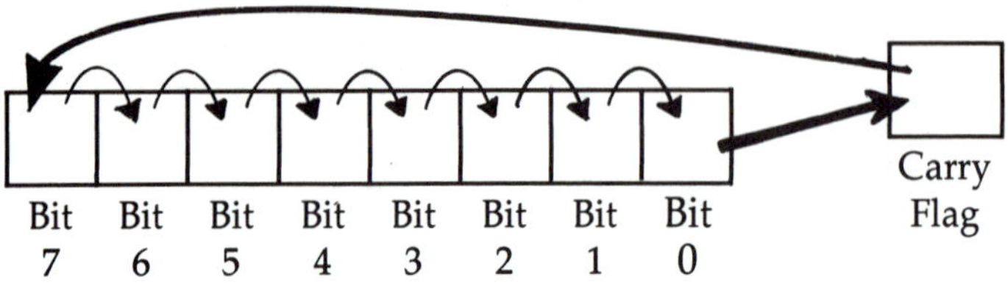

Major uses: To divide a byte by 2. ROR can be used with LSR to divide multiple-byte numbers since ROR puts any carry into bit 7. If an LSR resulted in a carry, it would be thus taken into account in the next lower byte in a multiple-byte number. (See Appendix E.)

Notice how the act of moving columns of binary numbers to the right has the effect of dividing by 2:

1000 (the number 8 in binary)
0100 (the number 4)

This same effect can be observed with decimal numbers, except the columns represent powers of 10:

1000 (the number 1000 in decimal)
0100 (the number 100)

Addressing Modes:

Name	Format	Opcode	Number of Bytes Used
Accumulator	ROR	$6A/106	1
Zero Page	ROR 15	$66/102	2
Zero Page,X	ROR 15,X	$76/118	2
Absolute	ROR 1500	$6E/110	3
Absolute,X	ROR 1500,X	$7E/126	3

Affected flags: N Z C

RTI

What it does: Returns from an interrupt.

Major uses: None. You might want to add your own routines to your machine's normal interrupt routines (see SEI below), but you won't be *generating* actual interrupts of your own. Consequently, you cannot ReTurn from Interrupts you never create.

Addressing Modes:

Name	Format	Opcode	Number of Bytes Used
Implied	RTI	$40/64	1

Affected flags: all (status register is retrieved from the stack).

RTS

What it does: Returns from a subroutine jump (caused by JSR).

Major uses: Automatically picks off the two top bytes on the stack and places them into the program counter. This reverses the actions taken by JSR (which put the program counter bytes onto the stack just before leaving for a subroutine). When RTS puts the return bytes into the program counter, the next event in the computer's world will be the instruction following the JSR which stuffed the return address onto the stack in the first place.

Addressing Modes:

Name	Format	Opcode	Number of Bytes Used
Implied	RTS	$60/96	1

Affected flags: none

SBC

What it does: Subtracts a byte in memory *from* the byte in the accumulator, and "borrows" if necessary. If a "borrow" takes place, the carry flag is cleared (set to 0). Thus, you always SEC (set the carry flag) before an SBC operation so you can tell if you need a "borrow." In other words, when an SBC operation clears the carry flag, it means that the byte in memory was *larger* than the byte in the accumulator. And since memory is subtracted from the accumulator in an SBC operation, if memory is the larger number, we must "borrow."

Major uses: Subtracts one number from another.

Addressing Modes:

Name	Format	Opcode	Number of Bytes Used
Immediate	SBC #15	$E9/233	2
Zero Page	SBC 15	$E5/229	2
Zero Page,X	SBC 15,X	$F5/245	2
Absolute	SBC 1500	$ED/237	3
Absolute,X	SBC 1500,X	$FD/253	3
Absolute,Y	SBC 1500,Y	$F9/249	3
Indirect,X	SBC (15,X)	$E1/225	2
Indirect,Y	SBC (15),Y	$F1/241	2

Affected flags: N Z C V

SEC

What it does: Sets the carry (C) flag (in the processor status register byte).

Major uses: This instruction is always used before any SBC operation to show if the result of the subtraction was negative (if the accumulator contained a smaller number than the byte in memory being subtracted from it). See SBC above.

Addressing Modes:

Name	Format	Opcode	Number of Bytes Used
Implied	SEC	$38/56	1

Affected flags: C

SED

What it does: Sets the decimal (D) flag (in the processor status register byte).

Major uses: Setting this flag puts the 6502 into decimal arithmetic mode. This mode can be easier to use when you are inputting or outputting decimal numbers (from the user of a program or to the screen). Simple addition and subtraction can be performed in decimal mode, but most programmers ignore this feature since more complicated math requires that you remain in the normal binary state of the 6502.

Note: Commodore computers automatically clear this mode when entering ML via SYS. However, Apple and Atari computers can enter ML in an indeterminant state. Since there is a possibility that the D flag might be set (causing havoc) on entry to an ML routine, it is sometimes suggested that owners of these two computers use the CLD instruction at the start of any ML program they write. Any ML programmer must CLD following any deliberate use of the decimal mode.

Addressing Modes:

Name	Format	Opcode	Number of Bytes Used
Implied	SED	$F8/248	1

Affected flags: D

SEI

What it does: Sets the interrupt disable flag (the I flag) in the processor status byte. When this flag is up, the 6502 will not acknowledge or act upon interrupt attempts (except a few nonmaskable interrupts which can take control in spite of this flag, like a reset of the entire computer). The operating systems of most computers will regularly interrupt the activities of the chip for necessary, high-priority tasks such as updating an internal clock, displaying things on the TV, receiving signals from the keyboard, etc. These interruptions of whatever the chip is doing normally occur 60 times every second. To find out what housekeeping routines your computer interrupts the chip to accomplish, look at the pointer in $FFFE/FFFF. It gives the starting address of the maskable interrupt routines.

Major uses: You can alter a RAM pointer so that it sends these interrupts to *your own ML routine,* and your routine then would conclude by pointing to the normal interrupt routines. In this way, you can add something you want (a click sound for each keystroke? the time of day on the screen?) to the normal actions of your operating system. The advantage of this method over normal SYSing is that your interrupt-driven routine is essentially transparent to whatever else you are doing (in whatever language). Your customization appears to have become part of the computer's ordinary habits.

However, if you try to alter the RAM pointer *while the other interrupts are active,* you will point away from the normal housekeeping routines in ROM, crashing the computer. This is where SEI comes in. You disable the interrupts while you LDA STA LDA STA the new pointer. Then CLI turns the interrupt back on and nothing is disturbed.

Interrupt processing is a whole subcategory of ML programming and has been widely discussed in magazine articles. Look there if you need more detail.

Addressing Modes:

Name	Format	Opcode	Number of Bytes Used
Implied	SEI	$78/120	1

Affected flags: I

STA

What it does: Stores the byte in the accumulator into memory.

Major uses: Can serve many purposes and is among the most used instructions. Many other instructions leave their results in the accumulator (ADC/SBC and logical operations like ORA), after which they are stored in memory with STA.

Addressing Modes:

Name	Format	Opcode	Number of Bytes Used
Zero Page	STA 15	$85/133	2
Zero Page,X	STA 15,X	$95/149	2
Absolute	STA 1500	$8D/141	3
Absolute,X	STA 1500,X	$9D/157	3
Absolute,Y	STA 1500,Y	$99/153	3
Indirect,X	STA (15,X)	$81/129	2
Indirect,Y	STA (15),Y	$91/145	2

Affected flags: none

STX

What it does: Stores the byte in the X register into memory.

Major uses: Copies the byte in X into a byte in memory.

Addressing Modes:

Name	Format	Opcode	Number of Bytes Used
Zero Page	STX 15	$86/134	2
Zero Page,Y	STX 15,Y	$96/150	2
Absolute	STX 1500	$8E/142	3

Affected flags: none

STY

What it does: Stores the byte in the Y register into memory.

Major uses: Copies the byte in Y into a byte in memory.

Addressing Modes:

Name	Format	Opcode	Number of Bytes Used
Zero Page	STY 15	$84/132	2
Zero Page,X	STY 15,X	$94/148	2
Absolute	STY 1500	$8C/140	3

Affected flags: none

TAX

What it does: Transfers the byte in the accumulator to the X register.

Major uses: Sometimes you can copy the byte in the accumulator into the X register as a way of briefly storing the byte until it's needed again by the accumulator. If X is currently unused, TAX is a convenient alternative to PHA (another temporary storage method).

However, since X is often employed as a loop counter, TAX is a relatively rarely used instruction.

Addressing Modes:

Name	Format	Opcode	Number of Bytes Used
Implied	TAX	$AA/170	1

Affected flags: N Z

TAY

What it does: Transfers the byte in the accumulator to the Y register.

Major uses: Sometimes you can copy the byte in the accumulator into the Y register as a way of briefly storing the byte until it's needed again by the accumulator. If Y is currently unused, TAY is a convenient alternative to PHA (another temporary storage method).

However, since Y is quite often employed as a loop counter, TAY is a relatively rarely used instruction.

Addressing Modes:

Name	Format	Opcode	Number of Bytes Used
Implied	TAY	$A8/168	1

Affected flags: N Z

TSX

What it does: Transfers the stack pointer to the X register.

Major uses: The stack pointer is a byte in the 6502 chip which points to where a new value (number) can be added to the stack. The stack pointer would be "raised" by two, for example, when you JSR and the two bytes of the program counter are pushed onto the stack. The next available space on the stack thus becomes two higher than it was previously. By contrast, an RTS will pull a two-byte return address off the stack, freeing up some space, and the stack pointer would then be "lowered" by two.

The stack pointer is always added to $0100 since the stack is located between addresses $0100 and $01FF.

Addressing Modes:

Name	Format	Opcode	Number of Bytes Used
Implied	TSX	$BA/186	1

Affected flags: N Z

TXA

What it does: Transfers the byte in the X register to the accumulator.

Major uses: There are times, after X has been used as a counter, when you'll want to compute something using the value of the counter. And you'll therefore need to transfer the byte in X to the accumulator. For example, if you search the screen for character $75:

```
CHARACTER = $75:SCREEN = $0400
LDX #0
LOOP LDA SCREEN,X:CMP #CHARACTER:BEQ MORE:INX
BEQ NOTFOUND          ; (this prevents an endless
                      loop
MORE TXA              ; (you now know the
                      character's location)
NOTFOUND BRK
```

In this example, we want to perform some action based on the location of the character. Perhaps we want to remember the location in a variable for later reference. This will require that we transfer the value of X to the accumulator so it can be added to the SCREEN start address.

Addressing Modes:

Name	Format	Opcode	Number of Bytes Used
Implied	TXA	$8A/138	1

Affected flags: N Z

TXS

What it does: Transfers the byte in X register into the stack pointer.

Major uses: Alters where, in the stack, the current "here's storage space" is pointed to. There are no common uses for this instruction.

Addressing Modes:

Name	Format	Opcode	Number of Bytes Used
Implied	TXS	$9A/154	1

Affected flags: none

TYA

What it does: Transfers the byte in the Y register to the accumulator.

Major uses: See TXA.

Addressing Modes:

Name	Format	Opcode	Number of Bytes Used
Implied	TYA	$98/152	1

Affected flags: N Z

Appendix B

How to Use LADS

How to Use LADS

Here is a step-by-step explanation of how to assemble machine language programs using the LADS assembler. As you familiarize yourself with its features and practice using it, you will likely discover things about the assembler which you'll want to change or features you'll want to add. For example, if you find yourself frequently using an impossible addressing mode like LDY (15,Y), you might want to insert an error trap for that into LADS source code. Appendix C, "Modifying LADS," shows you how these customizations can be accomplished. But here is a description of the features which are built into LADS.

General Instructions for Using LADS

LADS assembles from *source files.* They are particularly easy and convenient to create; just turn on your computer, if you are using DOS 3.3, BRUN LADS, and pretend you're writing a BASIC program. (ProDOS users, run Program B-1 to install the ProDOS version of LADS.) Apple LADS works with source files created exactly the way you would write a BASIC program (you must always BRUN LADS before creating source code). You use line numbers, you can use colons, you can insert new line numbers or delete. The only difference is that you're writing ML, so you use ML commands rather than BASIC commands. Here's an example:

```
10 *= $0300
15 .S
20 LDA #22:LDY #0
30 STA $1500,Y
40 .END TEST
```

Use line numbers, colons, and whatever programmer's aids (such as automatic line numbering) that you ordinarily use to write BASIC itself. But notice that if you use colons you should keep the instructions tight against the colons. (LDA #22 : LDY #0 would confuse LADS. Spaces following a colon won't cause any problems, but it's best to make a habit of using no spaces around colons.)

After you've typed in a program, save to disk in the normal way. (Tape drive users: See "Special Note to Tape Drive Users" at the end of this appendix.) Notice line 10 in the example above. *The first line of any LADS source file must provide the starting address,* the address where you want the ML program to begin in the computer's memory. You signify this with the *= symbol, which means "Program Counter equals." When LADS sees *=, it sets the program counter to the number following the equal sign. Remember also that *there must be a space between the = and the starting address.*

The only other fixed rule for every source code file is that *the last line of each LADS source file must contain either the .END pseudo-op or the .FILE pseudo-op.* Either of them links source files together in case you want to chain several files into one large ML program. However, .FILE names the next linked source file in the chain, whereas .END always specifies the first source file of the chain. If there is only one file (as in our example above), you still must end it with .END and give its name as the first file. More about this shortly.

Also notice that you can use either decimal or hexadecimal numbers interchangeably in LADS. Lines 10 and 30 contain hex; line 20 has decimal numbers.

After you've saved the source code to disk, you can assemble it by typing ASM *filename,* where *filename* is the name of the source file (or the first file in a chain) that you want assembled.

Let's go through the process of assembling step by step. Type in the little source program above as if you were writing a BASIC program. Save it by typing:

SAVE TEST
Then **ASM TEST**

You will see the assembler create the *object code,* the bytes which go into memory and comprise the ML program.

Note: Be sure to remember that every source code program must end with the **.END** ***NAME*** *pseudo-op. In our example, we concluded with* **.END TEST** *because TEST is the name of the only file in this source code. Also notice that you do not use quotes with these filenames.*

To review: Every source code program must contain the starting address in the first line (for example, 10 *= $0300) and must list the filename on the last line (for example, 500 .END SCREENPROG). If you chain several source code programs together using the .FILE pseudo-op, you end *only the final program in the chain* with the .END pseudo-op. These two rules will become clearer in a minute when we discuss the .END and .FILE pseudo-ops.

Features

There are a number of *pseudo-ops* available in LADS. Pseudo-ops are direct instructions to the assembler which make things easier for the programmer. The .S in line 15 is such an instruction. It tells LADS to print the results of an assembly to the screen. If you add the following lines to our test program, you will cause the listing to be in decimal instead of hex and cause LADS to save the object code (the runnable ML program) to a disk file called OBJ.

```
10 *= $0360
11 .NH
12 .D OBJ
15 .S
20 LDA #22:LDY #0
30 STA $1500,Y
40 .END TEST
```

The pseudo-op .NH means no hex (causing the listing to change from hex to decimal), and .D means create a disk file containing the ML program which results from the assembly process.

You can add REM-like comments by using a semicolon. And you can turn the screen listing *off* with .NS, anytime. Turn it on or off as much as you want:

```
10 *= $0360
11 .NH
12 .D OBJECTPROGRAM
15 .NS
20 LDA #22:LDY #0; load A with 22, load Y with zero
30 STA $1500,Y
40 .END TEST
```

You turn on printer listings with .P and turn them off with .NP. However, for the .P pseudo-op to work, the .S screen listings pseudo-op must also be turned on. In other words, you cannot have listings sent to the printer without the .S pseudo-op. The assembly will not appear on the screen when you use the .P and .S together. If you want screen echo while assembling to the printer, you'll need to use the system utilities on the IIc to configure the serial port; on other II's you'll need to set the switches on the printer interface. On the Apple super-serial card, set the switches to 40-column line width with screen echo. If you have another card you'll have to consult your interface and printer manual. Your printer interface must be in slot 1 for LADS to assemble to a printer.

To have the ML stored into memory during assembly, use .O and turn off these POKEs to memory with .NO. LADS will assemble somewhat faster if the .S and .P features are not used.

The pseudo-ops which turn the printer on and off; direct object code to disk, screen, and RAM; or switch between hex and decimal printout can be switched on and off within your source code wherever convenient. For example, you can turn on your printer anywhere within the program by inserting .P and turn it off anywhere with .NP. Among other things, this would allow you to specify that only a particular section of a large program be printed out. This can come in very handy if you're working on a 5000-byte program: You would have a long wait if you had to print out the whole thing.

Always put pseudo-ops on a line by themselves. Any other programming code can be put on a line in any fashion (divided by colons: LDA 15:STA 27:INY), but pseudo-ops should be the only thing on their lines. (The .BYTE pseudo-op is an exception—it can be on a multiple-statement line.)

100 .P .S (wrong)
100 .P (right)
110 .S (right)

And remember to keep your instructions right next to the colons, no spaces:

100 LDA #15 : STA 5000 : INY (wrong)
100 LDA #15:STA 5000:INY
(right)

Here's a summary of the commands you can give LADS:

.P	Turn on printer listing of object code (.S must be activated).
.NP	Turn off printer listing of object code.
.O	Turn on POKEs to memory. Object code is stored into RAM *during* assembly.
.NO	Turn off POKEs to memory.
.D ***filename***	Open a file and store object code to disk during assembly (use no quotes around filename).
.FILE ***filename***	Link one source file to the next in a chain so that they will all assemble together as a single large source program (end the chain with .END pseudo-op).
.END ***filename***	Link the last source file to first source file in a chain. If you are not assembling a chain of files (rather, are

	assembling from a single file), you must still give *its* filename as the .END so the assembler knows where to go for the second pass. Any source code must have .END as the last line in the program, whether the source code is contained within a single disk file or spread across a multiple-file chain.
.S	Turn on screen listing during assembly (required if you desire a hardcopy listing from a printer using the .P pseudo-op).
.NS	Turn off screen listing during assembly.
.H	Turn on hexadecimal output for screen or printer listing.
.NH	Turn off hexadecimal output for screen or printer listing. (As a result, the listings are in decimal.)
***=**	Set program counter to new address.

A Stable Buffer

The pseudo-op *= is mainly useful when you want to create data tables. The subprogram Tables in LADS (see Appendix D) source code is an example. (A subprogram is one of the source code files which, when linked together, form an entire ML program.) Most programmers locate an ML program's tables equates, buffers, and messages at the high end of the ML program the way LADS does with its Tables subprogram. Since you don't know what the highest RAM address will be while you're writing the program, you can set *= to some address perhaps 4K above the starting address. This gives you space to write the program below the tables. The advantage of creating these now-stable tables is that you can easily PEEK them, and this greatly assists debugging. You'll always know exactly where buffers and variables are going to end up in memory after an assembly—regardless of the changes you make in the program. After your program is debugged and running perfectly, you can remove the *= and assemble one last time, closing up the gap between the program and its tables.

Here's an example. Suppose you write:

```
10 *= $5000
20 STA BUFFER
30 *= $6000
40 BUFFER .BYTE 0 0 0 0 0 0 0 0 0 0 0 0 0 0
50 .END BUFFEREXAMPLE
```

This creates an ML instruction (STA buffer) at address $5000 (the starting address of this particular ML program), but places the buffer itself at $6000. When you add additional instructions after STA buffer, the location of the buffer itself will remain at address $6000. This means that you can write an entire program without having to worry that the location of the buffer is changing each time you add new instructions, new code. It's high enough so that it remains stable at $6000, and you can debug the program more easily. You can always check if something is being correctly sent into the buffer by just looking at $6000.

This fragment of code illustrates two other features of LADS. You can use the pseudo-op .BYTE to set aside some space in memory (the zeros above just make space to hold other things in a "buffer" during the execution of an ML program). You can also use .BYTE to define specific numbers in memory:

```
.BYTE 65 66 67 68
```

This would put these numbers (*you must always use decimal numbers with this pseudo-op*) into memory at the location of the .BYTE instruction. An easy way to create messages that you want to print to the screen is to use the .BYTE pseudo-op with quotes:

```
500 FIRSTLETTERS .BYTE "ABCD":.BYTE 0
```

Then, if you wanted to print this message, you could write:

```
  2 *= $0360
  5 LDY #0
 10 LOOP LDA FIRSTLETTERS,Y
 20 BEQ ENDMESSAGE
 30 STA $0400,Y; location of screen RAM
 40 INY
 50 JMP LOOP
 60 ENDMESSAGE RTS; finished printout
500 FIRSTLETTERS .BYTE "ABCD:.BYTE 0
900 .END MESSAGETEST
```

Note that using the second set of quotes is optional with the .BYTE pseudo-op: You can use either **.BYTE "ABCD:.BYTE 0** or **.BYTE "ABCD":.BYTE 0.** To POKE numbers instead of characters, just leave out the quotes: **.BYTE 10 15 75.** And since these numeric values are being POKEd directly into bytes in memory, they cannot be larger than 255.

Another convenient pseudo-op looks like this: #". It is

used when you want to specify a character instead of a number for immediate addressing. Say, you need to print a comma to the screen. You could LDA #44 (the ASCII code for a comma) and JSR PRINT.

But if you don't remember that a comma is the number 44 in the ASCII code, and you don't want to look it up, LADS will do it for you. Just use a quote after the # symbol: LDA #", (followed by the character you're after, in this case, the comma). The correct value for the character will be inserted into your object code. To print the letter *A*, you would LDA #"A and proceed to print it. Any character you type after the quotes will be translated into ASCII for you. *Note that this pseudo-op and the .BYTE " pseudo-op use* true ASCII, *which on the Apple screen will appear as reversed characters.* If you want normal characters sent to the screen, you'll have to look up the Apple version of ASCII in the table in Chapter 2.

Labels

With LADS, or with other assemblers that permit labels, you need not refer to locations in memory or numeric values by using numbers. You can use labels.

In the example above, line 10 starts off with the word LOOP. This means that you can use the word LOOP later on to refer to that location (see line 50). That's quite a convenience: The assembler remembers where the word LOOP is used, and you need not refer to an actual memory *address*; you can refer to the label instead. This kind of label is called a *PC-type* (for Program Counter) or *address-type* label.

The other type of label is defined with an assembly convention called an *equate* (an equal sign). This is quite similar to the way that BASIC allows you to assign value to words—it's called "assigning variables" when you do it in BASIC. In ML, the = pseudo-op works pretty much the way the = sign does in BASIC and these "equates" should be put at the very start of an ML program. (See the Defs subprogram in Appendix D.) Here's an example of equates, located at the start of the program, in lines 10 and 20:

```
5   *= $0300
10  SCREEN = $0400; the location of the first byte in RAM of the
    screen
20  LETTERA = $C1; the letter A
30; -----------------------
```

40 START LDA LETTERA; notice "START" (an address-type label)
50 STA SCREEN
60 RTS

Line 10 assigns the number $0400 (1024 decimal) to the word SCREEN. Anytime thereafter that you use the word SCREEN, LADS will substitute $0400 when it assembles your ML program. Line 20 "equates" the word LETTERA to the number $C1. So, when you LDA LETTERA in line 40, the assembler will put a C1 into your program. (Notice that, like BASIC, LADS requires equate labels to be a single word. You couldn't use LETTER A, since that's two words.)

Line 30 is just a REMark. The semicolon tells the assembler that what follows on that line is to be ignored. Nevertheless, blank lines or graphic dividers like line 30 can help to visually separate subroutines, tables, and equates from your actual ML program. In this case, we've used line 30 to separate the section of the program which defines labels (lines 10–20) from the program proper (lines 40–60). All this makes it easier to read and understand your source code later.

Automatic Math

There are times when you will want to have LADS do addition for you. That's where the + pseudo-op comes in. If you write "label+1" you will add 1 to the value of the label. Here's how it works:

```
10 *= 864
20 HIMEM = $73; top-of-memory pointer.
30; ----------------------------
40 LDA #0:STA HIMEM:LDA #$50:STA HIMEM+1
```

Here we are putting a new location into the top-of-memory pointer which the computer uses to decide where it can store things. (Doing that could protect an ML program which resides above the address stored in this pointer.) Like all pointers, it uses two bytes. If we want to store $5000 into this pointer, we store the lower half (the least significant byte) into MEMTOP. We'll want to put the number $50 into the most significant byte of the pointer—but we don't need to waste time making a new label. It's just one higher in memory than MEMTOP, hence, MEMTOP+1.

You'll also want to use the + pseudo-op command in constructions like this:

```
10  *= 864
15  SCREEN = $0400
17; ----------------------------
20  LDA #160; the blank character
30  LDA #0
40  START STA SCREEN,Y
50  STA SCREEN+256,Y
60  STA SCREEN+512,Y
70  STA SCREEN+768,Y
80  INY
90  BNE START
```

This is the fastest way to fill memory with a given byte. In this case we're clearing out the screen RAM by filling it with blanks. But it's easy to indicate multiples of 256 by just adding them to the label SCREEN.

A similar pseudo-op command is the #<. This refers to the least significant byte of a *label*. For example:

```
10 *= $0360
20 SCREEN = $0400
25 SCREENPOINTER = $FB
30 ;-------------------
40 LDA #<SCREEN; LSB (least significant byte of the label
   SCREEN, $11)
50 STA SCREENPOINTER
```

You'll find this technique used several times in the LADS source code. It puts the LSB (least signficant byte) or the MSB (most signficant byte) of a label into the LSB or MSB of a pointer. In the example above, we want to set up a pointer that will hold the address of the screen RAM. The pointer is called SCREENPOINTER, and we want to put $11 (the LSB of SCREEN) into SCREENPOINTER. So, we extract the LSB of SCREEN in line 40 by using # combined with the less-than symbol. We would complete the job with the greater-than symbol to fetch the MSB: 60 LDA #>SCREEN. Notice that these symbols must be attached to the label; *no space is allowed*. For example, LDA #> SCREEN would create problems. This LSB or MSB extraction from a label is something you'll need to do from time to time. The #< and #> pseudo-ops do it for you.

Chained Files

It is sometimes convenient to create several source code subprograms, to break the ML program source code into several pieces. LADS source code is divided into a number of program files: Array, Equate, Math, Pseudo, and so on. This way, you don't need to load the entire source code in the computer's memory when you just want to work on a particular part of it. It also allows you to assemble source code far larger than could fit into available RAM.

In the last line of each subprogram you want to link, you put the linking pseudo-op .FILE *NAME* (use no quotes) to tell the assembler which subprogram to assemble next. Subprograms, chained together in this fashion, will be treated as if they were one large program. The final subprogram in the chain ends with the special pseudo-op .END *NAME*, and this time the name is the filename of the first of the subprograms, the subprogram which begins the chain. It's like stringing pearls and then, at the end, tying thread so that the last pearl is next to the first, to form a necklace.

Remember that you always need to include the .END pseudo-op, even if you are assembling from a *single*, unlinked source code file. In that case (where you're working with a solo file), you don't need the linking .FILE pseudo-op. Instead, refer the file to itself with .END *NAME* where you list the solo file's name. Here's an illustration of how three subprograms would be linked to form a complete program:

```
 5 *= 864
10; FIRST--first program in chain
20;its first line must contain the start address
30;----------
40 LDA #20
50 STA $0400
60 .FILE SECOND
```

Then you save this subprogram to disk (it's handy to let the first remark line in each subprogram identify the subprogram's filename):

```
SAVE FIRST
```

Next, you create SECOND, the next link in the chain. But here, you use no starting address; you enter no *= since only one start address is needed for any program:

```
10 ; SECOND
20 INY:INX:DEY:DEX
30 .FILE THIRD
SAVE SECOND
```

Now write the final subprogram, ending it with the clasp pseudo-op .END *NAME* which links this last subprogram to the first:

```
10 ; THIRD
20 LDA #191:STA $0400
30 .END FIRST
SAVE THIRD
```

When you want to assemble this chain, just type ASM FIRST, and it will assemble the entire chain.

If you want the object code (the finished ML program) stored in the computer's memory during the LADS assembly, add this line to FIRST, above:

```
35 .O
```

If you want to save the object code as an ML program on disk that can be later loaded into the computer and run, add this line to FIRST:

```
36 .D PROGRAMNAME
```

When LADS is finished assembling, there will be an ML program on disk called PROGRAMNAME. You can BLOAD it and CALL 864 (that was the start address we gave this program), and the newly assembled ML program will execute.

Rules for LADS

Here are the rules you need to follow when writing ML for LADS to assemble:

1. *In general, all equate labels (labels using an equal sign) should be defined at the start of your program.* While this isn't absolutely necessary for labels with numbers above 255 (see SCREEN in the example below), it *is* the best programming practice. It makes it easier for you to modify your programs and simplifies debugging. LADS itself locates all its equate labels in the subprogram Defs (see Appendix D), the first subprogram in its chain of source code files.

   What's more, it is *necessary* that any equate label with a value lower than 256 be defined before any ML mnemonics reference that label. So, to be on the safe side, just get into the habit of putting all equate labels at the very start of your programs:

   ```
   10 *= 864
   20 ARRAYPOINTER = $FB; (251 decimal), a zero page address
   ```

```
30 OTHERPOINTER = $FD; (253 decimal), another zero page
   address
40 ;------------------------
50 LDY #0:LDA $41
60 STA ARRAYPOINTER,Y
70 SCREEN = $0400
```

Notice that it's permissible to define the label SCREEN anywhere in your program. It's not a zero page address. You do have to be careful, however, with zero page addresses (addresses lower than 255). So most ML programmers make it a habit to define all their equates at the start of their source code.

2. *Put only one pseudo-op on a line.* Don't use a colon to put two pseudo-ops on a single line:

```
10 *= 864
20 .O:.NH  (wrong)
30 .O      (right)
40 .NH     (right)
```

The main exception to this is the .BYTE pseudo-op. Normally, you'll set up messages with a zero at their end to *delimit* them, to show that the message is complete. When you delimit messages with a zero, you don't need to know the length of the message; you just branch when you come upon a zero:

```
10 *= 864
20 SCREEN = $0400
30 ;----------------------
40 LDY #0
50 LOOP LDA MESSAGE,Y:BEQ END; loading a zero signals
   end of message.
60 STA SCREEN,Y:INY: JMP LOOP; LADS ignores spaces after
   a colon.
70 ; --------- message area here ----------
80 MESSAGE .BYTE "PRINT THIS ON SCREEN":.BYTE 0
```

Any embedded pseudo-ops like + or = or #> can be used on multiple-statement lines. The only pseudo-ops which should be on a line by themselves are the I/O (input/output) instructions which direct communication to disk, screen, or printer, like .P, .S, .D, .END, and so forth.

Generally, it's important that you space things correctly. If you wrote

```
SCREEN= 864
```

LADS would think that your label was *screen=* instead of *screen*. So you need that space between the label and the equal sign. Likewise, you need to put *a single space* between labels, mnemonics, and arguments:

LOOP LDA MESSAGE

Running them together will confuse LADS:

LOOPLDA MESSAGE

and

LOOP LDAMESSAGE

are wrong.

Spaces within remarks are ignored. In fact, LADS ignores everything within remarks, everything following a semicolon on a line (see line 70). Thus, the semicolon should come after anything you want assembled. You couldn't rearrange line 50 above by putting the BEQ END after the remark message. It would be ignored because it followed the semicolon.

When using the text form of .BYTE, it's up to you whether you use a close quote:

50 MESSAGE .BYTE "PRINT THIS" (right)
60 MESSAGE .BYTE "PRINT THIS (also right)

However, the true ASCII values will be assembled by LADS, causing the text to flash when displayed on the screen. You'll have to look up the Apple ASCII values for the characters in the table in Chapter 2 and place these values after the .BYTE pseudo-op.

3. *The first character of any label must be a letter, not a number.* LADS knows when it comes upon a label because a number starts with a number; a label starts with a letter of the alphabet:

```
10 *= 864
20 LABEL = 255
30 LDA LABEL
40 LDA 255
```

Lines 30 and 40 accomplish the same thing and are correctly written. It would confuse LADS, however, if you wrote

20 5LABEL = 255 (wrong)

since the number 5 at the start of the word *label* would signal the assembler that it had come upon a number, not a label. You can use numbers anywhere else in a label name—just don't put a number at the start of the name. Also avoid using symbols like #, <, >, *, and other punctuation, shifted letters, or graphics symbols within labels. Stick with ordinary alphanumerics:

```
10 5LABEL   (wrong)
20 LABEL15 (right)
30 *LABEL* (wrong)
```

4. *Move the program counter forward, never backward.* The *= pseudo-op should be used to make space in memory. If you set the PC below its current address, you would be writing over previously assembled code:

```
10 *= 864
20 LDA #15
30 *= 900    (right)

10 *= 864
20 LDA #15
30 *= 864    (wrong, you'll assemble right over the LDA #15)
```

Special Note to Tape Drive Users

LADS will assemble source code from disk or RAM memory. It is possible to use the assembler with a tape drive, using the RAM memory-based version (see Appendix C). Of course, disk users can also assemble from RAM if they choose: That's an extremely fast way to create ML programs of small to moderate size. You'll find yourself writing, assembling, testing, and correcting your code at a rapid, efficient pace. But tape users must use RAMLADS.

There is a restriction when using a tape drive as the outboard memory device. You cannot link files together, forming a large, chained source code listing. The reason for this is that LADS, like all sophisticated assemblers, makes two passes through the source code. This means that tape containing the source code would have to be rewound at the end of the first pass.

It would be possible, of course, to have LADS pause at the end of pass 1, announce that it's time to rewind the tape, and then, when you press a key, start reading the source code from the start of the tape. But this causes a second problem: The object code cannot then be stored to tape. A tape drive cannot simultaneously read and write.

The best way to use LADS with a tape drive is to assemble from source code in RAM memory and to use the .O (store object code to RAM pseudo-op). Then, when the finished object code is in RAM, use the monitor program to save it to tape. If you have access to a disk drive, you could construct a version of LADS which automatically directs object code to tape during assembly using the .D pseudo-op. Note that if you make a RAM-based version of LADS, you won't use either the .FILE or .END pseudo-ops in your source programs.

Assembling Source Code

Once you have typed in Apple LADS, you must BSAVE it to disk. The start address of the 3.3 version is $79FD and the length is $1690; The ProDOS version starts at $7B00 and the length is $167C. To execute LADS you BRUN the binary file. (ProDOS users, RUN PROGRAMB.1.) After it loads and sets up its special wedge (see Appendix C for details on this wedge), you will be prompted with the BASIC prompt and a cursor. You can now type in your files and save them just as you would an Applesoft file. After saving the program to disk, you assemble it by typing:

ASM ***filename***

Make sure you have a space between ASM and your filename. If you do not have the space, you will get a SYNTAX ERROR. Remember, you must BRUN LADS before entering or saving source code; and you cannot enter, load, save, or run BASIC programs once you BRUN LADS since the BASIC tokenize routine will not execute.

Typing In LADS

LADS will run on any Apple II. There are two versions of LADS listed below. If you use the ProDOS operating system be sure to enter Program B-1 and Program B-2; the DOS 3.3 version is Program B-3. Program B-1 will reconfigure for LADS and BRUN LADS. This program must always be run to install LADS in memory with ProDOS. Both versions of LADS must be entered using "MLX," machine language editor. Complete instructions on how to enter the object code using MLX, as well as the MLX program, can be found in Appendix G.

MLX will ask for the starting and ending address of LADS. When asked enter the following:

DOS 3.3 LADS
Starting address: 79F8
Ending address: 9087
ProDOS LADS
Starting address: 7B00
Ending address: 917F

Be sure to use the MLX Loader program (see Appendix G) each time you use MLX to enter LADS object code.

LADS is a very long program. For those who prefer not to type it in, it can be purchased on disk, along with many of the other programs in this book, by calling COMPUTE! Publications toll-free at 1-800-334-0868 or by using the coupon in the back of this book. Be sure to state that you want the disk for the book *Apple Machine Language for Beginners.*

Running LADS

Once you have saved a copy of LADS using MLX on your disk, you are ready to run it. To run the 3.3 version of LADS, simply insert a disk that has DOS 3.3 on it and turn your Apple on. When the prompt appears, insert a disk with LADS on it and enter BRUN LADS (or whatever filename you used) and press RETURN.

To load the ProDOS version, first insert a disk with ProDOS on it and turn on your Apple. When the prompt appears, insert a disk which contains the Loader program, B-1, and LADS. Now run the Loader program; it will load and run LADS for you. Once the Loader has executed LADS, type NEW to delete the Loader from memory. Each time you want to write source code or assemble code with LADS, you must use the Loader program to load and run LADS.

(If you've purchased the *Apple Machine Language for Beginners* disk, you must have a disk with DOS 3.3 or ProDOS on it inserted in the disk drive when you turn on the computer—*the* Apple Machine Language for Beginners *disk does not contain DOS and will* ***not*** *boot.*)

Once LADS is executed, everything looks as if you were in BASIC. If you want to be sure you are actually operating under LADS, try this little test:

Enter this one-line program, **10 ? "THIS IS A TEST",** and press RETURN. Now type LIST. If you were in BASIC, your Apple would have changed the question mark into the word PRINT. If the question mark remains, you're in LADS.

Program B-1. ProDOS LADS Loader

```
10 REM LOADER FOR PRODOS ONLY
20 FOR I=768 TO I+5
30 READ A:POKE I,A
40 NEXT I
50 CALL 768
60 PRINT CHR$(4);"BRUN LADS"
70 DATA 169,31,32,245,190,96
```

Note that this Loader program should be changed when you are going to assemble a program larger than LADS itself (or create a new, expanded version of LADS as you do when adding the disassembler option described in Appendix C). Change the 31 in line 70 above to, say, 51 which will give you more protected memory.

Program B-2. ProDOS LADS Object Code

This program requires MLX, Appendix G, to be entered.

```
START ADDRESS: 7B00
END ADDRESS:   917F

7B00: 4C 10 84 A9 00 A0 32 99 CC
7B08: 9A 90 88 D0 FA A9 03 85 98
7B10: EB 85 4C 8D B0 90 A9 7B 57
7B18: 85 EC 85 4D 8D B1 90 A9 90
7B20: 01 8D C6 90 B9 00 04 C9 7C
7B28: A0 F0 07 99 38 91 C8 4C 0C
7B30: 24 7B 84 F9 20 CF 81 20 AB
7B38: 6B 84 A9 00 8D A0 90 20 6B
7B40: 21 85 AD B3 90 D0 3F 20 80
7B48: 63 8A A9 E6 20 BC 82 A9 D9
7B50: 4C 20 BC 82 A9 41 20 BC 84
7B58: 82 A9 44 20 BC 82 A9 53 1C
7B60: 20 BC 82 20 63 8A AD A9 33
7B68: 90 D0 0B A9 D0 85 FB A9 16
7B70: 8E 85 FC 20 94 84 AD A3 67
7B78: 90 85 FD 8D 9C 90 AD A4 D8
7B80: 90 85 FE 8D 9D 90 20 0A 53
7B88: 83 AD A0 90 F0 03 4C 9C 92
7B90: 7E 20 21 85 A9 00 8D A8 5C
7B98: 90 8D B2 90 AC B3 90 D0 C0
7BA0: 03 4C C0 7B 8C C7 90 AD 4E
7BA8: C5 90 F0 0C 20 6C 8A 20 6D
7BB0: 1D 8A 20 45 8A 20 1D 8A CA
7BB8: AD BE 90 F0 03 20 19 89 AB
7BC0: 4C 1D 84 AD 9B 90 F0 17 A8
7BC8: C9 03 D0 72 A9 01 8D 9B AE
7BD0: 90 AD D3 8E D0 68 A9 08 62
```

```
7BD8: 18 6D 9A 9Ø 8D 9A 9Ø 4C D7
7BEØ: AD 7D AD B3 9Ø FØ 39 AØ 5A
7BE8: FF C8 B9 DØ 8E FØ 2E 99 84
7BFØ: 38 91 C9 2Ø DØ F3 C8 B9 45
7BF8: DØ 8E C9 3D DØ Ø3 4C DD 12
7CØØ: 7D A2 ØØ 8E C7 9Ø 8A 99 78
7CØ8: 38 91 B9 DØ 8E FØ Ø8 9D AB
7C1Ø: DØ 8E E8 C8 4C ØA 7C 9D DF
7C18: DØ 8E 4C CØ 7B 2Ø 62 8Ø 54
7C2Ø: 2Ø Ø4 8Ø 4C CØ 7B AD 17 65
7C28: 8F C9 4Ø BØ Ø6 AD 18 8F 15
7C3Ø: EE B2 9Ø 49 8Ø 8D A1 9Ø Ø2
7C38: 2Ø A6 8Ø 4C B5 7C AØ ØØ AØ
7C4Ø: 8C A8 9Ø B9 D4 8E C9 41 ØD
7C48: 9Ø Ø3 EE A8 9Ø 99 17 8F 5B
7C5Ø: C8 B9 D4 8E FØ 16 99 17 C9
7C58: 8F C9 41 9Ø Ø3 EE A8 9Ø 72
7C6Ø: C8 B9 D4 8E FØ Ø6 99 17 99
7C68: 8F 4C 6Ø 7C 88 8C A7 9Ø 66
7C7Ø: AD A9 9Ø DØ 4Ø AD A8 9Ø 64
7C78: DØ AC A9 17 85 FB A9 8F AA
7C8Ø: 85 FC AØ ØØ AD 17 8F C9 42
7C88: 3Ø BØ Ø7 18 E6 FB 9Ø Ø2 72
7C9Ø: E6 FC B1 FB FØ 1Ø C9 29 B6
7C98: FØ ØC C9 2C FØ Ø8 C9 2Ø 64
7CAØ: FØ Ø4 C8 4C 92 7C 48 98 AØ
7CA8: 48 A9 ØØ 91 FB 2Ø 94 84 57
7CBØ: 68 A8 68 91 FB AD 17 8F 82
7CB8: C9 23 FØ 3F C9 28 FØ 17 59
7CCØ: AD 9B 9Ø C9 Ø8 FØ 37 C9 62
7CC8: Ø3 DØ 71 A9 Ø8 18 6D 9A 56
7CDØ: 9Ø 8D 9A 9Ø 4C AD 7D AC 92
7CD8: A7 9Ø B9 17 8F C9 29 FØ 59
7CEØ: 1Ø AD 9B 9Ø C9 Ø1 DØ Ø9 C6
7CE8: A9 1Ø 18 6D 9A 9Ø 8D 9A 61
7CFØ: 9Ø AD 9B 9Ø C9 Ø6 FØ 53 B5
7CF8: 4C 72 7D 4C 8D 7D AD B3 9A
7DØØ: 9Ø DØ Ø3 4C 72 7D 38 AD 44
7DØ8: A3 9Ø E5 FD 48 AD A4 9Ø 68
7D1Ø: E5 FE BØ ØE C9 FF FØ Ø4 E8
7D18: 68 4C EA 7F 68 1Ø ØC 4C 97
7D2Ø: 2E 7D FØ Ø4 68 4C EA 7F B9
7D28: 68 1Ø Ø3 4C EA 7F 38 E9 3Ø
7D3Ø: Ø2 8D A3 9Ø A9 ØØ 8D A4 1A
7D38: 9Ø 4C 72 7D AC A7 9Ø 88 62
7D4Ø: B9 17 8F C9 2C DØ Ø4 C8 E1
7D48: 4C E6 7E AD 9A 9Ø C9 4C C4
7D5Ø: DØ Ø3 4C 7B 7D AD A4 9Ø 32
7D58: DØ 59 AD 9B 9Ø C9 Ø9 FØ 3Ø
7D6Ø: 52 C9 Ø6 BØ ØD C9 Ø2 FØ 47
```

```
7D68: Ø9 A9 Ø4 18 6D 9A 9Ø 8D D8
7D7Ø: 9A 9Ø 2Ø 6Ø 89 2Ø 86 89 4A
7D78: 4C DD 7D AC A7 9Ø B9 17 95
7D8Ø: 8F C9 29 DØ Ø5 A9 6C 8D 1D
7D88: 9A 9Ø 4C D7 7D AD 18 8F 5E
7D9Ø: C9 22 DØ Ø6 AD 19 8F 8D F1
7D98: A3 9Ø AD 9B 9Ø C9 Ø1 DØ 77
7DAØ: D1 A9 Ø8 18 6D 9A 9Ø 8D F5
7DA8: 9A 9Ø 4C 72 7D 2Ø 6Ø 89 7C
7DBØ: 4C DD 7D AD 9B 9Ø C9 Ø2 88
7DB8: FØ Ø4 C9 Ø7 DØ ØC AD 9A 83
7DCØ: 9Ø 18 69 Ø8 8D 9A 9Ø 4C FB
7DC8: D7 7D C9 Ø6 BØ Ø9 AD 9A 48
7DDØ: 9Ø 18 69 ØC 8D 9A 9Ø 2Ø 2Ø
7DD8: 6Ø 89 2Ø AØ 89 AD B3 9Ø 6F
7DEØ: DØ Ø3 4C 99 7E AD C5 9Ø EE
7DE8: DØ Ø3 4C 99 7E AD C7 9Ø FA
7DFØ: DØ 3E AD C1 9Ø FØ 2A A9 FB
7DF8: 14 38 E5 24 8D B4 9Ø 2Ø 8B
7EØØ: F7 82 A2 Ø4 2Ø 9A 82 AC 4B
7EØ8: B4 9Ø 1Ø Ø5 AØ Ø2 4C 13 8E
7E1Ø: 7E A9 2Ø 2Ø BC 82 88 DØ 8E
7E18: FA 2Ø F7 82 A2 Ø1 2Ø 96 B1
7E2Ø: 82 A9 14 85 24 A9 38 85 61
7E28: FB A9 91 85 FC 2Ø ØC 8A 23
7E3Ø: A9 1E 38 E5 24 8D B5 9Ø 42
7E38: AD C1 9Ø FØ 1F 2Ø F7 82 89
7E4Ø: A2 Ø4 2Ø 9A 82 AC B5 9Ø FF
7E48: FØ ØA 3Ø Ø8 A9 2Ø 2Ø BC 91
7E5Ø: 82 88 DØ FA 2Ø F7 82 A2 Ø3
7E58: Ø1 2Ø 96 82 A9 1E 85 24 CD
7E6Ø: 2Ø 79 8A AD BF 9Ø FØ 11 2B
7E68: C9 Ø1 DØ Ø5 A9 3C 4C 73 3F
7E7Ø: 7E A9 3E 2Ø BC 82 2Ø 9E AF
7E78: 8A AD C8 9Ø FØ 13 2Ø 1D 79
7E8Ø: 8A A9 3B 2Ø BC 82 A9 ØØ D9
7E88: 85 FB A9 Ø2 85 FC 2Ø ØC Ø9
7E9Ø: 8A 2Ø 63 8A AD AØ 9Ø DØ D1
7E98: Ø3 4C 86 7B AD B3 9Ø DØ EØ
7EAØ: 1B EE B3 9Ø AD 9C 9Ø 85 EC
7EA8: FD AD 9D 9Ø 85 FE 2Ø F7 2D
7EBØ: 82 A9 Ø1 2Ø 1Ø 83 2Ø CF 1A
7EB8: 81 4C 37 7B 2Ø F7 82 A9 B7
7ECØ: Ø1 2Ø 1Ø 83 A9 Ø2 2Ø 1Ø 26
7EC8: 83 AD C1 9Ø FØ 15 2Ø F7 48
7EDØ: 82 A2 Ø4 2Ø 9A 82 A9 ØD 79
7ED8: 2Ø BC 82 2Ø F7 82 A9 Ø4 88
7EEØ: 2Ø 1Ø 83 4C DØ Ø3 B9 17 44
7EE8: 8F C9 58 FØ 62 88 88 B9 3A
7EFØ: 17 8F C9 29 DØ Ø3 4C D7 2C
```

```
7EF8: 7C AD A4 90 D0 0F AD 9B F6
7F00: 90 C9 02 F0 4F C9 05 F0 A5
7F08: 4B C9 01 F0 77 AD 9B 90 88
7F10: C9 01 D0 0C AD 9A 90 18 20
7F18: 69 18 8D 9A 90 4C D7 7D 10
7F20: AD 9B 90 C9 05 F0 08 A9 31
7F28: 31 20 BA 7F 4C 3B 7F AD 13
7F30: 9A 90 18 69 1C 8D 9A 90 17
7F38: 4C D7 7D 20 85 8A 20 6C 08
7F40: 8A A9 80 85 FB A9 90 85 84
7F48: FC 20 0C 8A 4C DD 7D AD 7A
7F50: A4 90 D0 33 AD 9B 90 C9 D9
7F58: 02 D0 0C A9 10 18 6D 9A FE
7F60: 90 8D 9A 90 4C 72 7D C9 58
7F68: 01 F0 10 C9 03 F0 0C C9 80
7F70: 05 F0 08 A9 32 20 BA 7F D0
7F78: 4C 3B 7F A9 14 18 6D 9A 6D
7F80: 90 8D 9A 90 4C 72 7D AD 5C
7F88: 9B 90 C9 02 D0 0C A9 18 F4
7F90: 18 6D 9A 90 8D 9A 90 4C 97
7F98: D7 7D C9 01 F0 10 C9 03 8A
7FA0: F0 0C C9 05 F0 08 A9 33 D2
7FA8: 20 BA 7F 4C 3B 7F A9 1C 62
7FB0: 18 6D 9A 90 8D 9A 90 4C B7
7FB8: D7 7D 8D B4 90 8C B6 90 B4
7FC0: 8E B5 90 A9 BA 20 BC 82 73
7FC8: 68 AA 68 A8 98 48 8A 48 81
7FD0: 98 20 24 ED AD B4 90 AC 95
7FD8: B6 90 AE B5 90 60 A0 00 CF
7FE0: 98 99 D0 8E C8 C0 FF D0 AF
7FE8: F8 60 20 63 8A 20 85 8A 21
7FF0: 20 6C 8A A9 EF 85 FB A9 3E
7FF8: 8F 85 FC 20 0C 8A 20 63 F0
8000: 8A 4C 72 7D A0 FF C8 B9 CF
8008: D0 8E F0 56 C9 20 D0 F6 FF
8010: C8 C8 8C AD 90 38 A5 EB B0
8018: ED AD 90 85 EB A5 EC E9 9F
8020: 00 85 EC A0 00 B9 D0 8E 41
8028: 49 80 91 EB C8 B9 D0 8E 3C
8030: C9 20 F0 05 91 EB 4C 2C 8D
8038: 80 C8 B9 D0 8E C9 3D F0 F6
8040: 32 88 A5 FD 91 EB C8 A5 84
8048: FE 91 EB AE AD 90 CA A0 7B
8050: 00 BD D0 8E F0 08 99 D0 6F
8058: 8E E8 C8 4C 51 80 99 D0 49
8060: 8E 60 20 85 8A A9 28 85 ED
8068: FB A9 90 85 FC 20 0C 8A 47
8070: 4C A1 80 88 8C AE 90 AD 86
8078: A9 90 D0 17 C8 C8 C8 8C 85
8080: A2 90 A9 D0 18 6D A2 90 85
```

```
8088: 85 FB A9 8E 69 00 85 FC BC
8090: 20 94 84 AC AE 90 AD A3 D8
8098: 90 91 EB AD A4 90 C8 91 29
80A0: EB 68 68 4C DD 7D AD B0 74
80A8: 90 85 ED AD B1 90 85 EE B5
80B0: 20 B4 81 A9 FF 8D C4 90 0A
80B8: 38 A5 EB E5 ED A5 EC E5 E0
80C0: EE B0 63 A2 00 38 A5 ED 16
80C8: E9 02 85 ED A5 EE E9 00 8B
80D0: 85 EE A0 00 B1 ED 30 0C 16
80D8: A5 ED D0 02 C6 EE C6 ED CF
80E0: E8 4C D4 80 A5 ED 8D B7 C3
80E8: 90 A5 EE 8D B8 90 B1 ED AB
80F0: CD A1 90 F0 03 4C 16 81 59
80F8: E8 8E A2 90 A2 01 AD B2 96
8100: 90 F0 04 C8 20 B4 81 C8 34
8108: B9 17 8F F0 53 C9 30 90 61
8110: 4F E8 D1 ED F0 F1 AD B7 70
8118: 90 85 ED AD B8 90 85 EE 5F
8120: 20 B4 81 4C B8 80 AD C4 3D
8128: 90 30 01 60 AD B3 90 D0 D3
8130: 02 F0 17 20 85 8A 20 6C 58
8138: 8A 20 1D 8A A9 18 85 FB 89
8140: A9 90 85 FC 20 0C 8A 20 23
8148: 63 8A 68 68 AD 9A 90 29 55
8150: 1F C9 10 F0 08 AD BF 90 6D
8158: D0 03 4C D7 7D 4C 72 7D 0B
8160: EC A2 90 F0 03 4C 16 81 9A
8168: EE C4 90 F0 03 20 BD 81 CA
8170: AC A2 90 AD B2 90 F0 01 1A
8178: C8 B1 ED 8D A3 90 C8 B1 85
8180: ED 8D A4 90 AD BF 90 F0 F9
8188: 0A C9 02 D0 1E AD A4 90 D1
8190: 8D A3 90 AD BE 90 F0 13 5D
8198: 18 AD BC 90 6D A3 90 8D 5C
81A0: A3 90 AD BD 90 6D A4 90 3F
81A8: 8D A4 90 AD B3 90 F0 01 4B
81B0: 60 4C 16 81 A5 ED D0 02 5A
81B8: C6 EE C6 ED 60 20 85 8A AB
81C0: A9 62 85 FB A9 90 85 FC 39
81C8: 20 0C 8A 20 63 8A 60 20 58
81D0: F7 82 A9 01 20 10 83 A9 A7
81D8: 92 20 75 82 8D C9 90 60 19
81E0: A9 96 20 75 82 8D CA 90 2A
81E8: 8D 15 91 20 00 BF D0 14 E0
81F0: 91 AD 9C 90 8D 26 91 AD 9A
81F8: 9D 90 8D 27 91 20 00 BF DF
8200: C3 21 91 60 A9 00 A6 36 38
8208: 85 36 A9 C1 A4 37 85 37 F2
8210: A9 8A 20 ED FD A9 50 8D 34
```

```
8218: 79 Ø5 A5 36 8D DF 82 86 AA
822Ø: 36 84 37 6Ø AD C9 9Ø 8D 91
8228: 1A 91 2Ø ØØ BF CA 19 91 8F
823Ø: AD 36 91 6Ø 8D 36 91 AD E7
8238: CA 9Ø 8D 1A 91 2Ø ØØ BF E6
824Ø: CB 19 91 6Ø AD C9 9Ø FØ 5Ø
8248: Ø8 2Ø 6Ø 82 A9 ØØ 8D C9 BF
825Ø: 9Ø 6Ø AD CA 9Ø FØ FA 2Ø 76
8258: 6Ø 82 A9 ØØ 8D CA 9Ø 6Ø 7C
826Ø: 8D ØD 91 2Ø ØØ BF CC ØC 48
8268: 91 6Ø A9 FØ 8D 3Ø BE A9 E6
827Ø: FD 8D 31 BE 6Ø 8D 12 91 D8
8278: A5 F9 8D 37 91 2Ø ØØ BF CØ
828Ø: C8 ØE 91 9Ø ØD C9 46 DØ 95
8288: Ø9 2Ø ØØ BF CØ ØØ 91 4C 8B
829Ø: 7D 82 AD 13 91 6Ø 8E 78 7F
8298: 91 6Ø 8A 8D 79 91 6Ø 8C Ø8
82AØ: 7B 91 8E B5 9Ø AD 78 91 B2
82A8: C9 Ø1 DØ ØC 2Ø 24 82 Ø8 4C
82BØ: AC 7B 91 AE B5 9Ø 28 6Ø A8
82B8: AC 7B 91 6Ø 8C 7B 91 8D 2E
82CØ: 7A 91 AD 79 91 C9 Ø2 DØ 3D
82C8: Ø9 AD 7A 91 2Ø 34 82 4C 49
82DØ: B8 82 AD 79 91 C9 Ø4 DØ AC
82D8: ØB AD 7A 91 Ø9 8Ø 2Ø ØØ C1
82EØ: C1 4C B8 82 AD C1 9Ø DØ 7F
82E8: Ø8 AD 7A 91 Ø9 8Ø 2Ø FØ 41
82FØ: FD AD 7A 91 4C B8 82 A9 BC
82F8: ØØ 8D 79 91 8D 78 91 A9 C4
83ØØ: BC 8D 3Ø BE A9 82 8D 31 5E
83Ø8: BE 6Ø AD ØØ CØ C9 83 6Ø DØ
831Ø: C9 Ø1 DØ Ø3 4C 44 82 C9 C8
8318: Ø2 DØ Ø3 4C 52 82 4C 6A 19
832Ø: 82 8D 7A 91 A9 ØØ C5 B8 C5
8328: DØ 1E A9 Ø2 C5 B9 DØ 18 43
833Ø: AØ ØØ B1 B8 C9 2Ø DØ Ø5 BE
8338: E6 B8 4C 32 83 C9 2F 9Ø BF
834Ø: Ø7 C9 3A BØ Ø3 4C D8 83 ØE
8348: AD ØØ Ø2 C9 41 DØ 74 AD E6
835Ø: Ø1 Ø2 C9 53 DØ 6D AD Ø2 6Ø
8358: Ø2 C9 4D DØ 66 AD Ø3 Ø2 7B
836Ø: C9 2Ø DØ 5F AØ ØØ B9 Ø4 EØ
8368: Ø2 C9 ØØ FØ Ø9 Ø9 8Ø 99 F8
837Ø: ØØ Ø4 C8 4C 66 83 A9 AØ 8B
8378: 99 ØØ Ø4 99 Ø1 Ø4 99 Ø2 B3
838Ø: Ø4 68 68 2Ø ØØ BF C7 2F 7Ø
8388: 91 AD 37 91 DØ 32 AD 3C AA
839Ø: BE ØA ØA ØA ØA AC 3D BE 97
8398: CØ Ø1 FØ Ø2 Ø9 8Ø 8D 33 17
83AØ: 91 2Ø ØØ BF C5 32 91 AD 3C
```

```
83A8: 38 91 29 ØF A8 C8 C8 A9 E9
83BØ: 2F 8C 37 91 8D 38 91 99 7C
83B8: 37 91 2Ø ØØ BF C6 2F 91 CC
83CØ: 4C Ø3 7B AD 7A 91 C9 3A EØ
83C8: BØ ØD C9 2Ø DØ Ø3 4C B1 83
83DØ: ØØ 38 E9 3Ø 38 E9 DØ 6Ø 91
83D8: A6 AF 86 69 A6 BØ 86 6A F5
83EØ: 18 2Ø ØC DA 2Ø EC 83 68 4F
83E8: 68 4C 6A D4 AØ ØØ 84 94 74
83FØ: A9 Ø2 85 95 B1 B8 91 94 7F
83F8: C8 C9 ØØ DØ F7 88 88 B1 88
84ØØ: 94 C9 2Ø FØ F9 C8 A9 ØØ 1F
84Ø8: 91 94 C8 C8 C8 C8 C8 6Ø FF
841Ø: A9 21 85 BB A9 83 85 BC C5
8418: A9 4C 85 BA 6Ø AØ ØØ A2 8D
842Ø: FF E8 B9 A8 8D CD DØ 8E F8
8428: FØ ØA C8 C8 C8 EØ 39 DØ DE
843Ø: FØ 4C E2 7B C8 B9 A8 8D E4
8438: CD D1 8E FØ Ø6 C8 C8 DØ 33
844Ø: EØ FØ EE C8 B9 A8 8D CD B9
8448: D2 8E FØ Ø5 C8 DØ D2 FØ EC
845Ø: EØ AD D3 8E C9 2Ø FØ Ø4 4D
8458: C9 ØØ DØ D5 BD 5Ø 8E 8D 97
846Ø: 9B 9Ø BC 88 8E 8C 9A 9Ø E7
8468: 4C C3 7B A2 Ø1 2Ø 96 82 5A
847Ø: A2 Ø4 8E B5 9Ø 2Ø 9F 82 BF
8478: AE B5 9Ø CA DØ F4 2Ø 9F 3F
848Ø: 82 C9 2A FØ ØE A9 DE 85 EB
8488: FB A9 8F 85 FC 2Ø ØC 8A 4F
849Ø: 4C BC 7E 6Ø AØ ØØ B1 FB 29
8498: FØ Ø4 C8 4C 96 84 8C DB B4
84AØ: 8F 88 A9 ØØ 8D A3 9Ø 8D 72
84A8: A4 9Ø A2 Ø1 8E B5 9Ø B1 AA
84BØ: FB 29 ØF 8D D9 8F 8D DC C1
84B8: 8F A9 ØØ 8D DA 8F 8D DD DA
84CØ: 8F CA FØ 12 2Ø E6 84 AD D6
84C8: D9 8F 8D DC 8F AD DA 8F 9A
84DØ: 8D DD 8F 4C C1 84 EE B5 82
84D8: 9Ø AE B5 9Ø 2Ø ØD 85 88 5E
84EØ: CE DB 8F DØ CA 6Ø 18 ØE 5D
84E8: D9 8F 2E DA 8F ØE D9 8F 2E
84FØ: 2E DA 8F 18 AD DC 8F 6D A8
84F8: D9 8F 8D D9 8F AD DD 8F AØ
85ØØ: 6D DA 8F 8D DA 8F ØE D9 4E
85Ø8: 8F 2E DA 8F 6Ø 18 AD D9 53
851Ø: 8F 6D A3 9Ø 8D A3 9Ø AD 85
8518: DA 8F 6D A4 9Ø 8D A4 9Ø Ø1
852Ø: 6Ø 2Ø DE 7F AØ ØØ 8C A9 FE
8528: 9Ø 8C C8 9Ø 8C BF 9Ø 8C D1
853Ø: BE 9Ø AD C3 9Ø DØ ØC 2Ø BØ
```

```
8538: 9F 82 8D 9E 9Ø 2Ø 9F 82 16
854Ø: 8D 9F 9Ø 2Ø 9F 82 C9 2Ø C8
8548: DØ Ø8 2Ø C5 86 68 68 4C 11
855Ø: 86 7B C9 2Ø 4C 5F 85 2Ø C3
8558: 9F 82 DØ Ø3 4C C5 86 C9 6E
856Ø: 3A DØ Ø3 4C Ø9 86 C9 3B 13
8568: DØ 73 8C B4 9Ø AD C1 9Ø E4
857Ø: FØ 55 8D C8 9Ø AD B4 9Ø BC
8578: FØ Ø6 2Ø A7 85 4C CF 85 7E
858Ø: 2Ø 9F 82 FØ ØE C9 7F 9Ø ØA
8588: Ø3 2Ø 17 86 99 DØ 8E C8 5E
859Ø: 4C 8Ø 85 2Ø 6C 8A 2Ø 1D 7F
8598: 8A 2Ø 79 8A 2Ø 63 8A A9 16
85AØ: ØØ 8D B4 9Ø 4C CF 85 8D E8
85A8: C8 9Ø 8D B4 9Ø AØ ØØ 2Ø 6Ø
85BØ: 9F 82 DØ Ø7 99 ØØ Ø2 AC 34
85B8: B4 9Ø 6Ø 1Ø Ø3 2Ø F4 88 5A
85CØ: 99 ØØ Ø2 C8 4C AF 85 2Ø B1
85C8: 9F 82 FØ Ø3 4C C7 85 2Ø 3F
85DØ: C5 86 AD B4 9Ø DØ Ø5 68 9B
85D8: 68 4C 86 7B 6Ø C9 3E FØ 4B
85EØ: 5B C9 3C FØ 5F C9 2B DØ EB
85E8: Ø3 EE BE 9Ø C9 2A DØ Ø3 AD
85FØ: 4C 4C 86 C9 2E FØ 16 C9 CD
85F8: 24 FØ 15 C9 7F 9Ø Ø3 2Ø F5
86ØØ: 17 86 99 DØ 8E C8 4C 57 Ø2
86Ø8: 85 8D C3 9Ø 6Ø 4C 69 87 4B
861Ø: 99 DØ 8E C8 4C E4 86 38 B7
8618: E9 7F 8D AC 9Ø A2 FF CE 54
862Ø: AC 9Ø FØ Ø8 E8 BD DØ DØ F6
8628: 1Ø FA 3Ø F3 E8 BD DØ DØ F1
863Ø: 3Ø Ø7 99 DØ 8E C8 4C 2C B3
8638: 86 29 7F 6Ø A9 Ø2 8D BF F8
864Ø: 9Ø 4C 57 85 A9 Ø1 8D BF 18
8648: 9Ø 4C 57 85 AD BF 9Ø FØ 72
865Ø: 2Ø A9 2A 99 DØ 8E C8 EE F7
8658: A9 9Ø AD BF 9Ø C9 Ø1 FØ AE
866Ø: Ø8 A5 FE 8D A3 9Ø 4C 57 E2
8668: 85 A5 FD 8D A3 9Ø 4C 57 89
867Ø: 85 2Ø 57 85 AD B3 9Ø FØ D9
8678: ØB A9 2A 2Ø BC 82 2Ø 79 66
868Ø: 8A 2Ø 63 8A AD A9 9Ø DØ F5
8688: 2Ø AØ ØØ B9 DØ 8E C9 2Ø DD
869Ø: FØ Ø4 C8 4C 8B 86 C8 84 81
8698: FB A9 DØ 18 65 FB 85 FB CB
86AØ: A9 8E 69 ØØ 85 FC 2Ø 94 48
86A8: 84 AD B3 9Ø FØ Ø8 AD CØ A6
86BØ: 9Ø FØ Ø3 2Ø B3 88 AD A3 63
86B8: 9Ø 85 FD AD A4 9Ø 85 FE 7B
86CØ: 68 68 4C 86 7B 99 DØ 8E 8Ø
```

```
86C8: C8 CØ FF DØ F8 99 DØ 8E D5
86DØ: 2Ø 9F 82 2Ø 9F 82 FØ Ø6 17
86D8: A9 ØØ 8D C3 9Ø 6Ø A9 Ø1 Ø3
86EØ: 8D AØ 9Ø 6Ø A2 ØØ 2Ø 9F E9
86E8: 82 FØ 2C C9 3A FØ 28 C9 45
86FØ: 2Ø FØ F3 C9 3B FØ 2Ø C9 ØD
86F8: 2C FØ ØF C9 29 FØ ØB 9D 97
87ØØ: BD 8F E8 99 DØ 8E C8 4C 27
87Ø8: E6 86 8E AA 9Ø 99 DØ 8E C3
871Ø: C8 2Ø 2B 87 4C 57 85 8D C1
8718: B4 9Ø A9 ØØ 8E AA 9Ø 99 B4
872Ø: DØ 8E 2Ø 2B 87 AD B4 9Ø DE
8728: 4C 5A 85 A9 ØØ 8D A3 9Ø 4D
873Ø: 8D A4 9Ø AA ØE A3 9Ø 2E 3A
8738: A4 9Ø ØE A3 9Ø 2E A4 9Ø DØ
874Ø: ØE A3 9Ø 2E A4 9Ø ØE A3 5B
8748: 9Ø 2E A4 9Ø BD BD 8F C9 96
875Ø: 41 9Ø Ø2 E9 Ø7 29 ØF ØD ØB
8758: A3 9Ø 8D A3 9Ø E8 EC AA F5
876Ø: 9Ø DØ D1 EE A9 9Ø A9 Ø1 F8
8768: 6Ø CØ ØØ FØ ØE AE B3 9Ø ØA
877Ø: DØ Ø9 48 98 48 2Ø Ø4 8Ø Ø8
8778: 68 A8 68 99 DØ 8E C8 2Ø FE
878Ø: 9F 82 99 DØ 8E C8 C9 42 AD
8788: DØ 68 A9 ØØ 8D B9 9Ø AD 71
879Ø: B3 9Ø FØ 17 8C B6 9Ø AD 3B
8798: C5 9Ø FØ ØF 2Ø 6C 8A 2Ø A5
87AØ: 1D 8A 2Ø 45 8A 2Ø 1D 8A D2
87A8: AC B6 9Ø 2Ø 9F 82 99 DØ DA
87BØ: 8E C8 C9 2Ø DØ F5 2Ø 9F B2
87B8: 82 99 DØ 8E C8 C9 22 DØ F4
87CØ: 45 2Ø 9F 82 DØ Ø3 4C 98 5A
87C8: 88 C9 3A DØ Ø3 4C 9B 88 EB
87DØ: C9 3B DØ ØC 2Ø A7 85 AE C7
87D8: C1 9Ø 8E C8 9Ø 4C 98 88 BA
87EØ: C9 22 DØ Ø3 4C C1 87 AE CE
87E8: B3 9Ø DØ Ø9 2Ø FE 89 4C FC
87FØ: C1 87 4C 69 8B 99 DØ 8E D5
87F8: AA 8C B6 9Ø 2Ø D6 89 AC 7C
88ØØ: B6 9Ø C8 4C C1 87 A2 ØØ DF
88Ø8: 8E BA 9Ø 9D D2 8F E8 AD 4F
881Ø: BA 9Ø DØ 75 2Ø 9F 82 FØ 89
8818: 43 C9 3A FØ 3F C9 3B DØ FB
882Ø: ØC 2Ø A7 85 AE C1 9Ø 8E B8
8828: C8 9Ø 4C 5C 88 8D 5F 8F D9
883Ø: AD B3 9Ø DØ ØD AD 5F 8F 91
8838: C9 2Ø DØ D3 2Ø FE 89 4C E9
884Ø: ØF 88 AD 5F 8F 99 DØ 8E B9
8848: C8 C9 2Ø FØ 18 C9 ØØ FØ 1C
885Ø: 14 C9 3A FØ 1Ø 9D D2 8F 6Ø
```

```
8858: E8 4C ØF 88 EE BA 9Ø 8D 6C
886Ø: 6Ø 8F 4C 2D 88 A9 D2 85 F7
8868: FB A9 8F 85 FC 8C B6 9Ø 44
887Ø: 2Ø 94 84 AE A3 9Ø 2Ø D6 A8
8878: 89 AC B6 9Ø A9 ØØ A2 Ø5 FØ
888Ø: 9D D2 8F CA DØ FA 4C ØF CD
8888: 88 AD B3 9Ø DØ Ø3 2Ø FE 9A
889Ø: 89 AD 6Ø 8F C9 3A FØ Ø3 F2
8898: 2Ø C5 86 8D C3 9Ø EE C7 DA
88AØ: 9Ø 68 68 AD B3 9Ø FØ Ø8 C5
88A8: AD C5 9Ø FØ Ø3 4C 5C 7E A3
88BØ: 4C 86 7B AD B3 9Ø C9 Ø2 49
88B8: DØ Ø1 6Ø 2Ø F7 82 A2 Ø2 91
88CØ: 2Ø 9A 82 38 AD A3 9Ø E5 5F
88C8: FD 8D A1 9Ø AD A4 9Ø E5 8Ø
88DØ: FE 8D A2 9Ø A9 ØØ 2Ø BC 6C
88D8: 82 AD A1 9Ø DØ Ø3 CE A2 A6
88EØ: 9Ø CE A1 9Ø DØ EE AD A2 6B
88E8: 9Ø DØ E9 2Ø F7 82 A2 Ø1 C5
88FØ: 2Ø 96 82 6Ø 38 E9 7F 8D Ø4
88F8: AC 9Ø A2 FF CE AC 9Ø FØ 14
89ØØ: Ø8 E8 BD DØ DØ 1Ø FA 3Ø Ø3
89Ø8: F3 E8 BD DØ DØ 3Ø Ø7 99 Ø3
891Ø: ØØ Ø2 C8 4C Ø9 89 29 7F C1
8918: 6Ø AØ ØØ A2 ØØ B9 DØ 8E C4
892Ø: C9 2B FØ Ø4 C8 4C 1D 89 7C
8928: C8 B9 DØ 8E 2Ø 38 89 BØ B6
893Ø: 12 9D BD 8F E8 4C 28 89 B6
8938: C9 3A BØ Ø6 38 E9 3Ø 38 37
894Ø: E9 DØ 6Ø A9 ØØ 9D BD 8F A4
8948: A9 BD 85 FB A9 8F 85 FC A3
895Ø: 2Ø 94 84 AD A3 9Ø 8D BC 3B
8958: 9Ø AD A4 9Ø 8D BD 9Ø 6Ø A1
896Ø: AD B3 9Ø DØ Ø4 2Ø FE 89 7E
8968: 6Ø AD C5 9Ø FØ 11 2Ø F7 DC
897Ø: 82 A2 Ø1 2Ø 96 82 AE 9A 46
8978: 9Ø 2Ø 26 8A 2Ø 1D 8A AE 82
898Ø: 9A 9Ø 2Ø D6 89 6Ø AD B3 53
8988: 9Ø DØ Ø4 2Ø FE 89 6Ø AD 27
899Ø: C5 9Ø FØ Ø6 AE A3 9Ø 2Ø 6E
8998: 26 8A AE A3 9Ø 4C D6 89 5E
89AØ: AD B3 9Ø DØ Ø7 2Ø FE 89 D6
89A8: 2Ø FE 89 6Ø AD C5 9Ø FØ 59
89BØ: Ø6 AE A3 9Ø 2Ø 26 8A AE 4D
89B8: A3 9Ø 2Ø D6 89 AD C5 9Ø 52
89CØ: FØ ØE AD C6 9Ø FØ Ø3 2Ø 6Ø
89C8: 1D 8A AE A4 9Ø 2Ø 26 8A Ø9
89DØ: AE A4 9Ø 4C D6 89 8E A2 D7
89D8: 9Ø AD C2 9Ø FØ Ø5 AØ ØØ DD
89EØ: 8A 91 FD AD CØ 9Ø FØ 16 78
```

```
89E8: 20 F7 82 A2 02 20 9A 82 CC
89F0: AD A2 90 20 BC 82 20 F7 BF
89F8: 82 A2 01 20 96 82 18 A9 B0
8A00: 01 65 FD 85 FD A9 00 65 03
8A08: FE 85 FE 60 A0 00 B1 FB 48
8A10: F0 0A 20 BC 82 20 98 8A 40
8A18: C8 4C 0E 8A 60 A9 20 20 19
8A20: BC 82 20 98 8A 60 8E B5 6A
8A28: 90 AD C6 90 F0 0B 8A 20 BB
8A30: 50 8B 20 C1 8A AE B5 90 7B
8A38: 60 A9 00 20 24 ED 20 C1 C4
8A40: 8A AE B5 90 60 AD C6 90 DD
8A48: F0 0E A5 FE 20 50 8B A5 FC
8A50: FD 20 50 8B 20 F4 8A 60 79
8A58: A6 FD A5 FE 20 24 ED 20 72
8A60: F4 8A 60 A9 0D 20 BC 82 1E
8A68: 20 98 8A 60 AE 9E 90 AD C9
8A70: 9F 90 20 24 ED 20 2A 8B 8F
8A78: 60 A9 D0 85 FB A9 8E 85 C3
8A80: FC 20 0C 8A 60 A9 07 20 1E
8A88: BC 82 A9 12 20 BC 82 20 0C
8A90: 79 8A A9 0D 20 BC 82 60 64
8A98: AE B3 90 D0 01 60 AE C1 B9
8AA0: 90 D0 01 60 8D B4 90 20 D8
8AA8: F7 82 A2 04 20 9A 82 AD 0D
8AB0: B4 90 20 BC 82 20 F7 82 1B
8AB8: A2 01 20 96 82 AD B4 90 91
8AC0: 60 AE B3 90 D0 01 60 AE 2B
8AC8: C1 90 D0 01 60 20 F7 82 03
8AD0: A2 04 20 9A 82 AD C6 90 CE
8AD8: F0 09 AD B5 90 20 50 8B EA
8AE0: 4C EB 8A A9 00 AE B5 90 B9
8AE8: 20 24 ED 20 F7 82 A2 01 E6
8AF0: 20 96 82 60 AE B3 90 D0 48
8AF8: 01 60 AE C1 90 D0 01 60 C2
8B00: 20 F7 82 A2 04 20 9A 82 F7
8B08: AE C6 90 F0 0D A5 FE 20 66
8B10: 50 8B A5 FD 20 50 8B 4C 6C
8B18: 21 8B A5 FE A6 FD 20 24 D8
8B20: ED 20 F7 82 A2 01 20 96 4D
8B28: 82 60 AE B3 90 D0 01 60 D3
8B30: AE C1 90 D0 01 60 20 F7 EF
8B38: 82 A2 04 20 9A 82 AD 9F 95
8B40: 90 AE 9E 90 20 24 ED 20 B5
8B48: F7 82 A2 01 20 96 82 60 21
8B50: 48 29 0F A8 B9 C0 8E AA DA
8B58: 68 4A 4A 4A 4A A8 B9 C0 4D
8B60: 8E 20 BC 82 8A 20 BC 82 57
8B68: 60 C9 46 D0 08 20 CC 8B DD
8B70: 68 68 4C 86 7B C9 45 D0 26
```

```
8B78: Ø6 2Ø 1F 8C 4C 7Ø 8B C9 4C
8B8Ø: 44 DØ Ø3 4C 57 8C C9 5Ø E3
8B88: DØ Ø3 4C AØ 8C C9 4E DØ 55
8B9Ø: Ø3 4C E1 8C C9 4F DØ Ø3 71
8B98: 4C CC 8C C9 53 DØ Ø3 4C 67
8BAØ: 79 8D C9 48 DØ Ø3 4C 93 54
8BA8: 8D 99 DØ 8E 2Ø 6C 8A 2Ø D7
8BBØ: 1D 8A 2Ø 45 8A 2Ø 85 8A BB
8BB8: 2Ø 79 8A A9 8Ø 85 FB A9 E5
8BCØ: 9Ø 85 FC 2Ø ØC 8A 2Ø 63 51
8BC8: 8A 4C B3 8C 2Ø 9F 82 C9 C5
8BDØ: 2Ø FØ Ø3 4C CC 8B AØ ØØ 2F
8BD8: 2Ø 9F 82 C9 ØØ FØ ØE C9 7E
8BEØ: 7F 9Ø Ø3 2Ø 17 86 99 DØ 15
8BE8: 8E C8 4C D8 8B 84 F9 AØ 93
8BFØ: ØØ B9 DØ 8E FØ Ø7 99 38 88
8BF8: 91 C8 4C F1 8B AD B3 9Ø BE
8CØØ: DØ Ø6 2Ø 45 8A 2Ø 1D 8A F4
8CØ8: 2Ø 79 8A 2Ø 63 8A 2Ø CF 38
8C1Ø: 81 A2 Ø1 2Ø 96 82 2Ø C5 79
8C18: 86 A2 ØØ 8E AØ 9Ø 6Ø A9 B7
8C2Ø: 2E 2Ø BC 82 A9 45 2Ø BC 77
8C28: 82 A9 4E 2Ø BC 82 A9 44 4Ø
8C3Ø: 2Ø BC 82 A9 2Ø 2Ø BC 82 FØ
8C38: 2Ø 9F 82 2Ø CC 8B AD B3 3F
8C4Ø: 9Ø FØ Ø3 EE AØ 9Ø EE B3 Ø6
8C48: 9Ø AD 9C 9Ø 85 FD AD 9D CE
8C5Ø: 9Ø 85 FE 2Ø 21 85 6Ø AD 82
8C58: B3 9Ø FØ 1E 2Ø 9F 82 99 8D
8C6Ø: DØ 8E AØ ØØ 2Ø 9F 82 FØ ØF
8C68: 14 C9 7F 9Ø Ø3 2Ø 17 86 44
8C7Ø: 99 DØ 8E 99 38 91 C8 4C DB
8C78: 64 8C 4C B3 8C 84 F9 2Ø 36
8C8Ø: 79 8A 2Ø 63 8A EE CØ 9Ø 55
8C88: 2Ø EØ 81 2Ø F7 82 A2 Ø1 2C
8C9Ø: 2Ø 96 82 2Ø C5 86 68 68 33
8C98: A2 ØØ 8E AØ 9Ø 4C 86 7B 1D
8CAØ: AD B3 9Ø FØ ØE 2Ø Ø4 82 1A
8CA8: EE C1 9Ø 2Ø F7 82 A2 Ø1 CD
8CBØ: 2Ø 96 82 2Ø 9F 82 FØ Ø7 C1
8CB8: C9 3A FØ Ø6 4C B3 8C 2Ø 2E
8CCØ: C5 86 68 68 A2 ØØ 8E AØ C4
8CC8: 9Ø 4C 86 7B A9 2E 2Ø BC C8
8CDØ: 82 A9 4F 2Ø BC 82 2Ø 63 15
8CD8: 8A A9 Ø1 8D C2 9Ø 4C B3 3F
8CEØ: 8C AD B3 9Ø FØ CD 2Ø 9F C9
8CE8: 82 C9 5Ø FØ ØC C9 4F FØ E5
8CFØ: 3A C9 53 FØ 6A C9 48 FØ ØF
8CF8: 4C A9 2E 2Ø BC 82 A9 4E FB
8DØØ: 2Ø BC 82 A9 5Ø 2Ø BC 82 44
```

```
8D08: 20 63 8A CE C1 90 20 F7 D2
8D10: 82 A2 04 20 9A 82 A9 0D D6
8D18: 20 BC 82 A9 04 20 10 83 A1
8D20: 20 F7 82 A2 01 20 96 82 FB
8D28: 4C B3 8C A9 2E 20 BC 82 70
8D30: A9 4E 20 BC 82 A9 4F 20 FC
8D38: BC 82 20 63 8A A9 00 8D 15
8D40: C2 90 4C B3 8C A9 2E 20 2D
8D48: BC 82 A9 4E 20 BC 82 A9 1F
8D50: 48 20 BC 82 20 63 8A A9 A4
8D58: 00 8D C6 90 4C B3 8C A9 AC
8D60: 2E 20 BC 82 A9 4E 20 BC DD
8D68: 82 A9 53 20 BC 82 20 63 2F
8D70: 8A A9 00 8D C5 90 4C B3 D0
8D78: 8C A9 2E 20 BC 82 A9 53 A2
8D80: 20 BC 82 20 63 8A AD B3 81
8D88: 90 F0 05 A9 01 8D C5 90 BD
8D90: 4C B3 8C A9 2E 20 BC 82 D8
8D98: A9 48 20 BC 82 20 63 8A 50
8DA0: A9 01 8D C6 90 4C B3 8C 98
8DA8: 4C 44 41 4C 44 59 4A 53 57
8DB0: 52 52 54 53 42 43 53 42 51
8DB8: 45 51 42 43 43 43 4D 50 59
8DC0: 42 4E 45 4C 44 58 4A 4D 63
8DC8: 50 53 54 41 53 54 59 53 71
8DD0: 54 58 49 4E 59 44 45 59 F9
8DD8: 44 45 58 44 45 43 49 4E CE
8DE0: 58 49 4E 43 43 50 59 43 C9
8DE8: 50 58 53 42 43 53 45 43 06
8DF0: 41 44 43 43 4C 43 54 41 B3
8DF8: 58 54 41 59 54 58 41 54 ED
8E00: 59 41 50 48 41 50 4C 41 CD
8E08: 42 52 4B 42 4D 49 42 50 CC
8E10: 4C 41 4E 44 4F 52 41 45 3D
8E18: 4F 52 42 49 54 42 56 43 E9
8E20: 42 56 53 52 4F 4C 52 4F 23
8E28: 52 4C 53 52 43 4C 44 43 28
8E30: 4C 49 41 53 4C 50 48 50 A7
8E38: 50 4C 50 52 54 49 53 45 73
8E40: 44 53 45 49 54 53 58 54 86
8E48: 58 53 43 4C 56 4E 4F 50 6E
8E50: 01 05 09 00 08 08 08 01 C1
8E58: 08 05 06 01 02 02 00 00 A3
8E60: 00 02 00 02 04 04 01 00 50
8E68: 01 00 00 00 00 00 00 00 06
8E70: 00 08 08 01 01 01 07 08 C2
8E78: 08 03 03 03 00 00 03 00 F0
8E80: 00 00 00 00 00 00 00 00 9D
8E88: A1 A0 20 60 B0 F0 90 C1 D4
8E90: D0 A2 4C 81 84 86 C8 88 B8
```

```
8E98: CA C6 E8 E6 CØ EØ E1 38 DD
8EAØ: 61 18 AA A8 8A 98 48 68 Ø4
8EA8: ØØ 3Ø 1Ø 21 Ø1 41 24 5Ø 8B
8EBØ: 7Ø 22 62 42 D8 58 Ø2 Ø8 33
8EB8: 28 4Ø F8 78 BA 9A B8 EA 3D
8ECØ: 3Ø 31 32 33 34 35 36 37 D5
8EC8: 38 39 41 42 43 44 45 46 98
8EDØ: ØØ ØØ ØØ ØØ ØØ ØØ ØØ ØØ ED
8ED8: ØØ ØØ ØØ ØØ ØØ ØØ ØØ ØØ F5
8EEØ: ØØ ØØ ØØ ØØ ØØ ØØ ØØ ØØ FD
8EE8: ØØ ØØ ØØ ØØ ØØ ØØ ØØ ØØ Ø6
8EFØ: ØØ ØØ ØØ ØØ ØØ ØØ ØØ ØØ ØE
8EF8: ØØ ØØ ØØ ØØ ØØ ØØ ØØ ØØ 16
8FØØ: ØØ ØØ ØØ ØØ ØØ ØØ ØØ ØØ 1F
8FØ8: ØØ ØØ ØØ ØØ ØØ ØØ ØØ ØØ 27
8F1Ø: ØØ ØØ ØØ ØØ ØØ ØØ ØØ ØØ 2F
8F18: ØØ ØØ ØØ ØØ ØØ ØØ ØØ ØØ 37
8F2Ø: ØØ ØØ ØØ ØØ ØØ ØØ ØØ ØØ 3F
8F28: ØØ ØØ ØØ ØØ ØØ ØØ ØØ ØØ 47
8F3Ø: ØØ ØØ ØØ ØØ ØØ ØØ ØØ ØØ 4F
8F38: ØØ ØØ ØØ ØØ ØØ ØØ ØØ ØØ 57
8F4Ø: ØØ ØØ ØØ ØØ ØØ ØØ ØØ ØØ 5F
8F48: ØØ ØØ ØØ ØØ ØØ ØØ ØØ ØØ 67
8F5Ø: ØØ ØØ ØØ ØØ ØØ ØØ ØØ ØØ 6F
8F58: ØØ ØØ ØØ ØØ ØØ ØØ ØØ ØØ 77
8F6Ø: ØØ ØØ ØØ ØØ ØØ ØØ ØØ ØØ 7F
8F68: ØØ ØØ ØØ ØØ ØØ ØØ ØØ ØØ 87
8F7Ø: ØØ ØØ ØØ ØØ ØØ ØØ ØØ ØØ 8F
8F78: ØØ ØØ ØØ ØØ ØØ ØØ ØØ ØØ 97
8F8Ø: ØØ ØØ ØØ ØØ ØØ ØØ ØØ ØØ 9F
8F88: ØØ ØØ ØØ ØØ ØØ ØØ ØØ ØØ A7
8F9Ø: ØØ ØØ ØØ ØØ ØØ ØØ ØØ ØØ AF
8F98: ØØ ØØ ØØ ØØ ØØ ØØ ØØ ØØ B7
8FAØ: ØØ ØØ ØØ ØØ ØØ ØØ ØØ ØØ BF
8FA8: ØØ ØØ ØØ ØØ ØØ ØØ ØØ ØØ C7
8FBØ: ØØ ØØ ØØ ØØ ØØ ØØ ØØ ØØ CF
8FB8: ØØ ØØ ØØ ØØ ØØ ØØ ØØ ØØ D7
8FCØ: ØØ ØØ ØØ ØØ ØØ ØØ ØØ ØØ DF
8FC8: ØØ ØØ ØØ ØØ ØØ ØØ ØØ ØØ E7
8FDØ: ØØ ØØ ØØ ØØ ØØ ØØ ØØ ØØ EF
8FD8: ØØ ØØ ØØ ØØ ØØ ØØ 4E 4F E3
8FEØ: 2Ø 53 54 41 52 54 2Ø 41 E8
8FE8: 44 44 52 45 53 53 ØØ 2D EE
8FFØ: 2D 2D 2D 2D 2D 2D 2D 2D 1Ø
8FF8: 2D 2D 2D 2D 2D 2D 2D 2D 18
9ØØØ: 2D 2D 2D 2Ø 42 52 41 4E D6
9ØØ8: 43 48 2Ø 4F 55 54 2Ø 4F 61
9Ø1Ø: 46 2Ø 52 41 4E 47 45 ØØ D4
9Ø18: 55 4E 44 45 46 49 4E 45 8D
9Ø2Ø: 44 2Ø 4C 41 42 45 4C ØØ C8
```

```
9Ø28: 1D 1D 1D 1D 1D 1D 1D 1D 49
9Ø3Ø: 1D 2Ø 4E 41 4B 45 44 2Ø DD
9Ø38: 4C 41 42 45 4C ØØ 1D 1D 26
9Ø4Ø: 1D 1D 1D 2Ø 3C 3C 3C 3C 64
9Ø48: 3C 3C 3C 3C 2Ø 44 49 53 D9
9Ø5Ø: 4B 2Ø 45 52 52 4F 52 2Ø 81
9Ø58: 3E 3E 3E 3E 3E 3E 3E 3E 79
9Ø6Ø: 2Ø ØØ 1D 1D 1D 1D 1D 2Ø BE
9Ø68: 2D 2D 2Ø 44 55 5Ø 4C 49 81
9Ø7Ø: 43 41 54 45 44 2Ø 4C 41 DE
9Ø78: 42 45 4C 2Ø 2D 2D 2Ø ØØ F5
9Ø8Ø: 1D 1D 1D 1D 1D 2Ø 2D 2D DD
9Ø88: 2Ø 53 59 4E 54 41 58 2Ø 17
9Ø9Ø: 45 52 52 4F 52 2Ø 2D 2D C2
9Ø98: 2Ø ØØ ØØ ØØ ØØ ØØ ØØ ØØ C9
9ØAØ: ØØ ØØ ØØ ØØ ØØ ØØ ØØ ØØ C1
9ØA8: ØØ ØØ ØØ ØØ ØØ ØØ ØØ ØØ C9
9ØBØ: ØØ ØØ ØØ ØØ ØØ ØØ ØØ ØØ D1
9ØB8: ØØ ØØ ØØ ØØ ØØ ØØ ØØ ØØ D9
9ØCØ: ØØ ØØ ØØ ØØ ØØ ØØ ØØ ØØ E1
9ØC8: ØØ ØØ ØØ FF ØØ ØØ ØØ ØØ E9
9ØDØ: ØØ ØØ ØØ ØØ ØØ ØØ ØØ ØØ F1
9ØD8: ØØ ØØ ØØ ØØ ØØ ØØ ØØ ØØ F9
9ØEØ: ØØ ØØ ØØ ØØ ØØ ØØ ØØ ØØ Ø2
9ØE8: ØØ ØØ ØØ ØØ ØØ ØØ ØØ ØØ ØA
9ØFØ: ØØ ØØ ØØ ØØ ØØ ØØ ØØ ØØ 12
9ØF8: ØØ ØØ ØØ ØØ ØØ ØØ ØØ ØØ 1A
91ØØ: Ø7 37 91 C3 Ø6 ØØ ØØ Ø1 14
91Ø8: ØØ ØØ ØØ ØØ Ø1 ØØ Ø3 37 7Ø
911Ø: 91 ØØ ØØ ØØ Ø2 ØØ ØØ ØØ ØC
9118: ØØ Ø4 ØØ 36 91 Ø1 ØØ ØØ 3Ø
912Ø: ØØ Ø7 37 91 C3 Ø6 ØØ ØØ 3B
9128: ØØ ØØ ØØ ØØ ØØ ØØ ØØ Ø1 4C
913Ø: 37 91 Ø2 ØØ 38 91 ØØ ØØ 9B
9138: ØØ ØØ ØØ ØØ ØØ ØØ ØØ ØØ 5B
914Ø: ØØ ØØ ØØ ØØ ØØ ØØ ØØ ØØ 63
9148: ØØ ØØ ØØ ØØ ØØ ØØ ØØ ØØ 6B
915Ø: ØØ ØØ ØØ ØØ ØØ ØØ ØØ ØØ 73
9158: ØØ ØØ ØØ ØØ ØØ ØØ ØØ ØØ 7B
916Ø: ØØ ØØ ØØ ØØ ØØ ØØ ØØ ØØ 83
9168: ØØ ØØ ØØ ØØ ØØ ØØ ØØ ØØ 8B
917Ø: ØØ ØØ ØØ ØØ ØØ ØØ ØØ ØØ 93
9178: ØØ ØØ ØØ ØØ ØØ ØØ ØØ ØØ 9B
```

Program B-3. DOS 3.3 LADS Object Code

This program requires MLX, Appendix G, to be entered.

```
START ADDRESS: 79F8
END ADDRESS:   9087

79F8: EA EA EA EA EA 4C 09 83 46
7A00: A9 00 A0 32 99 E2 8F 88 01
7A08: D0 FA A9 00 85 EB 85 4C 8C
7A10: 8D F8 8F A9 7A 85 EC 85 DF
7A18: 4D 8D F9 8F A9 01 8D 0E C9
7A20: 90 B9 00 04 C9 A0 F0 07 C5
7A28: 99 07 8F C8 4C 21 7A 99 9F
7A30: 07 8F C8 B9 00 04 C9 A0 85
7A38: D0 E7 88 84 F9 20 E9 80 8D
7A40: 20 6C 83 A9 00 8D E8 8F 03
7A48: 20 22 84 AD FB 8F D0 3F 40
7A50: 20 64 89 A9 E6 20 F5 81 5F
7A58: A9 4C 20 F5 81 A9 41 20 ED
7A60: F5 81 A9 44 20 F5 81 A9 AF
7A68: 53 20 F5 81 20 64 89 AD 39
7A70: F1 8F D0 0B A9 05 85 FB 75
7A78: A9 8E 85 FC 20 95 83 AD 72
7A80: EB 8F 85 FD 8D E4 8F AD AC
7A88: EC 8F 85 FE 8D E5 8F 20 BB
7A90: 43 82 AD E8 8F F0 03 4C 9E
7A98: A5 7D 20 22 84 A9 00 8D 3E
7AA0: F0 8F 8D FA 8F AC FB 8F 0A
7AA8: D0 03 4C C9 7A 8C 0F 90 A1
7AB0: AD 0D 90 F0 0C 20 6D 89 26
7AB8: 20 1E 89 20 46 89 20 1E 2F
7AC0: 89 AD 06 90 F0 03 20 1A 9D
7AC8: 88 4C 1E 83 AD E3 8F F0 1E
7AD0: 17 C9 03 D0 72 A9 01 8D FA
7AD8: E3 8F AD 08 8E D0 68 A9 0C
7AE0: 08 18 6D E2 8F 8D E2 8F C3
7AE8: 4C B6 7C AD FB 8F F0 39 55
7AF0: A0 FF C8 B9 05 8E F0 2E 5D
7AF8: 99 07 8F C9 20 D0 F3 C8 FF
7B00: B9 05 8E C9 3D D0 03 4C 03
7B08: E6 7C A2 00 8E 0F 90 8A 42
7B10: 99 07 8F B9 05 8E F0 08 6F
7B18: 9D 05 8E E8 C8 4C 13 7B 98
7B20: 9D 05 8E 4C C9 7A 20 7C B2
7B28: 7F 20 1E 7F 4C C9 7A AD CE
7B30: 4C 8E C9 40 B0 06 AD 4D 74
7B38: 8E EE FA 8F 49 80 8D E9 DB
7B40: 8F 20 C0 7F 4C BE 7B A0 0C
7B48: 00 8C F0 8F B9 09 8E C9 52
```

```
7B5Ø: 41 9Ø Ø3 EE FØ 8F 99 4C AØ
7B58: 8E C8 B9 Ø9 8E FØ 16 99 8E
7B6Ø: 4C 8E C9 41 9Ø Ø3 EE FØ CD
7B68: 8F C8 B9 Ø9 8E FØ Ø6 99 FE
7B7Ø: 4C 8E 4C 69 7B 88 8C EF 58
7B78: 8F AD F1 8F DØ 4Ø AD FØ AD
7B8Ø: 8F DØ AC A9 4C 85 FB A9 BD
7B88: 8E 85 FC AØ ØØ AD 4C 8E AF
7B9Ø: C9 3Ø BØ Ø7 18 E6 FB 9Ø E3
7B98: Ø2 E6 FC B1 FB FØ 1Ø C9 92
7BAØ: 29 FØ ØC C9 2C FØ Ø8 C9 85
7BA8: 2Ø FØ Ø4 C8 4C 9B 7B 48 Ø9
7BBØ: 98 48 A9 ØØ 91 FB 2Ø 95 8D
7BB8: 83 68 A8 68 91 FB AD 4C 4B
7BCØ: 8E C9 23 FØ 3F C9 28 FØ 47
7BC8: 17 AD E3 8F C9 Ø8 FØ 37 B3
7BDØ: C9 Ø3 DØ 71 A9 Ø8 18 6D A9
7BD8: E2 8F 8D E2 8F 4C B6 7C 9C
7BEØ: AC EF 8F B9 4C 8E C9 29 11
7BE8: FØ 1Ø AD E3 8F C9 Ø1 DØ C6
7BFØ: Ø9 A9 1Ø 18 6D E2 8F 8D FD
7BF8: E2 8F AD E3 8F C9 Ø6 FØ D9
7CØØ: 53 4C 7B 7C 4C 96 7C AD 5Ø
7CØ8: FB 8F DØ Ø3 4C 7B 7C 38 AE
7C1Ø: AD EB 8F E5 FD 48 AD EC 84
7C18: 8F E5 FE BØ ØE C9 FF FØ C5
7C2Ø: Ø4 68 4C Ø4 7F 68 1Ø ØC C8
7C28: 4C 37 7C FØ Ø4 68 4C Ø4 12
7C3Ø: 7F 68 1Ø Ø3 4C Ø4 7F 38 DE
7C38: E9 Ø2 8D EB 8F A9 ØØ 8D C7
7C4Ø: EC 8F 4C 7B 7C AC EF 8F DA
7C48: 88 B9 4C 8E C9 2C DØ Ø4 ØB
7C5Ø: C8 4C ØØ 7E AD E2 8F C9 8A
7C58: 4C DØ Ø3 4C 84 7C AD EC 2F
7C6Ø: 8F DØ 59 AD E3 8F C9 Ø9 55
7C68: FØ 52 C9 Ø6 BØ ØD C9 Ø2 57
7C7Ø: FØ Ø9 A9 Ø4 18 6D E2 8F 65
7C78: 8D E2 8F 2Ø 61 88 2Ø 87 D9
7C8Ø: 88 4C E6 7C AC EF 8F B9 73
7C88: 4C 8E C9 29 DØ Ø5 A9 6C 71
7C9Ø: 8D E2 8F 4C EØ 7C AD 4D 61
7C98: 8E C9 22 DØ Ø6 AD 4E 8E AE
7CAØ: 8D EB 8F AD E3 8F C9 Ø1 1A
7CA8: DØ D1 A9 Ø8 18 6D E2 8F FF
7CBØ: 8D E2 8F 4C 7B 7C 2Ø 61 4F
7CB8: 88 4C E6 7C AD E3 8F C9 93
7CCØ: Ø2 FØ Ø4 C9 Ø7 DØ ØC AD 55
7CC8: E2 8F 18 69 Ø8 8D E2 8F 7C
7CDØ: 4C EØ 7C C9 Ø6 BØ Ø9 AD Ø7
7CD8: E2 8F 18 69 ØC 8D E2 8F AC
```

```
7CEØ: 2Ø 61 88 2Ø A1 88 AD FB DB
7CE8: 8F DØ Ø3 4C A2 7D AD ØD 76
7CFØ: 9Ø DØ Ø3 4C A2 7D AD ØF Ø1
7CF8: 9Ø DØ 3E AD Ø9 9Ø FØ 2A A7
7DØØ: A9 14 38 E5 24 8D FC 8F 1B
7DØ8: 2Ø 3Ø 82 A2 Ø4 2Ø D3 81 63
7D1Ø: AC FC 8F 1Ø Ø5 AØ Ø2 4C 8E
7D18: 1C 7D A9 2Ø 2Ø F5 81 88 1C
7D2Ø: DØ FA 2Ø 3Ø 82 A2 Ø1 2Ø ØA
7D28: CF 81 A9 14 85 24 A9 Ø7 F8
7D3Ø: 85 FB A9 8F 85 FC 2Ø ØD 88
7D38: 89 A9 1E 38 E5 24 8D FD 82
7D4Ø: 8F AD Ø9 9Ø FØ 1F 2Ø 3Ø ØD
7D48: 82 A2 Ø4 2Ø D3 81 AC FD AB
7D5Ø: 8F FØ ØA 3Ø Ø8 A9 2Ø 2Ø DA
7D58: F5 81 88 DØ FA 2Ø 3Ø 82 Ø8
7D6Ø: A2 Ø1 2Ø CF 81 A9 1E 85 62
7D68: 24 2Ø 7A 89 AD Ø7 9Ø FØ Ø1
7D7Ø: 11 C9 Ø1 DØ Ø5 A9 3C 4C 27
7D78: 7C 7D A9 3E 2Ø F5 81 2Ø 26
7D8Ø: 9F 89 AD 1Ø 9Ø FØ 13 2Ø F2
7D88: 1E 89 A9 3B 2Ø F5 81 A9 63
7D9Ø: ØØ 85 FB A9 Ø2 85 FC 2Ø 47
7D98: ØD 89 2Ø 64 89 AD E8 8F 2B
7DAØ: DØ Ø3 4C 8F 7A AD FB 8F 59
7DA8: DØ 2C EE FB 8F 38 A5 FD 5B
7DBØ: ED E4 8F 8D 11 9Ø A5 FE BB
7DB8: ED E5 8F 8D 12 9Ø AD E4 Ø2
7DCØ: 8F 85 FD AD E5 8F 85 FE F6
7DC8: 2Ø 3Ø 82 A9 Ø1 2Ø 49 82 68
7DDØ: 2Ø E9 8Ø 4C 4Ø 7A 2Ø 3Ø 87
7DD8: 82 A9 Ø1 2Ø 49 82 A9 Ø2 4B
7DEØ: 2Ø 49 82 AD Ø9 9Ø FØ 15 EA
7DE8: 2Ø 3Ø 82 A2 Ø4 2Ø D3 81 44
7DFØ: A9 ØD 2Ø F5 81 2Ø 3Ø 82 D6
7DF8: A9 Ø4 2Ø 49 82 4C DØ Ø3 4C
7EØØ: B9 4C 8E C9 58 FØ 62 88 2F
7EØ8: 88 B9 4C 8E C9 29 DØ Ø3 C1
7E1Ø: 4C EØ 7B AD EC 8F DØ ØF ØC
7E18: AD E3 8F C9 Ø2 FØ 4F C9 AF
7E2Ø: Ø5 FØ 4B C9 Ø1 FØ 77 AD 4A
7E28: E3 8F C9 Ø1 DØ ØC AD E2 39
7E3Ø: 8F 18 69 18 8D E2 8F 4C ØD
7E38: EØ 7C AD E3 8F C9 Ø5 FØ 57
7E4Ø: Ø8 A9 31 2Ø D4 7E 4C 55 62
7E48: 7E AD E2 8F 18 69 1C 8D 71
7E5Ø: E2 8F 4C EØ 7C 2Ø 86 89 35
7E58: 2Ø 6D 89 A9 C8 85 FB A9 8A
7E6Ø: 8F 85 FC 2Ø ØD 89 4C E6 36
7E68: 7C AD EC 8F DØ 33 AD E3 38
```

```
7E70: 8F C9 02 D0 0C A9 10 18 34
7E78: 6D E2 8F 8D E2 8F 4C 7B 19
7E80: 7C C9 01 F0 10 C9 03 F0 FB
7E88: 0C C9 05 F0 08 A9 32 20 19
7E90: D4 7E 4C 55 7E A9 14 18 51
7E98: 6D E2 8F 8D E2 8F 4C 7B 39
7EA0: 7C AD E3 8F C9 02 D0 0C C0
7EA8: A9 18 18 6D E2 8F 8D E2 AD
7EB0: 8F 4C E0 7C C9 01 F0 10 B0
7EB8: C9 03 F0 0C C9 05 F0 08 86
7EC0: A9 33 20 D4 7E 4C 55 7E FE
7EC8: A9 1C 18 6D E2 8F 8D E2 CE
7ED0: 8F 4C E0 7C 8D FC 8F 8C 98
7ED8: FE 8F 8E FD 8F A9 BA 20 A3
7EE0: F5 81 68 AA 68 A8 98 48 50
7EE8: 8A 48 98 20 24 ED AD FC 83
7EF0: 8F AC FE 8F AE FD 8F 60 A6
7EF8: A0 00 98 99 05 8E C8 C0 A7
7F00: FF D0 F8 60 20 64 89 20 1E
7F08: 86 89 20 6D 89 A9 37 85 6E
7F10: FB A9 8F 85 FC 20 0D 89 CD
7F18: 20 64 89 4C 7B 7C A0 FF 45
7F20: C8 B9 05 8E F0 56 C9 20 10
7F28: D0 F6 C8 C8 8C F5 8F 38 86
7F30: A5 EB ED F5 8F 85 EB A5 2A
7F38: EC E9 00 85 EC A0 00 B9 24
7F40: 05 8E 49 80 91 EB C8 B9 1E
7F48: 05 8E C9 20 F0 05 91 EB 53
7F50: 4C 46 7F C8 B9 05 8E C9 4C
7F58: 3D F0 32 88 A5 FD 91 EB 35
7F60: C8 A5 FE 91 EB AE F5 8F BB
7F68: CA A0 00 BD 05 8E F0 08 1D
7F70: 99 05 8E E8 C8 4C 6B 7F AB
7F78: 99 05 8E 60 20 86 89 A9 35
7F80: 70 85 FB A9 8F 85 FC 20 DF
7F88: 0D 89 4C BB 7F 88 8C F6 E3
7F90: 8F AD F1 8F D0 17 C8 C8 37
7F98: C8 8C EA 8F A9 05 18 6D 74
7FA0: EA 8F 85 FB A9 8E 69 00 C3
7FA8: 85 FC 20 95 83 AC F6 8F 53
7FB0: AD EB 8F 91 EB AD EC 8F 0C
7FB8: C8 91 EB 68 68 4C E6 7C 43
7FC0: AD F8 8F 85 ED AD F9 8F C8
7FC8: 85 EE 20 CE 80 A9 FF 8D 6F
7FD0: 0C 90 38 A5 EB E5 ED A5 D3
7FD8: EC E5 EE B0 63 A2 00 38 8E
7FE0: A5 ED E9 02 85 ED A5 EE A9
7FE8: E9 00 85 EE A0 00 B1 ED D2
7FF0: 30 0C A5 ED D0 02 C6 EE A9
7FF8: C6 ED E8 4C EE 7F A5 ED 67
```

```
8000: 8D FF 8F A5 EE 8D 00 90 52
8008: B1 ED CD E9 8F F0 03 4C 48
8010: 30 80 E8 8E EA 8F A2 01 2B
8018: AD FA 8F F0 04 C8 20 CE 02
8020: 80 C8 B9 4C 8E F0 53 C9 38
8028: 30 90 4F E8 D1 ED F0 F1 F7
8030: AD FF 8F 85 ED AD 00 90 09
8038: 85 EE 20 CE 80 4C D2 7F 03
8040: AD 0C 90 30 01 60 AD FB 11
8048: 8F D0 02 F0 17 20 86 89 64
8050: 20 6D 89 20 1E 89 A9 60 BA
8058: 85 FB A9 8F 85 FC 20 0D B6
8060: 89 20 64 89 68 68 AD E2 76
8068: 8F 29 1F C9 10 F0 08 AD FD
8070: 07 90 D0 03 4C E0 7C 4C 8E
8078: 7B 7C EC EA 8F F0 03 4C 35
8080: 30 80 EE 0C 90 F0 03 20 C6
8088: D7 80 AC EA 8F AD FA 8F 92
8090: F0 01 C8 B1 ED 8D EB 8F 8B
8098: C8 B1 ED 8D EC 8F AD 07 09
80A0: 90 F0 0A C9 02 D0 1E AD 41
80A8: EC 8F 8D EB 8F AD 06 90 44
80B0: F0 13 18 AD 04 90 6D EB F5
80B8: 8F 8D EB 8F AD 05 90 6D 6B
80C0: EC 8F 8D EC 8F AD FB 8F 57
80C8: F0 01 60 4C 30 80 A5 ED 10
80D0: D0 02 C6 EE C6 ED 60 20 51
80D8: 86 89 A9 AA 85 FB A9 8F 5E
80E0: 85 FC 20 0D 89 20 64 89 D7
80E8: 60 20 30 82 A9 01 20 49 2B
80F0: 82 A9 15 85 2C A9 90 85 47
80F8: 2D 20 8C 81 EE 13 90 60 87
8100: A9 27 85 2C A9 90 85 2D DC
8108: 20 8C 81 EE 14 90 60 A9 AA
8110: 00 A6 36 85 36 A9 C1 A4 5C
8118: 37 85 37 A9 8A 20 ED FD 48
8120: A9 50 8D 79 05 A5 36 8D 0E
8128: 18 82 86 36 84 37 60 A9 77
8130: 39 85 2C A9 90 85 2D 20 66
8138: B7 81 20 DC 03 85 2B 84 52
8140: 2A A0 08 B1 2A 60 8D 53 DD
8148: 90 A9 4B 85 2C A9 90 85 6E
8150: 2D 20 B7 81 60 AD 13 90 71
8158: F0 10 A9 5D 85 2C A9 90 A3
8160: 85 2D 20 B7 81 A9 00 8D 31
8168: 13 90 60 AD 14 90 F0 FA BF
8170: A9 6F 85 2C A9 90 85 2D 5F
8178: 20 B7 81 A9 00 8D 14 90 33
8180: 60 A9 F0 8D 53 AA A9 FD AB
8188: 8D 54 AA 60 A0 08 B1 2C 77
```

```
8190: 85 2A C8 B1 2C 85 2B A9 8C
8198: Ø7 85 FB A9 8F 85 FC AØ C7
81AØ: ØØ A9 AØ 91 2A C8 CØ 1F 5Ø
81A8: DØ F9 AØ ØØ B1 FB Ø9 8Ø B6
81BØ: 91 2A C8 C4 F9 DØ F5 2Ø 8B
81B8: DC Ø3 85 2B 84 2A AØ ØØ 5C
81CØ: B1 2C 91 2A C8 CØ 12 DØ BA
81C8: F7 A2 ØØ 2Ø D6 Ø3 6Ø 8E 84
81DØ: 81 9Ø 6Ø 8A 8D 82 9Ø 6Ø 65
81D8: 8C 84 9Ø 8E FD 8F AD 81 49
81EØ: 9Ø C9 Ø1 DØ ØC 2Ø 2F 81 8C
81E8: Ø8 AC 84 9Ø AE FD 8F 28 69
81FØ: 6Ø AC 84 9Ø 6Ø 8C 84 9Ø B7
81F8: 8D 83 9Ø AD 82 9Ø C9 Ø2 7C
82ØØ: DØ Ø9 AD 83 9Ø 2Ø 46 81 BØ
82Ø8: 4C F1 81 AD 82 9Ø C9 Ø4 A8
821Ø: DØ ØB AD 83 9Ø Ø9 8Ø 2Ø F7
8218: ØØ C1 4C F1 81 AD Ø9 9Ø 9B
822Ø: DØ Ø8 AD 83 9Ø Ø9 8Ø 2Ø 47
8228: FØ FD AD 83 9Ø 4C F1 81 2E
823Ø: A9 ØØ 8D 82 9Ø 8D 81 9Ø 32
8238: A9 F5 8D 53 AA A9 81 8D Ø3
824Ø: 54 AA 6Ø AD ØØ CØ C9 83 1B
8248: 6Ø C9 Ø1 DØ Ø3 4C 55 81 92
825Ø: C9 Ø2 DØ Ø3 4C 6B 81 4C 64
8258: 81 81 8D 83 9Ø A9 ØØ C5 59
826Ø: B8 DØ 1B A9 Ø2 C5 B9 DØ 5F
8268: 15 AØ ØØ B1 B8 C9 2Ø DØ 39
827Ø: Ø5 E6 B8 4C 6B 82 C9 2F B5
8278: 9Ø Ø4 C9 3A 9Ø 53 AD ØØ DØ
828Ø: Ø2 C9 41 DØ 37 AD Ø1 Ø2 A2
8288: C9 53 DØ 3Ø AD Ø2 Ø2 C9 A7
829Ø: 4D DØ 29 AD Ø3 Ø2 C9 2Ø 44
8298: DØ 22 AØ ØØ B9 Ø4 Ø2 C9 4E
82AØ: ØØ FØ Ø9 Ø9 8Ø 99 ØØ Ø4 Ø2
82A8: C8 4C 9C 82 A9 AØ 99 ØØ E3
82BØ: Ø4 99 Ø1 Ø4 99 Ø2 Ø4 68 C3
82B8: 68 4C ØØ 7A AD 83 9Ø C9 13
82CØ: 3A BØ ØD C9 2Ø DØ Ø3 4C E3
82C8: B1 ØØ 38 E9 3Ø 38 E9 DØ 53
82DØ: 6Ø A6 AF 86 69 A6 BØ 86 DB
82D8: 6A 18 2Ø ØC DA 2Ø E5 82 83
82EØ: 68 68 4C 6A D4 AØ ØØ 84 12
82E8: 94 A9 Ø2 85 95 B1 B8 91 B1
82FØ: 94 C8 C9 ØØ DØ F7 88 88 AB
82F8: B1 94 C9 2Ø FØ F9 C8 A9 E1
83ØØ: ØØ 91 94 C8 C8 C8 C8 C8 4E
83Ø8: 6Ø A9 5A 85 BB A9 82 85 5C
831Ø: BC A9 4C 85 BA A9 FC 85 BD
8318: 73 A9 79 85 74 6Ø AØ ØØ 31
```

```
8320: A2 FF E8 B9 DD 8C CD Ø5 F2
8328: 8E FØ ØA C8 C8 C8 EØ 39 E4
8330: DØ FØ 4C EB 7A C8 B9 DD 6C
8338: 8C CD Ø6 8E FØ Ø6 C8 C8 9C
8340: DØ EØ FØ EE C8 B9 DD 8C 6A
8348: CD Ø7 8E FØ Ø5 C8 DØ D2 98
8350: FØ EØ AD Ø8 8E C9 2Ø FØ ØB
8358: Ø4 C9 ØØ DØ D5 BD 85 8D 1F
8360: 8D E3 8F BC BD 8D 8C E2 Ø5
8368: 8F 4C CC 7A A2 Ø1 2Ø CF B4
8370: 81 A2 Ø6 8E FD 8F 2Ø D8 D1
8378: 81 AE FD 8F CA DØ F4 2Ø 48
8380: D8 81 C9 2A FØ ØE A9 26 69
8388: 85 FB A9 8F 85 FC 2Ø ØD EC
8390: 89 4C D6 7D 6Ø AØ ØØ B1 59
8398: FB FØ Ø4 C8 4C 97 83 8C 3B
83AØ: 23 8F 88 A9 ØØ 8D EB 8F 66
83A8: 8D EC 8F A2 Ø1 8E FD 8F 9B
83BØ: B1 FB 29 ØF 8D 21 8F 8D 43
83B8: 24 8F A9 ØØ 8D 22 8F 8D 8C
83CØ: 25 8F CA FØ 12 2Ø E7 83 ØB
83C8: AD 21 8F 8D 24 8F AD 22 96
83DØ: 8F 8D 25 8F 4C C2 83 EE Ø4
83D8: FD 8F AE FD 8F 2Ø ØE 84 16
83EØ: 88 CE 23 8F DØ CA 6Ø 18 C7
83E8: ØE 21 8F 2E 22 8F ØE 21 AØ
83FØ: 8F 2E 22 8F 18 AD 24 8F D7
83F8: 6D 21 8F 8D 21 8F AD 25 91
84ØØ: 8F 6D 22 8F 8D 22 8F ØE 8B
84Ø8: 21 8F 2E 22 8F 6Ø 18 AD 49
841Ø: 21 8F 6D EB 8F 8D EB 8F 14
8418: AD 22 8F 6D EC 8F 8D EC F6
842Ø: 8F 6Ø 2Ø F8 7E AØ ØØ 8C 9F
8428: F1 8F 8C 1Ø 9Ø 8C Ø7 9Ø F5
843Ø: 8C Ø6 9Ø AD ØB 9Ø DØ ØC 36
8438: 2Ø D8 81 8D E6 8F 2Ø D8 1F
844Ø: 81 8D E7 8F 2Ø D8 81 C9 94
8448: 2Ø DØ Ø8 2Ø C6 85 68 68 1E
845Ø: 4C 8F 7A C9 2Ø 4C 6Ø 84 C6
8458: 2Ø D8 81 DØ Ø3 4C C6 85 41
846Ø: C9 3A DØ Ø3 4C ØA 85 C9 86
8468: 3B DØ 73 8C FC 8F AD Ø9 Ø5
847Ø: 9Ø FØ 55 8D 1Ø 9Ø AD FC 9C
8478: 8F FØ Ø6 2Ø A8 84 4C DØ Ø9
848Ø: 84 2Ø D8 81 FØ ØE C9 7F D9
8488: 9Ø Ø3 2Ø 18 85 99 Ø5 8E 4B
849Ø: C8 4C 81 84 2Ø 6D 89 2Ø 73
8498: 1E 89 2Ø 7A 89 2Ø 64 89 DD
84AØ: A9 ØØ 8D FC 8F 4C DØ 84 D3
84A8: 8D 1Ø 9Ø 8D FC 8F AØ ØØ CE
```

```
84B0: 20 D8 81 D0 07 99 00 02 DD
84B8: AC FC 8F 60 10 03 20 F5 12
84C0: 87 99 00 02 C8 4C B0 84 71
84C8: 20 D8 81 F0 03 4C C8 84 B6
84D0: 20 C6 85 AD FC 8F D0 05 F3
84D8: 68 68 4C 8F 7A 60 C9 3E D9
84E0: F0 5B C9 3C F0 5F C9 2B F9
84E8: D0 03 EE 06 90 C9 2A D0 2A
84F0: 03 4C 4D 85 C9 2E F0 16 8F
84F8: C9 24 F0 15 C9 7F 90 03 CF
8500: 20 18 85 99 05 8E C8 4C AB
8508: 58 84 8D 0B 90 60 4C 6A CB
8510: 86 99 05 8E C8 4C E5 85 17
8518: 38 E9 7F 8D F4 8F A2 FF AD
8520: CE F4 8F F0 08 E8 BD D0 01
8528: D0 10 FA 30 F3 E8 BD D0 91
8530: D0 30 07 99 05 8E C8 4C 6A
8538: 2D 85 29 7F 60 A9 02 8D 93
8540: 07 90 4C 58 84 A9 01 8D 5C
8548: 07 90 4C 58 84 AD 07 90 83
8550: F0 20 A9 2A 99 05 8E C8 7A
8558: EE F1 8F AD 07 90 C9 01 33
8560: F0 08 A5 FE 8D EB 8F 4C 12
8568: 58 84 A5 FD 8D EB 8F 4C DC
8570: 58 84 20 58 84 AD FB 8F B4
8578: F0 0B A9 2A 20 F5 81 20 92
8580: 7A 89 20 64 89 AD F1 8F EB
8588: D0 20 A0 00 B9 05 8E C9 E0
8590: 20 F0 04 C8 4C 8C 85 C8 5D
8598: 84 FB A9 05 18 65 FB 85 3E
85A0: FB A9 8E 69 00 85 FC 20 AC
85A8: 95 83 AD FB 8F F0 08 AD D2
85B0: 08 90 F0 03 20 B4 87 AD C2
85B8: EB 8F 85 FD AD EC 8F 85 F3
85C0: FE 68 68 4C 8F 7A 99 05 D5
85C8: 8E C8 C0 FF D0 F8 99 05 08
85D0: 8E 20 D8 81 20 D8 81 F0 B6
85D8: 06 A9 00 8D 0B 90 60 A9 2F
85E0: 01 8D E8 8F 60 A2 00 20 93
85E8: D8 81 F0 2C C9 3A F0 28 E2
85F0: C9 20 F0 F3 C9 3B F0 20 83
85F8: C9 2C F0 0F C9 29 F0 0B E2
8600: 9D F2 8E E8 99 05 8E C8 BF
8608: 4C E7 85 8E F2 8F 99 05 DC
8610: 8E C8 20 2C 86 4C 58 84 F7
8618: 8D FC 8F A9 00 8E F2 8F 67
8620: 99 05 8E 20 2C 86 AD FC E2
8628: 8F 4C 5B 84 A9 00 8D EB 18
8630: 8F 8D EC 8F AA 0E EB 8F F3
8638: 2E EC 8F 0E EB 8F 2E EC 51
8640: 8F 0E EB 8F 2E EC 8F 0E 61
```

```
8648: EB 8F 2E EC 8F BD F2 8E AB
865Ø: C9 41 9Ø Ø2 E9 Ø7 29 ØF 91
8658: ØD EB 8F 8D EB 8F E8 EC ØE
866Ø: F2 8F DØ D1 EE F1 8F A9 ØA
8668: Ø1 6Ø CØ ØØ FØ ØE AE FB 3F
867Ø: 8F DØ Ø9 48 98 48 2Ø 1E 63
8678: 7F 68 A8 68 99 Ø5 8E C8 C1
868Ø: 2Ø D8 81 99 Ø5 8E C8 C9 5B
8688: 42 DØ 68 A9 ØØ 8D Ø1 9Ø 5B
869Ø: AD FB 8F FØ 17 8C FE 8F EC
8698: AD ØD 9Ø FØ ØF 2Ø 6D 89 3E
86AØ: 2Ø 1E 89 2Ø 46 89 2Ø 1E 2F
86A8: 89 AC FE 8F 2Ø D8 81 99 7F
86BØ: Ø5 8E C8 C9 2Ø DØ F5 2Ø E9
86B8: D8 81 99 Ø5 8E C8 C9 22 63
86CØ: DØ 45 2Ø D8 81 DØ Ø3 4C BA
86C8: 99 87 C9 3A DØ Ø3 4C 9C 29
86DØ: 87 C9 3B DØ ØC 2Ø A8 84 3F
86D8: AE Ø9 9Ø 8E 1Ø 9Ø 4C 99 6F
86EØ: 87 C9 22 DØ Ø3 4C C2 86 CA
86E8: AE FB 8F DØ Ø9 2Ø FF 88 9C
86FØ: 4C C2 86 4C 6A 8A 99 Ø5 2Ø
86F8: 8E AA 8C FE 8F 2Ø D7 88 AE
87ØØ: AC FE 8F C8 4C C2 86 A2 CØ
87Ø8: ØØ 8E Ø2 9Ø 9D 1A 8F E8 61
871Ø: AD Ø2 9Ø DØ 75 2Ø D8 81 F4
8718: FØ 43 C9 3A FØ 3F C9 3B AØ
872Ø: DØ ØC 2Ø A8 84 AE Ø9 9Ø AA
8728: 8E 1Ø 9Ø 4C 5D 87 8D 94 12
873Ø: 8E AD FB 8F DØ ØD AD 94 15
8738: 8E C9 2Ø DØ D3 2Ø FF 88 B9
874Ø: 4C 1Ø 87 AD 94 8E 99 Ø5 5C
8748: 8E C8 C9 2Ø FØ 18 C9 ØØ 87
875Ø: FØ 14 C9 3A FØ 1Ø 9D 1A D6
8758: 8F E8 4C 1Ø 87 EE Ø2 9Ø 8Ø
876Ø: 8D 95 8E 4C 2E 87 A9 1A 2F
8768: 85 FB A9 8F 85 FC 8C FE 9F
877Ø: 8F 2Ø 95 83 AE EB 8F 2Ø 9E
8778: D7 88 AC FE 8F A9 ØØ A2 EØ
878Ø: Ø5 9D 1A 8F CA DØ FA 4C 91
8788: 1Ø 87 AD FB 8F DØ Ø3 2Ø DC
879Ø: FF 88 AD 95 8E C9 3A FØ D1
8798: Ø3 2Ø C6 85 8D ØB 9Ø EE ØB
87AØ: ØF 9Ø 68 68 AD FB 8F FØ 5C
87A8: Ø8 AD ØD 9Ø FØ Ø3 4C 65 63
87BØ: 7D 4C 8F 7A AD FB 8F C9 71
87B8: Ø2 DØ Ø1 6Ø 2Ø 3Ø 82 A2 8C
87CØ: Ø2 2Ø D3 81 38 AD EB 8F 4B
87C8: E5 FD 8D E9 8F AD EC 8F 37
87DØ: E5 FE 8D EA 8F A9 ØØ 2Ø 36
```

```
87D8: F5 81 AD E9 8F D0 03 CE 2C
87E0: EA 8F CE E9 8F D0 EE AD 0D
87E8: EA 8F D0 E9 20 30 82 A2 73
87F0: 01 20 CF 81 60 38 E9 7F D1
87F8: 8D F4 8F A2 FF CE F4 8F DC
8800: F0 08 E8 BD D0 D0 10 FA 69
8808: 30 F3 E8 BD D0 D0 30 07 58
8810: 99 00 02 C8 4C 0A 88 29 7F
8818: 7F 60 A0 00 A2 00 B9 05 A2
8820: 8E C9 2B F0 04 C8 4C 1E 59
8828: 88 C8 B9 05 8E 20 39 88 27
8830: B0 12 9D F2 8E E8 4C 29 DA
8838: 88 C9 3A B0 06 38 E9 30 67
8840: 38 E9 D0 60 A9 00 9D F2 83
8848: 8E A9 F2 85 FB A9 8E 85 EA
8850: FC 20 95 83 AD EB 8F 8D 9C
8858: 04 90 AD EC 8F 8D 05 90 61
8860: 60 AD FB 8F D0 04 20 FF 5C
8868: 88 60 AD 0D 90 F0 11 20 E6
8870: 30 82 A2 01 20 CF 81 AE 90
8878: E2 8F 20 27 89 20 1E 89 E7
8880: AE E2 8F 20 D7 88 60 AD E4
8888: FB 8F D0 04 20 FF 88 60 48
8890: AD 0D 90 F0 06 AE EB 8F 2F
8898: 20 27 89 AE EB 8F 4C D7 AD
88A0: 88 AD FB 8F D0 07 20 FF BC
88A8: 88 20 FF 88 60 AD 0D 90 F2
88B0: F0 06 AE EB 8F 20 27 89 25
88B8: AE EB 8F 20 D7 88 AD 0D 59
88C0: 90 F0 0E AD 0E 90 F0 03 8A
88C8: 20 1E 89 AE EC 8F 20 27 9A
88D0: 89 AE EC 8F 4C D7 88 8E 4A
88D8: EA 8F AD 0A 90 F0 05 A0 8C
88E0: 00 8A 91 FD AD 08 90 F0 46
88E8: 16 20 30 82 A2 02 20 D3 6C
88F0: 81 AD EA 8F 20 F5 81 20 80
88F8: 30 82 A2 01 20 CF 81 18 82
8900: A9 01 65 FD 85 FD A9 00 2C
8908: 65 FE 85 FE 60 A0 00 B1 65
8910: FB F0 0A 20 F5 81 20 99 30
8918: 89 C8 4C 0F 89 60 A9 20 DD
8920: 20 F5 81 20 99 89 60 8E 35
8928: FD 8F AD 0E 90 F0 0B 8A 9D
8930: 20 51 8A 20 C2 89 AE FD 92
8938: 8F 60 A9 00 20 24 ED 20 ED
8940: C2 89 AE FD 8F 60 AD 0E 34
8948: 90 F0 0E A5 FE 20 51 8A A1
8950: A5 FD 20 51 8A 20 F5 89 19
8958: 60 A6 FD A5 FE 20 24 ED 0E
8960: 20 F5 89 60 A9 0D 20 F5 EF
```

```
8968: 81 20 99 89 60 AE E6 8F 2B
8970: AD E7 8F 20 24 ED 20 2B 8C
8978: 8A 60 A9 05 85 FB A9 8E 6C
8980: 85 FC 20 0D 89 60 A9 07 92
8988: 20 F5 81 A9 12 20 F5 81 72
8990: 20 7A 89 A9 0D 20 F5 81 74
8998: 60 AE FB 8F D0 01 60 AE F9
89A0: 09 90 D0 01 60 8D FC 8F 49
89A8: 20 30 82 A2 04 20 D3 81 1C
89B0: AD FC 8F 20 F5 81 20 30 F3
89B8: 82 A2 01 20 CF 81 AD FC B4
89C0: 8F 60 AE FB 8F D0 01 60 6B
89C8: AE 09 90 D0 01 60 20 30 8E
89D0: 82 A2 04 20 D3 81 AD 0E 5E
89D8: 90 F0 09 AD FD 8F 20 51 2C
89E0: 8A 4C EC 89 A9 00 AE FD 2B
89E8: 8F 20 24 ED 20 30 82 A2 98
89F0: 01 20 CF 81 60 AE FB 8F E3
89F8: D0 01 60 AE 09 90 D0 01 D8
8A00: 60 20 30 82 A2 04 20 D3 B4
8A08: 81 AE 0E 90 F0 0D A5 FE 5A
8A10: 20 51 8A A5 FD 20 51 8A D2
8A18: 4C 22 8A A5 FE A6 FD 20 36
8A20: 24 ED 20 30 82 A2 01 20 8A
8A28: CF 81 60 AE FB 8F D0 01 3D
8A30: 60 AE 09 90 D0 01 60 20 B6
8A38: 30 82 A2 04 20 D3 81 AD 9B
8A40: E7 8F AE E6 8F 20 24 ED A4
8A48: 20 30 82 A2 01 20 CF 81 9D
8A50: 60 48 29 0F A8 B9 F5 8D 63
8A58: AA 68 4A 4A 4A 4A A8 B9 51
8A60: F5 8D 20 F5 81 8A 20 F5 A3
8A68: 81 60 C9 46 D0 08 20 CD A8
8A70: 8A 68 68 4C 8F 7A C9 45 F5
8A78: D0 06 20 26 8B 4C 71 8A D8
8A80: C9 44 D0 03 4C 6F 8B C9 D6
8A88: 50 D0 03 4C D5 8B C9 4E DD
8A90: D0 03 4C 16 8C C9 4F D0 B4
8A98: 03 4C 01 8C C9 53 D0 03 6B
8AA0: 4C AE 8C C9 48 D0 03 4C 8D
8AA8: C8 8C 99 05 8E 20 6D 89 22
8AB0: 20 1E 89 20 46 89 20 86 AF
8AB8: 89 20 7A 89 A9 C8 85 FB F9
8AC0: A9 8F 85 FC 20 0D 89 20 77
8AC8: 64 89 4C E8 8B 20 D8 81 9A
8AD0: C9 20 F0 03 4C CD 8A A0 70
8AD8: 00 20 D8 81 C9 00 F0 0E 67
8AE0: C9 7F 90 03 20 18 85 99 03
8AE8: 05 8E C8 4C D9 8A 84 F9 FD
8AF0: A0 00 B9 05 8E F0 07 99 BD
```

```
8AF8: 07 8F C8 4C F2 8A AD FB 6C
8B00: 8F D0 06 20 46 89 20 1E 8C
8B08: 89 20 7A 89 20 64 89 20 99
8B10: E9 80 A2 01 20 CF 81 20 04
8B18: D8 81 20 D8 81 20 C6 85 2D
8B20: A2 00 8E E8 8F 60 A9 2E 68
8B28: 20 F5 81 A9 45 20 F5 81 AF
8B30: A9 4E 20 F5 81 A9 44 20 6E
8B38: F5 81 A9 20 20 F5 81 20 DD
8B40: D8 81 20 CD 8A AD FB 8F 97
8B48: F0 03 EE E8 8F EE FB 8F C4
8B50: 38 A5 FD ED E4 8F 8D 11 1D
8B58: 90 A5 FE ED E5 8F 8D 12 7A
8B60: 90 AD E4 8F 85 FD AD E5 26
8B68: 8F 85 FE 20 22 84 60 AD 1C
8B70: FB 8F F0 1E 20 D8 81 99 6A
8B78: 05 8E A0 00 20 D8 81 F0 22
8B80: 14 C9 7F 90 03 20 18 85 5B
8B88: 99 05 8E 99 07 8F C8 4C 6D
8B90: 7C 8B 4C E8 8B 84 F9 20 63
8B98: 7A 89 20 64 89 EE 08 90 42
8BA0: 20 00 81 A2 02 20 D3 81 DB
8BA8: AD E4 8F 20 F5 81 AD E5 BA
8BB0: 8F 20 F5 81 AD 11 90 20 61
8BB8: F5 81 AD 12 90 20 F5 81 74
8BC0: 20 30 82 A2 01 20 CF 81 18
8BC8: 20 C6 85 68 68 A2 00 8E 35
8BD0: E8 8F 4C 8F 7A AD FB 8F D4
8BD8: F0 0E 20 0F 81 EE 09 90 4B
8BE0: 20 30 82 A2 01 20 CF 81 38
8BE8: 20 D8 81 F0 07 C9 3A F0 4A
8BF0: 06 4C E8 8B 20 C6 85 68 83
8BF8: 68 A2 00 8E E8 8F 4C 8F 83
8C00: 7A A9 2E 20 F5 81 A9 4F E0
8C08: 20 F5 81 20 64 89 A9 01 7E
8C10: 8D 0A 90 4C E8 8B AD FB 16
8C18: 8F F0 CD 20 D8 81 C9 50 A1
8C20: F0 0C C9 4F F0 3A C9 53 3A
8C28: F0 6A C9 48 F0 4C A9 2E 4C
8C30: 20 F5 81 A9 4E 20 F5 81 02
8C38: A9 50 20 F5 81 20 64 89 7C
8C40: CE 09 90 20 30 82 A2 04 EB
8C48: 20 D3 81 A9 0D 20 F5 81 87
8C50: A9 04 20 49 82 20 30 82 4F
8C58: A2 01 20 CF 81 4C E8 8B 9E
8C60: A9 2E 20 F5 81 A9 4E 20 AC
8C68: F5 81 A9 4F 20 F5 81 20 03
8C70: 64 89 A9 00 8D 0A 90 4C 55
8C78: E8 8B A9 2E 20 F5 81 A9 86
8C80: 4E 20 F5 81 A9 48 20 F5 44
```

```
8C88: 81 20 64 89 A9 00 8D 0E 06
8C90: 90 4C E8 8B A9 2E 20 F5 17
8C98: 81 A9 4E 20 F5 81 A9 53 05
8CA0: 20 F5 81 20 64 89 A9 00 16
8CA8: 8D 0D 90 4C E8 8B A9 2E 99
8CB0: 20 F5 81 A9 53 20 F5 81 AA
8CB8: 20 64 89 AD FB 8F F0 05 0C
8CC0: A9 01 8D 0D 90 4C E8 8B 84
8CC8: A9 2E 20 F5 81 A9 48 20 09
8CD0: F5 81 20 64 89 A9 01 8D 12
8CD8: 0E 90 4C E8 8B 4C 44 41 8C
8CE0: 4C 44 59 4A 53 52 52 54 DD
8CE8: 53 42 43 53 42 45 51 42 E5
8CF0: 43 43 43 4D 50 42 4E 45 27
8CF8: 4C 44 58 4A 4D 50 53 54 9F
8D00: 41 53 54 59 53 54 58 49 96
8D08: 4E 59 44 45 59 44 45 58 3C
8D10: 44 45 43 49 4E 58 49 4E 50
8D18: 43 43 50 59 43 50 58 53 A4
8D20: 42 43 53 45 43 41 44 43 D6
8D28: 43 4C 43 54 41 58 54 41 FA
8D30: 59 54 58 41 54 59 41 50 07
8D38: 48 41 50 4C 41 42 52 4B 99
8D40: 42 4D 49 42 50 4C 41 4E A1
8D48: 44 4F 52 41 45 4F 52 42 06
8D50: 49 54 42 56 43 42 56 53 F5
8D58: 52 4F 4C 52 4F 52 4C 53 CE
8D60: 52 43 4C 44 43 4C 49 41 62
8D68: 53 4C 50 48 50 50 4C 50 7B
8D70: 52 54 49 53 45 44 53 45 4F
8D78: 49 54 53 58 54 58 53 43 2B
8D80: 4C 56 4E 4F 50 01 05 09 AF
8D88: 00 08 08 08 01 08 05 06 5F
8D90: 01 02 02 00 00 00 02 00 F0
8D98: 02 04 04 01 00 01 00 00 4A
8DA0: 00 00 00 00 00 00 08 08 D3
8DA8: 01 01 01 07 08 08 03 03 7E
8DB0: 03 00 00 03 00 00 00 00 7D
8DB8: 00 00 00 00 00 A1 A0 20 BB
8DC0: 60 B0 F0 90 C1 D0 A2 4C 42
8DC8: 81 84 86 C8 88 CA C6 E8 09
8DD0: E6 C0 E0 E1 38 61 18 AA EB
8DD8: A8 8A 98 48 68 00 30 10 36
8DE0: 21 01 41 24 50 70 22 62 22
8DE8: 42 D8 58 02 08 28 40 F8 E0
8DF0: 78 BA 9A B8 EA 30 31 32 82
8DF8: 33 34 35 36 37 38 39 41 13
8E00: 42 43 44 45 46 00 00 00 1E
8E08: 00 00 00 00 00 00 00 00 25
8E10: 00 00 00 00 00 00 00 00 2D
```

```
8E18: ØØ ØØ ØØ ØØ ØØ ØØ ØØ ØØ 35
8E2Ø: ØØ ØØ ØØ ØØ ØØ ØØ ØØ ØØ 3D
8E28: ØØ ØØ ØØ ØØ ØØ ØØ ØØ ØØ 45
8E3Ø: ØØ ØØ ØØ ØØ ØØ ØØ ØØ ØØ 4D
8E38: ØØ ØØ ØØ ØØ ØØ ØØ ØØ ØØ 55
8E4Ø: ØØ ØØ ØØ ØØ ØØ ØØ ØØ ØØ 5D
8E48: ØØ ØØ ØØ ØØ ØØ ØØ ØØ ØØ 65
8E5Ø: ØØ ØØ ØØ ØØ ØØ ØØ ØØ ØØ 6D
8E58: ØØ ØØ ØØ ØØ ØØ ØØ ØØ ØØ 75
8E6Ø: ØØ ØØ ØØ ØØ ØØ ØØ ØØ ØØ 7D
8E68: ØØ ØØ ØØ ØØ ØØ ØØ ØØ ØØ 85
8E7Ø: ØØ ØØ ØØ ØØ ØØ ØØ ØØ ØØ 8D
8E78: ØØ ØØ ØØ ØØ ØØ ØØ ØØ ØØ 95
8E8Ø: ØØ ØØ ØØ ØØ ØØ ØØ ØØ ØØ 9D
8E88: ØØ ØØ ØØ ØØ ØØ ØØ ØØ ØØ A5
8E9Ø: ØØ ØØ ØØ ØØ ØØ ØØ ØØ ØØ AD
8E98: ØØ ØØ ØØ ØØ ØØ ØØ ØØ ØØ B5
8EAØ: ØØ ØØ ØØ ØØ ØØ ØØ ØØ ØØ BD
8EA8: ØØ ØØ ØØ ØØ ØØ ØØ ØØ ØØ C5
8EBØ: ØØ ØØ ØØ ØØ ØØ ØØ ØØ ØØ CD
8EB8: ØØ ØØ ØØ ØØ ØØ ØØ ØØ ØØ D5
8ECØ: ØØ ØØ ØØ ØØ ØØ ØØ ØØ ØØ DD
8EC8: ØØ ØØ ØØ ØØ ØØ ØØ ØØ ØØ E5
8EDØ: ØØ ØØ ØØ ØØ ØØ ØØ ØØ ØØ ED
8ED8: ØØ ØØ ØØ ØØ ØØ ØØ ØØ ØØ F5
8EEØ: ØØ ØØ ØØ ØØ ØØ ØØ ØØ ØØ FD
8EE8: ØØ ØØ ØØ ØØ ØØ ØØ ØØ ØØ Ø6
8EFØ: ØØ ØØ ØØ ØØ ØØ ØØ ØØ ØØ ØE
8EF8: ØØ ØØ ØØ ØØ ØØ ØØ ØØ ØØ 16
8FØØ: ØØ ØØ ØØ ØØ ØØ ØØ ØØ ØØ 1F
8FØ8: ØØ ØØ ØØ ØØ ØØ ØØ ØØ ØØ 27
8F1Ø: ØØ ØØ ØØ ØØ ØØ ØØ ØØ ØØ 2F
8F18: ØØ ØØ ØØ ØØ ØØ ØØ ØØ ØØ 37
8F2Ø: ØØ ØØ ØØ ØØ ØØ ØØ 4E 4F 2B
8F28: 2Ø 53 54 41 52 54 2Ø 41 3Ø
8F3Ø: 44 44 52 45 53 53 ØØ 2D 36
8F38: 2D 2D 2D 2D 2D 2D 2D 2D 57
8F4Ø: 2D 2D 2D 2D 2D 2D 2D 2D 5F
8F48: 2D 2D 2D 2Ø 42 52 41 4E 1D
8F5Ø: 43 48 2Ø 4F 55 54 2Ø 4F A7
8F58: 46 2Ø 52 41 4E 47 45 ØØ 1B
8F6Ø: 55 4E 44 45 46 49 4E 45 D3
8F68: 44 2Ø 4C 41 42 45 4C ØØ ØF
8F7Ø: 1D 1D 1D 1D 1D 1D 1D 1D 8F
8F78: 1D 2Ø 4E 41 4B 45 44 2Ø 24
8F8Ø: 4C 41 42 45 4C ØØ 1D 1D 6C
8F88: 1D 1D 1D 2Ø 3C 3C 3C 3C AA
8F9Ø: 3C 3C 3C 3C 2Ø 44 49 53 2Ø
8F98: 4B 2Ø 45 52 52 4F 52 2Ø C7
8FAØ: 3E 3E 3E 3E 3E 3E 3E 3E BF
```

```
8FA8: 2Ø ØØ 1D 1D 1D 1D 1D 2Ø Ø5
8FBØ: 2D 2D 2Ø 44 55 5Ø 4C 49 C7
8FB8: 43 41 54 45 44 2Ø 4C 41 25
8FCØ: 42 45 4C 2Ø 2D 2D 2Ø ØØ 3C
8FC8: 1D 1D 1D 1D 1D 2Ø 2D 2D 24
8FDØ: 2Ø 53 59 4E 54 41 58 2Ø 5D
8FD8: 45 52 52 4F 52 2Ø 2D 2D Ø9
8FEØ: 2Ø ØØ ØØ ØØ ØØ ØØ ØØ ØØ 1Ø
8FE8: ØØ ØØ ØØ ØØ ØØ ØØ ØØ ØØ Ø8
8FFØ: ØØ ØØ ØØ ØØ ØØ ØØ ØØ ØØ 1Ø
8FF8: ØØ ØØ ØØ ØØ ØØ ØØ ØØ ØØ 18
9ØØØ: ØØ ØØ ØØ ØØ ØØ ØØ ØØ ØØ 21
9ØØ8: ØØ ØØ ØØ ØØ ØØ ØØ ØØ ØØ 29
9Ø1Ø: ØØ ØØ ØØ ØØ ØØ Ø1 ØØ Ø1 36
9Ø18: ØØ ØØ Ø1 Ø6 Ø2 2D 93 ØØ A5
9Ø2Ø: ØØ ØØ 93 ØØ 92 ØØ ØØ Ø1 49
9Ø28: ØØ Ø1 ØØ ØØ Ø1 Ø6 Ø4 8Ø 32
9Ø3Ø: 95 ØØ ØØ 53 95 53 94 ØØ 74
9Ø38: ØØ Ø3 Ø1 ØØ ØØ ØØ ØØ ØØ 3A
9Ø4Ø: ØØ ØØ ØØ ØØ ØØ ØØ 93 ØØ 88
9Ø48: 92 ØØ 91 Ø4 Ø1 ØØ ØØ ØØ 2D
9Ø5Ø: ØØ ØØ ØØ ØØ ØØ ØØ ØØ 53 C4
9Ø58: 95 53 94 53 93 Ø2 ØØ ØØ 85
9Ø6Ø: ØØ ØØ ØØ ØØ ØØ ØØ ØØ ØØ 81
9Ø68: ØØ ØØ 93 ØØ 92 ØØ 91 Ø2 B5
9Ø7Ø: ØØ ØØ ØØ ØØ ØØ ØØ ØØ ØØ 91
9Ø78: ØØ ØØ ØØ 53 95 53 94 53 45
9Ø8Ø: 93 ØØ ØØ ØØ ØØ 7F 7F Ø1 69
```

Appendix C

Modifying LADS

Modifying LADS:
Adding Error Traps, RAM-Based Assembly, and a Disassembler

Imagine how nice it would be if you could add any additional commands to BASIC that you desired. You wouldn't just temporarily wedge the new commands into a frozen ROM BASIC. Instead, you would simply define the new commands, and they would then become a permanent part of your programming language.

This freedom to change a language is called *extensibility*. It's one of the best features of Forth and a few other languages. Extensibility opens up a language. It gives the programmer easy access to all aspects of the programming tool. LADS, too, is extensible since the internals of the assembler, its source code files, are thoroughly commented in this book. You can customize it at will, building in any features that you would find useful.

After exploring the details of the LADS assembler and using LADS to write your own machine language, you may have thought of some features or pseudo-ops that you would like to add. In this chapter, we'll show how to make several different kinds of modifications. These examples, even if they're not features of use to you, will demonstrate how to extend and customize the language. We'll add some new error traps, create a disassembler, and make a fundamental change to LADS—the capability of assembling directly from RAM. With the exception of the disassembler, all these modifications, including RAMLADS, are made the same way regardless of whether you are using the ProDOS or 3.3 operating system.

At the end of this chapter we'll cover the details of the Apple LADS source code where it becomes highly specific to the Apple and, thus, is of particular interest to programmers wishing to accomplish input/output from within ML.

But first, let's see some examples of how to customize LADS.

A Naked Mnemonic Error Trap

The original version of LADS notifies you of most serious errors: branch out of range, duplicated or undefined labels, naked labels (labels without arguments), invalid pseudo-ops, no starting address, file not found on disk, and various syntax errors. Other kinds of errors are forgiven by LADS since it can interpret what you meant to type in your source code. For example, LADS can interpret what you meant when you type errors like this:

100 INY #77; (Adding an argument to a one-byte opcode)

This source code will be correctly assembled. Also, if you forget to leave a space between a mnemonic and its argument (like LDA#15), that sort of error will be trapped and announced. However, to be on the safe side, generally keep your commands right up against colons in this fashion: 100 INY:LDA #15.

However, the original LADS didn't have a built-in trap for naked mnemonics. If you wrote

100 INC:INY:LDA #15; (that "INC" requires an argument)

the assembler would have crashed. No error message, no warning, just a crash.

Programmers who tested the early versions of LADS asked that this error be trapped. That is, if this mistake were made while you were typing in an ML program's source code, it shouldn't cause the assembler to go insane. You might want to make the following two error-trap modifications a permanent part of LADS. To make any changes to LADS, you change the source code, save the source code file, RENAME LADS on the disk (you're creating a new version; you can DELETE the old version later if you wish), check to see that DEFS contains a line 20 .D LADS (LOAD DEFS and check; the .D NAME is necessary to create a disk version of something), and finally type ASM DEFS. LADS will then create a new version of itself which incorporates your changes.

ProDOS users must relocate LADS lower in memory before attempting any modifications. The ProDOS Machine Language Interface Tables must be located at $9100. Inserting additional instructions and assembling may cause these tables to overwrite code when the start address for the tables is defined in line 858 of TABLES. Change line 10 in DEFS to

10 *= $7A00

The ProDOS Loader (Program B-1) must also be modified. Try changing the 31 in line 70 to a 51 to protect more memory.

To expose naked mnemonic errors, a special trap can be inserted into the Eval subprogram:

```
1474 LDA LABEL+3:CMP #32:BEQ GVEG:JMP L700
1480 GVEG LDA LABEL+4,Y
```

After Eval has determined (line 930 of Program D-2a) that the mnemonic under evaluation *does* require an argument (it's not like INY, which uses implied addressing and never has an argument), Eval then goes down to check to see if the argument is a label or a number (line 1460).

Here's where we can check to see if the programmer forgot to give an argument. If the mnemonic is followed by a colon or a zero (end of logical line), that's a sure signal that the argument has been left out. We can load in the character just after the mnemonic (see line 1474, above). If there is a space character (#32), all is well and we can continue (line 1480) with our assembly. If not, we jump to L700, the error-reporting routine which will print the error and ring the bell. Notice that we also have to modify line 1480, giving it a label. That's because we need to perform a branch test in line 1474 and have to invent a label, GVEG, to which to branch.

A Trap for Impossible Instructions

Another programmer who tested LADS was just starting to learn machine language. Unfamiliar with some of the mnemonics and addressing modes, he once tried to assemble a line like this:

100 LDA 15,Y

not knowing that zero page,Y addressing is a rare addressing mode, exclusively reserved for only two mnemonics, LDX and STX. But LADS didn't crash on this. Instead, it assembled an LDA 15,X (the correct addressing mode, but fatal to his particular program since he was trying to use the Y register as an index).

This trap:

```
5280 L760 LDA BUFFER+2,Y:CMP #89:BNE ML760
5282 LDA OP:CMP #182:BEQ ML760
5283 JMP L680
5284 ML760 JMP TWOS
```

was inserted into LADS to make a harmless substitution, to assemble an absolute,Y (at a zero page address). Thus, the programmer's intent is preserved, but the illegal addressing mode is replaced.

By the time Eval reaches this point, it has already filtered out many other possible addressing modes. Eval knows that the addressing mode is some form of ,X or ,Y and that it's zero page. Eval first checks to see if we are dealing with an attempted ,Y addressing mode (CMP #89, the Y character). If not, we continue with the assembly (line 5280) by a BNE to line 5284.

But if it is a ,Y, we check the opcode to see if it is LDX, the only correct opcode for this addressing mode. If so, we continue.

However, if it is some other mnemonic like LDA or STY, this ,Y addressing mode is illegal and we make the adjustment to absolute,Y by a JMP to the area of Eval where that addressing mode is accomplished.

Most illegal addressing will be reported by LADS. Nevertheless, if there's a peculiar error that you often make when programming and LADS doesn't alert you, just add an error-reporting trap or have the assembler automatically correct the problem.

If you want to make LADS also calculate subtraction, make the following changes to the source code and reassemble:

To Eval:

```
870 MX LDA PLUSFLAG:BNE MOWWA:LDA MINUSFLAG
890 MOWWA JSR MATH
```

To Array:

```
1170 BNE ARENW:LDA MINUSFLAG:BEQ AREND
1172 SEC:LDA RESULT:SBC ADDNUM:STA RESULT
1174 LDA RESULT+1:SBC ADDNUM+1:STA RESULT+1:JMP AREND
1180 ARENW CLC
```

To Math:

```
8Ø BEQ MATH2:CMP #45:BEQ MATH2
```

To Indisk:

```
91 STY MINUSFLAG
79Ø BNE COMM:INC PLUSFLAG
8ØØ COMM CMP #171:BNE COMO:INC MINUSFLAG
```

To Tables:

```
721 MINUSFLAG .BYTE Ø;
```

For ProDOS users, there is a special need for permitting <LABEL and >LABEL within the .BYTE pseudo-op. This will allow the programmer to stick in the required information when making calls to the MLI routines. (See the description of this technique at the end of this appendix.) This will make MLI-dependent programs like ProDOS LADS relocatable. Currently, ProDOS LADS freezes the MLI parameter list section of the Tables subprogram by using the *= pseudo-op. After adding label names to that parameter list, you could then refer to the addresses of the parameters by their labels rather than by their actual memory addresses. This, then, would make it no longer necessary to freeze the parameters and, thus, ProDOS LADS could be easily relocated anywhere in memory.

To make the .BYTE pseudo-op recognize and evaluate <LABEL or >LABEL, make the adjustments to the Indisk subprogram shown on page 274.

Remarkably Simple, Yet Radical, Change

Since LADS uses symbols instead of numbers, it's fairly easy to change, to make it what you want it to be. What's more, all the programs you write with LADS will also be symbolic and easily changed. Let's make a radical change to LADS and see how easy it is to profoundly alter the nature of the assembler.

As designed, LADS reads source code off a disk program file. While this is convenient for very large programs like LADS itself, which won't fit all at once in memory, it does slow down assembly. Most of your ML programming will involve writing smaller subprograms, modules you will later link together into a complete program. Any source code which will fit in memory can be more conveniently tested and assembled using the fast RAMLADS we'll create.

```
3425 DEX:STA BUFFER,X:INX
3480 WERK2 LDA #0:STA BUFFER,X:LDA NUBUF; GET 1ST CHAR IN BUFFER
3485 CMP #$3B:BCC WRK2:JMP LAAB; IS IT LESS THAN ASCII FOR <
3489 WRK2 LDA #<NUBUF; POINT TO THE ASCII NUMBER STORED IN BABUF
3580 LDX #7
3590 CLEX STA NUBUF,X:STA BUFFER,X
4410 LAAB CMP #$3C:BEQ LA3:LDA #2:BNE LA4:LA3 LDA #1; IS IT <
4420 LA4 STA BYTFLAG:LDA BUFFER:ORA #$80:STA WORK:JSR ARRAY:LDY Y:JMP REENTER
```

Let's make LADS read its source code from within the computer's RAM memory instead of from disk. This makes two things possible: First, you can change source code, then test it by a simple CALL. Second, tape drive users can use LADS.

This version of LADS isn't functionally different from the normal version since we'll still be reading through the same source files—they'll just reside in RAM rather than on disk. All the pseudo-ops will work the same way, *but do not use .FILE or .END, the disk-linking pseudo-ops. Simply end your source code wherever it ends.*

What's a radical change? You make a radical change whenever you change *= $300 to *= 5000 which puts your object code in an entirely new place in memory. You are making a small change at the beginning, the root, of your source code. But, after making this change, the entire program is assembled at address 5000 instead of address 768. The effect—in the usual sense of the term—is quite radical. The effort on your part, however, is rather minor. Likewise, we can drastically alter the way LADS works by making a few minor changes to the symbols in LADS.

Our goal is to make LADS read source code from memory instead of from disk files. First, we need to add two new pointers to the LADS zero page equates (in the Defs file). We create PMEM. It will serve as a dynamic pointer. It will always keep track of our current position in memory as we assemble source code.

Just for background information, LADS normally relies on the CHARIN routine in line 1040 of the Open1 subprogram to keep track of where we are in a file; whenever we call CHARIN, it increments a pointer so that the next CHARIN call will pull a new byte into A, the accumulator. But we're going to be reading from memory, so we'll need to update our own dynamic pointer. To create this pointer, we'll just type in a new line in the Defs subprogram which can serve as our pointer.

So, LOAD DEFS and add this new line:

157 PMEM = $E2

The other new pointer we need to define in zero page will tell LADS where your BASIC RAM memory starts, where a program in BASIC starts. We type this new line into Defs, too:

135 RAMSTART = $67

Here's what we've added to the Defs subprogram of Apple LADS:

135 RAMSTART = $67; POINTER TO START OF RAM MEMORY
157 PMEM = $E2; OUR DYNAMIC POINTER

One more change to Defs: We want to give our new version of LADS a new name, so change line 20 to read

20 .D RAMLADS

That's all we're changing in Defs, so SAVE DEFS which will replace the old DEFS and we're ready to move on. Now LOAD OPEN1.

A New CHARIN

In the OPEN1 file, we need to remove the CHARIN subroutine itself. As LADS normally runs, it goes to the disk get-a-byte subroutine whenever CHARIN is invoked. This won't work for memory-based source code. BASIC RAM cannot, alas, be OPENed as if it were a file. So, since LADS is peppered with references to CHARIN, we can just undefine CHARIN in the Open1 subprogram by putting a semicolon in front of it. Change line 1040 to read

1040 ;CHARIN STY Y1

Recall that LADS will ignore anything on a line following a semicolon. It's like REM. So, we can eliminate CHARIN by just sticking a semicolon in front of it. Similarly, CHKIN is scattered throughout LADS to reopen file 1, the read-code-from-disk file. We're not using file 1 in this version of LADS, so we add a semicolon to its definition, too. Change line 930 to read

930 ;CHKIN STX OPNI

That's all for Open1, so SAVE OPEN1, replacing the older version on the disk.

Now LOAD GETSA. Throughout LADS there are references to CHARIN and CHKIN. We need to write a new CHARIN and CHKIN to replace the ones we just obliterated. LADS will then have somewhere to go, something to do, as it comes upon CHARINs or CHKINs throughout the code. We do this by adding to the Getsa subprogram. Remove line 210 which would link us to the next file and add lines 220–660 to Getsa as shown in Listing C-1.

Listing C-1

```
220 ; MEMSA REPLACES GETSA
270 MEMSA LDA RAMSTART:STA PMEM:LDA RAMSTART+1:STA PMEM+1
280 LDX #3:MEM1 JSR CHARIN:DEX:BNE MEM1
300 JSR CHARIN:CMP #$2A:BEQ MMSA
310 LDA #<MNOSTART:STA TEMP:LDA #>MNOSTART:STA TEMP+1:JSR PRNTMESS
320 JMP FIN; GO BACK TO BASIC MODE
330 MMSA RTS
350 ; NEW CHARIN
390 CHARIN INC PMEM:BNE INCP1:INC PMEM+1
400 INCP1 STY Y:LDY #0:LDA (PMEM),Y:PHP:LDY Y:PLP:RTS; SAVE STATUS REGISTER
410 CHKIN RTS; REPLACES DISK ROUTINE
660 .FILE VALDEC
```

Then SAVE GETSA.

Line 410 is just an RTS. It's a placebo. We never want to reopen file 1 (CHKIN's normal job), so whenever LADS tries to do that, we JSR/RTS and nothing happens. Something does have to happen with CHARIN, however. CHARIN's job is to fetch the next byte in the source code and give it to the accumulator. So this new version of CHARIN **(390–400)** increments PMEM, our new RAM memory pointer, saves Y, loads the byte, saves the status register, restores Y, restores the status register, and returns. This effectively imitates the actions of the normal disk CHARIN, except it draws upon RAM for source code.

Here you can see one of those rare uses for PHP and PLP. There are times when it's not enough to save the A, Y, and X registers. This is one of those times. INDISK returns to Eval only when it finds a colon (end of source instruction), a semicolon (end of instruction, start of comment), or a zero (end of BASIC program line, hence end of source instruction). When we get a zero when we LDA, the zero flag will be set. But the LDY instruction will reset the zero flag. So, to preserve the effect of LDA on the zero flag, we PHP to store the flags on the stack. Then, after the LDY, we restore the status of the flags, using PLP before we return to the Indisk file. This way, whatever effect the LDA had on the flags will be intact. Indisk can thus expect to find the zero flag properly set if a particular LDA is pulling in the final zero which signifies the end of a line in the BASIC RAM source code.

After making these substitutions to LADS, we need to make three final changes to remove the two references to Open1 (the routine which opens a disk file for source code reading) in the Eval subprogram. These references are at lines 350 and 4360. We can simply remove them from assembly by putting a semicolon in front of them as we did earlier to remove CHARIN and CHKIN. LOAD EVAL and change these lines:

350 ;JSR OPEN1
4360 ;JSR OPEN1

Early in Eval, we have a JSR GETSA. This is the GET-Start-Address-from-disk routine. We want to change this to JSR MEMSA. GETSA isn't needed. MEMSA will perform the same job, but for memory-based source code instead of disk-based source code. (We added the MEMSA routine to the Getsa subprogram already.)

The first thing that MEMSA does is to put the start-of-BASIC-RAM pointer into PMEM (our dynamic pointer). This positions us to the first byte in the source code. Then it pulls off enough bytes to point to the * in the start address definition in the source code. This is just what GETSA does for a disk file. The rest of MEMSA is identical to GETSA.

So, we'll retype line 370:

```
370 SMORE JSR MEMSA
```

And then SAVE EVAL.

Second-Generation LADS

That's it. These few substitutions and LADS will read a source file from RAM memory. You can still use .D NAME to create a disk object code file. You can still send the object code disassembly to a printer with .P. All the other pseudo-ops *(except .FILE and .END which should not be used with RAMLADS)* still work fine. A radical change in ten minutes.

To create a RAMLADS: After you've made the above changes to the source code (and saved them to disk), just load in the normal disk version of LADS (if it's not in the computer already), type ASM DEFS. LADS Sr. will grind out a brand new baby called RAMLADS for you.

As always, when making a new version of your LADS assembler, be sure to direct object code to the disk (use the .D pseudo-op, not the .O) so that you won't overwrite the working LADS in the computer. Also be sure you've given the new version a filename that doesn't already exist on the disk. If you don't get a RAMLADS, or if it doesn't work correctly, you might check to be sure that your disk isn't full.

ProDOS users, change line 60 in Program B-1 to

```
60 PRINT CHR$(4);BRUN RAMLADS
```

Save this loader program with a new name and always use this program to execute RAMLADS.

When testing a new version of LADS, BRUN is preferable to BLOAD for pulling in the new version off the disk. This will protect the LADS Wedge that controls the LADS programming environment.

To use RAMLADS, just BRUN RAMLADS (except for ProDOS users) and type in some source code:

```
10 *= $300
20 .S
30 .O
40 LDA #$C1:STA $0400
50 RTS
```

Then type ASM T (LADS doesn't need any particular filename, but ASM requires an argument, something after the ASM, even if it's only a space). You'll then see how fast RAMLADS works. To try out this little test program (we made it save the resulting ML routine to memory by using the .O pseudo-op), you can just CALL 768 and you'll see the letter *A* in the upper left of the screen.

Using RAMLADS is a very efficient way to create, test, and modify ML programs. As this little example illustrates, you can observe the results, make modifications (change line 40 to use #$C2 if you want to put a letter *B* on the screen), add lines, and so on, and then almost instantly assemble and test the new version. By this process, you can craft your ML modules and, when you're satisfied, save them to disk.

A Disassembler

In a perfectly symmetrical universe, with a right hand for every left, and a north pole for every south, you could transform an assembler into a disassembler by just making it run backward.

Unfortunately, ours is not such a universe. Since LADS turns source code into object code, it would seem possible to tinker with it and adjust it a bit and make it turn object code back into source code, to disassemble. Not so. This one isn't a simple change. We have to link two new files onto LADS to add a disassembler function: Dis and Dtables.

Personal Programming Style

The disassembler in the Apple monitor works well. Adding a disassembler to LADS, however, serves as a good intermediate-level exercise. As it stands, you reassemble LADS with the addition of the DIS and DTABLES files. You should lower the *= starting address of LADS to make room for this new addition. Also, make a note of the address of DIS which will appear on the screen while your new version of LADS is assembling. This address is where you will CALL to activate the disassembler. The version of DIS printed here can be stopped only by hitting CONTROL-S or CONTROL–RESTORE.

DIS is an example of how a fairly complex ML program can be constructed using LADS. The relatively few comments reflect my personal style of programming. I find many of the variable names are meaningful enough to make the code understandable, especially since the purpose of the lookup tables in Dtables is fairly easy to see.

The relatively few comments in the compressed code in DIS also allow you to look at more source code instructions at the same time on the screen. This can help during debugging since you might be able to locate a fault in the overall logic of a program more quickly. Nevertheless, many programmers find such dense code hard to read, hard to debug, and generally inefficient.

Obviously, you should write the kind of source code that works for you. The degree of compression is a matter of programming style and personal preference. Some programming teachers insist on heavy commenting and airy, decompressed coding. Perhaps this emphasis is appropriate for students who are just starting out with computing for the same reasons that penmanship is stressed when students are just starting to learn how to write. But you needn't feel that there is only one programming style. There are many paths, many styles.

How to Use the Disassembler

The disassembler in your Apple monitor is perfectly functional for debugging purposes and, thus, adding this disassembler to LADS is essentially an object lesson in one way of writing fairly advanced ML. In practice, you'll probably do most of your debugging by looking at the source code or printouts of the object code from LADS. Disassembly, because it contains the same information as the source code, but without comments, is a less useful debugging tool. However, if you have a special interest in examining professional ML programs (where you won't have access to the source code), you might want to customize the LADS disassembler to suit your needs. Customizing LADS is an excellent way to increase your ML programming abilities.

For convenience, DIS for 3.3 is set to start at the very end of LADS's Tables subprogram (thus, at the very end of LADS). However, the ProDOS version must not reside in high memory, and so it should be assembled between DEFS and EVAL, at the start of LADS. Also, ProDOS users who want to BRUN DISLADS (the new LADS with the disassembler attached) should include, as the first line in the Dis subprogram, the command JMP SETUP so they will hook LADS into the wedge. To use LADS, they would type ASM as usual. To access the disassembler, they would CALL to the start address of DIS, plus three. In other words, if the DISLADS version were assembled at $7500, the disassembler would be turned on by CALL 29955 ($7503).

The version of the disassembler printed here is fully functional, but you might want to make modifications. As printed, it will ask for the *decimal* start address location in RAM of the object code you want to see listed. Notice that the object code must be residing in RAM to be disassembled. (It would be simple, though, to make a disassembler which operated on disk or tape code.) Then it will disassemble until you hit CONTROL-S or CONTROL–RESTORE. You might want to adjust it—you could have it assemble 20 instructions and then halt until a key was pressed. Or you might want to make it print disassemblies to the printer. Or it could ask for both starting and ending addresses before it begins. To have the disassembler you prefer, just modify the code.

The disassembler demonstrates compressed LADS source code and it also shows how LADS itself can be expanded while borrowing from existing LADS subroutines like STOPKEY and PRNTNUM.

The source code for LADS itself in Appendix D is somewhat artificial: Each line contains only one mnemonic followed by a description, a comment about the purpose of that line. Normally, such extensive commentary will not be necessary, and many lines can contain multiple statements separated by colons. Dis is an example of LADS source code as many programmers will probably write it.

To add the disassembler to 3.3 LADS, change the .END DEFS at the end of the Tables subprogram in LADS to **.FILE DIS.** This will cause the file for DIS to be assembled at the end of LADS. DIS will link to DTABLES, which ends with .END DEFS to permit the second pass through the combined LADS/DIS code. You should also change line 20 in DEFS to give a new name to the new LADS/DIS. Perhaps 20 .D NEWLADS and add line 86 to Defs—**86 PMEM = $E2.**

For the ProDOS version, lower the start of LADS in line 10 of Defs to, say, *= $7500. Then, change the last line in DEFS to .FILE DIS; have the last line of DTABLES read .FILE EVAL; and ASM DEFS. You'll also need to arrange to set aside extra memory for the enlarged ProDOS LADS/DISASSEMBLER you're trying to construct. The easiest way to do this is to change the second number in the DATA statement at the end of the LADS Loader program (Program B-1). Get into BASIC, load Program B-1, make the change, and run. Then you can safely start to assemble a new LADS at a new, lower location. (For more information on the ProDOS LADS Loader program, see the end of Appendix B.)

Keyboard Input

Let's briefly outline the structure and functions of the disassembler. It starts off by printing its prompt message called DISMESS **(30).** The actual message is located in line 710. PRNTMESS is a subroutine within LADS which prints any message pointed to by the variable TEMP.

Then $3F, the ? symbol, is printed and STARTDIS **(50)** sets the hexflag up so that numbers will be printed in hexadecimal. If you prefer decimal, LDA #0 and store it in HXFLAG.

Now there's an input loop to let the user input a decimal start address, character by character. If a carriage return is detected **(90),** we leave the loop to process the number. The number's characters are stored in the LABEL buffer and are also printed to the screen as they are entered **(100).**

When we finish getting the input, the LADS VALDEC routine changes the ASCII numbers into a two-byte integer in the variable RESULT. We pick up the two-byte number and store it in the variable SA which will be printed to the screen as the address of each disassembled mnemonic.

Line 150 is a bit obscure. It wasn't originally written this way, but testing revealed that the JSR GB in line 190 would increment the start address right off the bat (before anything was disassembled or printed). At the same time, putting that increment lower in the main loop was inconvenient. So the easiest thing was to simply accept a start address from the user, then decrement it. The disassembler will start off with a start address that is one lower than the user intends, but that early increment will fix things up. Thus, the variable PMEM will hold a number which is one lower than the variable SA. Both these variables are keeping track of where in memory we are currently disassembling. But we've got to distinguish in this way between SA which prints to the screen and PMEM which tells the computer the current location.

Battling Insects

This is a good place to observe that programming is never a smooth trip from the original concept to the final product. No programmer I've ever encountered is so well-prepared or knowledgeable that he or she simply sits down and calmly creates a workable program. If you find yourself scratching your head, circling around a bug and not trapping it, spending hours or days trying to see what could possibly be wrong—you're in good company. I've worked with some very experienced, very talented people and have yet to see someone fashion a program without snags. And the more sophisticated the program, the more snags it has.

All that can be done, when you hit a snag, is to single-step through the offending area of your program, or set BRK traps, or puzzle over the source code, or try making some tentative reassemblies (not knowing for sure if your changes will have any salutary effect), or sometimes even toss out an entire subroutine and start over.

For example, I wrote the rough draft, the first draft of this disassembler, in about two hours. I didn't have the final version working until I'd spent two full days battling bugs. Some were easy to fix, some were monsters. It took about ten minutes to cure that problem with the start address being one too high. But it took hours to locate an error in the disassembler tables, DTABLES.

After the user has input the start address, TEMP is made to point to the LABEL buffer and VALDEC is invoked. VALDEC leaves the result of an ASCII-to-integer conversion in the RESULT variable. That number is stored in PMEM and SA (140–150). One final adjustment restores SA to the original number input by the user. SA will only print addresses onscreen; PMEM is the real pointer to the current address during disassembly. The decrementing of PMEM, made necessary by that JSR GB early in the main loop, is not necessary for SA. (SA is not incremented by the GB subroutine.)

GETBYTE: The Main Loop

Now we arrive at the main loop. GETBYTE **(190)** first tests to see if the user wants to stop disassembly via the STOPKEY subroutine (in the Eval subprogram within LADS). Then the GB subroutine **(690)** raises the memory pointer PMEM and fetches a byte from memory. This byte is saved in the FILEN buffer and will act as an index, a pointer to the various tables in the Dtables subprogram. For purposes of illustration, let's assume that the byte we picked up held the number 1. One is the opcode for ORA (indirect,X). We can trace through the main loop of DIS and see what happens when DIS picks up a 1.

The 1 is transferred to the Y register **(200),** and we then load whatever value is in MTABLE+1 since we LDA MTABLE,Y and Y holds a 1. This turns out to be the number 2, signifying that we've come upon the second opcode (if the opcodes are arranged in ascending order). Notice that BNE will make us skip over the next couple of lines. Anytime we pull a 0 out of MTABLE it means that there is no valid opcode for that number, and we just print the address, the number, and a question mark ($3F). Then we raise the printout address pointer with INCSA and return to fetch the next byte **(210–220).**

However, in our example, we did find something other than a 0 in MTABLE. We've got a valid opcode. Now we have to find out its addressing mode and print a one- or two-byte argument, depending on that addressing mode. Is it immediate addressing like LDA #15 (one-byte argument) or absolute addressing like LDA 1500 (two-byte argument)?

Having found a valid opcode, we now extract the mnemonic from WORDTABLE and print it out **(240–330).** First, we multiply our number from MTABLE by 3 since each mnemonic has three letters. The number we found in MTABLE was a 2, so we have a 6 after the multiplication. That means that our mnemonic will start in the sixth position within WORDTABLE. We add 6 to the address of WORDTABLE **(280–290)** and leave the variable PARRAY pointing at the first letter *O* in WORDTABLE.

Now the SA (current disassembly address) is printed onscreen with PRNTSA and a space is printed **(300).** We then print ORA onscreen, one letter at a time **(310–330),** and print another space. Now we're ready to figure out the addressing mode.

Addressing Type

We had previously saved our original byte (the number 1 in our example) in FILEN **(190).** We now retrieve it, pull out the position value from MTABLE (getting the number 2), and load in the addressing mode type from TYPETABLE (see lines 360–410 in the Dtables subroutine listing at the end of this chapter). It turns out that the number 2 we're using in our example will pull out a number 4 from TYPETABLE. The number 4 identifies this as an indirect X addressing mode.

Between lines 380 and 410 we have a simple decision structure, much like BASIC's ON-GOTO structure. In our example, the CMP #4 in line 390 will now send us to a routine called DINDX which handles indirect X addressing.

DINDX **(460)** takes advantage of several routines which print symbols to the screen for us: LEPAR prints a left parenthesis; DOONE fetches and prints the next number in RAM memory (the argument for the current mnemonic); COMX prints a comma and an X; and RIPAR finishes things off with a right parenthesis. Now we have something like this onscreen:

0360 ORA (12,X)

so our disassembly of this particular instruction is complete. We JMP to ALLDONE **(600)** and print a carriage return and start the main loop over again to disassemble the next mnemonic.

Other mnemonics and other addressing modes follow a similar path through DIS as they are looked up in Dtables and then printed out.

Special I/O Notes

Finally, here are some general comments about what's Apple-specific in LADS. This will be of interest to those programmers who are planning to write sophisticated software which needs to access the disk.

LADS works on virtually any 6502 computer and there are versions of it for Atari and Commodore computers in my *Second Book of Machine Language*. However, disk access is computer-specific and it's in the Open1 subprogram of LADS where most of the changes need to be made to LADS to translate it to another machine. A similar translation was needed when moving from DOS 3.3 to ProDOS. First, we'll look at DOS 3.3 LADS input/output techniques and then ProDOS.

Program C-1. Dis—The Disassembler

```
10 ; DIS -- DISASSEMBLER
30 LDA #<DISMESS:STA TEMP:LDA #>DISMESS:STA TEMP+1:JSR PRNTMESS
40 JSR PRNTCR:LDA #$3F:JSR PRINT
50 STARTDIS LDA #1:STA HXFLAG:LDY #0:STY Y
60 DTM0 LDA 49168;    -- GET START ADDRESS (DECIMAL)
70 LOOPX LDA 49152:BPL LOOPX
80 CMP #$8D; CARRIAGE RETURN
90 BEQ DMO
100 LDY Y:STA LABEL,Y:JSR PRINT
110 INY:STY Y:JMP DTM0
120 DMO LDX Y:DEX:DEC LABEL,X:LDY Y:LDA #0:STA LABEL,Y:JSR PRNTCR
130 LDA #<LABEL:STA TEMP:LDA #>LABEL:STA TEMP+1:JSR VALDEC
140 LDY RESULT:STY PMEM
150 STY SA:LDA RESULT+1:STA SA+1:STA PMEM+1
160 ; NOW ADJUST PRINTED ADDRESS (SA) UP BY 1 (LOWERED IN LINE 120)
170 INC SA:BNE GETBYTE:INC SA+1
180 ;-------------- PULL IN A BYTE AND SEE IF IT IS A VALID OPCODE
190 GETBYTE JSR STOPKEY:JSR GB:STA FILEN;(SAVE AS INDEX)
200 TAY:LDA MTABLE,Y:BNE DMORE:JSR PRNTSA:JSR PRNTSPACE
210 LDX FILEN:LDA #0:JSR PRNTNUM:JSR PRNTSPACE
220 LDA #$3F:JSR PRINT:JSR INCSA:JMP ALLDONE; NOT A VALID OPCODE
230 ; CONTINUE ON, FOUND A VALID OPCODE-----
240 DMORE STA WORK:LDY #0:STY PARRAY+1:ASL:STA PARRAY:ROL PARRAY+1
250 ;              MULTIPLY Y BY THREE
260 LDA WORK:CLC:ADC PARRAY:STA PARRAY:LDA #0:ADC PARRAY+1:STA PARRAY+1
270 ;              ADD THIS TO WORDTABLE
280 CLC:LDA #<WORDTABLE:ADC PARRAY:STA PARRAY
290 LDA #>WORDTABLE:ADC PARRAY+1:STA PARRAY+1
300 JSR PRNTSA:JSR PRNTSPACE
310 LDY #0:LDA (PARRAY),Y:JSR PRINT:INY
```

```
320 LDA (PARRAY),Y:JSR PRINT:INY
330 LDA (PARRAY),Y:JSR PRINT:JSR PRNTSPACE
340 LDY FILEN:LDA MTABLE,Y; Ø MEANS NO ARGUMENT(INDIRECT OR ACCUMULATOR MODES)
350 TAY:DEY:LDA TYPETABLE,Y:BNE BRANCHES
360 JSR INCSA:JMP ALLDONE
370 BRANCHES LDA TYPETABLE,Y
380 CMP #1:BEQ DIMMED
390 CMP #2:BEQ DABSOL:CMP #3:BEQ DZERO:CMP #4:BEQ DINDX:CMP #5:BEQ DINDY
400 CMP #6:BEQ DZEROX:CMP #7:BEQ DABSOLX:CMP #8:BEQ DABSOLY:CMP #9:BEQ DREL
410 CMP #10:BEQ JDJUMPIND
420 JSR DOONE:JSR COMX:JMP ALLDONE; FALL-THROUGH TO TYPE 11 (ZERO,X)
430 DIMMED LDA #"#:JSR PRINT:JSR DOONE:JMP ALLDONE; IMMEDIATE (TYPE 1)
440 DABSOL JSR DOTWO:JMP ALLDONE:JDJUMPIND JMP DJUMPIND;ABSOLUTE (TYPE 2)
450 DZERO JSR DOONE:JMP ALLDONE; ZERO PG  (TYPE 3)
460 DINDX JSR LEPAR:JSR DOONE:JSR COMX:JSR RIPAR:JMP ALLDONE; IND.X (TYPE 4)
470 DINDY JSR LEPAR:JSR DOONE:JSR RIPAR:JSR COMY:JMP ALLDONE; IND. Y (TYPE 5)
480 DZEROX JSR DOONE:JSR COMX:JMP ALLDONE; ZERO X (TYPE 6)
490 DABSOLX JSR DOTWO:JSR COMX:JMP ALLDONE; ABSOLUTE X (TYPE 7)
500 DABSOLY JSR DOTWO:JSR COMY:JMP ALLDONE; ABSOLUTE Y (TYPE 8)
510 DREL JSR GB:BPL RELPL; RELATIVE (TYPE 8)
520 STA WORK:LDA #$FE:SEC:SBC WORK:STA WORK+1
530 SEC:LDA SA:SBC WORK+1:STA WORK
540 LDA SA+1:SBC #$00:TAX:JSR PRNTNUM
550 LDX WORK:JSR PRNTNUM:JSR INCSA:JSR INCSA:JMP ALLDONE
560 RELPL CLC:ADC SA:ADC #2:STA WORK:LDA #0:ADC SA+1
570 TAX:JSR PRNTNUM
580 LDX WORK:JSR PRNTNUM:JSR INCSA:JSR INCSA:JMP ALLDONE
590 DJUMPIND JSR LEPAR:JSR DOTWO:JSR RIPAR:JMP ALLDONE; IND. JUMP (TYPE 10)
600 ALLDONE JSR PRNTCR:LDX BABFLAG:CPX #1:BCC ALLD1:PLA:PLA:JMP FIN
610 ALLD1 JMP GETBYTE
620 DOONE JSR GB:TAX:LDA #0:JSR PRNTNUM:JSR INCSA:JSR INCSA:RTS
```

```
630 DOTWO JSR GB:PHA:JSR GB:TAX:LDA #Ø
640 JSR PRNTNUM:PLA:TAX:JSR PRNTNUM:JSR INCSA:JSR INCSA:JSR INCSA:RTS
650 COMX LDA #172:JSR PRINT:LDA #216:JSR PRINT:RTS
660 COMY LDA #172:JSR PRINT:LDA #217:JSR PRINT:RTS
670 LEPAR LDA #168:JSR PRINT:RTS
680 RIPAR LDA #169:JSR PRINT:RTS
690 GB INC PMEM:BNE DINCP1:INC PMEM+1;REPLACES CONVENTIONAL CHARIN/DISK
700 DINCP1 STY Y:LDY #Ø:LDA (PMEM),Y:PHP:LDY Y:PLP:RTS; SAVE STATUS REGISTER
710 DISMESS .BYTE "DISASSEMBLY START ADDRESS (DECIMAL)":.BYTE Ø
720 .FILE DTABLES
```

Program C-2. Dtables

```
10 ; "DTABLES"   TABLES FOR DISASSEMBLER
20 ;
30 ;        TABLE OF 256 POSSIBLE VALUES  (SOME ARE VALID ADDRESSING MODES)
40 ;
50 MTABLE .BYTE 1 2 Ø Ø Ø 3 4 Ø 5 6 7 Ø Ø 8 9 Ø
60 .BYTE 1Ø 11 Ø Ø Ø 12 13 Ø 14 15 Ø Ø Ø 16 17 Ø
70 .BYTE 18 19 Ø Ø 2Ø 21 22 Ø 23 24 25 Ø 26 27 28 Ø
80 .BYTE 29 3Ø Ø Ø Ø 31 32 Ø 33 34 Ø Ø Ø 35 36 Ø
90 .BYTE 37 38 Ø Ø Ø 39 4Ø Ø 41 42 43 Ø 44 45 46 Ø
100 .BYTE 47 48 Ø Ø Ø 49 5Ø Ø 51 52 Ø Ø Ø 53 54 Ø
110 .BYTE 55 56 Ø Ø Ø 57 58 Ø 59 6Ø 61 Ø 62 63 64 Ø
120 .BYTE 65 66 Ø Ø Ø 67 68 Ø 69 7Ø Ø Ø Ø 71 72 Ø
130 .BYTE Ø 73 Ø Ø 74 75 76 Ø 77 Ø 78 Ø 79 8Ø 81 Ø
140 .BYTE 82 83 Ø Ø 84 85 86 Ø 87 88 89 Ø Ø 9Ø Ø Ø
150 .BYTE 91 92 93 Ø 94 95 96 Ø 97 98 99 Ø 1ØØ 1Ø1 1Ø2 Ø
160 .BYTE 1Ø3 1Ø4 Ø Ø 1Ø5 1Ø6 1Ø7 Ø 1Ø8 1Ø9 11Ø Ø 111 112 113 Ø
170 .BYTE 114 115 Ø Ø 116 117 118 Ø 119 12Ø 121 Ø 122 123 124 Ø
```

```
180 .BYTE 125 126 Ø Ø Ø 127 128 Ø 129 130 Ø Ø Ø 131 132 Ø
190 .BYTE 133 134 Ø Ø 135 136 137 Ø 138 139 140 Ø 141 142 143 Ø
200 .BYTE 144 145 Ø Ø Ø 146 147 Ø 148 149 Ø Ø Ø 150 151 Ø
210 ;
220 ;            TABLE OF MNEMONICS (TIED TO THE NUMBERS IN TABLE ABOVE)
230 ;
240 WORDTABLE .BYTE "XXXBRKORAORAASLPHPORAASLORAASLBPLORAORAASL
250 .BYTE "CLCORAORAASLJSRANDBITANDROLPLPANDROLBIT
260 .BYTE "ANDROLBMIANDANDROLSECANDANDROLRTIEOR
270 .BYTE "EORLSRPHAEORLSRJMPEORLSRBVCEOREORLSRCLIEOR
280 .BYTE "EORLSRRTSADCADCRORPLAADCRORJMPADCRORBVSADC
290 .BYTE "ADCRORSEIADCADCRORSTASTYSTASTXDEYTXASTYSTA
300 .BYTE "STXBCCSTASTYSTASTXTYASTATXSSTALDYLDALDX
310 .BYTE "LDYLDALDXTAYLDATAXLDYLDALDXBCSLDALDYLDALDX
320 .BYTE "CLVLDATSXLDYLDALDXCPYCMPCPYCMPDECINYCMPDEXCPYCMPDEC
330 .BYTE "BNECMPCMPDECCLDCMPCMPDECCPXSBCCPXSBCINC
340 .BYTE "INXSBCNOPCPXSBCINCBEQSBCSBCINCSEDSBCSBCINC
350 ;
360 ;            TABLE OF MODE TYPES (TIED TO THE NUMBERS IN MTABLE ABOVE)
370 ;
380 ; (TYPE Ø = IMPLIED) (1 = IMMEDIATE) (2 = ABSOLUTE) (3 = ZERO PG.)
390 ; (TYPE 4 = INDIRECT X ) (5 = INDIRECT Y) (6 = ZERO X) (7 = ABSOLUTE X)
400 ; (TYPE 8 = ABSOLUTE Y ) (9 = RELATIVE)
410 ; (TYPE 10 = JMP INDIRECT) (11 = ZERO Y)
420 ;
430 TYPETABLE .BYTE Ø 4 3 3 Ø 1 Ø 2 2 9
440 .BYTE 5 6 6 Ø 8 7 7 2 4 3
450 .BYTE 3 3 Ø 1 Ø 2 2 2 9 5
460 .BYTE 6 6 Ø 8 7 7 Ø 4 3 3
470 .BYTE Ø 1 Ø 2 2 2 9 5 6 6
```

```
480 .BYTE Ø 8 7 7 Ø 4 3 3 Ø 1 Ø 1Ø
490 .BYTE 2 2 9 5 6 6 Ø 8 7 7 4 3 3
500 .BYTE 3 Ø Ø 2 2 2 9 5 6 6
510 .BYTE 11 Ø 8 Ø 7 1 4 1 3 3
520 .BYTE 3 Ø 1 Ø 2 2 2 9 5 6
530 .BYTE 6 11 Ø 8 Ø 7 7 8 1 4
540 .BYTE 3 3 3 Ø 1 Ø 2 2 2 9
550 .BYTE 5 6 6 Ø 8 7 7 1 4 3
560 .BYTE 3 3 Ø 1 Ø 2 2 2 9 5
570 .BYTE 6 6 Ø 8 7 7
580 .END DEFS
```

DOS 3.3

The Apple doesn't have the convenience of Kernal routines to access DOS, so special routines had to be written which could directly access the DOS file manager routines. This takes place in the Open1 subprogram, and is discussed below.

Also, because the Applesoft tokenize routine takes the spaces out of the text, it was necessary (if we wanted LADS source code to be entered by the user in the BASIC format) to put a wedge into Apple's CHRGET routine to intercept the BASIC tokenize routine. Also, the wedge includes a routine that puts the filename of the program you want to assemble to the top of the screen where LADS expects to find it.

Apple Disk Access

The Apple DOS file manager is the part of DOS that handles all file input and output to the disk. It calls RWTS (Read/Write to Track/Sector) and is called from the command interpreter. The command interpreter sends control bytes to the file manager through the file manager parameter list. You can access the file manager directly by sending it the parameters it requires.

To get the address of the parameter field you JSR to $03DC. This loads the accumulator with the high byte and the Y register with the low byte of the parameter field. You can then store these to a zero page location for easy transfer of the parameters.

Table C-1. Apple File Manager Parameter List

	Parameter											
	1	2	3/4	5	6	7	8	9/10	11	13/14	15/16	17/18
OPEN	1	*	*	*	*	*	*	*	*	*		
CLOSE	2								*	*	*	*
DELETE	5			*	*	*	*	*	*	*	*	*
CATALOG	6				*	*			*	*		
LOCK	7			*	*	*	*	*	*	*	*	
UNLOCK	8			*	*	*	*	*	*	*	*	
RENAME	9		*	*	*	*	*	*	*	*	*	
INIT	11	157		*	*	*			*	*		
VERIFY	12			*	*	*	*	*	*	*	*	*

	Parameter									
	1	2	3/4	5/6	7/8	9/10	11	13/14	15/16	17/18
READ 1 Byte	3	1				*	*	*	*	*
READ Range	3	2			*	*	*	*	*	*
POSITION and READ 1 Byte	3	3	*	*		*	*	*	*	*
POSITION and READ Range	3	4	*	*	*	*	*	*	*	*
WRITE 1 Byte	4	1				*	*	*	*	*
WRITE Range	4	2			*	*	*	*	*	*
POSITION and WRITE 1 Byte	4	3	*	*		*	*	*	*	*
POSITION and WRITE Range	4	4	*	*	*	*	*	*	*	*
POSITION	10		*	*			*	*		

Note: The numbers in the leftmost column represent the opcode; the numbers across the top of this chart represent byte positions relative to the start of the parameter list. Asterisks signify that a byte is required for the operation listed. A blank space means that this parameter can be ignored. Nevertheless, the byte positions must be maintained. For example, to DELETE, you do not need to worry about the second, third, or fourth bytes—anything can be in them—but they must exist. The first byte must contain a five, and the fifth through the eighteenth bytes must be set up as described below.

The parameters are expained in sections. The first section tells you about all the opcodes except for the read, write, and positions opcodes, because they are slightly different from the rest. The second section tells you about the read, write, and position opcodes; the third, about the last set of parameters that is common to all opcodes.

The first byte of the parameter field is the opcode type. This parameter can be in the range of 1 to 12.

The second parameter is used only with the INIT opcodes. If you are using a 48K Apple, the correct value for this parameter is 157.

The third and fourth parameters are used with the OPEN and RENAME opcodes. Together they hold the record length of a random access file. If you are not using a random access file, you should have a zero in both of these locations. With the RENAME opcode, these bytes hold the address of the new name.

The fifth byte holds the volume number. The sixth byte holds the drive number. The seventh byte holds the slot number. The eighth byte holds the file type.

The ninth and tenth bytes hold the address of the filename. The filename must be stored in the address pointed to by these bytes. It must be padded with spaces.

This section explains the read, write, and position opcodes.

The first byte holds the opcode. The second byte holds the subcode.

The next four bytes are used only when you require a position command. The third and fourth bytes hold the record number. The fifth and sixth bytes hold the byte offset. To reposition the pointer in an open file, you can use these bytes to calculate a new position. The new position is equal to the length of the file specified in the open opcode times the record number plus the byte offset.

The seventh and eighth bytes hold the length of the range of bytes. This is used only when reading or writing a range.

When reading or writing a range of bytes, the ninth and tenth bytes hold the start address of the range. If you are reading or writing only one byte, then the ninth byte holds the byte you read or the byte you are going to write.

The following are parameters for all the opcodes.

The eleventh byte is the error byte. It should be checked each time after you access the file manager. The errors are as follows:

0: NO ERROR
2: INVALID OPCODE
3: INVALID SUBCODE
4: WRITE PROTECTED
5: END OF DATA
6: FILE NOT FOUND
7: VOLUME MISMATCH
8: I/O ERROR
9: DISK FULL
10: FILE LOCKED

The twelfth byte is unused. The thirteenth and fourteenth bytes are used for the address of the work area buffer. This is a 45-byte buffer in one of the DOS buffers.

The fifteenth and sixteenth bytes hold the address of the track/sector list sector buffer. This is a 256-byte buffer in one of the DOS buffers.

The seventeenth and eighteenth bytes hold the address of the data sector buffer. This is another 256-byte buffer in one of the DOS buffers.

Once you have sent the correct parameters, you can call the file manager by a JSR to $03D6. You must specify if you want to create a new file on disk if the one you are accessing doesn't exist. This is done by loading the X register with a zero. If you don't want to create a new file, you can load the X register with a one. If you don't want to create a new file and you try to access a file that doesn't exist, you will receive an error number 6 in byte 11 of the parameter field.

Apple LADS uses the routines in the file manager that read or write one byte from or to the disk at a time. The general routine to transfer the parameters from Tables to the file manager can be found between lines 810 and 920 in the Open1 listing. This is called from the individual subroutines for opening, closing, reading, and writing. The OPEN routines require a filename. Lines 580–800 handle the transfer of the filename from the filename buffer to the specific buffer.

There is also a check to see whether a file about to be opened has been opened previously. This was needed because you cannot close a file unless it was previously opened. This is handled in the close routine **(370–570).**

The PRINT routine handles all output, and the CHARIN routine handles all input. There is one input and one output channel, and all input and output must be handled through a channel. The bytes which govern this event are set in the CHKIN and CHKOUT routine. The CHKIN routine **(930–940)** sets all input to come from that file. The CHKOUT routine **(950–1030)** sets all output to go to that file. The PRINT routine **(1170–1430)** and the CHARIN routine **(1040–1160)** check to see what channel is currently open, then go to that routine.

The BASIC wedge **(1700–2530)** handles the tokenizing of the BASIC text. It checks to see if the text pointer is at $200 (the input buffer). If not, it goes to the normal GETCHR routine. Otherwise, it checks to see if the first character is a number. If so, it goes to the insert line routine, and if not, it checks for the characters ASM. If that is found, the wedge concludes its work by putting the filename at the top of the screen and jumping to the start of LADS.

The insert line routine gets the line number, then jumps to the Apple tokenize routine, which loads the Y register with the length of the line plus six and then jumps to the normal line insert and tokenize routine.

The last subroutine in Open1 is the first thing that is called when you BRUN LADS. It initializes the wedge and sets HIMEM to the start of LADS.

Special ProDOS Notes

Like the DOS 3.3 operating system, ProDOS maintains a file buffer at the top of free RAM, just above where BASIC stores strings. This is where we want to locate LADS itself—above the ProDOS file buffer, but beneath ProDOS itself. This is accomplished by moving the file buffer downward before loading LADS. On the disk, there is a BASIC program, Program B-1, which POKEs a short ML program into memory. The ML program is CALLed and it causes ProDOS to lower the file buffer location. The ML program loads the accumulator with 31, to request 31 pages of memory (a page is 256 bytes, so we're requesting nearly 8K). Next, this little ML program CALLs the GETBUFR routine located at $BE38, and then we are returned to BASIC mode. Unlike the DOS 3.3 version of LADS, the ProDOS version does not have to change HIMEM (the location in zero page which tells the computer the address of the highest available RAM memory). The GETBUFR routine changes HIMEM for us when it relocates the file buffer location.

All requests for disk operations through ProDOS are made by calling its "Machine Language Interface," (MLI), located at $BF00. MLI is defined as a label in LADS: MLI = $BF00. Then, whenever you JSR MLI, you must follow this instruction (in the source code) with the call number and a pointer to a list of parameters. These three bytes are inserted into the source code itself by using the .BYTE pseudo-op. You will find several examples of this somewhat unusual technique in the source code listings for the Open1 subprogram (Appendix D).

These three bytes are inserted immediately following JSR MLI. While an ML program is running, the MLI itself will adjust the computer's stack so that the RTS instruction (at the end of the MLI subroutine) will correctly return control to six bytes beyond the JSR MLI instruction (this will cause the computer to skip over the three-bytes holding the call number and pointer).

There are a total of 24 MLI calls available; LADS makes use of 9 of them. These calls, and the format of their parameter lists, are thoroughly described in Apple's *ProDOS Technical Reference Manual.*

The first MLI call used by LADS is called ONLINE (call number $C5). This will fetch the volume name of the disk which is currently in the default drive. (That would be the disk most recently accessed prior to assembling.) ProDOS then stores the volume name in a location pointed to by this function's parameter list, called OLINLIST. The volume name is then used when you call SETPREFIX ($C6). SETPREFIX causes that volume to become the default volume for all subsequent disk operations. The parameter list for SETPREFIX is PREFLIST.

To open a disk file, for either reading or writing, LADS first calls OPEN ($C8), using OPENLIST. If the requested file is not located on the disk, a call to CREATE ($C0) using CRELIST will make a new file on the disk. If LADS is opening a "file number 2" (LADS's name for an object code file created by using the .D pseudo-op), LADS must make two more MLI calls. SETEOF ($D0) makes sure that the file is empty by setting its end-of-file pointer to the first byte in the file. Then, a call to SETFILEINFO ($C3) establishes the starting address of the object code, storing it in the file's auxiliary file type. The call to SETEOF uses SEOFLIST as its parameter list. The call to SETFILEINFO uses INFOLIST.

LADS accomplishes its actual file input and output by using the READ and WRITE MLI calls. These calls can transfer any number of bytes, but LADS does all of its I/O one byte at a time. The parameter list for both of these calls is RWLIST. Finally, files are closed by calling CLOSE with CLOSLIST as the parameter list.

Appendix D

LADS Source Code

LADS Source Code

The source code for LADS is divided into 13 sections, each of which accomplishes a particular task for the assembler. The DOS 3.3 version is listed, and any modifications required for ProDOS follow each section. If you are interested in studying or customizing the assembler, here is a brief overview of functions of the various sections:

- **Defs.** All the labels for zero-page pointers and ROM routines used by the assembler are defined here.
- **Eval.** The main routine. Most other sections of the assembler are called from within Eval to perform their various services. Eval starts assembly (line 30) and ends assembly (line 4260). In between, Eval takes each line of source code apart, determining the intended addressing mode.
- **Equate.** Builds the database of labels during the assembler's first pass through the source code.
- **Array.** Searchs through the label database on the second pass and locates a label name and its numeric value.
- **Open1.** Opens communication channels to disk and printer so that source code can be read from disk, and object code stored to disk or sent to printer.
- **Findmn.** A search routine to look through the list of 6502 mnemonics (in Tables below) to find the correct opcode.
- **Getsa.** Locates the start address as the first thing in the source code.
- **Valdec.** Transforms ASCII numerals from the source code into integers. Thus, the *characters* 2 5 become the *number* 25 after Valdec finishes with them.
- **Indisk.** The main input routine. Each line of source code is brought in, analyzed in various ways, and prepared for Eval.
- **Math.** Handles the + pseudo-op.
- **Printops.** Keeps track of our location within the object code and formats screen and printer output in various ways.
- **Pseudo.** Handles all pseudo-ops except + and .BYTE.
- **Tables.** LADS's internal database. Contains lookup tables of mnemonics, opcodes, and addressing-mode categories. Includes flags, pointers, error messages, and registers used by various routines.

Program D-1a. Defs

```
10 *= $79FD
20 .D LADS
30 .NO
40 ;APPLE VERSION
50 ; "DEFS"  EQUATES AND DEFINITIONS
60 ;-------------------------  MACHINE SPECIFIC ZERO PAGE EQUATES -----------
70 BMEMTOP = $4C; BASIC'S TOP OF MEMORY POINTER
80 TXTPTR = $B8; POINTER TO NEXT BYTE OF TEXT
85 FNAMELEN = $F9; LENGTH OF FILE NAME
90 CHRGET = $B1; GET NEXT BYTE OF TEXT
95 PRGEND = $AF; POINTER TO END OF PROGRAM
100 HIGHDS = $94; HIGH DESTINATION OF BLOCK TRANSFER UTILITY (BLTU)
110 VARTAB = $69; VARIABLE TABLE POINTER
130 CURPOS = 36; POSITION OF CURSOR ON A GIVEN SCREEN LINE
140 ;---------------------  LADS INTERNAL ZERO PAGE EQUATES -----------
150 TEMP = $FB:SA = $FD:MEMTOP = $EB:PARRAY = $ED
155 PARM = $2A:FMOP = $2C
160 ;------------------  MACHINE SPECIFIC ROM EQUATES -----------
170 TOBASIC = $3DØ; GO BACK TO BASIC
175 BABUF = $Ø2ØØ; BASIC'S INPUT BUFFER
180 KEYWDS = $DØDØ; START OF KEYWORD TABLE IN BASIC
190 OUTNUM = $ED24; PRINTS OUT A (MSB), X (LSB) NUMBER
200 CSWD = $AA53; ADDRESS OF CHARACTER OUTPUT ROUTINE
210 COUT = $FDFØ; OUTPUT ONE BYTE
240 LINGET = $DAØC; GET LINE NUMBER FROM TXTPTR INTO LINNUM
250 LININS = $D46A; INSERT BASIC LINE INTO BASIC TEXT
280 SCREEN = $Ø4ØØ; ADDRESS OF 1ST BYTE OF SCREEN RAM
640 .FILE EVAL
```

Program D-1b. Defs, ProDOS Changes

```
40 ;APPLE PRODOS VERSION
200 CSWD = $BE30; ADDRESS OF CHARACTER OUTPUT ROUTINE
290 MLI = $BF00 ;PRODOS MACHINE LANGUAGE INTERFACE
```

Program D-2a. Eval

```
10 ; "EVAL"  MAIN EVALUATION ROUTINE (SIMPLE ASSEMBLER)
20 ;---------------------------------------------------------------
25 SETUP JMP EDITSU; START THE WEDGE
30 START LDA #0
40 LDY #50
50 STRTLP STA OP,Y;      -- LOOP TO CLEAR FLAGS --
60 DEY
70 BNE STRTLP; --------
80 LDA #<START; STORE BOTTOM OF LADS INTO TOP OF ARRAY/MEMORY.  PROTECT IT.
90 STA MEMTOP
100 STA BMEMTOP
110 STA ARRAYTOP
120 LDA #>START
130 STA MEMTOP+1
140 STA BMEMTOP+1
150 STA ARRAYTOP+1;--------
160 LDA #1;                -- SET DEFAULTS --
170 ; HERE YOU CAN SET ANY ADDITIONAL DEFAULTS YOU WISH
180 STA HXFLAG; TURN ON HEX LISTING FLAG
190 STM0 LDA SCREEN,Y;                -- GET SOURCE FILE NAME --
200 CMP #$A0
210 BEQ STM1; CHECK FOR ANOTHER BLANK
```

```
250 STM3 STA FILEN,Y; STORE CHARACTER IN FILE NAME BUFFER
260 INY
270 JMP STMØ; GET ANOTHER CHARACTER
280 STM1 STA FILEN,Y; CHECK FOR 2ND BLANK
290 INY
300 LDA SCREEN,Y
310 CMP #$AØ; IF NO SECOND BLANK SPACE
320 BNE STMØ;              THEN GO BACK FOR MORE NAME (MIGHT BE 2 WORDS)
330 DEY
340 STY FNAMELEN;  STORE FILE NAME LENGTH
350 JSR OPEN1; OPEN READ FILE (SOURCE CODE FILE ON DISK)
360 ;-------------------  RE-ENTRY POINT FOR PASS 2 -------
370 SMORE JSR GETSA; POINT DISKFILE TO 1ST CHARACTER IN SOURCE CODE
380 LDA #Ø
390 STA ENDFLAG; SET LADS-IS-OVER FLAG TO DOWN
400 JSR INDISK; GET A SINGLE LINE OF SOURCE CODE
410 LDA PASS; IF 2ND PASS
420 BNE STARTLINE;          THEN JUMP OVER PRINTING OF LADS NAME
430 JSR PRNTCR; PRINT CARRIAGE RETURN
440 LDA #230; PRINT BLOCK GRAPHICS SYMBOL
450 JSR PRINT
460 LDA #76;        L
470 JSR PRINT
480 LDA #65;        A
490 JSR PRINT
500 LDA #68;        D
510 JSR PRINT
520 LDA #83;        S
530 JSR PRINT
540 JSR PRNTCR; ANOTHER CARRIAGE RETURN
550 CKHEX LDA HEXFLAG; IF START ADDRESS NUMBER IS HEX, IT'S ALREADY TRANSLATED
```

```
560 BNE STAR1
570 LDA #<LABEL; IN THE LABEL BUFFER IS SOMETHING LIKE: *= 864
580 STA TEMP; PUT THE ADDRESS OF THE BUFFER INTO THE POINTER CALLED TEMP
590 LDA #>LABEL
600 STA TEMP+1
610 JSR VALDEC; TURN ASCII NUMBER INTO A TWO-BYTE INTEGER IN "RESULT"
620 STAR1 LDA RESULT;     -- STORE OBJECT CODE'S STARTING ADDRESS IN SA,TA --
630 STA SA
640 STA TA
650 LDA RESULT+1
660 STA SA+1
670 STA TA+1
680 ;----------------    ENTRY POINT FOR EACH NEW LINE OF SOURCE CODE  ----
690 STARTLINE JSR STOPKEY:LDA ENDFLAG:BEQ EVIND:JMP FINI; END LADS ASSEMBLY IF
700 ; EITHER THE STOP (BREAK) KEY IS PRESSED OR IF THE ENDFLAG IS UP.
710 ;
720 EVIND JSR INDISK; OTHERWISE GO TO PULL IN A LINE FROM SOURCE CODE
730 LDA #0
740 STA EXPRESSF; SET DOWN THE FLAG THAT SIGNALS A LABEL ARGUMENT LIKE LDA P
750 STA BUFLAG; SET DOWN THE FLAG THAT SIGNALS # OR ( DURING ARRAY CHECK.
760 LDY PASS;ON PASS 1, WE DON'T PRINT LINE NUMBERS, ADDR. OR ANYTHING ELSE
770 BNE MOREEV
780 JMP MOE4
790 MOREEV STY LOCFLAG; ZERO ADDRESS-TYPE LABEL FLAG (LIKE: LABEL INY)
800 ;                   THIS IS FOR THE INLINE SUBROUTINE BELOW.
810 LDA SFLAG; SHOULD WE PRINT TO THE SCREEN
820 BEQ MX; IF NOT, SKIP THIS PART
830 JSR PRNTLINE; PRINT LINE NUMBER
840 JSR PRNTSPACE; PRINT SPACE
850 JSR PRNTSA; PRINT PC (PROGRAM COUNTER)."SA" IS THE VARIABLE.
860 JSR PRNTSPACE
```

```
870 MX LDA PLUSFLAG; DO WE HAVE A + PSEUDO OP
880 BEQ MOE4; IF NOT SKIP
890 JSR MATH; IF SO, HANDLE IT IN SUBPROGRAM "MATH"
900 MOE4 JMP FINDMN; LOOK UP MNEMONIC (OR, NOT FINDING ONE, IT'S A LABEL)
910 ; --------  EVALUATE ARGUMENT
920 EVAR LDA TP
930 BEQ TP1JMP; CHECK TYPE, IF 1, NO ARGUMENT
940 CMP #3; IF NOT TYPE 3, THEN CONTINUE EVALUATION
950 BNE EVGO
960 LDA #1; OTHERWISE, REPLACE 3 WITH 1 IN TP (TYPE)
970 STA TP
980 LDA LABEL+3; IS THERE SOMETHING (NOT A ZERO) IN 4TH POSITION
990 BNE EVGO; EVGO = ARGUMENT (IF NOT, THERE'S NO ARGUMENT,IT'S IMPLIED
1000 LDA #8; OTHERWISE, RAISE OP (OPCODE) BY 8
1010 CLC
1020 ADC OP
1030 STA OP
1040 TP1JMP JMP TP1; AND JUMP TO TYPE 1 (SINGLE BYTE TYPES)
1050 ;-------------------
1060 EQLABEL LDA PASS; MOE4 FOUND IT TO BE A LABEL, NOT A MNEMONIC
1070 BEQ EQLAB1; ON PASS 1 WE DON'T CARE WHICH KIND OF LABEL IT IS SO WE
1080 LDY #255; GO DOWN AND STORE IT IN THE ARRAY (VIA EQLAB1)
1090 EVX1 INY; BUT ON PASS 2, WE NEED TO DECIDE IF IT'S A PC ADDRESS TYPE
1100 LDA LABEL,Y; LABEL (LIKE: LABEL INY) OR AN EQUATE TYPE (LABEL = 15)
1110 BEQ GONOAR; SO IN THIS LOOP WE LOOK FOR A BLANK WHILE STORING THE
1120 STA FILEN,Y; LABEL NAME IN THE "FILEN" BUFFER.  F WE FIND A Ø, IT'S
1130 CMP #32; A NAKED LABEL (NO ARGUMENT TO IT) WHICH CAUSES US TO PRINT
1140 BNE EVX1;OUT THAT ERROR MESSAGE (AT NOAR, IN EQUATE).OTHERWISE, WE FIND A
1150 INY; BLANK AND FALL THROUGH TO THIS LINE.
1160 LDA LABEL,Y; WE RAISE Y BY 1 AND CHECK FOR AN = SIGN.
1170 CMP #$3D
```

```
1180 BNE NOTEQ; IF NOT, IT'S A PC ADDRESS TYPE (SO SET LOCFLAG)
1190 JMP INLINE; IF SO,WAS = TYPE SO IGNORE IT (ON PASS 2) ----------
1200 NOTEQ LDX #0
1210 STX LOCFLAG;(SHOWS PRINTOUT TO DO THIS TYPE OF LABEL ON SCREEN/PRINTER)
1220 TXA; PUT A ZERO IN AT THE END OF THE LABEL NAME (AS A DELIMITER)
1230 STA FILEN,Y; NOW WE HAVE TO MOVE THE ARGUMENT PORTION OF THIS LINE
1240 EVX5 LDA LABEL,Y; OVER TO THE START OF THE "LABEL" BUFFER FOR FURTHER
1250 BEQ EVX4; ANALYSIS (0 DELIMITER HERE)
1260 STA LABEL,X; WE CAN IGNORE THE PC LABEL (THIS IS PASS 2), BUT WE
1270 INX; NEED TO EVALUATE THE REST OF THE LINE FOLLOWING THAT LABEL.
1280 INY
1290 JMP EVX5;-------------------
1300 EVX4 STA LABEL,X
1310 JMP MOE4; JUMP TO CONTINUE EVALUATION
1320 GONOAR JSR NOAR; PRINT NO ARGUMENT MESSAGE (A SPRINGBOARD);----------
1330 EQLAB1 JSR EQUATE; PUT LABEL AND ITS VALUE INTO THE ARRAY (PASS 1)
1340 JMP MOE4; CONTINUE EVALUATION
1350 ;------------------ TRANSLATE ARGUMENT LABELS INTO NUMBERS
1360 EVEXLAB LDA BUFFER; IS THIS 1ST CHARACTER ALPHABETIC (>64)
1370 CMP #64
1380 BCS EVE1; IF SO, GO DOWN TO FIND ITS VALUE.
1390 LDA BUFFER+1; IF NOT, IT MUST HAVE BEEN A ( OR # SYMBOL
1400 INC BUFLAG; TO TELL ARRAY THAT ( OR # WAS FOUND (AND TO IGNORE THEM)
1410 EVE1 EOR #$80; SET 7TH BIT IN 1ST CHAR. (TO MATCH ARRAY STORAGE METHOD)
1420 STA WORK; SAVE IT HERE TEMPORARILY TO COMPARE WITH ARRAY WORDS
1430 JSR ARRAY;  EVAL. EXPRESSION LABEL, SHIFTED 1ST CHAR.
1440 JMP L340; THEN CONTINUE ON WITH EVALUATION (AFTER VALUE IS IN "RESULT")
1450 ;--------------- IS ARGUMENT NUMERIC OR A LABEL
1460 EVGO LDY #0
1470 STY EXPRESSF; TURN OFF THE "IT'S A LABEL" FLAG
1480 LDA LABEL+4,Y; CHECK 5TH CHAR. (LDA NAME OR LDA 25) (THE "N" OR "2")
```

```
1490 CMP #65; IF LESS THAN 65 (ASCII FOR "A") THEN IT'S A NUMBER
1500 BCC EVMO2A
1510 INC EXPRESSF; >65 = ALPHABETIC ARG (LABEL) SO RAISE THIS FLAG
1520 EVMO2A STA BUFFER,Y; STORE 1ST CHAR. OF ARGUMENT IN "BUFFER" BUFFER
1530 INY
1540 LDA LABEL+4,Y; LOOK AT 2ND CHAR. IN THE ARGUMENT
1550 BEQ EVMO3; IF ZERO, WE'RE AT THE END SO MOVE ON
1560 STA BUFFER,Y; OTHERWISE, STORE 2ND CHAR.
1570 CMP #65; IF LOWER THAN 65, DON'T RAISE LABEL-ARGUMENT FLAG
1580 BCC EVMO2
1590 INC EXPRESSF; IF HIGHER, DO RAISE IT
1600 EVMO2 INY; NOW MOVE REST OF ARGUMENT UP TO "BUFFER" BUFFER
1610 LDA LABEL+4,Y; LOOP TO MOVE THE ARGUMENT INTO THE BUFFER
1620 BEQ EVMO3; EVMO3 TAKES OVER AFTER END OF ARGUMENT IS REACHED
1630 STA BUFFER,Y
1640 JMP EVMO2; RETURN FOR MORE ARGUMENT CHARACTERS.
1650 ;----------------
1660 EVMO3 DEY
1670 STY ARGSIZE; REMEMBER NUMBER OF CHARACTERS IN ARGUMENT
1680 LDA HEXFLAG; IF IT'S HEX, INDISK SUBPROGRAM ALREADY TRANSLATED IT FOR US
1690 BNE L340; SO GO ON TO EVALUATE ADDRESS MODE.
1700 LDA EXPRESSF; IF IT'S A LABEL (NOT A NUMBER) THEN GO TO THE ROUTINE
1710 BNE EVEXLAB; WHICH EVALUATES EXPRESSION (ARGUMENT) LABELS, "EVEXLAB"
1720 ; ----------  CALCULATE ARGUMENT'S VALUE (IF IT'S A DECIMAL NUMBER)
1730 LDA #<BUFFER; MAKE "TEMP" POINTER POINT TO "BUFFER"
1740 STA TEMP
1750 LDA #>BUFFER
1760 STA TEMP+1
1770 LDY #0
1780 LDA BUFFER; IS 1ST CHARACTER HIGHER THAN 48 (ASCII FOR THE NUMBER ZERO)
1790 CMP #48
```

```
1800 BCS MCAL; IF SO, SKIP THIS PART
1810 CLC; IF NOT, THE 1ST CHARACTER MUST BE # OR ( ..... SO WE NEED TO
1820 INC TEMP; MAKE "TEMP" POINT 1 CHARACTER HIGHER IN "BUFFER" TO
1830 BCC MCAL; AVOID HAVING THE ASCII TO INTEGER SUBROUTINE THINK THAT THE
1840 INC TEMP+1; NUMBER STARTS WITH A # OR ( --- THAT WOULD MESS THINGS UP.
1850 MCAL LDA (TEMP),Y; NOW LOOK FOR THE END OF THE NUMBER:  -----------
1860 BEQ MCAL1; IT COULD END WITH A 0 (DELIMITER) OR
1870 CMP #41; WITH A ) LEFT PARENTHESIS OR
1880 BEQ MCAL1
1890 CMP #44; WITH A , COMMA (AS IN: 15,Y) OR
1900 BEQ MCAL1
1905 CMP #32; WITH BLANK SPACE (AS IN: #15  ;COMMENT)
1907 BEQ MCAL1
1910 INY; IF WE'VE NOT YET FOUND ONE OF THESE 4 THINGS, CONTINUE LOOKING
1920 JMP MCAL;----------------------------
1930 MCAL1 PHA; SAVE ACCUMULATOR
1940 TYA
1950 PHA;SAVE Y REGISTER(BY NOW, Y IS POINTING AT THE SPACE JUST AFTER THE #)
1960 LDA #0; PUT DELIMITER ZERO INTO BUFFER JUST FOLLOWING NUMBER.
1970 STA (TEMP),Y
1980 JSR VALDEC;GO TO THE ASCII-NUMBER-TO-INTEGER-NUMBER-IN-"RESULT" ROUTINE
1990 PLA; RESTORE THE A AND Y REGISTERS
2000 TAY
2010 PLA
2020 STA (TEMP),Y; RESTORE A "," OR ")" TO THE BUFFER (FOR THE ADDR. ANALYSIS)
2030 ;---------------  ANALYZE THE ARGUMENT TO DETERMINE ADDRESSING MODE
2040 ; (THIS ESSENTIALLY AMOUNTS TO MODIFYING THE ORIGINAL OPCODE TO
2050 ;  REFLECT THE CORRECT ADDRESSING MODE.  ADJUSTMENTS TO THE OPCODE "OP"
2060 ;  APPEAR FROM HERE ON RATHER FREQUENTLY.  THEIR LOGIC WILL NOT BE
2070 ;  EXPLAINED.  DDING 4,8,16, OR 24 TO AN "OP" IS BASED ON THEIR
2080 ;  RELATIONSHIPS WITHIN THE OPCODE TABLE).
```

```
2Ø9Ø ;
21ØØ L34Ø LDA BUFFER; 1ST CHAR. OF THE ARGUMENT (THE "#" IN LDA #15)
211Ø CMP #35
212Ø BEQ JIMMED; # SYMBOL FOUND (SO IMMEDIATE MODE).  BRANCH TO SPRINGBOARD
213Ø CMP #4Ø; IS IT A "(" LEFT PARENTHESIS.  IF SO, GO TO INDIRECT ADDR.
214Ø BEQ INDIR
215Ø LDA TP; IS IT A RELATIVE ADDR. MODE (LIKE BNE, BEQ).
216Ø CMP #8
217Ø BEQ REL; IF SO, GO TO WHERE THEY ARE HANDLED.
218Ø CMP #3; ADD 8 TO OP AT THIS POINT IF IT'S A TYPE 3
219Ø BNE EVMO5
22ØØ LDA #8
221Ø CLC
222Ø ADC OP
223Ø STA OP
224Ø JMP TP1; AND JUMP TO THE SINGLE BYTE TYPES (IMPLIED ADDRESSING)
225Ø INDIR LDY ARGSIZE; HANDLE INDIRECT ADDRESSING-------------------
226Ø LDA BUFFER,Y; LOOK AT THE LAST CHARACTER IN THE ARGUMENT.
227Ø CMP #41; IS IT A ")" LEFT PARENTHESIS
228Ø BEQ MINDIR; IF SO, HANDLE THAT TYPE.
229Ø LDA TP
23ØØ CMP #1; IF TYPE 1, ADD 16 AT THIS POINT TO OPCODE
231Ø BNE MINDIR
232Ø LDA #16
233Ø CLC
234Ø ADC OP
235Ø STA OP
236Ø MINDIR LDA TP; TYPE 6 IS A JUMP INSTRUCTION
237Ø CMP #6
238Ø BEQ JJUMP; SO GO TO THE JUMP-HANDLING ROUTINE
239Ø JMP TWOS; OTHERWISE, IT MUST BE A 2-BYTE TYPE SO PRINT/POKE IT.;-------
```

```
2400 JIMMED JMP IMMED; SPRINGBOARD TO IMMEDIATE MODE TYPES.
2410 ;------------------------------- HANDLE RELATIVE ADDRESS (BNE) TYPES
2420 REL LDA PASS; ON PASS 1, DON'T BOTHER, JUST INCREASE PC BY 2
2430 BNE MREL
2440 JMP TWOS
2450 MREL SEC; ON PASS 2, SUBTRACT PC FROM ARGUMENT TO GET REL. BRANCH
2460 LDA RESULT
2470 SBC SA
2480 PHA; SAVE LOW BYTE ANSWER
2490 LDA RESULT+1
2500 SBC SA+1
2510 BCS FOR; IF ARGUMENT > CURRENT PC, THEN IT'S A BRANCH FORWARD
2540 CMP #$FF
2550 BEQ MPXS
2560 PLA
2570 JMP DOBERR
2580 MPXS PLA; OTHERWISE, CHECK FOR OUT OF RANGE BRANCH ATTEMPT
2590 BPL BERR; OUT OF RANGE (PRINT ERROR MESSAGE "BERR")
2600 JMP RELM; AND JUMP TO REL CONCLUSION ROUTINE
2610 FOR BEQ MPXS1; CHECK FORWARD BRANCH OUT OF RANGE
2620 PLA
2630 JMP DOBERR
2640 MPXS1 PLA
2650 BPL RELM; WITHIN RANGE----------------
2660 BERR JMP DOBERR; PRINT "BRANCH OUT OF RANGE" ERROR MESSAGE
2670 RELM SEC
2690 SBC #2; CORRECT FOR THE FACT THAT BRANCHES ARE CALCULATED FROM THE
2700 STA RESULT; INSTRUCTION FOLLOWING THEM:  BNE LOOP:LDA 15 WOULD BE
2710 LDA #0;     CALCULATED FROM THE PC OF THE LDA 15
2720 STA RESULT+1
2730 JMP TWOS; NOW GO TO THE 2-BYTE PRINT/POKE (WITH CORRECT ARGUMENT)
```

```
2740 ;------------------------------ CONTINUE ADDR. MODE ANALYSIS
2750 EVMO5 LDY ARGSIZE
2760 DEY
2770 LDA BUFFER,Y; LOOK AT LAST CHARACTER OF ARGUMENT
2780 CMP #44; IF IT'S NOT A COMMA, THEN THIS MUST BE A JUMP INSTRUCTION
2790 BNE JJUMP; SO GO TO THE JUMP-HANDLING ROUTINE
2800 INY
2810 JMP XYTYPE; OTHERWISE, IT MUST BE A ,X OR ,Y TYPE;--------------
2820 JJUMP LDA OP; HANDLE JMP MNEMONIC
2830 CMP #76; IF THE OPCODE ISN'T 76, IT'S NOT A JUMP
2840 BNE MEV; SO LOOK FOR SOMETHING ELSE
2850 JMP JUMP; NOW SPRINGBOARD TO THE JUMP-HANDLING ROUTINE.----------
2860 MEV LDA RESULT+1; IF HIGH BYTE OF RESULT ISN'T ZERO (ZERO PG. ADDR)
2870 BNE PREPTHREES; THEN GO TO THE 3-BYTE INSTRUCTIONS (LINE 400)
2880 LDA TP; OTHERWISE, IT'S ZERO PAGE MODE
2885 CMP #9:BEQ PREPTHREES
2890 CMP #6; IF HIGHER THAN TYPE 6, IT'S AN ORDINARY 2-BYTE TYPE
2900 BCS TWOS; SO GO THERE.
2910 CMP #2; IF TYPE 2, ALSO GO THERE.
2920 BEQ TWOS
2930 LDA #4; OTHERWISE, ADD 4 TO OPCODE AND FALL THROUGH INTO TWO-BYTE TYPE
2940 CLC
2950 ADC OP
2960 STA OP
2970 ;------------------------------  2 BYTE TYPES (LIKE LDA 12)
2980 TWOS JSR FORMAT; PRINT/POKE OPCODE
2990 JSR PRINT2; THEN PRINT/POKE ARGUMENT
3000 JMP INLINE; AND FINALLY PREPARE TO FETCH NEW LINE OF SOURCECODE (2000)
3010 ;------------------------------  HANDLE JMP
3020 JUMP LDY ARGSIZE; IS IT JMP 1500 OR JMP (1500)
3030 LDA BUFFER,Y; A ")" AT THE END PROVES IT'S AN INDIRECT JUMP SO
```

```
3040 CMP #41
3050 BNE JUMO
3060 LDA #108;          WE MUST CHANGE THE OPCODE FROM 76 TO 108
3070 STA OP
3080 JUMO JMP THREES; TREAT IT AS A NORMAL 3-BYTE INSTRUCTION
3090 ;-------------------------------- IMMEDIATE ADDRESSING (# TYPE)
3100 IMMED LDA BUFFER+1
3110 CMP #""; IS THIS A CHARACTER LOAD PSEUDO-OP LIKE: LDA #"A
3120 BNE IMMEDX
3130 LDA BUFFER+2; IF SO, PUT THE ASCII CHAR. INTO "RESULT" (ARGUMENT)
3140 STA RESULT
3150 IMMEDX LDA TP
3160 CMP #1
3170 BNE TWOS; IF IT'S TYPE 1, ADJUST OPCODE BY ADDING 8 TO IT.
3180 LDA #8
3190 CLC:ADC OP:STA OP
3200 JMP TWOS
3210 ;-------------------------------- 1 BYTE TYPES
3220 TP1 JSR FORMAT; JUST POKE OPCODE FOR THESE, THERE'S NO ARGUMENT
3230 JMP INLINE; (LINE 1000)
3240 ;-------------------------------- 3 BYTE TYPES
3250 PREPTHREES LDA TP; SEVERAL OPCODE ADJUSTMENTS (BASED ON TYPE)
3260 CMP #2
3270 BEQ PTT
3280 CMP #7; (LINE 430)
3290 BNE PT1
3300 PTT LDA OP
3310 CLC
3320 ADC #8
3330 STA OP
3340 JMP THREES
```

```
3350 PT1 CMP #6
3360 BCS THREES
3370 LDA OP
3380 CLC
3390 ADC #12
3400 STA OP
3410 THREES JSR FORMAT; PRINT/POKE OPCODE
3420 JSR PRINT3; PRINT/POKE 2 BYTES OF THE ARGUMENT   (3000)
3430 ;------------------------------------- PREPARE TO GET A NEW LINE
3440 ;PRINT MAIN INPUT AND COMMENTS, THEN TO STARTLINE
3450 INLINE LDA PASS; ON PASS 1, IGNORE THIS WHOLE PRINTOUT THING.
3460 BNE NLOX1
3470 JMP JST
3480 NLOX1 LDA SFLAG; LIKEWISE, IF SCREENFLAG IS DOWN, IGNORE.
3490 BNE NLOX
3500 JMP JST
3510 NLOX LDA LOCFLAG; ANY PC ADDRESS LABEL TO PRINT
3520 BNE PRMMX1; NO LOC TO PRINT (RVS FLAG USAGE, FOR SPEED)
3530 LDA PRINTFLAG; PRINT TO PRINTER
3540 BEQ PRMM
3550 LDA #20
3560 SEC
3570 SBC CURPOS; SUBTRACT CURRENT CURSOR POSITION
3580 STA A; MOVE THE CURSOR TO 20TH COLUMN ON THE SCREEN
3590 JSR CLRCHN; PREPARE PRINTER TO PRINT BLANKS
3600 LDX #4
3610 JSR CHKOUT
3620 LDY A
3630 BPL PRXM1
3640 LDY #2
3650 JMP PRMLOP
```

```
3660 PRXM1 LDA #32
3670 PRMLOP JSR PRINT;---------------- PRINT BLANKS TO PRINTER
3680 DEY
3690 BNE PRMLOP; PRINT MORE BLANKS TO PRINTER;---------------
3700 JSR CLRCHN; RESTORE NORMAL I/O
3710 LDX #1
3720 JSR CHKIN
3730 PRMM LDA #20; PUT 20 INTO CURRENT SCREEN CURSOR POSITION
3740 STA CURPOS
3750 LDA #<FILEN; POINT "TEMP" TO PC ADDRESS LABEL FOR PRINTOUT
3760 STA TEMP
3770 LDA #>FILEN
3780 STA TEMP+1
3790 JSR PRNTMESS; PRINT LOCATION LABEL;----------
3800 PRMMX1 LDA #30; MOVE CURSOR TO 30TH COLUMN
3810 SEC
3820 SBC CURPOS
3830 STA X; SAVE OFFSET FROM CURRENT POSITION (30-POSITION) FOR PRINTER
3860 LDA PRINTFLAG; DO WE NEED TO PRINT BLANKS TO THE PRINTER
3870 BEQ PRMMFIN
3880 JSR CLRCHN; ALERT PRINTER TO RECEIVE BLANKS
3890 LDX #4
3900 JSR CHKOUT
3910 LDY X
3920 BEQ PXMX; HANDLE NO BLANKS (IGNORE)
3930 BMI PXMX; HANDLE TOO MANY BLANKS (>127) (IGNORE)
3940 LDA #32
3950 PRMLOPX JSR PRINT; PRINT BLANKS TO PRINTER FOR FORMATTING--------
3960 DEY
3970 BNE PRMLOPX; PRINT MORE BLANKS----------
3980 PXMX JSR CLRCHN; RESTORE NORMAL I/O
```

```
3990 LDX #1
4000 JSR CHKIN;-------------------------------------------------
4003 PRMMFIN LDA #30
4006 STA CURPOS; SET SCREEN CURSOR POSITION TO 30
4010 JSR PRNTINPUT; PRINT MAIN INPUT BUFFER (BULK OF SOURCE LINE)
4020 LDA BYTFLAG; IS THERE A < OR > PSEUDO-OP TO PRINT --------------
4030 BEQ PRXM; HANDLE < AND >
4040 CMP #1; 1 IN BYTFLAG MEANS <
4050 BNE MO5
4060 LDA #60
4070 JMP PRMO
4080 MO5 LDA #62; PRINT >
4090 PRMO JSR PRINT
4100 JSR PTP1; PRINT > OR <.  PTP1 IS TO PRINTER----------
4110 PRXM LDA BABFLAG; IS THERE ANY COMMENT TO PRINT (SOMETHING FOLLOWING ;)
4120 BEQ RETTX; IF NOT, SKIP THIS.
4130 JSR PRNTSPACE; PRINT A SPACE--------PRINT COMMENTS FIELD----------
4140 LDA #59; PRINT A SEMICOLON
4150 JSR PRINT
4160 LDA #<BABUF; POINT "TEMP" TO THE COMMENTS BUFFER "BABUF"
4170 STA TEMP
4180 LDA #>BABUF
4190 STA TEMP+1
4200 JSR PRNTMESS; PRINT WHAT'S IN THE COMMENTS BUFFER
4210 RETTX JSR PRNTCR; PRINT CARRIAGE RETURN
4220 LDA ENDFLAG; IF ENDFLAG IS UP, JUMP TO THE SHUTDOWN ROUTINE
4230 BNE FINI
4240 JST JMP STARTLINE; OTHERWISE GO BACK UP TO GET THE NEXT SOURCE LINE.
4250 ;------------------------------- THE END OF A PASS (1 OR 2)
4260 FINI LDA PASS
4270 BNE FIN; IF IT'S PASS 2, SHUT EVERYTHING DOWN.
```

```
4280 INC PASS; OTHERWISE, CHANGE PASS 1 TO PASS TWO (IN THE FLAG)
4282 SEC; SAVE THE LENGTH OF THE CODE
4283 LDA SA; FOR THE THIRD AND FOURTH
4284 SBC TA; BYTES OF THE BINARY
4285 STA LENPTR; FILE CREATED BY THE
4286 LDA SA+1; .D PSEUDOP
4287 SBC TA+1
4288 STA LENPTR+1
4290 LDA TA; PUT THE ORIGINAL START ADDR. INTO THE PC PROGRAM COUNTER (SA)
4300 STA SA
4310 LDA TA+1
4320 STA SA+1
4330 JSR CLRCHN; RESTORE ORDINARY I/O CONDITIONS
4340 LDA #1
4350 JSR CLOSE; CLOSE INPUT FILE
4360 JSR OPEN1; OPEN INPUT FILE (POINT IT TO THE 1ST BYTE IN THE FILE)
4370 JMP SMORE; PASS 1 FINISHED, START PASS 2 (ENTRY POINT FOR PASS 2)------
4380 ;
4390 ;------------------- SHUT DOWN LADS OPERATIONS AND RETURN TO BASIC ------
4400 FIN JSR CLRCHN; RESTORE NORMAL I/O
4410 LDA #1
4420 JSR CLOSE; CLOSE SOURCE CODE INPUT FILE
4430 LDA #2
4440 JSR CLOSE; CLOSE OBJECT CODE OUTPUT FILE (IF ANY)
4450 LDA PRINTFLAG; IS THE PRINTER ACTIVE
4460 BEQ FINFIN; IF NOT, JUST RETURN TO BASIC
4470 JSR CLRCHN; OTHERWISE SHUT DOWN PRINTER, GRACEFULLY.
4480 LDX #4
4490 JSR CHKOUT
4500 LDA #13;        BY PRINTING A CARRIAGE RETURN
4510 JSR PRINT
```

```
4520 JSR CLRCHN
4530 LDA #4
4540 JSR CLOSE
4550 FINFIN JMP TOBASIC; RETURN TO BASIC
4560 ;
4570 ;------------------------------------  ,X OR ,Y ADDRESSING TYPE
4580 XYTYPE LDA BUFFER,Y; LOOK AT LAST CHAR. IN ARGUMENT
4590 CMP #88; IS IT AN X
4600 BEQ L720
4610 DEY; OTHERWISE, LOOK AT THE 3RD CHAR. FROM END OF ARGUMENT
4620 DEY
4630 LDA BUFFER,Y; IS IT A ")" LEFT PARENTHESIS
4640 CMP #41
4650 BNE ZEROY; IF NOT, IT'S NOT AN INDIRECT ADDR. MODE
4660 JMP INDIR; IF SO, IT IS AN INDIRECT ADDRESSING MODE
4670 ZEROY LDA RESULT+1; CHECK HIGH BYTE OF RESULT (ZERO PG. OR NOT)
4680 BNE L680; ZERO Y TYPE
4690 LDA TP; ADJUST OPCODE BASED ON TYPE
4700 CMP #2
4710 BEQ L730
4720 CMP #5
4730 BEQ L730
4740 CMP #1
4750 BEQ L760
4760 L680 LDA TP
4770 CMP #1
4780 BNE L690
4790 LDA OP
4800 CLC
4810 ADC #24
4820 STA OP
```

```
4830 JMP THREES
4840 L690 LDA TP
4850 CMP #5
4860 BEQ M6
4870 LDA #$31
4880 JSR P
4890 JMP L700
4900 M6 LDA OP
4910 CLC
4920 ADC #28
4930 STA OP
4940 JMP THREES
4950 ;----------- PRINT A SYNTAX ERROR MESSAGE ------------------
4960 L700 JSR ERRING; RING ERROR BELL AND TURN ON REVERSE CHARACTERS
4970 JSR PRNTLINE; PRINT LINE NUMBER
4980 LDA #<MERROR; POINT "TEMP" TO SYNTAX ERROR MESSAGE
4990 STA TEMP
5000 LDA #>MERROR
5010 STA TEMP+1
5020 JSR PRNTMESS; PRINT THE MESSAGE
5030 JMP INLINE; GO TO THE GET-THE-NEXT-LINE ROUTINE
5040 ;------------------------------- CONTINUE ANALYSIS OF ADDR. MODE
5050 L720 LDA RESULT+1; MAKE FURTHER ADJUSTMENTS TO OPCODE
5060 BNE L780; NOT ZERO PAGE
5070 L730 LDA TP
5080 CMP #2
5090 BNE L740
5100 LDA #16
5110 CLC
5120 ADC OP
5130 STA OP
```

```
5140 JMP TWOS
5150 L740 CMP #1
5160 BEQ L759
5170 CMP #3
5180 BEQ L759
5190 CMP #5
5200 BEQ L759
5210 L750 LDA #$32
5220 JSR P
5230 JMP L700
5240 L759 LDA #20
5250 CLC
5260 ADC OP
5270 STA OP
5280 L760 JMP TWOS
5290 L780 LDA TP
5300 CMP #2
5310 BNE L790
5320 LDA #24
5330 CLC
5340 ADC OP
5350 STA OP
5360 JMP THREES
5370 L790 CMP #1
5380 BEQ L809
5390 CMP #3
5400 BEQ L809
5410 CMP #5
5420 BEQ L809
5430 L800 LDA #$33
5440 JSR P
```

```
5450 JMP L700
5460 L809 LDA #28
5470 CLC
5480 ADC OP
5490 STA OP
5500 JMP THREES;    END OF ADDR. MODE EVALUATIONS AND ADJUSTMENTS
5510 ;
5520 ;-------------------- ERROR REPORTING FOR DEBUGGING (PRINTS PC)
5530 P STA A; WHEN YOU INSERT A "JSR P" INTO YOUR SOURCE CODE, THIS ROUTINE
5540 STY Y; WILL PRINT THE PC FROM WHICH YOU JSR'ED.
5550 STX X;  AFTER AN RTS, THIS WILL REVEAL THE JSR ADDR.
5560 LDA #$BA; PRINT A GRAPHICS SYMBOL TO SIGNAL THAT THE PC IS TO FOLLOW
5570 JSR PRINT
5580 PLA; SAVE THE RTS ADDRESS (TO KEEP THE STACK INTACT)
5590 TAX
5600 PLA
5610 TAY
5620 TYA
5630 PHA
5640 TXA
5650 PHA
5660 TYA
5670 JSR OUTNUM; PRINT THE PC ADDRESS.
5680 LDA A; RESTORE THE REGISTERS.
5690 LDY Y
5700 LDX X
5710 RTS
5720 ;--------------------------
5730 CLEANLAB LDY #0; FILLS MAIN INPUT BUFFER ("LABEL") WITH ZERO. CLEANS IT.
5740 TYA
5750 CLEMORE STA LABEL,Y
```

```
5760 INY
5770 CPY #255
5780 BNE CLEMORE
5790 RTS
5800 ;---------------------------
5810 DOBERR JSR PRNTCR; PRINT "BRANCH OUT OF RANGE" ERROR MESSAGE
5820 JSR ERRING
5830 JSR PRNTLINE; PRINT THE LINE NUMBER
5840 LDA #<MBOR; POINT "TEMP" TO THE ERROR MESSAGE "MBOR"
5850 STA TEMP; (MESSAGE BRANCH OUT OF RANGE, MBOR)
5860 LDA #>MBOR
5870 STA TEMP+1
5880 JSR PRNTMESS; PRINT THE MESSAGE
5890 JSR PRNTCR; PRINT A CARRIAGE RETURN AND
5900 JMP TWOS; BUNGLE AS AN ORDINARY 2-BYTE EVENT (TO KEEP PC CORRECT)
5910 ;------------------
5920 .FILE EQUATE
```

Program D-2b. Eval, ProDOS Changes

```
DELETE THE FOLLOWING LINES FROM
PROGRAM D-2A:
280 TO 330
4282 TO 4288
AND REPLACE LINE 340 WITH:
340 STM1 STY FNAMELEN; STORE FILE NAME LENGTH
```

Program D-3. Equate

```
10 ; "EQUATE"  EVALUATE LABEL OF EQUATE TYPE
20 ; COULD BE PC (ADDRESS) TYPE OR EQUATE TYPE.  STORE IN ARRAY.
25 ; NAME/2-BYTE INTEGER VALUE/NAME/2-BYTE VALUE/ETC...
30 ;-------------
40 EQUATE LDY #255; PREPARE Y TO ZERO AT START OF LOOP
50 EQ1 INY; Y GOES TO ZERO 1ST TIME THRU LOOP
60 LDA LABEL,Y; LOOK AT THE WORD, THE LABEL
70 BEQ NOAR; END OF LINE (SO THERE'S A NAKED LABEL, NOTHING FOLLOWS IT)
80 CMP #32; FOUND A SPACE, SO RAISE Y BY 2 AND SET LABEL SIZE (LABSIZE)
90 BNE EQ1; OTHERWISE, KEEP LOOKING FOR A SPACE.
100 INY
110 INY
120 STY LABSIZE
130 ;-------------------- LOWER MEMTOP POINTER WITHIN ARRAY (BY LABEL SIZE)
140 SUBMEM SEC; SUBTRACT LABEL SIZE FROM ARRAY POINTER TO MAKE ROOM FOR LABEL
150 LDA MEMTOP
160 SBC LABSIZE
170 STA MEMTOP
180 LDA MEMTOP+1
190 SBC #0
200 STA MEMTOP+1;--------------
205 ;SHIFT 7TH BIT OF 1ST CHAR. TO SIGNIFY START OF LABEL'S NAME
210 LDY #0
220 LDA LABEL,Y
230 EOR #$80
240 STA (MEMTOP),Y; STORE SHIFTED 1ST LETTER
250 EQ3 INY
260 LDA LABEL,Y; IF SPACE, STOP STORING LABEL NAME IN ARRAY.
270 CMP #32
```

```
280 BEQ EQ2
290 STA (MEMTOP),Y; OTHERWISE, PUT NEXT LETTER INTO ARRAY &
300 JMP EQ3; CONTINUE.
310 EQ2 INY; NOW CHECK FOR = (SIGNIFYING EQUATE TYPE) (LABEL = 15)
320 LDA LABEL,Y
330 CMP #$3D; IF EQUATE TYPE, GO TO FIND ITS VALUE.
340 BEQ EQUAL
350 DEY; OTHERWISE, IT'S PC TYPE (LABEL LDA 15)
360 LDA SA; SO THE PC VARIABLE (SA) CONTAINS THE VALUE OF THIS LABEL
370 STA (MEMTOP),Y; STORE IT RIGHT AFTER LABEL NAME WITHIN ARRAY.
380 INY
390 LDA SA+1
400 STA (MEMTOP),Y
410 LDX LABSIZE; NOW, USING LABELSIZE AS INDEX, ERASE THE PC-TYPE LABEL
420 DEX;          FROM THE BUFFER.  FOR EXAMPLE, (LABEL LDA 15) NOW
430 LDY #0;       BECOMES (LDA 15).  THE LABEL NAME IS COVERED OVER
440 EQ5 LDA LABEL,X; TO PREPARE THE REST OF THE LINE TO BE ANALYZED
450 BEQ EQ4; NORMALLY BY EVAL.
460 STA LABEL,Y
470 INX
480 INY
490 JMP EQ5
500 EQ4 STA LABEL,Y
510 RTS; RETURN TO EVAL -------------------------
520 NOAR JSR ERRING; NAKED LABEL FOUND (NO ARGUMENT) SO RING BELL &
530 LDA #<NOARG; AND PRINT NAKED LABEL ERROR MESSAGE.
540 STA TEMP
550 LDA #>NOARG
560 STA TEMP+1
570 JSR PRNTMESS
580 JMP EQRET; RETURN TO EVAL-----------------------
```

```
584 ;
585 ;---------------- HANDLE EQUATE TYPES HERE (LABEL = 15)
590 EQUAL DEY
600 STY LABPTR; TELLS US HOW FAR FROM MEMTOP WE SHOULD STORE ARGUMENT VALUE
610 LDA HEXFLAG; HEX NUMBERS ALREADY HANDLED BY INDISK ROUTINE, SO SKIP OVER.
620 BNE FINEQ; HEX FLAG UP, SO GO TO EQUATE EXIT ROUTINE BELOW.
630 INY; OTHERWISE, WE NEED TO FIGURE OUT THE ARGUMENT (LABEL = 15)
640 INY; THERE ARE THREE CHARS. ( = ) BETWEEN LABEL & ARGUMENT, SO
650 INY; INY THRICE.
660 STY WORK+1; POINT TO LOCATION OF ASCII NUMBER (IN LABEL BUFFER)
670 LDA #<LABEL; SET UP TEMP POINTER TO POINT TO ASCII NUMBER
680 CLC
690 ADC WORK+1
700 STA TEMP
710 LDA #>LABEL
720 ADC #0
730 STA TEMP+1
740 JSR VALDEC; CALCULATE ASCII NUMBER VALUE AND STORE IN RESULT
750 FINEQ LDY LABPTR; STORE INTEGER VALUE JUST AFTER LABEL NAME IN ARRAY
760 LDA RESULT
770 STA (MEMTOP),Y
780 LDA RESULT+1
790 INY
800 STA (MEMTOP),Y
810 EQRET PLA;PULL OFF THE RTS (FROM EVAL) AND JUMP DIRECTLY TO INLINE
820 PLA;       IGNORING ANY FURTHER EVALUATION OF THIS LINE SINCE EQUATE TYPE
830 JMP INLINE; LABELS ARE FOLLOWED BY NOTHING TO EVALUATE
840 .FILE ARRAY
```

Program D-4. Array

```
10 ; "ARRAY" LOOKS THROUGH LABEL TABLE AND PUTS VALUE IN RESULT.
20 ;  (USED IN BOTH PASS 1 AND PASS 2)
30 ARRAY LDA ARRAYTOP;PUT TOP-OF-ARRAY VALUE INTO THE DYNAMIC POINTER (PARRAY)
40 STA PARRAY; IN OTHER WORDS, MAKE PARRAY POINT TO THE HIGHEST WORD IN THE
50 LDA ARRAYTOP+1; LABELS ARRAY
60 STA PARRAY+1
70 JSR DECPAR
80 LDA #$FF; SET UP FOR BMI TEST IF NO MATCH FOUND
90 STA FOUNDFLAG
100 STARTLK SEC; START LOOKING FOR LABEL NAME
110 LDA MEMTOP; CHECK TO SEE IF WE'RE AT THE BOTTOM OF THE ARRAY
120 SBC PARRAY
130 LDA MEMTOP+1
140 SBC PARRAY+1
150 BCS ADONE; IF SO, CHECK IF WE FOUND THE LABEL (OR FOUND IT TWICE)
160 LDX #0; SET LABEL NAME SIZE COUNTER TO ZERO
170 SEC; GO DOWN 2 BYTES IN MEMORY (PAST THE INTEGER VALUE OF A LABEL)
180 LDA PARRAY
190 SBC #2
200 STA PARRAY
210 LDA PARRAY+1
220 SBC #0
230 STA PARRAY+1
240 LDY #0
250 ;---------------------------
260 LPAR LDA (PARRAY),Y; LOOK FOR A 7TH BIT SET (START OF LABEL NAME)
270 BMI FOUNDONE; IF YES, WE'VE GOT TO THE START OF A NAME.
280 LDA PARRAY; OTHERWISE GO DOWN 1 BYTE IN ARRAY
290 BNE MDECX
```

```
300 DEC PARRAY+1
310 MDECX DEC PARRAY
320 INX; INCREASE LABEL NAME SIZE COUNTER
330 JMP LPAR
340 ;------------------------
350 FOUNDONE LDA PARRAY; WE'VE LOCATED A LABEL NAME IN THE ARRAY
360 STA PT; REMEMBER ITS STARTING LOCATION
370 LDA PARRAY+1
380 STA PT+1
390 LDA (PARRAY),Y
400 CMP WORK; COMPARE THE 1ST LETTER WITH THE 1ST LETTER OF THE TARGET WORD
410 BEQ LKMORE; LOOK MORE CLOSELY AT THE WORD, IF 1ST LETTER MATCHED
420 JMP STARTOVER; IF IT DIDN'T MATCH, GO DOWN IN THE TABLE & FIND NEXT WORD.
430 ;----------------------------
440 LKMORE INX; RAISE LENGTH COUNTER BY 1
450 STX WORK+1; REMEMBER IT
460 LDX #1
470 LDA BUFLAG;THIS MEANS THAT # OR ( COME BEFORE THE NAME IN THE BUFFER
480 BEQ LKM1; IF THEY DON'T WE DON'T NEED TO RAISE Y IN ORDER TO IGNORE THEM
490 INY
500 JSR DECPAR; LOWER THE INDEX TO COMPENSATE FOR THE INY
510 ;
520 LKM1 INY
530 LDA BUFFER,Y; CHECK BUFFER-HELD LABEL
540 BEQ FOUNDIT; IF WE'RE AT THE END OF THE WORD (0), THEN WE'VE FOUND A MATCH
550 CMP #48; OR THERE'S A MATCH IF IT'S A CHARACTER LOWER THAN ASCII 0 (,OR+)
560 BCC FOUNDIT
570 ; NOT YET THE END OF THE "BUFFER" HELD LABEL
580 INX
590 CMP (PARRAY),Y; IF ARRAY WORD STILL AGREES WITH BUFFER WORD, THEN
600 BEQ LKM1; CONTINUE LOOKING AT THESE WORDS
```

```
610 ;---------------------------  NO MATCH, SO LOOK AT NEXT WORD DOWN -----
620 STARTOVER LDA PT; PUT PREVIOUS WORD'S START ADDR. INTO POINTER
630 STA PARRAY
640 LDA PT+1
650 STA PARRAY+1
660 JSR DECPAR; LOWER POINTER BY 1 (STARTLK WILL LOWER IT ALSO, BELOW VALUE)
670 JMP STARTLK; TRY ANOTHER WORD IN THE ARRAY
680 ;-----------------------
690 ADONE LDA FOUNDFLAG
700 BMI AD1; DIDN'T FIND THE LABEL
710 RTS; ALL IS WELL.  RETURN TO EVAL.
720 AD1 LDA PASS
730 BNE AD1X; 2ND PASS-- GO AHEAD AND PRINT ERROR MESSAGE
740 BEQ ADONE1; ON 1ST PASS, MIGHT NOT YET BE DEFINED (RAISE INCSA/2S OR 3S)
750 AD1X JSR ERRING; LABEL NOT IN TABLE.  (TREAT IT AS A 2-BYTE ADDRESS)
760 JSR PRNTLINE
770 JSR PRNTSPACE
780 LDA #<NOLAB
790 STA TEMP
800 LDA #>NOLAB
810 STA TEMP+1
820 JSR PRNTMESS; RING BELL AND PRINT NOT FOUND MESSAGE
830 JSR PRNTCR
840 ADONE1 PLA
850 PLA;
860 LDA OP
870 AND #31
880 CMP #16
890 BEQ ADO2; CHECK IF BRANCH INSTRUCT.
900 LDA BYTFLAG
910 BNE ADO2; < OR > PSEUDO
```

```
920 JMP THREES
930 ADO2 JMP TWOS
940 ;
950 FOUNDIT CPX WORK+1;CHECK LABEL LENGTH AGAINST TARGET WORD LENGTH
960 BEQ FOUNDF; THEY MUST EQUAL TO SIGNIFY A MATCH. (PRINT/PRIN WOULD FAIL)
970 JMP STARTOVER; FAILED MATCH
980 FOUNDF INC FOUNDFLAG; RAISE FLAG TO ZERO (FIRST MATCH)
990 BEQ FOFX; IF HIGHER THAN 0, PRINT DUPLICATION LABEL ERROR MESSAGE
1000 JSR DUPLAB
1010 FOFX LDY WORK+1
1020 LDA BUFLAG; COMPENSATE FOR # AND (
1030 BEQ FOF
1040 INY
1050 FOF LDA (PARRAY),Y; PUT TABLE LABEL'S VALUE IN RESULT
1060 STA RESULT
1070 INY
1080 LDA (PARRAY),Y
1090 STA RESULT+1
1100 LDA BYTFLAG
1110 BEQ CMPMO; IS IT > OR < PSEUDOPRINT
1120 CMP #2
1130 BNE AREND
1140 LDA RESULT+1; STORE HIGH BYTE INTO LOW BYTE
1150 STA RESULT
1160 CMPMO LDA PLUSFLAG; DO ADDITION + PSEUDO OP
1170 BEQ AREND
1180 CLC; ADD THE + NUMBER "ADDNUM" TO RESULT
1190 LDA ADDNUM
1200 ADC RESULT
1210 STA RESULT
1220 LDA ADDNUM+1
```

```
123Ø ADC RESULT+1
124Ø STA RESULT+1
125Ø AREND LDA PASS; ON 2ND PASS, DON'T CHECK FOR DUPS
126Ø BEQ ARENX
127Ø RTS; GO BACK TO EVAL
128Ø ARENX JMP STARTOVER; ON PASS 1, LOOK FOR DUPS (SO CONTINUE IN ARRAY)
129Ø ;------------------------------
13ØØ DECPAR LDA PARRAY; LOWER ARRAY POINTER BY 1
131Ø BNE MDEC
132Ø DEC PARRAY+1
133Ø MDEC DEC PARRAY
134Ø RTS
135Ø ; -----------------
136Ø DUPLAB JSR ERRING; RING BELL AND PRINT DUP LABEL MESSAGE
137Ø LDA #<MDUPLAB
138Ø STA TEMP
139Ø LDA #>MDUPLAB
14ØØ STA TEMP+1
141Ø JSR PRNTMESS
142Ø JSR PRNTCR
143Ø RTS;
144Ø .FILE OPEN1
```

Program D-5a. Open1, 3.3 Version

```
5 ;OPEN INPUT FILE
1Ø OPEN1 JSR CLRCHN
2Ø LDA #1; CLOSE FILE IF ALREADY OPEN
3Ø JSR CLOSE
4Ø LDA #<OPNREAD
```

```
50 STA FMOP
60 LDA #>OPNREAD
70 STA FMOP+1
80 JSR FMDRVR0
90 INC FOPEN1; SET INPUT FILE TO OPEN
100 RTS
105 ; OPEN OUTPUT FILE
110 OPEN2 LDA #<OPNWRIT
120 STA FMOP
130 LDA #>OPNWRIT
140 STA FMOP+1
150 JSR FMDRVR0
160 INC FOPEN2; SET OUTPUT FILE OPEN
170 RTS
175 OPEN4 LDA #0; SETUP CARD IN SLOT1
176 LDX $36; SAVING OLD OUTPUT LINK
177 STA $36
178 LDA #$C1
179 LDY $37
180 STA $37
181 LDA #$8A:JSR $FDED; SEND LINE FEED
182 LDA #$50:STA $579; SET LINE LEN TO 80 COLUMNS
183 LDA $36
184 STA PBYTE+1; SET PRINTING ADDRESS
185 STX $36; RESET OUTPUT LINK
186 STY $37
187 RTS
188 ; READ ONE BYTE FROM INPUT FILE
190 RDBYTE LDA #<RD1B
200 STA FMOP
210 LDA #>RD1B
```

```
220 STA FMOP+1
230 JSR FMDRVR
240 JSR $3DC
250 STA PARM+1
260 STY PARM
270 LDY #08
280 LDA (PARM),Y; GET THE BYTE
290 RTS
295 ; WRITE ONE BYTE TO OUTPUT FILE
300 WRBYTE STA WRDATA
310 LDA #<WR1B
320 STA FMOP
330 LDA #>WR1B
340 STA FMOP+1
350 JSR FMDRVR
360 RTS
365 ; CLOSE INPUT FILE
370 CLOSE1 LDA FOPEN1; CHECK TO SEE IF INPUT FILE IS OPEN
380 BEQ NOCLOSE; IF NOT EXIT
390 LDA #<CLOSER
400 STA FMOP
410 LDA #>CLOSER
420 STA FMOP+1
430 JSR FMDRVR
440 LDA #0
450 STA FOPEN1; SET INPUT FILE TO CLOSED
460 NOCLOSE RTS
465 ; CLOSE OUTPUT FILE
470 CLOSE2 LDA FOPEN2; CHECK TO SEE IF OUTPUT FILE IS OPEN
480 BEQ NOCLOSE; IF NOT EXIT
490 LDA #<CLOSEW
```

```
500 STA FMOP
510 LDA #>CLOSEW
520 STA FMOP+1
530 JSR FMDRVR
540 LDA #0
550 STA FOPEN2; SET OUTPUT FILE TO CLOSED
560 RTS
570 CLOSE4 LDA #<COUT
572 STA CSWD; RESTORE NORMAL SCREEN OUTPUT
574 LDA #>COUT
576 STA CSWD+1
578 RTS
580 FMDRVR0 LDY #08; PUT FILENAME INTO PARAMETER FIELD
590 LDA (FMOP),Y
600 STA PARM
610 INY
620 LDA (FMOP),Y
630 STA PARM+1
640 LDA #<FILEN
650 STA TEMP
660 LDA #>FILEN
670 STA TEMP+1
680 LDY #00
690 LDA #$A0
700 PADFN STA (PARM),Y; FIRST FILL WITH SPACES
710 INY
720 CPY #31
730 BNE PADFN
740 LDY #00
750 FM0 LDA (TEMP),Y; THEN PUT FILENAME IN PARM
760 ORA #$80; MAKE SURE HIGH BIT SET
```

```
770 STA (PARM),Y
780 INY
790 CPY FNAMELEN
800 BNE FMØ
810 FMDRVR JSR $3DC; GET START ADDRESS TO PARAMETER FIELD
820 STA PARM+1
830 STY PARM
840 LDY #ØØ
850 PARMSU LDA (FMOP),Y; PUT PARMS INTO PARM
860 STA (PARM),Y
870 INY
880 CPY #18
890 BNE PARMSU
900 LDX #ØØ
910 JSR $3D6; JSR TO FILE MANAGER IN DOS
920 RTS
925 ; SET CURRENT INPUT CHANNEL
930 CHKIN STX OPNI
940 RTS
945 ; SET CURRENT OUTPUT CHANNEL
950 CHKOUT TXA
960 STA OPNO
1030 CHKOUTO RTS
1035 ; GET ONE BYTE FROM CURRENTLY OPEN CHANNEL
1040 CHARIN STY Y1
1050 STX X; SAVE X & Y REG
1060 LDA OPNI; CHECK TO SEE IF INPUT CHANNEL
1070 CMP #1
1080 BNE CTOUT; IF NOT EXIT
1090 JSR RDBYTE
1100 PHP
```

```
1110 LDY Y1
1120 LDX X
1130 PLP
1140 RTS
1150 CTOUT LDY Y1
1160 RTS
1165 ; OUTPUT ONE BYTE TO CURRENTLY OPEN CHANNEL
1170 PRINT STY Y1; SAVE REG
1180 STA A1
1190 LDA OPNO; CHECK TO SEE IF TO OUTPUT FILE
1200 CMP #02
1210 BNE NXT1
1220 LDA A1; YES, WRITE THE BYTE
1230 JSR WRBYTE
1240 JMP CTOUT
1340 NXT1 LDA OPNO; CHECK TO SEE IF TO PRINTER
1350 CMP #4
1360 BNE NXT2
1370 LDA A1; YES, PRINT TO PRINTER
1375 ORA #$80
1380 PBYTE JSR $C100; LOBYTE GETS MODIFIED BY OPEN4
1390 JMP CTOUT
1400 NXT2 LDA PRINTFLAG; NO, MUST BE TO SCREEN
1402 BNE RPRINTING; CARD DOES IT FOR US IF WE'RE PRINTING
1404 LDA A1
1410 ORA #$80
1420 JSR COUT
1425 RPRINTING LDA A1; RESTORE ACCUM
1430 JMP CTOUT
1435 ; CLOSE ALL INPUT AND OUTPUT CHANNELS
1440 CLRCHN LDA #00
```

```
1450 STA OPNO
1460 STA OPNI
1470 LDA #<PRINT; RESET OUTPUT ROUTINE
1480 STA CSWD
1490 LDA #>PRINT
1500 STA CSWD+1
1510 RTS
1515 ;CHECK FOR STOP KEY
1520 STOPKEY LDA $C000
1530 CMP #$83
1540 RTS
1545 ; CLOSE OPEN FILES
1550 CLOSE CMP #01
1560 BNE CL2; CLOSE INPUT FILE?
1570 JMP CLOSE1
1580 CL2 CMP #02; NO, CLOSE OUTPUT FILE?
1590 BNE CL4
1600 JMP CLOSE2
1610 CL4 JMP CLOSE4; NO, MUST BE PRINTER
1700 ; BASIC WEDGE
1710 WEDGE STA A1
1720 LDA #$00; IS TXTPTR AT $200?
1730 CMP TXTPTR
1740 BNE OUT
1750 LDA #02
1760 CMP TXTPTR+1
1770 BNE OUT; NO, EXIT
1775 LDY #0
1780 NXTCHR LDA (TXTPTR),Y; IGNORE LEADING SPACES
1781 CMP #32
1782 BNE ISLNUM
```

```
1783 INC TXTPTR
1784 JMP NXTCHR
1790 ISLNUM CMP #$2F; IS IT A NUMBER?
1800 BCC OUT; NO, EXIT
1810 CMP #$3A
1820 BCC INSLIN
1830 OUT LDA $200; IS IT "ASM "?
1840 CMP #65
1850 BNE OUT1
1860 LDA $201
1870 CMP #83
1880 BNE OUT1
1890 LDA $202
1900 CMP #77
1910 BNE OUT1
1920 LDA $203
1930 CMP #32
1940 BNE OUT1; NO, EXIT
1950 LDY #0; YES
1960 TFRNAM LDA $204,Y; TRANSFER NAME TO TOP OF SCREEN
1970 CMP #0
1980 BEQ ASM
1990 ORA #$80
2000 STA $400,Y
2010 INY
2020 JMP TFRNAM
2030 ASM LDA #$A0; PUT FOLLOWING 3 SPACES
2040 STA $400,Y
2050 STA $401,Y
2060 STA $402,Y
2070 PLA; PULL RETURN ADDRESS AND JUMP TO START
```

```
2080 PLA
2090 JMP START
2100 OUT1 LDA A1; NORMAL CHRGET
2110 CMP #$3A
2120 BCS EXIT
2130 CMP #$20
2140 BNE NXT
2150 JMP CHRGET
2160 NXT SEC
2170 SBC #$30
2180 SEC
2190 SBC #$D0
2200 EXIT RTS
2210 INSLIN LDX PRGEND; FOUND LINE NUMBER, NOW INSERT LINE
2220 STX VARTAB
2230 LDX PRGEND+1
2240 STX VARTAB+1
2250 CLC
2260 JSR LINGET; GET LINE NUMBER
2270 JSR TOKNIZ
2280 PLA
2290 PLA
2300 JMP LININS; JUMP TO NORMAL INSERT LINE AND RESET LINE LINK ADDRESSES
2310 TOKNIZ LDY #00; TOKENIZE LINE
2320 STY HIGHDS
2330 LDA #02
2340 STA HIGHDS+1
2350 TK3 LDA (TXTPTR),Y
2360 STA (HIGHDS),Y
2370 INY
2380 CMP #00; END OF LINE
```

```
2390 BNE TK3
2400 DEY; YES
2410 TK4 DEY
2420 LDA (HIGHDS),Y; IGNORE FOLLOWING SPACES
2430 CMP #32
2440 BEQ TK4
2450 INY
2460 LDA #0
2470 STA (HIGHDS),Y
2480 INY
2490 INY
2500 INY
2510 INY
2520 INY; Y-REG HOLDS LINE LENGTH +6
2530 RTS
2540 EDITSU LDA #<WEDGE; INITIALIZE WEDGE
2550 STA $BB
2560 LDA #>WEDGE
2570 STA $BC
2580 LDA #$4C; "JMP"
2590 STA $BA
2592 LDA #$FC:STA 115; SET HIMEM
2595 LDA #$79:STA 116
2600 RTS
2610 .FILE FINDMN
```

Program D-5b. Open1, ProDOS Version

```
5 ;OPEN INPUT FILE
10 OPEN1 JSR CLRCHN
20 LDA #1; CLOSE FILE IF ALREADY OPEN
30 JSR CLOSE
40 LDA #$92; BUFFER1 AT $9200
50 JSR OPENFILE
60 STA FOPEN1
100 RTS
105 ; OPEN OUTPUT FILE
110 OPEN2 LDA #$96; BUFFER2 AT $9600
120 JSR OPENFILE
130 STA FOPEN2
140 STA SEOFLIST+1
150 JSR MLI ;ERASE OLD CONTENTS
160 ;.BYTE $D0 <SEOFLIST >SEOFLIST
165 .BYTE 208 20 145
166 LDA TA
167 STA INFOLIST+5
168 LDA TA+1
169 STA INFOLIST+6
170 JSR MLI; PUT START ADDRESS IN AUX FILE TYPE
171 ;.BYTE $C3 <INFOLIST >INFOLIST
172 .BYTE 195 33 145
173 RTS
175 OPEN4 LDA #0; SETUP CARD IN SLOT1
176 LDX $36; SAVE OLD OUTPUT LINK
177 STA $36
178 LDA #$C1
179 LDY $37
```

```
180 STA $37
181 LDA #$8A:JSR $FDED; SEND LINE FEED
182 LDA #$50:STA $579; SET LINE LEN TO 80 COLUMNS
183 LDA $36
184 STA PBYTE+1; SET PRINTING ADDRESS
185 STX $36; RESTORE OUTPUT LINK
186 STY $37
187 RTS
188 ; READ ONE BYTE FROM INPUT FILE
190 RDBYTE LDA FOPEN1
200 STA RWLIST+1
210 JSR MLI
220 ;.BYTE $CA <RWLIST >RWLIST
225 .BYTE 202 25 145
230 LDA DATABUFF
240 RTS
295 ; WRITE ONE BYTE TO OUTPUT FILE
300 WRBYTE STA DATABUFF
310 LDA FOPEN2
320 STA RWLIST+1
330 JSR MLI
340 ;.BYTE $CB <RWLIST >RWLIST
345 .BYTE 203 25 145
350 RTS
365 ; CLOSE INPUT FILE
370 CLOSE1 LDA FOPEN1; CHECK TO SEE IF INPUT FILE IS OPEN
380 BEQ NOCLOSE; IF NOT EXIT
390 JSR CLOSIT
400 LDA #0
410 STA FOPEN1; SET INPUT FILE TO CLOSED
420 NOCLOSE RTS
```

```
430 ; CLOSE OUTPUT FILE
440 CLOSE2 LDA FOPEN2; CHECK TO SEE IF OUTPUT FILE IS OPEN
450 BEQ NOCLOSE; IF NOT EXIT
460 JSR CLOSIT
465 ; CLOSE OUTPUT FILE
470 LDA #0
480 STA FOPEN2; SET OUTPUT FILE TO CLOSED
490 RTS
500 CLOSIT STA CLOSLIST+1
510 JSR MLI
520 ;.BYTE $CC <CLOSLIST >CLOSLIST
525 .BYTE 204 12 145
530 RTS
570 CLOSE4 LDA #<COUT
572 STA CSWD; RESTORE NORMAL SCREEN OUTPUT
574 LDA #>COUT
576 STA CSWD+1
578 RTS
580 OPENFILE STA OPENLIST+4
590 LDA FNAMELEN
600 STA NAMEBUFF
670 ATTOPEN JSR MLI
680 ;.BYTE $C8 <OPENLIST >OPENLIST
685 .BYTE 200 14 145
690 BCC OPENSUCC ;IF FILE NOT FOUND
700 CMP #$46
710 BNE OPENSUCC
720 JSR MLI ;MAKE ONE
730 ;.BYTE $C0 <CRELIST >CRELIST
735 .BYTE 192 0 145
740 JMP ATTOPEN
```

```
75Ø OPENSUCC LDA OPENLIST+5 ;RETURN FILE ID
76Ø RTS
925 ; SET CURRENT INPUT CHANNEL
93Ø CHKIN STX OPNI
94Ø RTS
945 ; SET CURRENT OUTPUT CHANNEL
95Ø CHKOUT TXA
96Ø STA OPNO
1Ø3Ø CHKOUTO RTS
1Ø35 ; GET ONE BYTE FROM CURRENTLY OPEN CHANNEL
1Ø4Ø CHARIN STY Y1
1Ø5Ø STX X; SAVE X & Y REG
1Ø6Ø LDA OPNI; CHECK TO SEE IF INPUT CHANNEL
1Ø7Ø CMP #1
1Ø8Ø BNE CTOUT; IF NOT EXIT
1Ø9Ø JSR RDBYTE
11ØØ PHP
111Ø LDY Y1
112Ø LDX X
113Ø PLP
114Ø RTS
115Ø CTOUT LDY Y1
116Ø RTS
1165 ; OUTPUT ONE BYTE TO CURRENTLY OPEN CHANNEL
117Ø PRINT STY Y1; SAVE REG
118Ø STA A1
119Ø LDA OPNO; CHECK TO SEE IF TO OUTPUT FILE
12ØØ CMP #Ø2
121Ø BNE NXT1
122Ø LDA A1; YES, WRITE THE BYTE
123Ø JSR WRBYTE
```

```
1240 JMP CTOUT
1340 NXT1 LDA OPNO; CHECK TO SEE IF TO PRINTER
1350 CMP #4
1360 BNE NXT2
1370 LDA A1; YES, PRINT TO PRINTER
1375 ORA #$80
1380 PBYTE JSR $C100
1390 JMP CTOUT
1400 NXT2 LDA PRINTFLAG; NO, MUST BE TO SCREEN
1402 BNE RPRINTING; CARD DOES IT FOR US IF WE'RE PRINTING
1404 LDA A1
1410 ORA #$80
1420 JSR COUT
1425 RPRINTING LDA A1; RESTORE ACCUM
1430 JMP CTOUT
1435 ; CLOSE ALL INPUT AND OUTPUT CHANNELS
1440 CLRCHN LDA #00
1450 STA OPNO
1460 STA OPNI
1470 LDA #<PRINT
1480 STA CSWD
1490 LDA #>PRINT
1500 STA CSWD+1
1510 RTS
1515 ;CHECK FOR STOP KEY
1520 STOPKEY LDA $C000
1530 CMP #$83
1540 RTS
1545 ; CLOSE OPEN FILES
1550 CLOSE CMP #01
1560 BNE CL2; CLOSE INPUT FILE?
```

```
1570 JMP CLOSE1
1580 CL2 CMP #02; NO, CLOSE OUTPUT FILE?
1590 BNE CL4
1600 JMP CLOSE2
1610 CL4 JMP CLOSE4; NO, MUST BE PRINTER
1700 ; BASIC WEDGE
1710 WEDGE STA A1
1720 LDA #$00; IS TXTPTR AT $200?
1730 CMP TXTPTR
1740 BNE OUT
1750 LDA #02
1760 CMP TXTPTR+1
1770 BNE OUT; NO, EXIT
1775 LDY #0
1780 NXTCHR LDA (TXTPTR),Y; IGNORE LEADING SPACES
1781 CMP #32
1782 BNE ISLNUM
1783 INC TXTPTR
1784 JMP NXTCHR
1790 ISLNUM CMP #$2F; IS IT A NUMBER?
1800 BCC OUT; NO, EXIT
1810 CMP #$3A
1820 BCS OUT
1825 JMP INSLIN
1830 OUT LDA $200; IS IT "ASM "?
1840 CMP #65
1850 BNE OUT1
1860 LDA $201
1870 CMP #83
1880 BNE OUT1
1890 LDA $202
```

```
1900 CMP #77
1910 BNE OUT1
1920 LDA $203
1930 CMP #32
1940 BNE OUT1; NO, EXIT
1950 LDY #0; YES
1960 TFRNAM LDA $204,Y; TRANSFER NAME TO TOP OF SCREEN
1970 CMP #0
1980 BEQ ASM
1990 ORA #$80
2000 STA $400,Y
2010 INY
2020 JMP TFRNAM
2030 ASM LDA #$A0; PUT FOLLOWING 3 SPACES
2040 STA $400,Y
2050 STA $401,Y
2060 STA $402,Y
2070 PLA; PULL RETURN ADDRESS AND JUMP TO START
2080 PLA
2081 JSR MLI; IS PREFIX?
2082 ;.BYTE $C7 <PREFLIST >PREFLIST
2083 .BYTE 199 47 145
2084 LDA NAMEBUFF
2085 BNE GOASSM; IS ONE
2086 LDA $BE3C:ASL:ASL:ASL:ASL
2087 LDY $BE3D; DEFAULT DRIVE
2088 CPY #1
2089 BEQ SLOT1
2090 ORA #$80
2091 SLOT1 STA OLINLIST+1
2092 JSR MLI; FIND NAME OF VOLUME
```

```
2093 ;.BYTE $C5 <OLINLIST >OLINLIST
2094 .BYTE 197 50 145
2095 LDA NAMEBUFF+1:AND #$F
2096 TAY:INY:INY
2097 LDA #$2F; ADD "/"'S
2098 STY NAMEBUFF
2099 STA NAMEBUFF+1
2100 STA NAMEBUFF,Y
2101 JSR MLI; MAKE IT PREFIX
2102 ;.BYTE $C6 <PREFLIST >PREFLIST
2103 .BYTE 198 47 145
2104 GOASSM JMP START
2105 OUT1 LDA A1; NORMAL CHRGET
2110 CMP #$3A
2120 BCS EXIT
2130 CMP #$20
2140 BNE NXT
2150 JMP CHRGET
2160 NXT SEC
2170 SBC #$30
2180 SEC
2190 SBC #$D0
2200 EXIT RTS
2210 INSLIN LDX PRGEND; FOUND LINE NUMBER, NOW INSERT LINE
2220 STX VARTAB
2230 LDX PRGEND+1
2240 STX VARTAB+1
2250 CLC
2260 JSR LINGET; GET LINE NUMBER
2270 JSR TOKNIZ
2280 PLA
```

```
2290 PLA
2300 JMP LININS; JUMP TO NORMAL INSERT LINE AND RESET LINE LINK ADDRESSES
2310 TOKNIZ LDY #00; TOKENIZE LINE
2320 STY HIGHDS
2330 LDA #02
2340 STA HIGHDS+1
2350 TK3 LDA (TXTPTR),Y
2360 STA (HIGHDS),Y
2370 INY
2380 CMP #00; END OF LINE
2390 BNE TK3
2400 DEY; YES
2410 TK4 DEY
2420 LDA (HIGHDS),Y; IGNORE FOLLOWING SPACES
2430 CMP #32
2440 BEQ TK4
2450 INY
2460 LDA #0
2470 STA (HIGHDS),Y
2480 INY
2490 INY
2500 INY
2510 INY
2520 INY; Y-REG HOLDS LINE LENGTH +6
2530 RTS
2540 EDITSU LDA #<WEDGE; INITIALIZE WEDGE
2550 STA $BB
2560 LDA #>WEDGE
2570 STA $BC
2580 LDA #$4C; "JMP"
```

```
2590 STA $BA
2600 RTS
2610 .FILE FINDMN
```

Program D-6. Findmn

```
10 ; "FINDMN" -- LOOKS THROUGH MNEMONICS FOR MATCH TO LABEL.
20 ; WE JMP TO THIS FROM EVAL.  & JMP BACK TO 1 OF 2 LOCATIONS (JMP FOR SPEED)
30 FINDMN LDY #0
40 LDX #255; PREPARE X TO GO TO ZERO AT START OF LOOP
50 LOOP INX; X RAISED TO ZERO AT START OF LOOP
60 LDA MNEMONICS,Y; LOOK IN TABLE OF MNEMONICS
70 CMP LABEL; COMPARE IT TO 1ST CHAR. OF WORD IN LABEL BUFFER
80 BEQ MORE; IF =, COMPARE 2ND LETTERS OF TABLE VS. BUFFER
90 INY; OTHERWISE GO UP THREE IN THE TABLE TO FIND THE NEXT MNEMONIC
100 INY
110 INY
120 CPX #57; HAVE WE CHECKED ALL 56 MNEMONICS.
130 BNE LOOP; IF NOT, CONTINUE TRYING TO FIND A MATCH
140 NOMATCH JMP EQLABEL; DIDN'T FIND A MATCH (SO GO BACK TO EVAL)
150 MORE INY; COMPARE 2ND LETTER
160 LDA MNEMONICS,Y
170 CMP LABEL+1
180 BEQ MORE1; IF =, GO ON TO COMPARE 3RD AND FINAL LETTER
190 INY
200 INY
210 BNE LOOP; 2ND LETTER DIDN'T MATCH, TRY NEXT MNEMONIC (Y <> 0)
220 BEQ NOMATCH ; IF Y = 0, WE'VE GONE PAST TABLE (RETURN TO EVAL)
230 MORE1 INY; COMPARE 3RD LETTER
240 LDA MNEMONICS,Y
```

```
250 CMP LABEL+2
260 BEQ FOUND; IF 3RD LETTERS ARE =, WE'VE FOUND OUR MATCH
270 INY
280 BNE LOOP; OTHERWISE TRY NEXT MNEMONIC
290 BEQ NOMATCH
300 FOUND LDA LABEL+3; THE 4TH CHAR. MUST BE A BLANK FOR THIS TO BE A MNEMONIC
310 CMP #32
320 BEQ FO1; IF SO, STORE DATA ABOUT THIS MNEMONIC & RETURN TO EVAL.
330 CMP #0; OR IF END OF LINE, IT WOULD BE AN IMPLIED ADDR. MNEMONIC LIKE INY
340 BNE NOMATCH; OTHERWISE, NO MATCH FOUND (IT'S NOT A MNEMONIC).
350 FO1 LDA TYPES,X; STORE ADDR. TYPE.
360 STA TP
370 LDY OPS,X; STORE OPCODE
380 STY OP
390 END JMP EVAR; MATCH FOUND SO JUMP TO EVAR ROUTINE IN EVAL
400 .FILE GETSA
```

Program D-7a. Getsa

```
10 ; "GETSA" GET STARTING ADDRESS FROM DISK (LEAVES DISK POINTING AT-
20 ;                  *= THIS SPACE (START ADDRESS)
30 ;   (EXPECTS FILE #1 TO BE ALREADY OPENED).
40 ; -------------------------
50 GETSA LDX #1; SET UP INPUT CHANNEL FOR A DEVICE (TO GET BYTES)
60 JSR CHKIN; BASIC'S ROUTINE
70 LDX #6; WE NEED TO THROW AWAY THE 1ST 6 BYTES ON A DISK FILE (SECTOR LINK,
75 LSA STX X
80 JSR CHARIN; RAM START ADDRESS, AND LINE LINK) (CHARINIS "GET BYTE")
85 LDX X
90 DEX; COUNT DOWN UNTIL WE'VE PULLED OFF THE
```

```
100 BNE LSA; 1ST 6 BYTES...THEN-------------------
110 JSR CHARIN; PULL IN NEXT BYTE
120 CMP #$2A; IS IT THE * SYMBOL
130 BEQ MSA; IF SO, GO BACK TO CALLER (EVAL SUBPROGRAM CALLS GETSA)
140 LDA #<MNOSTART; OTHERWISE, PRINT ERROR MESSAGE WHICH
150 STA TEMP; SAYS "NO START ADDRESS". POINT TO THIS ERROR MESSAGE IN
160 LDA #>MNOSTART; THE POINTER,"TEMP," AND PRINT THE MESSAGE (PRNTMESS)
170 STA TEMP+1; (NOTE: THIS NO-START-ADDRESS CONDITION OCCURS 2 WAYS: (EITHER
180 JSR PRNTMESS; (YOU FORGOT TO WRITE ONE OR YOU GAVE THE WRONG FILE NAME)
190 JMP FIN; GO BACK TO BASIC VIA THE SHUTDOWN ROUTINE WITHIN EVAL;-------
200 MSA RTS
210 .FILE VALDEC
```

Program D-7b. Getsa, ProDOS Changes

```
70 LDX #4; WE NEED TO THROW AWAY THE 1ST 4 BYTES ON A DISK FILE
```

Program D-8. Valdec

```
10 ; "VALDEC"  TRANSLATE ASCII INPUT TO A TWO-BYTE INTEGER IN RESULT
20 ;  SETUP/TEMP MUST POINT TO ASCII NUMBER (WHICH ENDS IN ZERO).
30 ;  RESULTS/ RESULT HOLDS 2-BYTE RESULT
40 ; --------------------------
50 VALDEC LDY #0
55 ; READ ASCII FROM LEFT TO RIGHT--DECREMENTING Y --(TO FIND LENGTH)
60 VGETZERO LDA (TEMP),Y
70 BEQ VZERO; 0 DELIMITER FOUND
80 INY
```

```
90 JMP VGETZERO;----------------  (FOR EXAMPLE, ASSUME ASCII IS "15")
110 VZERO STY VREND; SAVE LENGTH OF ASCII NUMBER  (IN THE EXAMPLE, LEN = 2)
120 DEY
130 LDA #0; CLEAN "RESULT" VARIABLE (SET TO 0)
140 STA RESULT
150 STA RESULT+1
160 LDX #1; USE "X" VARIABLE AS A MULTIPLY-X10-HOW-MANY-TIMES COUNTER
170 STX X
180 VALLOOP LDA (TEMP),Y; LOAD IN THE RIGHTMOST ASCII CHARACTER (EX: "5")
190 AND #$0F; AS ASCII, 5 = $35.  O STRIP OFF THE 3, LEAVING THE 5.
200 STA RADD; STORE IN MULTIPLICATION REGISTER
210 STA TSTORE; STORE IN "REMEMBER IT" REGISTER
220 LDA #0; PUT 0 IN BOTH THESE REGISTERS (IN THEIR HIGH BYTES)
230 STA RADD+1
240 STA TSTORE+1;----------------- MULTIPLY X10 AS MUCH AS NECESSARY------
250 VLOOP DEX; LOWER THE COUNTER. (IN THE EXAMPLE, X NOW = 0 FOR 1ST CHAR)
260 BEQ VGOON; SO WE DON'T JSR TO THE X10 SUBROUTINE IN THIS CASE)
270 JSR TEN; OTHERWISE,WE'D MULTIPLY THE NUMBER X10 AS MANY TIMES AS NECESSARY
280 LDA RADD; MOVE RESULT OF MULTIPLICATION INTO STORAGE REGISTER
290 STA TSTORE
300 LDA RADD+1
310 STA TSTORE+1; SAVING RESULTS OF MOST RECENT MULTIPLICATION
320 JMP VLOOP; CONTINUE MULTIPLYING X10 UNTIL X IS DOWN TO ZERO.---------
330 VGOON INC X; RAISE X BY 1 (SINCE WE'RE MOVING LEFT AND EACH NUMBER WILL
335 ;                               BE 10X THE ONE TO ITS RIGHT).
340 LDX X
350 JSR VALADD; ADD RADD TO RESULT (ADD IN RESULTS OF THE MULTIPLICATION)
360 DEY; MOVE INDEX OVER BY 1 (TO POINT TO NEXT ASCII CHAR. TO THE LEFT)
370 DEC VREND; LOWER LENGTH POINTER.  IF IT'S NOT YET ZERO, THEN
380 BNE VALLOOP; CONTINUE PROCESSING THIS ASCII NUMBER
390 RTS; OTHERWISE RETURN TO CALLER.
```

```
400 ;----------------    MULTIPLY BY 10
410 TEN CLC
420 ASL RADD;       MULTIPLY RADD X 4
430 ROL RADD+1
440 ASL RADD
450 ROL RADD+1;----------------
460 CLC
470 LDA TSTORE;PULL OUT ORIGINAL NUMBER AND ADD IT TO RESULT OF X4 (GIVING X5)
480 ADC RADD
490 STA RADD
500 LDA TSTORE+1
510 ADC RADD+1
520 STA RADD+1;------------ NOW, MULTIPLY X2.  ((N*4+N)*2) IS N*10
530 ASL RADD
540 ROL RADD+1
550 RTS
560 ;------------- ADD RESULTS OF THE MULTIPLICATION TO THE INTEGER ANSWER
570 VALADD CLC
580 LDA RADD
590 ADC RESULT
600 STA RESULT
610 LDA RADD+1
620 ADC RESULT+1
630 STA RESULT+1
640 RTS
650 .FILE INDISK
```

Program D-9. Indisk

```
1Ø ; "INDISK" MAIN GET-INPUT-FROM-DISK ROUTINE
2Ø ;SETUP/EXPECTS DISK TO POINT TO 1ST CHAR IN A NEW LINE (OR BEYOND COLON)
3Ø ;RESULTS/EITHER FLAGS END OF PROG. OR FILLS LABEL+ WITH LINE OF CODE
4Ø ;------------------
5Ø INDISK JSR CLEANLAB; FILL LABEL WITH ZEROS (ROUTINE IN EVAL)
6Ø LDY #Ø
7Ø STY HEXFLAG; PUT HEXFLAG DOWN
75 STY BABFLAG
8Ø STY BYTFLAG; PUT FLAG SHOWING < OR > DOWN
9Ø STY PLUSFLAG; PUT ARITHMETIC PSEUDO OP (+) FLAG DOWN
1ØØ LDA COLFLAG; IF THERE WAS A COLON JUST PRIOR TO THIS, REMOVE ANY BLANKS
11Ø BNE NOBLANKS; (THIS TAKES CARE OF: INY:  LDA 15:    LDX 17 TYPE ERRORS)
12Ø JSR CHARIN; OTHERWISE, PULL IN THE 1ST CHARACTER (FROM DISK OR RAM)
13Ø STA LINEN; STORE LOW BYTE OF LINE NUMBER
14Ø JSR CHARIN
15Ø STA LINEN+1; STORE HIGH BYTE OF LINE NUMBER
16Ø NOBLANKS JSR CHARIN; ROUTINE TO ELIMINATE BLANKS FOLLOWING A COLON
17Ø CMP #32; (OR FOLLOWING A LINE NUMBER)
175 BNE COOLOOK
176 JSR ENDPRO; THIS HANDLES COLONS PLACED ACCIDENTALLY AT THE END OF LINE
177 PLA:PLA:JMP STARTLINE
18Ø COOLOOK CMP #32; (OR FOLLOWING A LINE NUMBER)
19Ø JMP MOI1; SKIP TO CHECK FOR COLON (IT'S EQUIVALENT TO AN END OF LINE Ø)
2ØØ STINDISK JSR CHARIN; ENTRY POINT WITHIN LINE (NOT AT START OF LINE)
21Ø MOINDI BNE MOI1; IF NOT ZERO, LOOK FOR COLON
22Ø JMP ENDPRO; FOUND A Ø END OF LINE. CHECK FOR END OF PROGRAM (3 ZEROS)
23Ø MOI1 CMP #58; IS IT A COLON
24Ø BNE XMO1; IF NOT, CHECK FOR SEMICOLON
25Ø JMP COLON; FOUND A COLON
```

```
260 XMO1 CMP #59; IS IT A SEMICOLON
270 BNE COMOA; IF NOT CONTINUE ON
280 STY A; FOUND A SEMICOLON (REM)
290 LDA PRINTFLAG; IF PRINTOUT NOT REQUESTED, THEN DON'T STORE THE REMARKS
300 BEQ PULLRX
305 STA BABFLAG
310 LDA A; OTHERWISE, CHECK Y (SAVED ABOVE).  IF ZERO, IS A SEMICOLON AT
320 BEQ PUX; START OF THE LINE (NO LABELS OR MNEMONICS, JUST A BIG COMMENT)
330 JSR PULLREST; OTHERWISE SAVE COMMENTS FOLLOWING THE SEMICOLON
340 JMP MPULL; AND THEN RETURN TO EVAL ---------------------------
350 PUX JSR CHARIN; PUT NON-COMMENT DATA INTO LABEL BUFFER
360 BEQ PUX1; END OF LINE, SO EXIT
370 CMP #127; 7TH BIT NOT SET (SO IT'S NOT A KEYWORD IN BASIC)
380 BCC PUX2
390 JSR KEYWORD; IT IS A KEYWORD, SO EXTEND IT OUT AS AN ASCII WORD
400 PUX2 STA LABEL,Y; PUT THE CHAR. INTO THE MAIN BUFFER
410 INY
420 JMP PUX; RETURN TO LOOP FOR MORE CHARACTERS---------------------
430 PUX1 JSR PRNTLINE; PRINT THE LINE NUMBER
440 JSR PRNTSPACE; PRINT A SPACE
450 JSR PRNTINPUT; PRINT THE CHARACTERS IN THE LABEL BUFFER (MAIN BUFFER)
460 JSR PRNTCR; PRINT A CARRIAGE RETURN
470 LDA #0; SET A VARIABLE TO ZERO TO SIGNIFY NOTHING FOR EVAL TO EVALUATE
480 STA A
490 JMP MPULL; GO TO EXIT ROUTINE--------------------------------
495 PULLREST STA BABFLAG
500 STA A
510 LDY #0
530 PAX1 JSR CHARIN; GET CHARACTER
540 BNE PAX; IF NOT ZERO, CONTINUE
550 STA BABUF,Y; OTHERWISE, WE'RE AT THE END OF THE COMMENT
```

```
560 LDY A
570 RTS; Y MUST HOLD OFFSET FOR ZERO FILL (ENDPRO)-----------------
580 PAX BPL PAXA; NOT A KEYWORD (7TH BIT NOT SET)
600 JSR KEYWAD; OTHERWISE, EXTEND KEYWORD INTO AN ASCII STRING
610 PAXA STA BABUF,Y; STORE CHAR. IN REMARK BUFFER
620 INY
630 JMP PAX1; RETURN TO LOOP TO GET ANOTHER CHARACTER--------------
640 PULLRX JSR CHARIN; JUST PULL IN REMARK CHARACTERS, IGNORING THEM
650 BEQ MPULL; LOOKING FOR THE END OF LINE ZERO
660 JMP PULLRX;-------------------------
670 MPULL JSR ENDPRO; CHECK FOR END OF PROGRAM AND THEN
680 LDA A; SEE IF Y = 0.  IF SO, THE SEMICOLON WAS AT THE START OF A LINE
690 BNE MPULL1
700 PLA; Y = 0 SO JUMP BACK TO EVAL TO PREPARE TO GET NEXT LINE
710 PLA
720 JMP STARTLINE; SEMI @ START SO RETURN TO EVAL TO GET NEXT LINE---------
730 MPULL1 RTS; SEMICOLON, BUT NOT AT START OF LINE (RETURN TO CALLER)
740 COMOA CMP #$3E;------------------ CHECK FOR OTHER ODD CHARACTERS
750 BEQ HI; FOUND >
760 CMP #$3C
770 BEQ LO; FOUND <
780 CMP #$2B
790 BNE COMO
800 INC PLUSFLAG; FOUND +
810 COMO CMP #$2A
820 BNE COMO1
830 JMP STAR; FOUND *
840 COMO1 CMP #46
850 BEQ PSEUDOO; FOUND PSEUDO-OP
860 CMP #36
870 BEQ HEXX; FOUND HEX NUMBER
```

```
880 CMP #127; NOT A KEYWORD (7TH BIT NOT UP)
890 BCC ADDLAB
900 JSR KEYWORD; FOUND KEYWORD, SO EXTEND IT INTO AN ASCII STRING
910 ADDLAB STA LABEL,Y; PUT THE CHARACTER INTO THE MAIN BUFFER AND
920 INY; RAISE THE POINTER AND
930 JMP STINDISK; RETURN TO GET ANOTHER CHARACTER (BUT NOT A LINE NUMBER)
940 ;----------------------
950 COLON STA COLFLAG; SIGNIFY COLON BY SETTING COLFLAG
960 RTS;----------------------
970 PSEUDOO JMP PSEUDOJ; SPRINGBOARD TO PSEUDO-OP HANDLING ROUTINES
980 HEXX STA LABEL,Y; SPRINGBOARD TO HEX NUMBER TRANSLATOR
990 INY
1000 JMP HEX
1010 ;-------- TRANSLATE A SINGLE-BYTE KEYWORD TOKEN INTO ASCII STRING
1020 KEYWORD SEC; FIND NUMBER OF KEYWORD (IS IT 1ST, 5TH, OR WHAT)
1030 SBC #$7F
1040 STA KEYNUM; STORE NUMBER (POSITION) IN BASIC'S KEYWORD TABLE
1050 LDX #255
1060 SKEY DEC KEYNUM; REDUCE NUMBER BY 1 (WHEN ZERO, WE'VE FOUND IT IN TABLE)
1070 BEQ FKEY; AND WE EXIT THIS SEARCH ROUTINE AND STORE THE ASCII WORD
1080 KSX INX; BRING X UP TO ZERO AT START OF LOOP
1090 LDA KEYWDS,X; LOOK AT CHAR. IN BASIC'S TABLE.
1100 BPL KSX;DID NOT FIND A SHIFTED BYTE(1ST CHAR. IS SHIFTED IN THE TABLE)
1110 BMI SKEY; DID FIND START-OF-KEYWORD SHIFTED CHARACTER -------------
1120 FKEY INX; STORE THE KEYWORD INTO LADS' MAIN BUFFER (LABEL)
1130 LDA KEYWDS,X
1140 BMI KSET; A SHIFTED CHAR. INDICATES END OF KEYWORD, START OF NEXT KEYWORD
1150 STA LABEL,Y; PUT CHAR. INTO LADS' BUFFER
1160 INY
1170 JMP FKEY; LOOP AGAIN FOR NEXT CHAR.---------------------
```

```
1180 KSET AND #$7F
1190 RTS; CLEAR OUT BIT 7 AND RETURN TO CALLING ROUTINE
1200 ;------------------- HANDLE > AND < PSEUDO-OPS
1210 HI LDA #2;        THE BYTFLAG HAS 3 POSSIBLE STATES:
1220 STA BYTFLAG;               Ø = LINE DOESN'T CONTAIN A > OR < PSEUDO
1230 JMP STINDISK;              1 = < (LOW BYTE) TYPE
1240 LO LDA #1;                 2 = > (HIGH BYTE) TYPE
1250 STA BYTFLAG;          (ACTION IS TAKEN ON THIS PSEUDO-OP WITHIN THE
1260 JMP STINDISK;              EQUATE SUBPROGRAM).  O WE FETCH THE NEXT CHAR.
1270 ;-------------------  HANDLE * PSEUDO OP (CHANGE THE PC)
1280 STAR LDA BYTFLAG; IF NOT *> OR *< TYPE THEN
1290 BEQ STARM; CONTINUE ON
1300 LDA #42; OTHERWISE PUT * SYMBOL INTO LABEL (MAIN BUFFER)
1310 STA LABEL,Y;------------- HANDLE *> OR *< TYPE
1320 INY
1330 INC HEXFLAG; SET HEXFLAG TO PREVENT EVAL FROM TRYING TO FIGURE OUT ARG.
1340 LDA BYTFLAG; SEE WHICH <> PSEUDO-OP IT IS
1350 CMP #1
1360 BEQ STARLO; LOW BYTE TYPE PUTS LOW BYTE OF PC INTO RESULT
1370 LDA SA+1; HIGH BYTE TYPE PUTS HIGH BYTE OF PC INTO RESULT
1380 STA RESULT
1390 JMP STINDISK; AND RETURN FOR NEXT CHAR.------------------------
1400 STARLO LDA SA
1410 STA RESULT
1420 JMP STINDISK; WAS LDA #<* TYPE --------
1430 STARM JSR STINDISK;------------- HANDLE *= PSEUDO-OP (CHANGE THE PC)
1440 LDA PASS; ON PASS 1, DON'T PRINT OUT DATA TO SCREEN
1450 BEQ STARN
1460 LDA #42; PRINT *
1470 JSR PRINT
1480 JSR PRNTINPUT; PRINT STRING IN LABEL BUFFER
```

```
1490 JSR PRNTCR; PRINT CARRIAGE RETURN
1500 STARN LDA HEXFLAG; IF HEX, THE ARGUMENT HAS ALREADY BEEN FIGURED
1510 BNE STARR; SO JUMP OVER THIS NEXT PART
1520 LDY #0
1530 STAF LDA LABEL,Y
1540 CMP #32
1550 BEQ STAF1
1560 INY
1570 JMP STAF; FIND NUMBER (BY LOOKING FOR THE BLANK: *= 15)
1580 STAF1 INY
1590 STY TEMP; POINT TO ASCII NUMBER
1600 LDA #<LABEL
1610 CLC
1620 ADC TEMP
1630 STA TEMP
1640 LDA #>LABEL
1650 ADC #0
1660 STA TEMP+1
1670 JSR VALDEC; TRANSLATE ASCII NUMBER INTO INTEGER (IN RESULT)
1680 STARR LDA PASS; ON PASS 1, LEAVE DISK OBJECT FILE ALONE.
1690 BEQ STARRX
1700 LDA DISKFLAG; ON PASS 2, WE'VE GOT TO STUFF THE DISK OBJECT FILE
1710 BEQ STARRX; IF THE DISKFLAG IS UP (WE ARE CREATING AN OBJECT CODE FILE)
1720 JSR FILLDISK; FILLDISK DOES THIS FOR US.
1730 STARRX LDA RESULT; PUT THE ARGUMENT OF *= INTO THE PC (SA)
1740 STA SA
1750 LDA RESULT+1
1760 STA SA+1
1770 PLA; PULL OFF THE RTS AND
1780 PLA
1790 JMP STARTLINE; RETURN TO EVAL FOR THE NEXT LINE OF CODE
```

```
18ØØ ;------------------- IS THIS THE END OF THE ENTIRE SOURCE CODE
181Ø ENDPRO STA LABEL,Y; PUT THE ZERO (THAT SENT US HERE) INTO THE MAIN BUFFER
182Ø INY
183Ø CPY #255
184Ø BNE ENDPRO; FILL REST OF BUFFER WITH ØØS
185Ø STA LABEL,Y
186Ø JSR CHARIN; PULL IN THE NEXT 2 BYTES.  IF THEY ARE BOTH ZEROS, THEN
187Ø JSR CHARIN; WE HAVE, IN FACT, FOUND THE END OF OUR SOURCE CODE FILE
188Ø BEQ INEND; AND WE BEQ TO INEND
189Ø LDA #Ø; OTHERWISE WE PUT THE COLFLAG (COLON) DOWN, BECAUSE THIS IS
19ØØ STA COLFLAG; AN END OF LINE CONDITION, NOT A COLON
191Ø RTS; AND RETURN TO CALLER
192Ø INEND LDA #1;-------- SET END OF SOURCE CODE FILE FLAG TO UP CONDITION
193Ø STA ENDFLAG
194Ø RTS; AND RETURN TO CALLER
195Ø ;----------------------- CHANGE A HEX NUMBER TO A 2-BYTE INTEGER
196Ø ; PULL IN NEXT FEW BYTES, TURNING THEM INTO AN INTEGER IN RESULT
197Ø HEX LDX #Ø; PUTS INTEGER EQUIVALENT OF INCOMING HEX INTO RESULT
198Ø H1 JSR CHARIN
199Ø BEQ DECI; END OF LINE (SO STOP LOOKING)
2ØØØ CMP #58
2Ø1Ø BEQ DECI; COLON (SO STOP LOOKING)
2Ø12 CMP #32
2Ø14 BEQ H1
2Ø2Ø CMP #59
2Ø3Ø BEQ DECI; SEMICOLON (SO STOP LOOKING)
2Ø4Ø CMP #44
2Ø5Ø BEQ DECIT; COMMA (SO STOP LOOKING, BUT GO TO A DIFFERENT PLACE)
2Ø6Ø CMP #41; (THIS "DIFFERENT PLACE" HANDLES A NOT-END-OF-LINE CONDITION).
2Ø7Ø BEQ DECIT; CLOSE PARENTHESIS ) (SO STOP LOOKING)
2Ø8Ø STA HEXBUF,X; OTHERWISE, PUT THE ASCII-STYLE-HEX CHAR. IN BUFFER AND
```

```
2090 INX; RAISE THE INDEX AND
2100 STA LABEL,Y; ALSO STORE IT INTO MAIN BUFFER FOR PRINTOUT AND
2110 INY; RAISE THIS INDEX TOO
2120 JMP H1; THEN KEEP ON PUTTING HEX NUMBER INTO HEXBUFFER-----------
2130 DECIT STX HEXLEN; SAVE LENGTH OF ASCII-HEX NUMBER
2140 STA LABEL,Y; FINISH STORING CHARS. INTO MAIN BUFFER (, OR ) IN THIS CASE)
2150 INY
2160 JSR STARTHEX; TRANSLATE ASCII-HEX NUMBER INTO INTEGER IN RESULT VARIABLE
2170 JMP STINDISK; RETURN TO PULL IN REST OF THE LINE;-----------
2180 DECI STA A; SAVE THE END OF LINE, COLON, OR SEMICOLON CHAR. FOR LATER
2190 LDA #0
2200 STX HEXLEN; SAVE LENGTH OF ASCII-HEX NUMBER
2210 STA LABEL,Y; FINISH STORING CHARS. INTO MAIN BUFFER (0 IN THIS CASE)
2220 JSR STARTHEX; TRANSLATE ASCII-HEX NUMBER INTO INTEGER IN RESULT VARIABLE
2230 LDA A; RETRIEVE 0 OR COLON OR SEMICOLON AND GO BACK UP TO MOINDI WHICH
2240 JMP MOINDI;----------------- BEHAVES ACCORDING TO WHICH SYMBOL A HOLDS.
2250 STARTHEX LDA #0;----------------- HEX-ASCII TO INTEGER TRANSLATOR------
2260 STA RESULT; SET RESULT TO ZERO
2270 STA RESULT+1
2280 TAX; SET X TO ZERO
2290 HXLOOP ASL RESULT; SHIFT AND ROLL (MOVES 2-BYTE BITS TO THE LEFT)-----
2300 ROL RESULT+1; DOING THIS 8 TIMES HAS THE EFFECT OF BRINGING IN
2310 ASL RESULT; THE ASCII NUMBER, 1 BYTE AT A TIME, AND TRANSFORMING IT
2320 ROL RESULT+1; INTO A 2-BYTE INTEGER WITHIN THIS 2-BYTE VARIABLE WE'RE
2330 ASL RESULT; CALLING "RESULT."
2340 ROL RESULT+1
2350 ASL RESULT
2360 ROL RESULT+1
2370 LDA HEXBUF,X; GET A BYTE FROM THE ASCII-HEX NUMBER
2380 CMP #65; IF IT'S LOWER THAN 65, IT'S NOT AN ALPHABETIC (A-F) HEX NUMBER
2390 BCC HXMORE; SO DON'T SUBTRACT 7 FROM IT
```

```
2400 SBC #7; BUT IF IT'S > 65, THEN -7.   = 65.  65-7 = 58.
2410 HXMORE AND #15; WHEN YOU 58 AND 15, YOU GET 10 (THE VALUE OF A)
2420 ORA RESULT; #15 (00001111) AND #58 (00111010)  = 00001010 (TEN)
2430 STA RESULT; PUT THE BYTE INTO RESULT
2440 INX; RAISE THE INDEX
2450 CPX HEXLEN; ARE WE AT THE END OF OUR ASCII-HEX NUMBER
2460 BNE HXLOOP; IF NOT, CONTINUE
2470 INC HEXFLAG; IF SO, RAISE HEXFLAG (TO SHOW RESULT HAS THE ANSWER)
2480 LDA #1; AND RETURN TO CALLER
2490 RTS
2500 ;-----------------------
2510 ; HANDLE PSEUDOS.  (.BYTE TYPES)
2520 PSEUDOJ CPY #0; IF Y = 0 THEN IT'S NOT A PC LABEL LIKE (LABEL .BYTE 0 0)
2530 BEQ PSE2
2540 LDX PASS; OTHERWISE, ON 1ST PASS, STORE LABEL NAME AND PC ADDR. IN ARRAY
2550 BNE PSE2
2560 PHA; SAVE A AND Y REGISTERS
2570 TYA
2580 PHA
2590 JSR EQUATE; NAME AND PC ADDR. STORED IN ARRAY
2600 PLA; PULL OUT A AND Y REGISTERS (RESTORE THEM)
2610 TAY
2620 PLA
2630 PSE2 STA LABEL,Y; STORE . CHAR.
2640 INY
2650 JSR CHARIN; GET CHAR. FOLLOWING THE PERIOD (.)
2660 STA LABEL,Y
2670 INY
2680 CMP #66; IS IT "B" FOR .BYTE
2690 BNE PSEUD1; WASN'T .BYTE
2700 LDA #0; RESET FLAG WHICH WILL DISTINGUISH BETWEEN .BYTE 0 AND .BYTE "A
```

```
2710 STA BNUMFLAG; " TYPE, OR 00 08 15 172 TYPE (THE TWO .BYTE TYPES)
2720 LDA PASS; PRINT NOTHING TO SCREEN ON PASS 1
2730 BEQ CLB
2740 STY Y; SAVE Y REGISTER (OUR INDEX)
2760 LDA SFLAG; SHOULD WE PRINT TO SCREEN
2770 BEQ CLB; NO
2780 JSR PRNTLINE; YES, PRINT LINE NUMBER
2790 JSR PRNTSPACE; PRINT SPACE
2800 JSR PRNTSA; PRINT PC ADDRESS
2810 JSR PRNTSPACE; PRINT SPACE
2820 LDY Y; RECOVER Y INDEX
2830 CLB JSR CHARIN; PULL IN CHARACTER FROM DISK/RAM
2840 STA LABEL,Y; STORE IN MAIN BUFFER
2850 INY
2860 CMP #32; IS IT A SPACE
2870 BNE CLB; IF NOT, CONTINUE PULLING IN MORE CHARACTERS-----------
2880 JSR CHARIN; (WE'RE LOOKING FOR THE 1ST SPACE AFTER .BYTE)
2890 STA LABEL,Y; STORE FOR PRINTING
2900 INY
2910 CMP #34; IS THE CHARACTER A QUOTE (").  IF SO, IT'S A .BYTE "ABCD TYPE
2920 BNE BNUMWERK; OTHERWISE IT'S NOT THE " TYPE
2930 BY1 JSR CHARIN;----------  HANDLE ASCII STRING .BYTE TYPES
2940 BNE BY2
2950 JMP BENDPRO; FOUND A 0 END OF LINE (OR PROGRAM)
2960 BY2 CMP #58; FOUND A COLON "END OF LINE"
2970 BNE BY2X
2980 JMP BEN1; FOUND A COLON
2990 BY2X CMP #59; FOUND A SEMICOLON "END OF LINE"
3000 BNE BY3
3010 JSR PULLREST; STORE COMMENTS IN COMMENT BUFFER (BABUF)
3012 LDX PRINTFLAG
```

```
3014 STX BABFLAG
3020 JMP BENDPRO; A SEMICOLON SO END THIS ROUTINE IN THAT WAY.
3030 BY3 CMP #34; HAVE WE FOUND A CONCLUDING QUOTE (")
3040 BNE BY3X
3050 JMP BY1; FOUND A " SO IGNORE IT
3060 BY3X LDX PASS; ON PASS 1, JUST RAISE PC COUNTER (INCSA); DON'T POKE IT.
3070 BNE PSLOOP
3080 JSR INCSA
3090 JMP BY1;-----------------
3100 PSEUD1 JMP PSEUDO; SOME OTHER PSEUDO TYPE, NOT .BYTE (A SPRINGBOARD)
3110 PSLOOP STA LABEL,Y; STORE A CHARACTER IN MAIN BUFFER;------------
3120 TAX
3130 STY Y; SAVE Y INDEX
3140 JSR POKEIT; PASS 2, SO POKE IT INTO MEMORY (THE ASCII CHARACTER)
3150 LDY Y; RESTORE Y
3160 INY; RAISE INDEX AND
3170 JMP BY1; GET NEXT CHARACTER
3180 BNUMWERK LDX #0;-------- HANDLE .BYTE 1 2 3 (NUMERIC TYPE)
3190 STX BFLAG; PUT DOWN BFLAG (END OF LINE SIGNAL)
3200 STA NUBUF,X
3210 INX
3220 WERK1 LDA BFLAG; IF BFLAG IS UP, WE'RE DONE.
3230 BNE BBEND; SO GO TO END ROUTINE
3240 WK0 JSR CHARIN; OTHERWISE, GET A CHARACTER FROM DISK/RAM
3250 BEQ BSFLAG; IF ZERO (END OF LINE) SET BFLAG UP.
3260 CMP #58; LIKEWISE IF COLON
3270 BEQ BSFLAG
3280 CMP #59; SEMICOLON REQUIRES THAT WE FIRST FILL THE COMMENT BUFFER
3290 BNE WK1;          BEFORE SETTING THE BFLAG (IN THE BSFLAG ROUTINE)
3300 JSR PULLREST; HERE'S WHERE THE COMMENT BUFFER IS FILLED
3302 LDX PRINTFLAG
```

```
3304 STX BABFLAG
3310 JMP BSFLAG; FOUND SEMICOLON
3320 WK1 STA BUFM; PUT CHAR. INTO "BUFM" BUFFER
3330 LDA PASS; ON PASS 1, RAISE THE PC ONLY (INCSA), NO POKES
3340 BNE WERK5
3350 LDA BUFM
3360 CMP #32; IS IT A SPACE
3370 BNE WERK1; IF NOT, RETURN FOR MORE OF THE NUMBER (Ø VS 555)
3380 JSR INCSA; RAISE PC COUNTER BY 1
3390 JMP WERK1; GET NEXT NUMBER
3400 WERK5 LDA BUFM; PUT CHAR. INTO PRINTOUT MAIN BUFFER
3410 STA LABEL,Y
3420 INY
3430 CMP #32; IS IT A SPACE
3440 BEQ WERK2
3450 CMP #Ø; IS IT END OF LINE
3460 BEQ WERK2
3470 CMP #58; IS IT COLON
3480 BEQ WERK2
3490 STA NUBUF,X; OTHERWISE, STORE IT
3500 INX
3510 JMP WERK1; AND RETURN FOR MORE OF THE NUMBER----------------
3520 BSFLAG INC BFLAG; RAISE UP THE END OF LINE FLAG
3530 STA BUFM+1; SAVE COLON, SEMICOLON, OR WHATEVER FOR LATER USE
3540 JMP WK1; RETURN FOR MORE (BUT THIS TIME IT WILL END LINE);---------
3550 WERK2 LDA #<NUBUF; POINT TO THE ASCII NUMBER STORED IN NUBUF
3560 STA TEMP
3570 LDA #>NUBUF
3580 STA TEMP+1
3590 STY Y
3600 JSR VALDEC; TURN THE ASCII INTO AN INTEGER IN RESULT
```

```
3610 LDX RESULT
3620 JSR POKEIT; POKE THE RESULT INTO MEMORY (OR DISK OBJECT FILE)
3630 LDY Y; ERASE THE NUMBER IN HEXBUF
3640 LDA #Ø
3650 LDX #5
3660 CLEX STA NUBUF,X
3670 DEX
3680 BNE CLEX
3690 JMP WERK1; AND THEN RETURN TO FETCH THE NEXT NUMBER;--------------
3700 BBEND LDA PASS; END .BYTE LINE.  ON PASS 1, RAISE PC (POKEIT RAISES IT
3710 BNE BBEND1;                       ON PASS 2).
3720 JSR INCSA
3730 BBEND1 LDA BUFM+1; IF END OF LINE SIGNAL WAS A COLON, THEN
3740 CMP #58
3750 BEQ BEN1; DON'T LOOK FOR LINE NUMBER OR END OF SOURCE CODE FILE (ENDPRO)
3760 BENDPRO JSR ENDPRO
3770 BEN1 STA COLFLAG; SET IT (COLON) OR NOT (ENDPRO RETURNS WITH Ø IN A)
3780 INC LOCFLAG; RAISE PRINT-A-PC-LABEL FLAG
3790 PLA; PULL RTS FROM STACK
3800 PLA
3810 LDA PASS; ON PASS 1, DON'T PRINT ANY COMMENTS
3820 BEQ NOPR
3830 LDA SFLAG; IF SCREENFLAG IS DOWN, DON'T PRINT ANY COMMENTS
3840 BEQ NOPR
3850 JMP PRMMFIN; BACK TO EVAL (WHERE COMMENTS ARE PRINTED)
3860 NOPR JMP STARTLINE; BACK TO EVAL (BYPASSING PRINTOUT)
3870 ;-----------------------  FOR CHANGE OF PC
3880 FILLDISK LDA PASS; A CHANGE OF PC REQUIRES FILLING A DISK OBJECT FILE
3890 CMP #2;             WITH THE REQUISITE NUMBER OF BYTES TO MAKE UP FOR
3900 BNE FILLX;          THE ADVANCING OF THE PROGRAM COUNTER (PC)
3910 RTS; NOT AT START OF 3RD PASS (3RD PASS IS JUST BEFORE SHUT DOWN)
```

```
3920 FILLX JSR CLRCHN
3930 LDX #2
3940 JSR CHKOUT; PUT SPACERS IN DISKFILE FOR *=
3950 SEC; FIND OUT HOW MANY SPACERS TO SEND TO DISK BY SUBTRACTING:RESULT-SA
3960 LDA RESULT
3970 SBC SA
3980 STA WORK; ANSWER HELD IN "WORK" VARIABLE
3990 LDA RESULT+1
4000 SBC SA+1
4010 STA WORK+1
4020 PUTSPCR LDA #0
4030 JSR PRINT; PRINT SPACER TO DISK
4040 LDA WORK; LOWER WORK BY 1
4050 BNE DECWORKX
4060 DEC WORK+1
4070 DECWORKX DEC WORK
4080 BNE PUTSPCR
4090 LDA WORK+1
4100 BNE PUTSPCR; PUT MORE SPACERS IN UNTIL "WORK" IS DECREMENTED TO ZERO.
4110 RESFILL JSR CLRCHN
4120 LDX #1; RESTORE NORMAL I/O
4130 JSR CHKIN
4140 RTS
4150 ;----------------------
4160 KEYWAD SEC; SEE KEYWORD ABOVE (SAME KEWORD TO ASCII STRING ROUTINE)
4170 SBC #$7F; THIS IS A VERSION OF KEYWORD, BUT FOR COMMENTS(PUTS IT IN BABUF
4180 STA KEYNUM;                         INSTEAD OF LABEL BUFFER).
4190 LDX #255
4200 SKEX DEC KEYNUM
4210 BEQ FKEX
4220 KSXX INX
```

```
4230 LDA KEYWDS,X
4240 BPL KSXX
4250 BMI SKEX
4260 FKEX INX
4270 LDA KEYWDS,X
4280 BMI KSEX
4290 STA BABUF,Y
4300 INY
4310 JMP FKEX
4320 KSEX AND #$7F
4330 RTS
4340 ;-------------------
4350 .FILE MATH
```

Program D-10. Math

```
10 ; "MATH"  THIS ROUTINE HANDLES +   IT COMES FROM EVAL AFTER INDISK
20 ; IT LEAVES THE INTENDED ADDITION IN THE VARIABLE "ADDNUM"
30 ; (ADDNUM IS ADDED TO "RESULT" IN THE VALDEC SUBPROGRAM)
40 MATH LDY #0; SET INDEXES TO ZERO
50 LDX #0
60 MATH1 LDA LABEL,Y; LOOK FOR LOCATION OF "+" SYMBOL--------
70 CMP #43
80 BEQ MATH2
90 INY
100 JMP MATH1;------------- NOW POINT TO 1ST NUMBER FOLLOWING +
110 MATH2 INY
120 LDA LABEL,Y
130 JSR RANGECK; CHECK TO SEE IF THIS IS BETWEEN 48 - 58 (ASCII FOR 0-9)
```

```
140 BCS VALIT; IF NOT, EXIT THIS ROUTINE (WE'VE STORED THE NUMBER AND HAVE
150 STA HEXBUF,X; LOCATED SOMETHING OTHER THAN AN ASCII NUMBER)
160 INX; KEEP STORING VALID ASCII NUMBERS IN HEXBUF BUFFER
170 JMP MATH2;-------------------
180 RANGECK CMP #58;-------------- IS THIS >47 AND <58
190 BCS MATH3
200 SEC
210 SBC #48
220 SEC
230 SBC #208; IS IT > 47 & < 58
240 MATH3 RTS
250 VALIT LDA #0;---------- TURN IT FROM ASCII INTO A 2-BYTE INTEGER
260 STA HEXBUF,X; PUT ZERO AT END OF ASCII NUMBER (AS DELIMITER)
270 LDA #<HEXBUF; POINT "TEMP" POINTER TO ASCII NUMBER IN BUFFER
280 STA TEMP
290 LDA #>HEXBUF
300 STA TEMP+1
310 JSR VALDEC; ROUTINE WHICH TURNS ASCII NUMBER INTO INTEGER IN "RESULT"
320 LDA RESULT; MOVE RESULT TO TEMPORARY ADDITION VARIABLE, "ADDNUM"
330 STA ADDNUM
340 LDA RESULT+1
350 STA ADDNUM+1
360 RTS; RETURN TO CALLER
370 .FILE PRINTOPS
```

Program D-11. Printops

```
10 ; "PRINTOPS"   PRINTS & POKES VALUES (BOTH OPCODES & ARGUMENTS)
20 FORMAT LDA PASS; ON PASS 2, IGNORE INCSA (RAISES PC) SINCE
30 BNE PRM; ON PASS 2, WE JSR TO POKEIT (IT GOES TO INCSA)
40 JSR INCSA; BUT ON PASS 1, WE DON'T PRINT OR POKE ANYTHING, WE JUST
50 RTS; RAISE THE PC AND RETURN --------------
60 PRM LDA SFLAG; SHOULD WE PRINT TO SCREEN
70 BEQ PRMX; IF NOT, SKIP THIS NEXT PART (PRINT TO SCREEN)
80 JSR CLRCHN; OTHERWISE, RESET NORMAL I/O CONDITION
90 LDX #1; (FILE #1 FOR INPUT, SCREEN FOR OUTPUT)
100 JSR CHKIN
110 LDX OP; LOAD THE OPCODE
120 JSR PRNTNUM; PRINT IT
130 JSR PRNTSPACE; PRINT A SPACE
140 PRMX LDX OP;----------- NOW POKE THE OPCODE INTO RAM/DISK MEMORY
150 JSR POKEIT
160 RTS;--------------------------------------
170 ; PRINT TWO BYTES (THE OPCODE AND A 1-BYTE ARGUMENT)-----------------
180 PRINT2 LDA PASS; ON PASS 2, WE SKIP INCSA (SEE LINE 20 ABOVE)
190 BNE P2M
200 JSR INCSA
210 RTS;--------------------
220 P2M LDA SFLAG; IF SCREEN PRINT FLAG IS DOWN, SKIP PRINTING TO SCREEN
230 BEQ P2MX
240 LDX RESULT; OTHERWISE PRINT THE LOW-BYTE OF "RESULT" (THE ARGUMENT)
250 JSR PRNTNUM
260 P2MX LDX RESULT; AND ALSO POKE THE LOW-BYTE TO RAM/DISK MEMORY
270 JMP POKEIT; A JMP TO POKEIT WILL RTS US BACK TO THE CALLER------------
280 ; PRINT THREE BYTES (THE OPCODE AND A 2-BYTE ARGUMENT)-----------------
290 PRINT3 LDA PASS; ON PASS 2, SKIP INCSA (SEE LINE 20 ABOVE)
```

```
300 BNE P3M
310 JSR INCSA; RAISE PC BY 2
320 JSR INCSA
330 RTS;--------------------
340 P3M LDA SFLAG; SHOULD WE PRINT TO SCREEN
350 BEQ P3MX
360 LDX RESULT; PRINT AND POKE LOW BYTE OF ARGUMENT
370 JSR PRNTNUM
380 P3MX LDX RESULT
390 JSR POKEIT
400 LDA SFLAG; SHOULD WE PRINT TO SCREEN
410 BEQ P3MXX
420 LDA HXFLAG; ARE WE PRINTING OPCODES AND ARGUMENTS IN HEX
430 BEQ P3MX2; IF SO, DON'T PRINT A SPACE HERE
440 JSR PRNTSPACE; OTHERWISE, PRINT A SPACE
450 P3MX2 LDX RESULT+1; PRINT AND POKE THE HIGH BYTE OF THE ARGUMENT
460 JSR PRNTNUM
470 P3MXX LDX RESULT+1
480 JMP POKEIT; AND A JUMP TO POKEIT WILL RTS US BACK TO CALLER
490 POKEIT STX WORK+1;-------------POKE IN A BYTE TO RAM/DISK---------------
500 LDA POKEFLAG; ARE WE SUPPOSED TO POKE TO RAM
510 BEQ DISP; IF NOT, SKIP IT
520 LDY #0; OTHERWISE, SEND THE BYTE TO RAM MEMORY AT CURRENT PC ADDRESS (SA)
530 TXA
540 STA (SA),Y;----------------
550 DISP LDA DISKFLAG; ARE WE SUPPOSED TO POKE TO A DISK OBJECT FILE
560 BEQ INCSA; IF NOT, SKIP IT
570 JSR CLRCHN; IF SO, ALERT FILE #2 (WRITE FILE ON DISK)
580 LDX #2
590 JSR CHKOUT
600 LDA WORK+1; PUT THE BYTE TO BE SENT TO DISK IN THE A REGISTER
```

```
610 JSR PRINT; PRINT (AFTER LINES 550-570 ABOVE) PRINTS TO DISK FILE #2
620 JSR CLRCHN; RESTORE NORMAL I/O (PRINT TO SCREEN AND
630 LDX #1; READ FROM FILE #1
640 JSR CHKIN
650 INCSA CLC;------------------- RAISE THE PC COUNTER (SA) BY 1 --------
660 LDA #1
670 ADC SA
680 STA SA
690 LDA #0
700 ADC SA+1
710 STA SA+1
720 RTS
730 ;------------------------  PRINTOUT ROUTINES (TO SCREEN) ----------
740 PRNTMESS LDY #0; PRINT A MESSAGE (ERRORS USUALLY) TO THE SCREEN
750 MESSLOOP LDA (TEMP),Y; THESE MESSAGES ARE DELIMITED BY 0 AND ARE POINTED
760 BEQ MESSDONE; TO BY THE VARIABLE "TEMP"
770 JSR PRINT
780 JSR PTP; AFTER PRINTING A CHARACTER TO SCREEN, CHECK TO SEE IF IT SHOULD
790 INY;                       ALSO BE PRINTED TO THE PRINTER
800 JMP MESSLOOP
810 MESSDONE RTS;----------------------------
820 PRNTSPACE LDA #32; PRINT A SPACE CHARACTER
830 JSR PRINT
840 JSR PTP; SEE IF IT SHOULD ALSO GO TO THE PRINTER
850 RTS;-------------------------------------------
860 PRNTNUM STX X; PRINT A NUMBER (LOW BYTE IN X, HIGH BYTE IN A)
870 LDA HXFLAG; IF WE'RE PRINTING IN HEX, NOT DECIMAL, THEN
880 BEQ PRNTNUMD; USE THE HEXPRINT SUBROUTINE.  OTHERWISE, GO TO PRNTNUMD
890 TXA
900 JSR HEXPRINT
910 JSR PTPNU; CHECK IF NUMBER SHOULD BE PRINTED TO PRINTER AS WELL
```

```
920 LDX X; RESTORE NUMBER IN X BEFORE
930 RTS; RETURNING TO CALLER------------------------
940 PRNTNUMD LDA #0; PRINT A DECIMAL NUMBER
950 JSR OUTNUM; BASIC'S LINE NUMBER PRINTOUT ROUTINE
960 JSR PTPNU; SHOULD WE ALSO PRINT IT TO PRINTER
970 LDX X; RESTORE VALUE IN X BEFORE
980 RTS; RETURNING TO THE CALLER ---------------------------------
990 PRNTSA LDA HXFLAG; PRINT THE SA (PC, PROGRAM COUNTER)
1000 BEQ PRNTSAD; IF NOT HEX PRINTOUT, THEN USE DECIMAL ROUTINE BELOW
1010 LDA SA+1; OTHERWISE, PRINT LOW AND HIGH BYTES OF SA (AS HEX)
1020 JSR HEXPRINT; HIGH BYTE 1ST
1030 LDA SA
1040 JSR HEXPRINT
1050 JSR PTPSA; SHOULD WE ALSO PRINT SA TO PRINTER
1060 RTS;----------------
1070 PRNTSAD LDX SA; PRINT SA (DECIMAL VERSION)
1080 LDA SA+1
1090 JSR OUTNUM
1100 JSR PTPSA; PRINT TO PRINTER, TOO
1110 RTS;-----------------------------------------------
1120 PRNTCR LDA #13;                          PRINT A CARRIAGE RETURN
1130 JSR PRINT
1140 JSR PTP; SHOULD WE DO IT ON THE PRINTER TOO
1150 RTS;----------------------------------------------
1160 PRNTLINE LDX LINEN;                      PRINT A SOURCE CODE LINE NUMBER
1170 LDA LINEN+1
1180 JSR OUTNUM; BASIC ROUTINE (LOW BYTE IN X, HIGH IN A)
1190 JSR PTPLI; SHOULD WE ALSO PRINT LINE NUMBER TO PRINTER
1200 RTS; ---------------------------------------------
1210 PRNTINPUT LDA #<LABEL;                   PRINT CONTENTS OF MAIN INPUT
1220 STA TEMP;                                BUFFER ("LABEL")
```

```
1230 LDA #>LABEL; POINT "TEMP" TO THE BUFFER AND THEN
1240 STA TEMP+1
1250 JSR PRNTMESS; USE GENERAL MESSAGE PRINTING ROUTINE
1260 RTS
1270 ;-------------------------   ERROR PRINTOUT PREPARATIONS
1280 ERRING LDA #7; RING BELL
1290 JSR PRINT
1300 LDA #18; TURN ON REVERSE PRINTING TO HIGHLIGHT ERROR
1310 JSR PRINT
1320 JSR PRNTINPUT; PRINT CONTENTS OF MAIN INPUT BUFFER
1330 LDA #13; PRINT A CARRIAGE RETURN
1340 JSR PRINT
1350 RTS
1360 ;--------------------------------------- PRINTOUT (TO PRINTER)
1370 ;(PTP PRINTS A SINGLE CHARACTER TO THE PRINTER).
1380 PTP LDX PASS; ON PASS 1, DO NO PRINTING TO PRINTER
1390 BNE PTP1
1400 RTS
1410 PTP1 LDX PRINTFLAG; IF PRINTFLAG IS DOWN, DO NOTHING, RETURN TO CALLER
1420 BNE MPTP
1430 RTS;---------
1440 MPTP STA A; SAVE CONTENTS OF ACCUMULATOR
1450 JSR CLRCHN; ALERT PRINTER
1460 LDX #4
1470 JSR CHKOUT
1480 LDA A; RECOVER A
1490 JSR PRINT; PRINT TO PRINTER
1500 JSR CLRCHN; RESTORE NORMAL I/O
1510 LDX #1
1520 JSR CHKIN
1530 RETT LDA A; RECOVER A
```

```
1540 RTS; RETURN TO CALLER
1550 ;--------------------   NUMBERS TO PRINTER
1560 PTPNU LDX PASS; SAME LOGIC AS LINES 1350+ ABOVE
1570 BNE PTPN1
1580 RTS
1590 PTPN1 LDX PRINTFLAG
1600 BNE MPTPN
1610 RTS
1620 MPTPN JSR CLRCHN
1630 LDX #4
1640 JSR CHKOUT
1650 LDA HXFLAG; HEX OR DECIMAL MODE
1660 BEQ MPTPND
1670 LDA X
1680 JSR HEXPRINT
1690 JMP FINPTP
1700 MPTPND LDA #0
1710 LDX X
1720 JSR OUTNUM
1730 FINPTP JSR CLRCHN
1740 LDX #1
1750 JSR CHKIN
1760 RTS
1770 ;-------------------  SA TO PRINTER
1780 PTPSA LDX PASS; SAME LOGIC AS LINES 1350+ ABOVE
1790 BNE PTPS1
1800 RTS
1810 PTPS1 LDX PRINTFLAG
1820 BNE MPTPSA
1830 RTS
1840 MPTPSA JSR CLRCHN
```

```
1850 LDX #4
1860 JSR CHKOUT
1870 LDX HXFLAG; HEX OR DECIMAL PRINTOUT
1880 BEQ MPTPSAD
1890 LDA SA+1
1900 JSR HEXPRINT
1910 LDA SA
1920 JSR HEXPRINT
1930 JMP FINPTPSA
1940 MPTPSAD LDA SA+1
1950 LDX SA
1960 JSR OUTNUM
1970 FINPTPSA JSR CLRCHN
1980 LDX #1
1990 JSR CHKIN
2000 RTS
2010 ;------------------- LINE NUMBER TO PRINTER
2020 PTPLI LDX PASS; SAME LOGIC AS LINES 1350+ ABOVE
2030 BNE PTPL1
2040 RTS
2050 PTPL1 LDX PRINTFLAG
2060 BNE MPTPL
2070 RTS
2080 MPTPL JSR CLRCHN
2090 LDX #4
2100 JSR CHKOUT
2110 LDA LINEN+1
2120 LDX LINEN
2130 JSR OUTNUM
2140 JSR CLRCHN
2150 LDX #1
```

```
2160 JSR CHKIN
2170 RTS
2180 ;-----------------------------------  HEX NUMBER PRINTOUT
2190 ; PRINT THE NUMBER IN THE ACCUMULATOR AS A HEX DIGIT (AS ASCII CHARS.)
2200 HEXPRINT PHA; STORE NUMBER
2210 AND #$0F; CLEAR HIGH BITS (10101111 BECOMES 00001111, FOR EXAMPLE)
2220 TAY; NOW WE KNOW WHICH POSITION IN THE STRING OF HEX NUMBERS ("HEXA")
2230 LDA HEXA,Y; THIS NUMBER IS.  SO PULL IT OUT AS AN ASCII CHARACTER
2240 ; (HEXA LOOKS LIKE THIS: "0123456789ABCDEF")
2250 TAX; SAVE LOW-BITS VALUE INTO X
2260 PLA; PULL OUT THE ORIGINAL NUMBER, BUT THIS TIME
2270 LSR;SHIFT RIGHT 4 TIMES (MOVING THE 4 HIGH BITS INTO THE 4 LOW BITS AREA)
2280 LSR; (10101111 BECOMES 00001010, FOR EXAMPLE)
2290 LSR
2300 LSR
2310 TAY; AGAIN, PUT POSITION OF THIS VALUE INTO THE Y INDEX
2320 LDA HEXA,Y; PULL OUT THE RIGHT ASCII CHARACTER FROM "HEXA" STRING
2330 JSR PRINT; PRINT HIGH VALUE (FIRST) (A HOLDS HIGH VALUE AFTER LINE 2280)
2340 TXA; (X HELD LOW VALUE AFTER LINE 2210)
2350 JSR PRINT; PRINT LOW VALUE
2360 RTS; RETURN TO CALLER
2370 .FILE PSEUDO
```

Program D-12a. Pseudo

```
10 ; "PSEUDO" HANDLE ALL PSEUDOPS EXCEPT .BYTE
20 ; JMP HERE FROM INDISK
30 ; (INDISK WAS JSR'ED TO FROM EVAL). / Y HOLDS POINTER TO LABEL
40 ; -------------------------
50 PSEUDO CMP #70; IS IT "F" FOR .FILE
```

```
60 BNE PSE1
70 JSR FILE; F MEANS GO TO NEXT LINKED FILE -----------------
80 GOBACK PLA; RETURN TO EVAL TO GET NEXT LINE
90 PLA
100 JMP STARTLINE;------------------------
110 PSE1 CMP #69; IS IT .END
120 BNE PSEE
130 JSR PEND; 128 IS TOKEN FOR END (END OF CHAIN PSEUDO)
140 JMP GOBACK; RETURN TO EVAL
150 PSEE CMP #68; IS IT "D" FOR .DISK (CREATE OBJECT CODE FILE ON DISK)
160 BNE PSEE1
170 JMP PDISK; OPEN FILE ON DISK FOR OBJECT CODE STORAGE
180 PSEE1 CMP #80; IS IT "P" FOR .P (PRINTER OUTPUT)
190 BNE PSEE2
200 JMP PPRINTER; TURN ON PRINTER LISTING
210 PSEE2 CMP #78; IS IT "N" FOR .NH OR .NS OR SOME OTHER "TURN IT OFF"
220 BNE PSEE3
230 JMP NIX; TURN SOMETHING OFF
240 PSEE3 CMP #79; IS IT "O" FOR OUTPUT (POKE OBJECT CODE INTO RAM)
250 BNE PSEE4
260 JMP OPON; START POKING OBJECT CODE (DEFAULT)
270 PSEE4 CMP #83; IS IT "S" FOR PRINT TO SCREEN
280 BNE PSEE5
290 JMP SCREIN; TURN ON SCREEN PRINTING
300 PSEE5 CMP #72; IS IT "H" FOR HEX NUMBERS DURING PRINTOUTS
310 BNE PSE9
320 JMP HEXIT; TURN ON HEX PRINTING
330 ;------------------------  PRINT ERROR MESSAGE (NO SUCH PSEUDO-OP)
340 PSE9 STA LABEL,Y; STORE CHAR. FOR PRINTOUT
350 JSR PRNTLINE
360 JSR PRNTSPACE
```

```
370 JSR PRNTSA
380 JSR ERRING
390 JSR PRNTINPUT
400 LDA #<MERROR
410 STA TEMP
420 LDA #>MERROR
430 STA TEMP+1
440 JSR PRNTMESS
450 JSR PRNTCR
460 JMP PULLINE; PULL IN (& IGNORE) REST OF LINE, THEN BACK TO EVAL
470 ;-------------------------  HANDLE .FILE PSEUDO-OP ----------------
480 FILE JSR CHARIN
490 CMP #32; LOOK FOR END OF THE WORD .FILE (TO LOCATE FILENAME)
500 BEQ FI0
510 JMP FILE; CONTINUE LOOKING FOR BLANK
520 FI0 LDY #0
530 FI1 JSR CHARIN
540 CMP #0; END OF LINE
550 BEQ FI2
560 CMP #127; KEYWORD, SO STRETCH IT OUT
570 BCC FII1
580 JSR KEYWORD
590 FII1 STA LABEL,Y; STORE CHAR. OF FILENAME
600 INY
610 JMP FI1; CONTINUE STORING FILENAME IN MAIN BUFFER (LABEL)
620 FI2 STY FNAMELEN; STORE FILENAME LENGTH
630 LDY #0
640 FILO LDA LABEL,Y;------- PUT FILENAME INTO PROPER BUFFER (FILEN)
650 BEQ FILO1
660 STA FILEN,Y
670 INY
```

```
680 JMP FILO
690 FILO1 LDA PASS; ON PASS 2, DON'T PRINT OUT PC
700 BNE FI5
710 JSR PRNTSA; PRINT .FILE AND THE FILE NAME
720 JSR PRNTSPACE
730 FI5 JSR PRNTINPUT
740 JSR PRNTCR; CARRIAGE RETURN
750 JSR OPEN1; OPEN NEXT LINKED FILE ON DISK (FOR CONTINUED READING OF SOURCE)
760 LDX #1
770 JSR CHKIN
780 JSR CHARIN; PULL IN NEXT TWO BYTES AND
790 JSR CHARIN
800 JSR ENDPRO; CHECK FOR END OF PROGRAM
810 LDX #0
820 STX ENDFLAG; SET END OF PROGRAM FLAG TO ZERO
830 RTS
840 ;------------------------- HANDLE .END PSEUDO-OP ---------
850 PEND LDA #46; PRINT OUT .END
860 JSR PRINT
870 LDA #69
880 JSR PRINT
890 LDA #78
900 JSR PRINT
910 LDA #68
920 JSR PRINT
930 LDA #32
940 JSR PRINT
950 JSR CHARIN
960 JSR FILE; GET FILENAME, ETC. JUST AS .FILE PSEUDO-OP DOES
970 LDA PASS; ON PASS 1, DON'T SET THE ENDFLAG UP.
980 BEQ PEND1; BUT ON PASS 2, IT'S NECESSARY (TO END THE ENTIRE PROGRAM)
```

```
990 INC ENDFLAG
1000 PEND1 INC PASS; RAISE PASS FROM PASS 1 TO PASS 2
1002 SEC; SAVE LENGTH OF FILE
1003 LDA SA; FOR THIRD AND FOUTH
1004 SBC TA; BYTES OF BINARY FILE
1005 STA LENPTR; CREATED BY .D
1006 LDA SA+1; PSEUDO-OP
1007 SBC TA+1
1008 STA LENPTR+1
1010 LDA TA; PUT ORIGINAL START ADDRESS BACK INTO PC (SA) FOR RESTART OF
1020 STA SA; ASSEMBLY ON PASS 2.
1030 LDA TA+1
1040 STA SA+1
1050 JSR INDISK; SET UP NEXT LINE
1060 RTS
1070 ;-------------------- HANDLE .D FILENAME PSEUDO-OP (OBJECT CODE FILE)
1080 PDISK LDA PASS; ON PASS 1, DON'T STORE ANYTHING TO DISK
1090 BEQ PULLJ; PULLJ IS A SPRINGBOARD (JUMPS TO PULLINE)
1100 JSR CHARIN; POINT TO FILENAME
1110 STA LABEL,Y
1120 LDY #0
1130 PDLOOP JSR CHARIN
1140 BEQ PD1; END OF LINE
1150 CMP #127; IT'S A KEYWORD (WITHIN THE FILENAME) IF >127
1160 BCC PDIX
1170 JSR KEYWORD
1180 PDIX STA LABEL,Y; KEEP STORING FILENAME INTO PRINTOUT BUFFER (LABEL)
1190 STA FILEN,Y; AS WELL AS OPEN1 BUFFER (FILEN)
1200 INY
1210 JMP PDLOOP; KEEP STORING FILENAME;-------------------
1220 PULLJ JMP PULLINE;-------- SPRINGBOARD TO IGNORE FILENAME
```

```
1350 PD1 STY FNAMELEN
1360 JSR PRNTINPUT; PRINT OUT THE LINE
1370 JSR PRNTCR; CARRIAGE RETURN
1380 INC DISKFLAG; RAISE DISKFLAG TO SHOW THAT FUTURE POKES SHOULD GO TO DISK
1390 JSR OPEN2; OPEN A SECOND DISK FILE (THIS ONE FOR WRITING TO)
1400 LDX #2
1410 JSR CHKOUT
1420 LDA TA; PRINT OBJECT CODE'S STARTING ADDRESS TO DISK FILE
1430 JSR PRINT
1440 LDA TA+1
1450 JSR PRINT
1455 LDA LENPTR; WRITE LENGTH OF
1456 JSR PRINT; BINARY FILE
1457 LDA LENPTR+1
1458 JSR PRINT
1460 EDISK JSR CLRCHN
1470 LDX #1; RESTORE NORMAL I/O
1480 JSR CHKIN
1500 JSR ENDPRO; GET NEXT LINE NUMBER
1510 PLA; PULL RTS
1520 PLA
1530 LDX #0
1540 STX ENDFLAG; RESET END OF PROGRAM FLAG
1550 JMP STARTLINE; AND RETURN TO EVAL TO GET NEXT LINE
1560 ;------------------------- HANDLE .P (PRINTER) PSEUDO-OP -------
1570 PPRINTER LDA PASS; ON PASS 1, DO NO PRINTER OUTPUT
1580 BEQ PULLINE; GET RID OF REST OF LINE AND GO ON.
1590 JSR OPEN4; PASS 2, SO OPEN PRINTER TO HEAR FROM COMPUTER
1600 INC PRINTFLAG; RAISE PRINTER OUTPUT FLAG (SO PRINT WILL SEND BYTES TO
1610 JSR CLRCHN;                THE PRINTER AS WELL AS THE SCREEN).
1620 LDX #1; RESTORE NORMAL I/O
```

```
1630 JSR CHKIN
1640 ;---------------------- SUCTION ROUTINE.  GET RID OF REST OF A LINE
1650 PULLINE JSR CHARIN; IGNORE ALL BYTES, JUST LOCATE NEXT LINE
1660 BEQ ENDPULL; ZERO END OF LINE SHOULD GO TO ENDPRO FOR NEXT LINE #
1670 CMP #58; WHEREAS A COLON END OF LINE SKIPS THAT STEP
1680 BEQ ENDPULR; (COLON)
1690 JMP PULLINE; NEITHER COLON NOR ZERO (SO PULL IN MORE CHARACTERS)
1700 ENDPULL JSR ENDPRO
1710 ENDPULR PLA; PULL RTS OFF STACK
1720 PLA
1730 LDX #0
1740 STX ENDFLAG; SET ENDFLAG DOWN
1750 JMP STARTLINE; RETURN TO EVAL (TO GET NEXT LINE OF SOURCE CODE)
1760 ;-------------------------- HANDLE .O (POKE BYTES TO RAM) PSEUDO-OP
1770 OPON LDA #46; PRINT .O
1780 JSR PRINT
1790 LDA #79; "O"
1800 JSR PRINT
1810 JSR PRNTCR; CARRIAGE RETURN
1820 LDA #1
1830 STA POKEFLAG; RAISE POKE-TO-RAM FLAG
1840 JMP PULLINE; IGNORE REST OF LINE
1850 ;-------------------------- HANDLE .N(SOMETHING),TURN-IT-OFF PSEUDO-OPS
1860 NIX LDA PASS; ON PASS 1, DON'T BOTHER WITH ANY OF THIS
1870 BEQ PULLINE
1880 JSR CHARIN; ON PASS 2, SEE WHICH THING IS BEING TURNED OFF
1890 CMP #80; IS IT ".NP" TO "NOT PRINT TO PRINTER"
1900 BEQ NIXPRINT
1910 CMP #79; IS IT ".NO" TO "NOT POKE OBJECT BYTES TO RAM"
1920 BEQ NIXOP
1930 CMP #83; IS IT ".NS" TO "NOT PRINT TO SCREEN"
```

```
1940 BEQ NIXSCREEN
1950 CMP #72; IS IT ".NH" TO "NOT PRINTOUT HEX" (THUS SWITCH TO DECIMAL)
1960 BEQ NIXHEX
1970 ;------------------------- TURN OFF PRINTER OUTPUT
1980 NIXPRINT LDA #46; PRINT ".NP" TO SCREEN
1990 JSR PRINT
2000 LDA #78; "N"
2010 JSR PRINT
2020 LDA #80; "P"
2030 JSR PRINT
2040 JSR PRNTCR; CARRIAGE RETURN
2050 DEC PRINTFLAG; LOWER PRINT-TO-SCREEN FLAG
2060 JSR CLRCHN; TURN OFF PRINTER
2070 LDX #4
2080 JSR CHKOUT
2090 LDA #13
2100 JSR PRINT
2110 LDA #4
2120 JSR CLOSE
2130 JSR CLRCHN
2140 LDX #1; RESTORE NORMAL I/O
2150 JSR CHKIN
2160 JMP PULLINE; IGNORE REST OF LINE (AND RETURN TO EVAL)
2170 ;------------------------- STOP POKING OBJECT BYTES TO RAM
2180 NIXOP LDA #46; PRINT ".NO"
2190 JSR PRINT
2200 LDA #78;       "N"
2210 JSR PRINT
2220 LDA #79;       "O"
2230 JSR PRINT
2240 JSR PRNTCR;CARRIAGE RETURN
```

```
2250 LDA #0
2260 STA POKEFLAG; TURN OFF POKE FLAG
2270 JMP PULLINE; IGNORE REST OF LINE (AND RETURN TO EVAL)
2280 ;-------------------------- STOP HEX PRINTOUTS (START DECIMAL)
2290 NIXHEX LDA #46; PRINT ".NH"
2300 JSR PRINT
2310 LDA #78;      "N"
2320 JSR PRINT
2330 LDA #72;      "H"
2340 JSR PRINT
2350 JSR PRNTCR; CARRIAGE RETURN
2360 LDA #0
2370 STA HXFLAG; PUT HEXFLAG DOWN
2380 JMP PULLINE; IGNORE REST OF LINE (AND RETURN TO EVAL)
2390 ;-------------------------- STOP SCREEN PRINTOUTS
2400 NIXSCREEN LDA #46; PRINT ".NS"
2410 JSR PRINT
2420 LDA #78;      "N"
2430 JSR PRINT
2440 LDA #83;      "S"
2450 JSR PRINT
2460 JSR PRNTCR;CARRIAGE RETURN
2470 LDA #0
2480 STA SFLAG; PUT DOWN SCREEN PRINTOUT FLAG
2490 JMP PULLINE; IGNORE REST OF LINE (AND RETURN TO EVAL)
2660 ;--------------- HANDLE .S PSEUDO-OP (TURN ON SCREEN PRINTOUT)
2670 SCREIN LDA #46; PRINT ".S"
2680 JSR PRINT
2690 LDA #83;        "S"
2700 JSR PRINT
2710 JSR PRNTCR; CARRIAGE RETURN
```

```
2720 LDA PASS; ON PASS 1, NO SCREEN PRINTOUT
2730 BEQ SCREX
2740 LDA #1; OTHERWISE, RAISE SCREEN PRINTOUT (LISTING) FLAG
2750 STA SFLAG
2760 SCREX JMP PULLINE; IGNORE REST OF LINE (AND RETURN TO EVAL)
2770 ;-------------- HANDLE .H PSEUDO-OP (HEX NUMBERS DURING PRINTOUT)
2780 HEXIT LDA #46; PRINT ".H"
2790 JSR PRINT
2800 LDA #72;      "H"
2810 JSR PRINT
2820 JSR PRNTCR; CARRIAGE RETURN
2830 LDA #1
2840 STA HXFLAG; SET HEXFLAG UP
2850 JMP PULLINE; IGNORE REST OF LINE (AND RETURN TO EVAL)
2860 .FILE TABLES
```

Program D-12b. Pseudo, ProDOS Changes

Delete the following lines from from Program D-12a:

780–790
1002–1008
1400–1458

Program D-13a. Tables, 3.3 Version

```
10 ; "TABLES"
20 ;  TABLE OF MNEMONICS AND PARALLEL TABLE OF OPCODE/ADDRESS TYPE DATA
30 ;  BUFFERS AND MESSAGES, FLAGS, POINTERS, REGISTERS
40 ;------------------------  MNEMONICS, TYPES, ADDRESS MODE OPCODES
50 MNEMONICS .BYTE "LDALDYJSRRTSBCSBEQBCCCMP
```

```
60 .BYTE "BNELDXJMPSTASTYSTXINYDEY
70 .BYTE "DEXDECINXINCCPYCPXSBCSEC
80 .BYTE "ADCCLCTAXTAYTXATYAPHAPLA
90 .BYTE "BRKBMIBPLANDORAEORBITBVC
100 .BYTE "BVSROLRORLSRCLDCLIASLPHP
110 .BYTE "PLPRTISEDSEITSXTXSCLVNOP
120 TYPES .BYTE 1 5 9 Ø 8 8 8 1
130 .BYTE 8 5 6 1 2 2 Ø Ø
140 .BYTE Ø 2 Ø 2 4 4 1 Ø
150 .BYTE 1 Ø Ø Ø Ø Ø Ø Ø
160 .BYTE Ø 8 8 1 1 1 7 8
170 .BYTE 8 3 3 3 Ø Ø 3 Ø
180 .BYTE Ø Ø Ø Ø Ø Ø Ø Ø
190 OPS .BYTE 161 16Ø 32 96 176 24Ø 144 193
200 .BYTE 2Ø8 162 76 129 132 134 2ØØ 136
210 .BYTE 2Ø2 198 232 23Ø 192 224 225 56
220 .BYTE 97 24 17Ø 168 138 152 72 1Ø4
230 .BYTE Ø 48 16 33 1 65 36 8Ø
240 .BYTE 112 34 98 66 216 88 2 8
250 .BYTE 4Ø 64 248 12Ø 186 154 184 234
260 ;--------------------- HEX ROUTINE TABLE ------------------
270 HEXA .BYTE "Ø123456789ABCDEF"
280 ;--------------------- BUFFERS ------------------------------
290 LABEL .BYTE Ø Ø Ø Ø Ø Ø Ø Ø Ø Ø Ø Ø Ø Ø Ø Ø Ø Ø
     Ø Ø Ø
295 .BYTE Ø Ø Ø Ø Ø Ø Ø Ø Ø Ø Ø Ø Ø Ø Ø Ø Ø Ø Ø Ø Ø
     Ø Ø Ø Ø Ø Ø Ø Ø Ø Ø Ø Ø Ø Ø Ø Ø Ø Ø Ø Ø Ø Ø Ø
    Ø Ø Ø Ø Ø Ø
300 BUFFER .BYTE Ø Ø Ø Ø Ø Ø Ø Ø Ø Ø Ø Ø Ø Ø Ø Ø Ø
    Ø Ø Ø
```

```
305 .BYTE Ø Ø Ø Ø Ø Ø Ø Ø Ø Ø Ø Ø Ø Ø Ø Ø Ø Ø Ø Ø Ø
     Ø Ø Ø Ø Ø Ø Ø Ø Ø Ø Ø Ø Ø Ø Ø Ø Ø Ø Ø Ø Ø Ø Ø
    Ø Ø Ø Ø Ø Ø Ø Ø
310 BUFM .BYTE Ø Ø Ø Ø Ø Ø Ø Ø Ø Ø Ø Ø Ø Ø Ø Ø Ø Ø
    Ø Ø
315 .BYTE Ø Ø Ø Ø Ø Ø Ø Ø Ø Ø Ø Ø Ø Ø Ø Ø Ø Ø Ø Ø Ø
     Ø Ø Ø Ø Ø Ø Ø Ø Ø Ø Ø Ø Ø Ø Ø Ø Ø Ø Ø Ø Ø Ø Ø
    Ø Ø Ø Ø Ø Ø Ø Ø Ø Ø Ø Ø Ø Ø Ø Ø Ø Ø Ø Ø Ø Ø Ø Ø
     Ø Ø Ø Ø Ø Ø
320 HEXBUF .BYTE Ø Ø Ø Ø Ø Ø Ø Ø Ø Ø Ø Ø Ø Ø Ø Ø Ø Ø Ø Ø Ø
330 FILEN .BYTE Ø Ø Ø Ø Ø Ø Ø Ø Ø Ø Ø Ø Ø Ø Ø Ø Ø Ø Ø
340 NUBUF .BYTE Ø Ø Ø Ø Ø Ø Ø
350 ;-----  REGISTERS USED BY VALDEC -------
360 RADD .BYTE Ø Ø;TEMPORARY REGISTER FOR DOUBLE ADDITION
370 VREND .BYTE Ø; TEMP REG TO HOLD END OF PROGRAM COUNTER
380 TSTORE .BYTE Ø Ø; TEMPORARY REGISTER FOR MULTIPLY
390 ;---- MESSAGES TO PRINT TO SCREEN ---------------------------
400 MNOSTART .BYTE "NO START ADDRESS":.BYTE Ø
410 MBOR .BYTE "-------------------- BRANCH OUT OF RANGE":.BYTE Ø
420 NOLAB .BYTE "UNDEFINED LABEL":.BYTE Ø
430 NOARG .BYTE " NAKED LABEL":.BYTE Ø
440 MDISER .BYTE " <<<<<<<< DISK ERROR >>>>>>>> ":.BYTE Ø
450 MDUPLAB .BYTE " -- DUPLICATED LABEL -- ":.BYTE Ø
460 MERROR .BYTE " -- SYNTAX ERROR -- ":.BYTE Ø
470 ;-----------  FLAGS, POINTERS, REGISTERS  ---------------------
480 OP .BYTE Ø;          OPCODE
490 TP .BYTE Ø;          TYPE
500 TA .BYTE Ø Ø;          START ADDRESS
510 LINEN .BYTE Ø Ø;       CURRENT LINE #
520 ENDFLAG .BYTE Ø;     END-OF-PROG FLAG
530 WORK .BYTE Ø Ø;        TEMP WORK AREA
```

```
540 RESULT .BYTE Ø Ø;        TEMP ANSWER AREA
550 ARGN .BYTE Ø Ø;          VALUE OF ARGUMENT
560 ARGSIZE .BYTE Ø;       LENGTH OF ARGUMENT
570 EXPRESSF .BYTE Ø;      IS IT AN EXPRESS LABEL
580 HEXFLAG .BYTE Ø;       HEX NUMBER FLAG
590 HEXLEN .BYTE Ø;        LENGTH OF HEX NUMBER
600 NUMSIZE .BYTE Ø;       LENGTH OF ASCII NUMBER IN BUFFER (FOR VALDEC)
610 KEYNUM .BYTE Ø;        POSITION OF KEYWORD IN BASIC'S TABLE
620 LABSIZE .BYTE Ø;       SIZE OF LABEL (EQUATE TYPE)
630 LABPTR .BYTE Ø Ø;        POINTS TO ARRAY POSITION FOR ARG STORAGE
640 ARRAYTOP .BYTE Ø Ø;      TOP OF ARRAYS--SAME AS MEMTOP BEFORE LABELS.
650 BUFLAG .BYTE Ø;        AVOID # OR ( DURING ARRAYS ANALYSIS
660 PASS .BYTE Ø;          WHICH PASS WE'RE ON.
670 A .BYTE Ø:X .BYTE Ø:Y .BYTE Ø; TO HOLD REGISTERS DURING P SUBR. CHECKER
680 PT .BYTE Ø Ø;            TEMPORARILY HOLDS PARRAY (IN "ARRAY") 2-BYTE
690 BNUMFLAG .BYTE Ø;      FOR .BYTE IN "INDISK"
700 BFLAG .BYTE Ø Ø;         FOR NUMWERK IN "INDISK"
710 ADDNUM .BYTE Ø Ø;        NUMBER TO ADD FOR + PSEUDO
720 PLUSFLAG .BYTE Ø;      FLAG SHOWS THAT + PSEUDO HAPPENED.
730 BYTFLAG .BYTE Ø;       SHOWS THAT < OR > HAPPENED.
740 DISKFLAG .BYTE Ø;      SHOWS TO SEND BYTES TO DISK OBJECT FILE
750 PRINTFLAG .BYTE Ø;     SHOWS TO SEND BYTES TO PRINTER
760 POKEFLAG .BYTE Ø;      SHOWS TO SEND BYTES TO MEMORY (OBJECT CODE)
770 COLFLAG .BYTE Ø;       ENCOUNTERED A COLON (USED BY INDISK)
780 FOUNDFLAG .BYTE Ø;     DUPLCATED LABEL NAME (USED BY ARRAY)
790 SFLAG .BYTE Ø;         SHOWS TO SEND SOURCECODE TO SCREEN
800 HXFLAG .BYTE Ø;        SHOWS TO PRINT SA AND OPCODES IN HEX
810 LOCFLAG .BYTE Ø;       SHOWS TO PRINT A PC ADDRESS LABEL
820 BABFLAG .BYTE Ø;       SHOWS TO PRINT A REM AFTER PRNTINPUT IN EVAL
830 LENPTR .BYTE Ø Ø;      HOLDS LENGTH OF BINARY PROGRAM
840 FOPEN1 .BYTE Ø;        HOLDS THE CURRENT INPUT FILE
```

```
850 FOPEN2 .BYTE Ø;      HOLDS THE CURRENT OUTPUT FILE
855 ;------------ DOS-MANAGER CONTROL BYTES ------------------
860 OPNREAD .BYTE 1 Ø 1 Ø Ø 1 6 2
870 .BYTE 45 147 Ø Ø Ø 147 Ø 146 Ø Ø
880 OPNWRIT .BYTE 1 Ø 1 Ø Ø 1 6 4
890 .BYTE 128 149 Ø Ø 83 149 83 148 Ø Ø
900 RD1B .BYTE 3 1 Ø Ø Ø Ø Ø Ø Ø Ø Ø Ø
910 .BYTE Ø 147 Ø 146 Ø 145
920 WR1B .BYTE 4 1 Ø Ø Ø Ø Ø Ø
930 WRDATA .BYTE Ø Ø Ø Ø 83 149 83 148 83 147
940 CLOSER .BYTE 2 Ø Ø Ø Ø Ø Ø Ø Ø Ø Ø Ø Ø 147 Ø 146 Ø 145
950 CLOSEW .BYTE 2 Ø Ø Ø Ø Ø Ø Ø Ø Ø Ø Ø 83 149 83 148 83 147
960 OPNI .BYTE Ø;        HOLDS THE FILE # OF THE CURRENT INPUT DEVICE
970 OPNO .BYTE Ø;        HOLDS THE FILE # OF THE CURRENT OUTPUT DEVICE
980 A1 .BYTE Ø;          TEMP STORAGE OF ACC
990 Y1 .BYTE Ø;          TEMP STORAGE OF Y-REG
1000 ;---------------------
1010 .END DEFS
```

Program D-13b. Tables, ProDOS Version

```
10 ; PRODOS TABLES
20 ;  TABLE OF MNEMONICS AND PARALLEL TABLE OF OPCODE/ADDRESS TYPE DATA
30 ;  BUFFERS AND MESSAGES, FLAGS, POINTERS, REGISTERS
40 ;------------------------  MNEMONICS, TYPES, ADDRESS MODE OPCODES
50 MNEMONICS .BYTE "LDALDYJSRRTSBCSBEQBCCCMP
60 .BYTE "BNELDXJMPSTASTYSTXINYDEY
70 .BYTE "DEXDECINXINCCPYCPXSBCSEC
80 .BYTE "ADCCLCTAXTAYTXATYAPHAPLA
90 .BYTE "BRKBMIBPLANDORAEORBITBVC
```

```
100 .BYTE "BVSROLRORLSRCLDCLIASLPHP
110 .BYTE "PLPRTISEDSEITSXTXSCLVNOP
120 TYPES .BYTE 1 5 9 0 8 8 8 1
130 .BYTE 8 5 6 1 2 2 0 0
140 .BYTE 0 2 0 2 4 4 1 0
150 .BYTE 1 0 0 0 0 0 0 0
160 .BYTE 0 8 8 1 1 1 7 8
170 .BYTE 8 3 3 3 0 0 3 0
180 .BYTE 0 0 0 0 0 0 0 0
190 OPS .BYTE 161 160 32 96 176 240 144 193
200 .BYTE 208 162 76 129 132 134 200 136
210 .BYTE 202 198 232 230 192 224 225 56
220 .BYTE 97 24 170 168 138 152 72 104
230 .BYTE 0 48 16 33 1 65 36 80
240 .BYTE 112 34 98 66 216 88 2 8
250 .BYTE 40 64 248 120 186 154 184 234
260 ;--------------------- HEX ROUTINE TABLE ------------------
270 HEXA .BYTE "0123456789ABCDEF"
280 ;--------------------- BUFFERS -----------------------------
290 LABEL .BYTE 0 0 0 0 0 0 0 0 0 0 0 0 0 0 0 0 0 0
     0 0 0
295 .BYTE 0 0 0 0 0 0 0 0 0 0 0 0 0 0 0 0 0 0 0 0 0
     0 0 0 0 0 0 0 0 0 0 0 0 0 0 0 0 0 0 0 0 0 0 0
    0 0 0 0 0 0
300 BUFFER .BYTE 0 0 0 0 0 0 0 0 0 0 0 0 0 0 0 0 0
    0 0 0
305 .BYTE 0 0 0 0 0 0 0 0 0 0 0 0 0 0 0 0 0 0 0 0 0
     0 0 0 0 0 0 0 0 0 0 0 0 0 0 0 0 0 0 0 0 0 0 0
    0 0 0 0 0 0 0 0
310 BUFM .BYTE 0 0 0 0 0 0 0 0 0 0 0 0 0 0 0 0 0 0
    0 0
```

```
315 .BYTE Ø Ø Ø Ø Ø Ø Ø Ø Ø Ø Ø Ø Ø Ø Ø Ø Ø Ø Ø Ø Ø
     Ø Ø Ø Ø Ø Ø Ø Ø Ø Ø Ø Ø Ø Ø Ø Ø Ø Ø Ø Ø Ø Ø Ø
    Ø Ø Ø Ø Ø Ø Ø Ø Ø Ø Ø Ø Ø Ø Ø Ø Ø Ø Ø Ø Ø Ø Ø Ø
     Ø Ø Ø Ø Ø Ø Ø
320 HEXBUF .BYTE Ø Ø Ø Ø Ø Ø Ø Ø Ø Ø Ø Ø Ø Ø Ø Ø Ø
    Ø Ø Ø Ø
340 NUBUF .BYTE Ø Ø Ø Ø Ø Ø Ø
350 ;-----  REGISTERS USED BY VALDEC -------
360 RADD .BYTE Ø Ø;TEMPORARY REGISTER FOR DOUBLE ADDITION
370 VREND .BYTE Ø; TEMP REG TO HOLD END OF PROGRAM COUNTER
380 TSTORE .BYTE Ø Ø; TEMPORARY REGISTER FOR MULTIPLY
390 ;---- MESSAGES TO PRINT TO SCREEN ----------------------------
400 MNOSTART .BYTE "NO START ADDRESS":.BYTE Ø
410 MBOR .BYTE "--------------------- BRANCH OUT OF RANGE":.BYTE Ø
420 NOLAB .BYTE "UNDEFINED LABEL":.BYTE Ø
430 NOARG .BYTE " NAKED LABEL":.BYTE Ø
440 MDISER .BYTE " <<<<<<<< DISK ERROR >>>>>>>> ":.BYTE Ø
450 MDUPLAB .BYTE " -- DUPLICATED LABEL -- ":.BYTE Ø
460 MERROR .BYTE " -- SYNTAX ERROR -- ":.BYTE Ø
470 ;-----------  FLAGS, POINTERS, REGISTERS  ---------------------
480 OP .BYTE Ø;           OPCODE
490 TP .BYTE Ø;           TYPE
500 TA .BYTE Ø Ø;           START ADDRESS
510 LINEN .BYTE Ø Ø;        CURRENT LINE #
520 ENDFLAG .BYTE Ø;      END-OF-PROG FLAG
530 WORK .BYTE Ø Ø;         TEMP WORK AREA
540 RESULT .BYTE Ø Ø;       TEMP ANSWER AREA
550 ARGN .BYTE Ø Ø;         VALUE OF ARGUMENT
560 ARGSIZE .BYTE Ø;      LENGTH OF ARGUMENT
570 EXPRESSF .BYTE Ø;     IS IT AN EXPRESS LABEL
580 HEXFLAG .BYTE Ø;      HEX NUMBER FLAG
```

```
590 HEXLEN .BYTE Ø;       LENGTH OF HEX NUMBER
600 NUMSIZE .BYTE Ø;      LENGTH OF ASCII NUMBER IN BUFFER (FOR VALDEC)
610 KEYNUM .BYTE Ø;       POSITION OF KEYWORD IN BASIC'S TABLE
620 LABSIZE .BYTE Ø;      SIZE OF LABEL (EQUATE TYPE)
630 LABPTR .BYTE Ø Ø;       POINTS TO ARRAY POSITION FOR ARG STORAGE
640 ARRAYTOP .BYTE Ø Ø;     TOP OF ARRAYS--SAME AS MEMTOP BEFORE LABELS.
650 BUFLAG .BYTE Ø;       AVOID # OR ( DURING ARRAYS ANALYSIS
660 PASS .BYTE Ø;         WHICH PASS WE'RE ON.
670 A .BYTE Ø:X .BYTE Ø:Y .BYTE Ø; TO HOLD REGISTERS DURING P SUBR. CHECKER
680 PT .BYTE Ø Ø;           TEMPORARILY HOLDS PARRAY (IN "ARRAY") 2-BYTE
690 BNUMFLAG .BYTE Ø;     FOR .BYTE IN "INDISK"
700 BFLAG .BYTE Ø Ø;        FOR NUMWERK IN "INDISK"
710 ADDNUM .BYTE Ø Ø;       NUMBER TO ADD FOR + PSEUDO
720 PLUSFLAG .BYTE Ø;     FLAG SHOWS THAT + PSEUDO HAPPENED.
730 BYTFLAG .BYTE Ø;      SHOWS THAT < OR > HAPPENED.
740 DISKFLAG .BYTE Ø;     SHOWS TO SEND BYTES TO DISK OBJECT FILE
750 PRINTFLAG .BYTE Ø;    SHOWS TO SEND BYTES TO PRINTER
760 POKEFLAG .BYTE Ø;     SHOWS TO SEND BYTES TO MEMORY (OBJECT CODE)
770 COLFLAG .BYTE Ø;      ENCOUNTERED A COLON (USED BY INDISK)
780 FOUNDFLAG .BYTE Ø;    DUPLCATED LABEL NAME (USED BY ARRAY)
790 SFLAG .BYTE Ø;        SHOWS TO SEND SOURCECODE TO SCREEN
800 HXFLAG .BYTE Ø;       SHOWS TO PRINT SA AND OPCODES IN HEX
810 LOCFLAG .BYTE Ø;      SHOWS TO PRINT A PC ADDRESS LABEL
820 BABFLAG .BYTE Ø;      SHOWS TO PRINT A REM AFTER PRNTINPUT IN EVAL
840 FOPEN1 .BYTE Ø;       HOLDS THE CURRENT INPUT FILE
850 FOPEN2 .BYTE Ø;       HOLDS THE CURRENT OUTPUT FILE
855 ;------------ PRODOS MLI PARAMETER LISTS -------------------
857 .BYTE 255; MARKER
858 *= $91ØØ; FIX LOCATIONS OF PARAMETER LISTS
860 ;CRELIST .BYTE 7 <NAMEBUFF >NAMEBUFF $C3 6 Ø Ø 1 Ø Ø Ø Ø
865 CRELIST .BYTE 7 55 145 195 6 Ø Ø 1 Ø Ø Ø Ø
```

```
870 CLOSLIST .BYTE 1 Ø
880 ;OPENLIST .BYTE 3 <NAMEBUFF >NAMEBUFF Ø Ø Ø
885 OPENLIST .BYTE 3 55 145 Ø Ø Ø
890 SEOFLIST .BYTE 2 Ø Ø Ø Ø
900 ;RWLIST .BYTE 4 Ø <DATABUFF >DATABUFF 1 Ø Ø Ø
905 RWLIST .BYTE 4 Ø 54 145 1 Ø Ø Ø
910 ;INFOLIST .BYTE 7 <NAMEBUFF >NAMEBUFF $C3 6 Ø Ø Ø Ø Ø Ø Ø Ø Ø
915 INFOLIST .BYTE 7 55 145 195 6 Ø Ø Ø Ø Ø Ø Ø Ø Ø
916 ;PREFLIST .BYTE 1 <NAMEBUFF >NAMEBUFF
917 PREFLIST .BYTE 1 55 145
918 ;OLINLIST .BYTE 2 Ø <NAMEBUFF+1 >NAMEBUFF+1
919 OLINLIST .BYTE 2 Ø 56 145
920 DATABUFF .BYTE Ø
924 NAMEBUFF .BYTE Ø
925 FILEN .BYTE Ø Ø Ø Ø Ø Ø Ø Ø Ø Ø Ø Ø Ø Ø Ø Ø
930 .BYTE Ø Ø Ø Ø Ø Ø Ø Ø Ø Ø Ø Ø Ø Ø Ø Ø
940 .BYTE Ø Ø Ø Ø Ø Ø Ø Ø Ø Ø Ø Ø Ø Ø Ø Ø
950 .BYTE Ø Ø Ø Ø Ø Ø Ø Ø Ø Ø Ø Ø Ø Ø Ø Ø
960 OPNI .BYTE Ø;         HOLDS THE FILE # OF THE CURRENT INPUT DEVICE
970 OPNO .BYTE Ø;         HOLDS THE FILE # OF THE CURRENT OUTPUT DEVICE
980 A1 .BYTE Ø;           TEMP STORAGE OF ACC
990 Y1 .BYTE Ø;           TEMP STORAGE OF Y-REG
1000 ;---------------------
1010 .END DEFS
```

Appendix E

Library of Subroutines

Library of Subroutines

Here is a collection of techniques you'll need to use in many of your ML programs. Those techniques which are not inherently easy to understand are followed by an explanation.

Increment and Decrement Double-Byte Numbers

You'll often want to raise or lower a number by 1. To *increment* a number, you add 1 to it: Incrementing 5 results in 6. Decrement lowers a number by 1. Single-byte numbers are easy; you just use INC or DEC. But you'll often want to increment two-byte numbers which hold addresses, game scores, pointers, or some other number which requires two bytes. Two bytes, ganged together and seen as a single number, can hold values from 0 ($0000) up to 65535 ($FFFF). Here's how to raise a two-byte number by 1, to increment it:

(Let's assume that the number you want to increment or decrement is located in addresses $0605 and $0606, and the ML program segment performing the action is located at $5000.)

```
5000 INCREMENT INC $0605 (Raise the low byte.)
5003 BNE GOFORTH         (If not zero, leave high byte alone.)
5005 INC $0606           (Raise high byte.)
5008 GOFORTH...          (Continue with program.)
```

The trick in this routine is the BNE. If the low byte isn't raised to 0 (from 255), we don't need to add a carry to the high byte, so we jump over it. However, if the low byte does turn into a 0, the high byte must then be raised. This is similar to the way an ordinary decimal increment creates a carry when you add 1 to 9 (or to 99 or 999). The lower number turns to 0, and the next column over is raised by 1.

To double-decrement, you need an extra step. The reason it's more complicated is that the 6502 chip has no way to test if you've crossed over to $FF, down from $00. BNE and BEQ will test if something is 0, but nothing tests for $FF. (The N flag *is* turned on when you go from $00 to $FF, and BPL or BMI could test it.) The problem with it, though, is that the N flag isn't limited to sensing $FF. It is sensitive to *any* number higher than 127 decimal ($7F).

So, here's the way to handle double-deckers:

```
5000 LDA $0605           (Load in the low byte, affecting the
                          zero flag.)
```

5003 BNE FIXLOWBYTE	(If it's not zero, lower it, skipping high byte.)
5005 DEC $0606	(Zero in low byte forces this.)
5008 FIXLOWBYTE DEC $0605	(Always dec the low byte.)

Here we *always* lower the low byte, but lower the high byte only when the low byte is found to be zero. If you think about it, that's the way any subtraction would work.

Comparison

Comparing a single-byte against another single-byte is easily achieved with CMP. Double-byte comparison can be handled this way:

(Assume that the numbers you want to compare are located in addresses $0605,0606 and $0700,0701. The ML program segment performing the comparison is located at $5000.)

5000 SEC	
5001 LDA $0605	(Low byte of first number)
5004 SBC $0700	(Low byte of second number)
5007 STA $0800	(Temporary holding place for this result)
500A LDA $0606	(High byte of first number)
500D SBC $0701	(High byte of second number, leave result in A)
5010 ORA $0800	(Results in zero if A and $0800 were both zero)

The flags in the status register are left in various states after this routine—you can test them with the B instructions and branch according to the results. The ORA sets the Z (zero) flag if the results of the first subtraction (left in $0800) and the second subtraction (in A, the accumulator) were both zero. This would happen only if the two numbers tested were identical, and BEQ would test for this (Branch if EQual).

If the first number is lower than the second, the carry flag would have been cleared, so BCC (Branch if Carry Clear) will test for that possibility. If the first number is higher than the second, BCS (Branch if Carry Set) will be true. You can therefore branch with BEQ for =, BCC for <, and BCS for >. Just keep in mind which number you are considering the *first* and which the *second* in this test.

Double-Byte Addition

CLC ADC and SEC SBC will add and subtract one-byte numbers. To add two-byte numbers, use:

(Assume that the numbers you want to add are located in addresses

$0605,0606 and $0700,0701. The ML program segment performing the addition is located at $5000.)

```
5000  CLC         (Always do this before any addition.)
5001  LDA $0605
5004  ADC $0700
5007  STA $0605   (The result will be left in $0605,0606.)
500A  LDA $0606
500D  ADC $0701
5010  STA $0606
```

It's not necessary to put the result on top of the number in $0605,0606—you can put it anywhere. But you'll often be adding a particular value to another and not needing the original any longer—adding ten points to a score for every blasted alien is an example. If this were the case, following the logic of the routine above, you would have a 10 in $0701,0702:

```
0701 0A  (The ten points you get for hitting an alien)
0702 00
```

You'd want that 10 to remain undisturbed throughout the game. The score, however, keeps changing during the game and, held in $0605,0606, it can be covered over, replaced with each addition.

Double-Byte Subtraction

This is quite similar to double-byte addition. Since subtracting one number from another is also a comparison of those two numbers, you could combine subtraction with the double-byte comparison routine above (using ORA). In any event, this is the way to subtract double-byte numbers. Be sure to keep straight which number is being subtracted from the other. We'll call the number *being subtracted* the *second number.*

(Assume that the number you want to subtract [the "second number"] is located in addresses $0700,0701, and the number it is being subtracted from [the "first number"] is held in $0605,0606. The result will be left in $0605,0606. The ML program segment performing the subtraction is located at $5000.)

```
5000  SEC         (Always do this before any subtraction.)
5001  LDA $0605   (Low byte of first number)
5004  SBC $0700   (Low byte of second number)
5007  STA $0605   (The result will be left in $0605,0606.)
500A  LDA $0606   (High byte of first number)
```

```
500D SBC $0701   (High byte of second number)
5010 STA $0606   (High byte of final result)
```

Multibyte Addition and Subtraction

Using the methods for adding and subtracting illustrated above, you can manipulate larger numbers than can be held within two bytes (65535 is the largest possible two-byte integer). Here's how to subtract one four-byte-long number from another. The locations and conditions are the same as for the two-byte subtraction example above, except the "first number" (the *minuend*) is held in the four-byte chain, $0605,0606,0607,0608, and the "second number" (the *subtrahend*, the number being subtracted from the first number) is in $0700,0701,0702,0703.

Also observe that the most significant byte is held in $0703 and $0608. We'll use the Y register for indirect Y addressing, four bytes in zero page as pointers to the two numbers, and the X register as a counter to make sure that all four bytes are dealt with. This means that X must be loaded with the length of the chains we're subtracting—in this case, 4.

```
5000 LDX #4               (Length of the byte chains)
5002 LDY #0               (Set Y)
5004 SEC                  (Always before subtraction)
5005 LOOP LDA (FIRST),Y
5007 SBC (SECOND),Y
5009 STA (FIRST),Y        (The answer will be left in
                          $0605–0608.)
500B INY                  (Raise index to chains)
500C DEX                  (Lower counter)
5010 BNE LOOP             (Haven't yet done all four bytes)
```

Before this will work, the pointers in zero page must have been set up to allow the indirect Y addressing. This is one way to do it:

```
2000 FIRST = $FB       (Define zero page pointers at $FB and $FD)
2000 SECOND = $FD
2000 SETUP LDA #5      (Set up pointer to $0605)
2002 STA FIRST
2004 LDA #6
2006 STA FIRST+1
2008 LDA #0            (Set up pointer to $0700)
200A STA SECOND
200C LDA #7
200E STA SECOND+1
```

Multiplication

× 2

ASL (no argument used, "accumulator addressing mode") will multiply the number in the accumulator by 2.

× 3

(To multiply by 3, use a temporary variable byte we'll call TEMP.)

5000 STA TEMP (Put the number into the variable)
5003 ASL (Multiply it by 2)
5004 ADC TEMP ((X * 2 + X = X * 3) the answer is in A.)

× 4

(To multiply by 4, just ASL twice.)

5000 ASL (* 2)
5001 ASL (* 2 again)

× 4 (Two Byte)

(To multiply a two-byte integer by 4, use a two-byte variable we'll call TEMP and TEMP+1.)

5000 ASL TEMP (Multiply the low byte by 2)
5003 ROL TEMP+1 (Moving any carry into the high byte)
5006 ASL TEMP (Multiply the low byte by 2 again)
5009 ROL TEMP+1 (Again acknowledge any carry)

× 10

(To multiply a two-byte integer by 10, use an additional two-byte variable we'll call STORE.)

5000 (First, put the number into STORE for safekeeping.)
5000 LDA TEMP:STA STORE:LDA TEMP+1:STA STORE+1
500C (Then multiply it by 4.)
500C ASL TEMP (Multiply the low byte by 2)
500F ROL TEMP+1 (moving any carry into the high byte.)
5012 ASL TEMP (Multiply the low byte by 2 again.)
5015 ROL TEMP+1; (Again acknowledge any carry.)
5018 (Then add the original, resulting in X * 5.)
5018 LDA STORE
501B ADC TEMP
501E STA TEMP
5021 LDA STORE+1
501D ADC TEMP+1

```
5024  STA TEMP+1
5027                         (Then just multiply by 2 since (5 * 2 = 10).)
5027  ASL TEMP
502A  ROL TEMP+1
```

× ?

(To multiply a two-byte integer by other odd values, just use a similar combination of addition and multiplication which results in the correct amount of multiplication.)

× 100

(To multiply a two-byte integer by 100, just go through the above subroutine twice.)

× 256

(To multiply a one-byte integer by 256, just transform it into a two-byte integer.)

```
5000 LDA TEMP
5003 STA TEMP+1
5006 LDA #0
5008 STA TEMP
```

Division

÷ 2

LSR (no argument used, "accumulator addressing mode") will divide the number in the accumulator by 2.

÷ 4

(To divide by 4, just LSR twice.)

```
5000 LSR  (/ 2)
5001 LSR  (/ 2 again)
```

÷ 4 (Two Byte)

(To divide a two-byte integer, called TEMP, by 2)

```
5000 LSR TEMP+1  (Shift high byte right)
5001 ROR TEMP    (pulling any carry into the low byte.)
```

Appendix F

Number Tables

Number Tables

This lookup table should make it convenient when you need to translate hex, binary, or decimal numbers. The first column lists the decimal numbers between 1 and 255. The second column is the hexadecimal equivalent. The third column is the decimal equivalent of a hex *most significant byte,* or MSB. The fourth column is the binary.

If you need to find out the decimal equivalent of the hex number $FD15, look up $FD in the hex column and you'll see that the MSB is 64768. Then look up the $15 in the hex column to get the LSB (it's 21 decimal) and add 21+64768 to get the answer: 64789.

Going the other way, from decimal to hex, you could translate 64780 into hex by looking in the MSB column for the closest number (it must be smaller, however). In this case, the closest smaller number is 64768, so jot down $FD as the hex MSB. Then subtract 64768 from 64780 to get the LSB: 12. Look up 12 in the decimal column (it is $0C hex) and put the $FD MSB together with the $0C LSB for your answer: $FD0C.

With a little practice, you can use this chart for fairly quick conversions between the number systems. Most of your translations will only involve going from hex to decimal or vice versa with the LSB of hex numbers, the first 255 numbers, which require no addition or subtraction. Just look them up in the table.

Table F-1. Number Tables

Decimal (LSB)	Hex	Decimal (MSB)	Binary
1	Ø1	256	ØØØØØØØ1
2	Ø2	512	ØØØØØØ1Ø
3	Ø3	768	ØØØØØØ11
4	Ø4	1Ø24	ØØØØØ1ØØ
5	Ø5	128Ø	ØØØØØ1Ø1
6	Ø6	1536	ØØØØØ11Ø
7	Ø7	1792	ØØØØØ111
8	Ø8	2Ø48	ØØØØ1ØØØ
9	Ø9	23Ø4	ØØØØ1ØØ1
1Ø	ØA	256Ø	ØØØØ1Ø1Ø
11	ØB	2816	ØØØØ1Ø11
12	ØC	3Ø72	ØØØØ11ØØ
13	ØD	3328	ØØØØ11Ø1
14	ØE	3584	ØØØØ111Ø
15	ØF	384Ø	ØØØØ1111

Decimal (LSB)	Hex	Decimal (MSB)	Binary
16	10	4096	00010000
17	11	4352	00010001
18	12	4608	00010010
19	13	4864	00010011
20	14	5120	00010100
21	15	5376	00010101
22	16	5632	00010110
23	17	5888	00010111
24	18	6144	00011000
25	19	6400	00011001
26	1A	6656	00011010
27	1B	6912	00011011
28	1C	7168	00011100
29	1D	7424	00011101
30	1E	7680	00011110
31	1F	7936	00011111
32	20	8192	00100000
33	21	8448	00100001
34	22	8704	00100010
35	23	8960	00100011
36	24	9216	00100100
37	25	9472	00100101
38	26	9728	00100110
39	27	9984	00100111
40	28	10240	00101000
41	29	10496	00101001
42	2A	10752	00101010
43	2B	11008	00101011
44	2C	11264	00101100
45	2D	11520	00101101
46	2E	11776	00101110
47	2F	12032	00101111
48	30	12288	00110000
49	31	12544	00110001
50	32	12800	00110010
51	33	13056	00110011
52	34	13312	00110100
53	35	13568	00110101
54	36	13824	00110110
55	37	14080	00110111
56	38	14336	00111000
57	39	14592	00111001
58	3A	14848	00111010
59	3B	15104	00111011
60	3C	15360	00111100
61	3D	15616	00111101
62	3E	15872	00111110
63	3F	16128	00111111

Decimal (LSB)	Hex	Decimal (MSB)	Binary
64	40	16384	01000000
65	41	16640	01000001
66	42	16896	01000010
67	43	17152	01000011
68	44	17408	01000100
69	45	17664	01000101
70	46	17920	01000110
71	47	18176	01000111
72	48	18432	01001000
73	49	18688	01001001
74	4A	18944	01001010
75	4B	19200	01001011
76	4C	19456	01001100
77	4D	19712	01001101
78	4E	19968	01001110
79	4F	20224	01001111
80	50	20480	01010000
81	51	20736	01010001
82	52	20992	01010010
83	53	21248	01010011
84	54	21504	01010100
85	55	21760	01010101
86	56	22016	01010110
87	57	22272	01010111
88	58	22528	01011000
89	59	22784	01011001
90	5A	23040	01011010
91	5B	23296	01011011
92	5C	23552	01011100
93	5D	23808	01011101
94	5E	24064	01011110
95	5F	24320	01011111
96	60	24576	01100000
97	61	24832	01100001
98	62	25088	01100010
99	63	25344	01100011
100	64	25600	01100100
101	65	25856	01100101
102	66	26112	01100110
103	67	26368	01100111
104	68	26624	01101000
105	69	26880	01101001
106	6A	27136	01101010
107	6B	27392	01101011
108	6C	27648	01101100
109	6D	27904	01101101
110	6E	28160	01101110

Decimal (LSB)	Hex	Decimal (MSB)	Binary
111	6F	28416	Ø11Ø1111
112	7Ø	28672	Ø111ØØØØ
113	71	28928	Ø111ØØØ1
114	72	29184	Ø111ØØ1Ø
115	73	2944Ø	Ø111ØØ11
116	74	29696	Ø111Ø1ØØ
117	75	29952	Ø111Ø1Ø1
118	76	3Ø2Ø8	Ø111Ø11Ø
119	77	3Ø464	Ø111Ø111
12Ø	78	3Ø72Ø	Ø1111ØØØ
121	79	3Ø976	Ø1111ØØ1
122	7A	31232	Ø1111Ø1Ø
123	7B	31488	Ø1111Ø11
124	7C	31744	Ø11111ØØ
125	7D	32ØØØ	Ø11111Ø1
126	7E	32256	Ø111111Ø
127	7F	32512	Ø1111111
128	8Ø	32768	1ØØØØØØØ
129	81	33Ø24	1ØØØØØØ1
13Ø	82	3328Ø	1ØØØØØ1Ø
131	83	33536	1ØØØØØ11
132	84	33792	1ØØØØ1ØØ
133	85	34Ø48	1ØØØØ1Ø1
134	86	343Ø4	1ØØØØ11Ø
135	87	3456Ø	1ØØØØ111
136	88	34816	1ØØØ1ØØØ
137	89	35Ø72	1ØØØ1ØØ1
138	8A	35328	1ØØØ1Ø1Ø
139	8B	35584	1ØØØ1Ø11
14Ø	8C	3584Ø	1ØØØ11ØØ
141	8D	36Ø96	1ØØØ11Ø1
142	8E	36352	1ØØØ111Ø
143	8F	366Ø8	1ØØØ1111
144	9Ø	36864	1ØØ1ØØØØ
145	91	3712Ø	1ØØ1ØØØ1
146	92	37376	1ØØ1ØØ1Ø
147	93	37632	1ØØ1ØØ11
148	94	37888	1ØØ1Ø1ØØ
149	95	38144	1ØØ1Ø1Ø1
15Ø	96	384ØØ	1ØØ1Ø11Ø
151	97	38656	1ØØ1Ø111
152	98	38912	1ØØ11ØØØ
153	99	39168	1ØØ11ØØ1
154	9A	39424	1ØØ11Ø1Ø
155	9B	3968Ø	1ØØ11Ø11
156	9C	39936	1ØØ111ØØ
157	9D	4Ø192	1ØØ111Ø1
158	9E	4Ø448	1ØØ1111Ø

Decimal (LSB)	Hex	Decimal (MSB)	Binary
159	9F	40704	10011111
160	A0	40960	10100000
161	A1	41216	10100001
162	A2	41472	10100010
163	A3	41728	10100011
164	A4	41984	10100100
165	A5	42240	10100101
166	A6	42496	10100110
167	A7	42752	10100111
168	A8	43008	10101000
169	A9	43264	10101001
170	AA	43520	10101010
171	AB	43776	10101011
172	AC	44032	10101100
173	AD	44288	10101101
174	AE	44544	10101110
175	AF	44800	10101111
176	B0	45056	10110000
177	B1	45312	10110001
178	B2	45568	10110010
179	B3	45824	10110011
180	B4	46080	10110100
181	B5	46336	10110101
182	B6	46592	10110110
183	B7	46848	10110111
184	B8	47104	10111000
185	B9	47360	10111001
186	BA	47616	10111010
187	BB	47872	10111011
188	BC	48128	10111100
189	BD	48384	10111101
190	BE	48640	10111110
191	BF	48896	10111111
192	C0	49152	11000000
193	C1	49408	11000001
194	C2	49664	11000010
195	C3	49920	11000011
196	C4	50176	11000100
197	C5	50432	11000101
198	C6	50688	11000110
199	C7	50944	11000111
200	C8	51200	11001000
201	C9	51456	11001001
202	CA	51712	11001010
203	CB	51968	11001011
204	CC	52224	11001100
205	CD	52480	11001101

Decimal (LSB)	Hex	Decimal (MSB)	Binary
2Ø6	CE	52736	11ØØ111Ø
2Ø7	CF	52992	11ØØ1111
2Ø8	DØ	53248	11Ø1ØØØØ
2Ø9	D1	535Ø4	11Ø1ØØØ1
21Ø	D2	5376Ø	11Ø1ØØ1Ø
211	D3	54Ø16	11Ø1ØØ11
212	D4	54272	11Ø1Ø1ØØ
213	D5	54528	11Ø1Ø1Ø1
214	D6	54784	11Ø1Ø11Ø
215	D7	55Ø4Ø	11Ø1Ø111
216	D8	55296	11Ø11ØØØ
217	D9	55552	11Ø11ØØ1
218	DA	558Ø8	11Ø11Ø1Ø
219	DB	56Ø64	11Ø11Ø11
22Ø	DC	5632Ø	11Ø111ØØ
221	DD	56576	11Ø111Ø1
222	DE	56832	11Ø1111Ø
223	DF	57Ø88	11Ø11111
224	EØ	57344	111ØØØØØ
225	E1	576ØØ	111ØØØØ1
226	E2	57856	111ØØØ1Ø
227	E3	58112	111ØØØ11
228	E4	58368	111ØØ1ØØ
229	E5	58624	111ØØ1Ø1
23Ø	E6	5888Ø	111ØØ11Ø
231	E7	59136	111ØØ111
232	E8	59392	111Ø1ØØØ
233	E9	59648	111Ø1ØØ1
234	EA	599Ø4	111Ø1Ø1Ø
235	EB	6Ø16Ø	111Ø1Ø11
236	EC	6Ø416	111Ø11ØØ
237	ED	6Ø672	111Ø11Ø1
238	EE	6Ø928	111Ø111Ø
239	EF	61184	111Ø1111
24Ø	FØ	6144Ø	1111ØØØØ
241	F1	61696	1111ØØØ1
242	F2	61952	1111ØØ1Ø
243	F3	622Ø8	1111ØØ11
244	F4	62464	1111Ø1ØØ
245	F5	6272Ø	1111Ø1Ø1
246	F6	62976	1111Ø11Ø
247	F7	63232	1111Ø111
248	F8	63488	11111ØØØ
249	F9	63744	11111ØØ1
25Ø	FA	64ØØØ	11111Ø1Ø
251	FB	64256	11111Ø11
252	FC	64512	111111ØØ

Decimal (LSB)	Hex	Decimal (MSB)	Binary
253	FD	64768	11111101
254	FE	65024	11111110
255	FF	65280	11111111

The following program will print copies of this number table. You might need to make some adjustments to line 90 depending in which slot you have your printer card. As the program is written, it will print to PR #1. If you just want to print to the screen, either delete line 90 or enter RUN 100.

Program F-1. Number Tables

```
90 PRINT CHR$ (4);"PR#1": REM CHANGE THIS TO MATCH
   THE LOCATION OF YOUR PRINTER CARD
100 HE$ = "0123456789ABCDEF"
110 FOR X = 1 TO 255
120 B = 2:C = 1
122 IF X < 10 THEN PRINT "  ";: GOTO 130
124 IF X < 100 THEN PRINT " ";
130 PRINT X;" ";:DE = X: GOSUB 240
135 REM CREATE BINARY
138 Z = X:L = 7
140 FOR Q = 0 TO 7:T = INT (X / 2)
150 K$(L) = CHR$ (48 + (X - T * 2))
160 L = L - 1:X = T: NEXT Q
165 X = Z: PRINT TAB( 5);
170 FOR I = 0 TO 7: PRINT K$(I);: NEXT I: PRINT
220 NEXT X: PRINT CHR$ (4);"PR#0"
230 END : REM  TRANSFORM TO HEX
240 H$ = "": FOR M = 1 TO 0 STEP - 1:N% = DE / (16
   ^ M):DE = DE - N% * 16 ^ M
250 H$ = H$ + MID$ (HE$,N% + 1,1): NEXT M
260 PRINT H$" ";:DE = X * 256
262 IF DE < 1000 THEN PRINT "  ";: GOTO 270
264 IF DE < 10000 THEN PRINT " ";
270 PRINT DE" ";: RETURN
```

Appendix G

Machine Language Entry Program, MLX

Machine Language Entry Program, MLX

Tim Victor

A machine language (ML) program like LADS is usually listed as a long series of numbers. It's hard to keep your place and even harder to avoid making mistakes as you type in the listing, since an incorrect line looks almost identical to a correct one. To make error-free entry easier, COMPUTE! Publications lists ML programs in a format designed to be typed in with a utility called "MLX." The MLX program uses a checksum system to catch typing errors almost as soon as they happen.

Apple MLX checks your typing on a line-by-line basis. It won't let you enter invalid characters or let you continue if there's a mistake in a line. It won't even let you enter a line or digit out of sequence. Best of all, you don't have to know anything about machine language to enter ML programs with MLX. Apple MLX makes typing ML programs almost foolproof.

Using Apple MLX

Type in and save some copies of Apple MLX (Program G-3) on disk with the filename MLX. It doesn't matter whether you type it in on a disk formatted for DOS 3.3 or ProDOS. Programs entered with Apple MLX, however, must be saved to a disk formatted with the same operating system as Apple MLX itself.

Next, type in and save the MLX Loader program listed below. Be sure to use the correct Loader program for your operating system.

Program G-1. MLX Loader, DOS 3.3 Version

```
10 REM DOS 3.3 MLX LOADER
20 REM FOR USE TO TYPE IN LADS
30 HIMEM: 31228
40 PRINT CHR$(4);"RUN MLX"
```

Program G-2. MLX Loader, ProDOS Version

```
10 REM ProDOS MLX LOADER
20 REM FOR USE TO TYPE IN LADS
30 FOR I= 768 to I+5
```

```
40 READ A: POKE I,A
50 NEXT I
60 CALL 768
70 PRINT CHR$(4);"RUN MLX"
80 DATA 169,31,32,245,190,96
```

If you have an Apple IIe or IIc, make sure that the key marked CAPS LOCK is in the down position. Run the Loader program for your operating system. (The Loader programs are necessary only when using MLX to enter LADS. If you use MLX to enter other ML programs from other COMPUTE! publications, the Loaders printed here are not necessary.)

The Loader program will set up your Apple and load MLX. You'll be asked for the starting and ending addresses of the ML program. These values are

DOS 3.3 LADS

Starting address: 79F8
Ending address: 9087

ProDOS LADS

Starting address: 7B00
Ending address: 917F

The next thing you'll see is a menu asking you to select a function. The first is (E)NTER DATA. If you're just starting to type in a program, pick this. Press the E key, and the program asks for the address where you want to begin entering data. Type the first number in the first line of the program listing if you're just starting, or the line number where you left off if you've already typed in part of a program. Hit the RETURN key and begin entering the data.

Once you're in Enter mode, Apple MLX prints the address for each program line for you. You then type in all nine numbers on that line, beginning with the first two-digit number after the colon (:). Each line represents eight bytes and a checksum. When you enter a line and hit RETURN, Apple MLX recalculates the checksum from the eight bytes and the address. If you enter more or less than nine numbers, or the checksum doesn't exactly match, Apple MLX erases the line you just entered and prompts you again for the same line.

Invalid Characters Banned

Apple MLX is fairly flexible about how you type in the numbers. You can put extra spaces between numbers or leave the spaces out entirely, compressing a line into 18 keypresses. Be careful not to put a space between two digits in the middle of a number. Apple MLX will read two single-digit numbers instead of one two-digit number (F 6 means F *and* 6, not F6).

You can't enter an invalid character with Apple MLX. Only the numerals 0–9 and the letters A–F can be typed in. If you press any other key (with some exceptions noted below), nothing happens. This safeguards against entering extraneous characters. Even better, Apple MLX checks for transposed characters. If you're supposed to type in A0 and instead enter 0A, Apple MLX will catch your mistake.

Apple MLX also checks to make sure you're typing in the right line. The address (the number to the left of the colon) is part of the checksum recalculation. If you accidentally skip a line and try to enter incorrect values, Apple MLX won't let you continue. Just make sure you enter the correct starting address; if you don't, you won't be able to enter any of the following lines. Apple MLX will stop you.

Editing Features

Apple MLX also includes some editing features. The left- and right-arrow keys allow you to back up and go forward on the line that you are entering, so you can retype data. Pressing the CONTROL (CTRL) and D keys at the same time (*delete*) removes the character under the cursor, shortening the line by one character. Pressing CTRL-I (*insert*) puts a space under the cursor and shifts the rest of the line to the right, making the line one character longer. If the cursor is at the right end of the line, neither CTRL-D nor CTRL-I has any effect.

When you've entered the entire listing (up to the ending address that you specified earlier), Apple MLX automatically leaves Enter mode and redisplays the functions menu. If you want to leave Enter mode before then, press the RETURN key when Apple MLX prompts you with a new line address. (For instance, you may want to leave Enter mode to enter a program listing in more than one sitting; see below.)

Display Data

The second menu choice, (D)ISPLAY DATA, examines memory and shows the contents in the same format as the program listing. You can use it to check your work or to see how far you've got. When you press D, Apple MLX asks you for a starting address. Type in the address of the first line you want to see and hit RETURN. Apple MLX displays program lines until you press any key or until it reaches the end of the program.

Save and Load

Two more menu selections let you save programs on disk and load them back into the computer. These are (S)AVE FILE and (L)OAD FILE. When you press S or L, Apple MLX asks you for the filename. The first time you save an ML program, the name you assign will be the program's filename on the disk. If you press L and specify a filename that doesn't exist on the disk, you'll see a disk error message.

If you're not sure why a disk error has occurred, check the drive. Make sure there's a formatted disk in the drive and that it was formatted by the same operating system you're using for Apple MLX (ProDOS or DOS 3.3). If you're trying to save a file and see an error message, the disk might be full. Either save the file on another disk or quit Apple MLX (by pressing the Q key), delete an old file or two, then run Apple MLX again. Your typing should still be safe in memory.

Program G-3. MLX

```
100 N = 9: HOME : NORMAL : PRINT "APPLE MLX": POKE
     34,2: ONERR GOTO 610
110 VTAB 1: HTAB 20: PRINT "START ADDRESS";: GOSUB
     530: IF A = 0 THEN PRINT CHR$ (7): GOTO 110
120 S = A
130 VTAB 2: HTAB 20: PRINT "END ADDRESS  ";: GOSUB
     530: IF S > = A OR A = 0 THEN PRINT CHR$ (7): G
     OTO 130
140 E = A
150 PRINT : PRINT "CHOOSE:(E)NTER DATA";: HTAB 22:
     PRINT "(D)ISPLAY DATA": HTAB 8: PRINT "(L)OAD F
     ILE  (S)AVE FILE  (Q)UIT": PRINT
160 GET A$: FOR I = 1 TO 5: IF A$ < > MID$ ("EDLSQ"
     ,I,1) THEN NEXT : GOTO 160
170 ON I GOTO 270,220,180,200: POKE 34,0: END
180 INPUT "FILENAME: ";A$: IF A$ < > "" THEN PRINT
     CHR$ (4);"BLOAD";A$;",A";S
190 GOTO 150
200 INPUT "FILENAME: ";A$: IF A$ < > "" THEN PRINT
     CHR$ (4);"BSAVE";A$;",A";S;",L";E - S
210 GOTO 150
220 GOSUB 590: IF B = 0 THEN 150
230 FOR B = B TO E STEP 8:L = 4:A = B: GOSUB 580: P
     RINT A$;": ";:L = 2
```

```
240 FOR F = Ø TO 7:V(F + 1) = PEEK (B + F): NEXT :
    GOSUB 56Ø:V(9) = C
25Ø FOR F = 1 TO N:A = V(F): GOSUB 58Ø: PRINT A$" "
    ;: NEXT : PRINT : IF PEEK (49152) < 128 THEN NE
    XT
26Ø POKE 49168,Ø: GOTO 15Ø
27Ø GOSUB 59Ø: IF B = Ø THEN 15Ø
28Ø FOR B = B TO E STEP 8
29Ø HTAB 1:A = B:L = 4: GOSUB 58Ø: PRINT A$;": ";:
    CALL 64668:A$ = "":P = Ø: GOSUB 33Ø: IF L = Ø T
    HEN 15Ø
3ØØ GOSUB 47Ø: IF F < > N THEN PRINT CHR$ (7);: GOT
    O 29Ø
31Ø IF N = 9 THEN GOSUB 56Ø: IF C < > V(9) THEN PRI
    NT CHR$ (7);: GOTO 29Ø
32Ø FOR F = 1 TO 8: POKE B + F - 1,V(F): NEXT : PRI
    NT : NEXT : GOTO 15Ø
33Ø IF LEN (A$) = 33 THEN A$ = O$:P = O: PRINT CHR$
     (7);
34Ø L = LEN (A$):O$ = A$:O = P:L$ = "": IF P > Ø TH
    EN L$ = LEFT$ (A$,P)
35Ø R$ = "": IF P < L - 1 THEN R$ = RIGHT$ (A$,L -
    P - 1)
36Ø HTAB 7: PRINT L$;: FLASH : IF P < L THEN PRINT
    MID$ (A$,P + 1,1);: NORMAL : PRINT R$;
37Ø PRINT " ";: NORMAL
38Ø K = PEEK (49152): IF K < 128 THEN 38Ø
39Ø POKE 49168,Ø:K = K - 128
4ØØ IF K = 13 THEN HTAB 7: PRINT A$;" ";: RETURN
41Ø IF K = 32 OR K > 47 AND K < 58 OR K > 64 AND K
    < 71 THEN A$ = L$ + CHR$ (K) + R$:P = P + 1
42Ø IF K = 4 THEN A$ = L$ + R$
43Ø IF K = 9 THEN A$ = L$ + " " + MID$ (A$,P + 1,1)
     + R$
44Ø IF K = 8 THEN P = P - (P > Ø)
45Ø IF K = 21 THEN P = P + (P < L)
46Ø GOTO 33Ø
47Ø F = 1:D = Ø: FOR P = 1 TO LEN (A$):C$ = MID$ (A
    $,P,1): IF F > N AND C$ < > " " THEN RETURN
48Ø IF C$ < > " " THEN GOSUB 52Ø:V(F) = J + 16 * (D
     = 1) * V(F):D = D + 1
49Ø IF D > Ø AND C$ = " " OR D = 2 THEN D = Ø:F = F
     + 1
5ØØ NEXT : IF D = Ø THEN F = F - 1
51Ø RETURN
52Ø J = ASC (C$):J = J - 48 - 7 * (J > 64): RETURN
53Ø A = Ø: INPUT A$:A$ = LEFT$ (A$,4): IF LEN (A$)
     = Ø THEN RETURN
54Ø FOR P = 1 TO LEN (A$):C$ = MID$ (A$,P,1): IF C$
     < "Ø" OR C$ > "9" AND C$ < "A" OR C$ > "Z" THE
    N A = Ø: RETURN
```

```
550 GOSUB 520:A = A * 16 + J: NEXT : RETURN
560 C = INT (B / 256):C = B - 254 * C - 255 * (C >
    127):C = C - 255 * (C > 255)
570 FOR F = 1 TO 8:C = C * 2 - 255 * (C > 127) + V(
    F):C = C - 255 * (C > 255): NEXT : RETURN
580 I = FRE (Ø):A$ = "": FOR I = 1 TO L:T = INT (A
    / 16):A$ = MID$ ("Ø123456789ABCDEF",A - 16 * T
    + 1,1) + A$:A = T: NEXT : RETURN
590 PRINT "FROM ADDRESS ";: GOSUB 530: IF S > A OR
    E < A OR A = Ø THEN B = Ø: RETURN
6ØØ B = S + 8 * INT ((A - S) / 8): RETURN
61Ø PRINT "DISK ERROR": GOTO 15Ø
```

Index

To order your copy of the Apple Machine Language for Beginners Disk call our toll-free US order line: 1-800-334-0868 (in NC call 919-275-9809) or send your prepaid order to:

Apple Machine Language for Beginners Disk
COMPUTE! Publications
P.O. Box 5058
Greensboro, NC 27403

All orders must be prepaid (check, charge, or money order). NC residents add 4.5% sales tax.

Send ____ copies of the Apple Machine Language for Beginners Disk at $12.95 per copy. (0025AML)

Subtotal $__________

Shipping & Handling: $2.00/disk $__________

Sales tax (if applicable) $__________

Total payment enclosed $__________

□ Payment enclosed
Charge □ Visa □ MasterCard □ American Express

Acct. No. ______________________ Exp. Date ______ (Required)

Name ______________________________

Address ______________________________

City ________________ State ________ Zip ______

Please allow 4-5 weeks for delivery.

4570023